Dictionary of
Financial
Engineering

Wiley Series in Financial Engineering

Derivatives Demystified: Using Structured Financial Products
John C. Braddock

Option Pricing Models
Les Clewlow and Chris Strickland

Derivatives for Decision Makers: Strategic Management Issues
George Crawford and Bidyut Sen

Currency Derivatives: Pricing Theory, Exotic Options, and Hedging Applications
David F. DeRosa

Options on Foreign Exchange, Second Edition
David DeRosa

The Handbook of Equity Derivatives, Revised Edition
Jack Francis, William Toy, and J. Gregg Whittaker

Dictionary of Financial Engineering
John F. Marshall

Interest-Rate Option Models: Understanding, Analyzing, and Using Models for Exotic Interest-Rate Options
Ricardo Rebonato

Derivatives Handbook: Risk Management and Control
Robert J. Schwartz and Clifford W. Smith, Jr.

Dynamic Hedging: Managing Vanilla and Exotic Options
Nassim Taleb

Credit Derivatives: A Guide to Instruments and Applications:
Janet Tavakoli

Pricing Financial Instruments: The Finite Difference Method
Domingo Tavella and Curt Randall

Dictionary of
Financial
Engineering

John F. Marshall, Ph.D.

Marshall, Tucker & Associates, LLC

John Wiley & Sons
New York ■ Chichester ■ Weinheim
Brisbane ■ Singapore ■ Toronto

Library of Congress Cataloging-in-Publication Data:

Marshall, John F. (John Francis), 1952–
    Dictionary of financial engineering / John F. Marshall.
        p. cm. — (Wiley series in financial engineering)
    ISBN 0-471-24291-8 (cloth : alk. paper)
    1. Financial engineering—Dictionaries.   I. Title.   II. Series.
HG176.7 .M368   2000
658.15—dc21   00-043326

Printed in the United States of America
10 9 8 7 6 5 4 3 2 1

To all my students—past, present, and future.
Jack

ABOUT THE AUTHOR

John F. Marshall is Professor of Finance at St. John's University and Director of the University's Center for Financial Engineering. Dr. Marshall is also a principal of Marshall, Tucker & Associates, LLC, a financial engineering and derivatives consulting firm with offices in New York, Chicago, Boston, San Francisco, and Philadelphia; and he is a member of the Board of Directors of the International Securities Exchange, the first SEC-approved screen-based options exchange in the United States. Dr. Marshall is the author of sixteen books on financial products, markets, and analytics including *Futures and Option Contracting* (South Western), *Investment Banking & Brokerage* (McGraw Hill), *Understanding Swaps* (Wiley), and *Financial Engineering: A Complete Guide to Financial Innovation* (Simon & Schuster). He has also authored several dozen articles published in professional journals and he is a frequently requested speaker for financial conferences.

Dr. Marshall is an accomplished financial innovator. He contributed to the development of the mathematical underpinnings of cash/index arbitrage using stock index futures (sometimes called program trading), and to the development of the first published pricing models for both equity swaps and CMT swaps. He is the originator or co-originator of seasonal swaps, synthetic barter, and macroeconomic swaps. He also participated in the development of several mortgage product variants.

From 1992 to 1998, Dr. Marshall served as the Executive Director of the International Association of Financial Engineers (IAFE). During his time as its Executive Director, the IAFE grew from 40 founding members to over 2000 members worldwide. From 1997 through 1999 he served on the Board of Directors of the Fischer Black Memorial Foundation. From 1991 to 1995, Dr. Marshall served as the managing trustee for Health Care Equity Trust, a closed-end limited-life investment company sponsored by Paine Webber.

From 1994 to 1996, Dr. Marshall served as Visiting Professor of Financial Engineering at Polytechnic University where he created the first Master of Science degree program in Financial Engineering under a grant from the Alfred P. Sloan Foundation. During 1992 he held the post of Distinguished Visiting Professor of Finance at the Moscow Institute of Physics and Technology, a unit of the Russian Academy of Sciences.

Dr. Marshall has been an invited lecturer at the Wharton School of Business of the University of Pennsylvania, the Stern School of Business at New York University, and the Graduate School of Business of the University of Chicago. Outside the United States, he has lectured in Zurich, London, Toronto, Bucharest, and Tokyo. As a consultant, Dr. Marshall has worked for the United States Treasury Department, the United States Justice Department, the Federal Home Loan Bank, The First Boston Corporation (now CS First Boston), the Chase Manhattan Bank, Chemical Bank, Smith Barney (now Salomon Smith Barney), Merrill Lynch, Goldman Sachs, Morgan Stanley Dean Witter, Paine Webber, Union Bank of Switzerland, and JP Morgan, among others.

Dr. Marshall earned his undergraduate degree in Biology/Chemistry from Fordham University in 1973. He earned an MBA in Finance from St. John's University in 1977 and an M.A. in Quantitative Economics from the State University of New York in 1978. He was awarded his doctoral degree in Financial Economics from the State University of New York at Stony Brook in 1982 while also a dissertation fellow of the Center for the Study of Futures Markets at Columbia University.

CONTENTS

In November 1993, I accepted an invitation from John Wiley & Sons to serve as the Series Editor for the *Wiley Series in Financial Engineering*. As we envisioned it at the time, this book series would grow to cover the full range of topics encompassed by the rapidly evolving field of financial engineering. As the *Series* grew, with several new titles added each year, it became obvious that the series needed a dictionary that would provide short definitions of the many terms used by financial engineers so that users of the series, and others, could get a quick sense of their meaning. Financial engineering terms often have meanings very different from the way they are used by other branches of finance and the outside world.

Unfortunately, try as I might, I was unable to recruit authors to compile such a dictionary. Eventually, I decided that my staff and I would, in our spare time, compile it from the books that were already included in the series, augmented with terms from my earlier publications and various other public sources. We took on this task in April 1997 and thought we would have it done within two years. Of course, when you try to do anything in your spare time, it almost certainly won't get done. Not surprisingly, we slipped further and further behind our target date for completion. This was complicated further by the fact that, with every new book in the series, a list of additional terms had to be worked into the dictionary. Eventually, we decided to make completion of the dictionary a priority project and focus almost exclusively on it for several months. At the same time, we recognized that the dictionary would never be truly complete because the language, like the profession, of financial engineering continues to evolve.

With that background, let me tell you what this dictionary is and what it is not. It is an attempt to gather several thousand terms that are used by financial engineers and others involved in finance and to provide a short definition of each. When terms have multiple meanings, many of the meanings are listed. For example, if there are multiple meanings for a term, they will be separated by numbers (1), (2), etc. Each number refers to an alternative usage of the term. Very frequently, many terms mean the same thing and in many situations one term is a special case of another. We have tried to cross-reference these so that the user can make the connections. We have also included many acronyms with their meanings.

This book is not meant to be encyclopedic. That is, we do not provide a long or detailed explanation for each term. The reader should refer to the books in the series, or other sources, if greater detail is required. This book is also not intended to provide legal guidance with respect to the usage of any term contained within it.

Because of the limited scope of this work, we cannot guarantee the accuracy of any given term, nor that the term does not have meanings other than those included. The book is also not complete and never could be for the reasons noted above. For this reason, we see it as an ongoing work in progress. We would appreciate it if readers would forward via e-mail any terms they think should be included in future editions of this dictionary together with a citation of the source. We would also appreciate any suggestions for improvements of the definitions and descriptions that have already been included.

Financial engineering makes extensive use of derivative financial instruments and, not surprisingly, many of the books in the series are concerned with derivatives. Additionally, financial engineering makes extensive use of fixed income analytics, including yields, spot rates, and forward rates. For the benefit of the uninitiated, this dictionary includes some tutorial material on financial engineering, derivatives, and fixed income analytics. The tutorial material dealing with financial engineering and derivatives is drawn from a series of articles I authored (with Kevin Wynne) between 1995 and 1998 for *Derivatives: Tax, Regulation, Finance* (published by Warren, Gorham & Lamont). The tutorial material dealing with fixed income analytics comes from an article I authored (with Alan Tucker) for *Derivatives Risk Management Services* (published by Warren, Gorham & Lamont). They follow the dictionary.

I would like to thank all of my staff, particularly Mary Freeman, for the time spent digging through reference material for terms I missed. I would also like to thank the editors at John Wiley & Sons, particularly Pamela van Giessen and Claudio Campuzano, for their remarkable patience with me.

John F. Marshall, Ph.D.
Compiler
marshall@mtaglobal.com

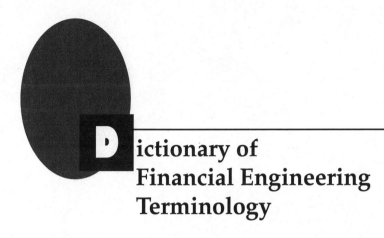

Dictionary of
Financial Engineering
Terminology

abandonment Allowing an option to expire unexercised. Generally this will happen only if the option is out-of-the-money at expiry or if the option is in-the-money at expiry by less than the transaction costs associated with exercising it.

ABS See *asset-backed securities.*

absolute advantage The ability of one country to produce more of a given good with its endowed resources. In the context of swaps, the ability of one party to borrow at a lower rate of interest in a given currency than another party. This is in contrast to comparative advantage. See also *comparative advantage* for contrast.

absolute priority rule The principle that senior creditors are paid in full before junior creditors are paid anything. Generally, this would require that secured creditors be paid first, then unsecured creditors, and finally equity holders.

absolute quotation The quotation of the rate on an instrument, such as the coupon rate on an interest rate swap, in which the quotation is an explicit rate such as 6.80%. This is in contrast to a quotation in the form of a spread over another instrument, such as a Treasury. The latter form of quotation is called a *relative quotation.* For example, suppose that the equivalent maturity Treasury to the swap quoted above is 6.20%. Then, if the swap is quoted at TN + 60 bps (i.e., the Treasury note yield plus 60 basis points), the quotation would be a relative quotation. See *relative quotation.*

academic arbitrage See *pure arbitrage.*

accelerated depreciation The depreciation of an asset at a rate faster than simple straight-line depreciation. Over the years, a number of different accelerated depreciation methods have been permitted under tax rules and generally accepted accounting principles (GAAP). Presently in the United States a method of accelerated depreciation called the modified accelerated cost recovery system or MACRS is the permissible method. Accelerating depreciation has the advantage of reducing reported profit in the years immediately following the purchase of new capital equipment, thereby reducing corporate income taxes and increasing corporate cash flow. However, by accelerating depreciation, out-year profits and taxes will be greater and cash flow will be lower than they would have been under straight-line depreciation.

acceleration A clause in a contractual obligation, such as a swap contract, that provides for the early termination of the contract with an appropriately specified termination process. Early termination is usually triggered by some credit event such as an outright default or a credit downgrading.

accounting risk The risk of variability in reported profits of a corporation or a bank as a consequence of a change in either the accounting rules or their interpretation. For example, users of derivatives for hedging purposes employ hedge accounting. For some years, the FASB debated new rules before releasing its FAS 133, which addressed the issue. FAS 133 itself is difficult to interpret and employ and dramatically changes the rules concerning hedge accounting. See *FAS 133.*

accredited investor An investor who meets the requirements of Regulation D spelled out in the Securities Act of 1933 such that the investor may participate in the purchase of securities through private placements. Such investors must possess a minimum level of wealth and/or a minimum level of annual income and/or be prepared to invest at a substantial level. Sometimes called a *qualified investor*.

accreting notional swap Any swap in which the notional principal increases over time, under a prespecified schedule. Also known as an *accumulation swap*, an *appreciating swap*, a *step-up swap*, or simply an accreting swap. The opposite of an *amortizing swap*.

accretion An increase in the carrying value (i.e., the principal) of a security.

accretion bond A tranche of a CMO that does not receive interest or principal for some period of time. Instead, the interest that would otherwise flow to the tranche accrues. Once the tranche becomes the fastest-pay tranche, it begins to receive interest and principal. Such tranches are also known as *accrual bonds* and *Z bonds*.

accrual accounting An accounting system that recognizes revenue when the right to receive the revenue has been earned and recognizes expenses when obligations are incurred. This is in contrast to a cash accounting system that recognizes revenue when cash is received and expenses when obligations are paid.

accrual bond See *accretion bond*.

accrual note Also known as a *range note*. A type of medium-term note (usually three years) that pays a high rate as long as some short-term reference rate stays within a defined range, but pays a different and much lower rate whenever the reference rate strays outside the range. For example, an accrual note might pay a fixed rate of 8% while the T-bill rate stays between 5.50% and 6.50% but would fall to 2% should the T-bill rate go below 5.50% or above 6.50%. If the note pays a fixed rate when the reference rate is within the range and a different but fixed rate when the reference rate is outside the range, the note is called a *binary accrual note*. The illustration above is this sort of accrual note. The term *range floater* is used if the instrument pays a floating rate. See *range floater*.

accrual swap An interest rate swap in which interest accrual on one leg of the swap is conditional upon one or more specific conditions being met.

accrued interest The interest that has been earned by the holder of a debt instrument or interest rate derivative but which has not yet been paid. Rules for calculating accrued interest differ for different types of instruments and are very dependent on the interest accrual day count convention. The day count convention can be actual/actual, actual/360, or 30/360. See *day count*, *actual/actual*, *actual/360*, and *30/360*.

accumulation swap See *accreting notional swap*.

acquiree In an acquisition of one company by another, the company that is to be purchased or acquired is the acquiree. Prior to completion of the acquisition, the acquiree is often called the *target*. See also *acquirer*.

acquirer In an acquisition of one company by another, the company making the purchase is called the acquirer. The company that is purchased is called the *acquiree*. Prior to the completion of the acquisition, the acquirer is often described as a *suitor* (if the acquisition is friendly) or as a *raider* (if the acquisition is hostile). Prior to completion of the acquisition, the acquiree is called the *target*.

acquisition The purchase of one company by another company. The purchasing company is called the *acquirer* and the purchased company is called the *acquiree*. Acquisitions can result in a parent-subsidiary relationship or they can be a prelude to a merger.

act of God bonds Bonds, most often issued by insurance companies, that contain the following clause: If the issuer suffers significant losses, for example, due to excessive claims payout, the interest on the bond can be reduced or delayed without triggering default. Principal repayments may also be delayed without triggering default.

active portfolio management An effort by a portfolio manager to buy securities that are expected to outperform some benchmark and to sell securities that are expected to underperform the benchmark in order to generate performance for the portfolio that exceeds the benchmark's performance. This is in contrast to passive portfolio management, which simply seeks to match a benchmark by replicating the contents of the benchmark.

actual rate swap Also known as a *zebra basis risk swap* or *zebra swap* and sometimes called a *perfect swap*. A swap, usually involving a municipality that has issued floating rate debt, such that the municipality pays a fixed rate and receives a floating rate that precisely offsets the floating rate it is contracted to pay on its floating rate debt.

actual/360 A day count convention that counts the actual number of days that have elapsed since the start of an inter-

est accrual period and then divides this number by 360 as part of the process for determining the amount of interest that has accrued on a debt instrument. This day count convention is used, for example, in calculating the interest due on Eurodollar deposits, CDs, and repurchase agreements.

actual/actual A day count convention that counts the actual number of days that have elapsed since the start of an interest accrual period and then divides this number by the actual number of days in the entire interest accrual period or in the entire year (depending on the application and the type of instrument). This day count convention is employed in calculating the accrued interest on coupon-bearing U.S. Treasury notes and bonds, but not on U.S. Treasury bills.

actuals Also known as *physicals* and as *spot*. The term is used to distinguish between commodities and securities that are real and those that are purely hypothetical. The latter are known as *notionals*.

actuarial rate A rate of return that is expected to be earned. It is used to calculate the contributions to be made to a pension plan or the premiums to be paid on an insurance policy.

ad valorem tax A tax based on value, such as a tax on the value of real estate or personal property.

adaptive mesh model A lattice-like numerical process for valuing derivative instruments, such as options, in which regions of high resolution are embedded in critical regions of a lower resolution structure. Developed by Figlewski and Gao.

add-on factor Part of the bank capital guidelines adopted by the Federal Reserve in 1989. In the case of swaps and other off–balance sheet positions, it is a percentage of the notional principal and is intended to provide for an increase in market risk that might occur over time. This measure predates the later approach to regulatory capital that is based on VaR and VaR-like measures.

add-on interest Interest that is paid at the end of a loan. That is, at the end of the loan period, the borrower repays the lender the principal and pays the lender the accrued interest. Sometimes called *add-on yield*.

add-on yield See *add-on interest*.

adjustable rate debt See *floating rate debt*.

adjustable rate instruments Any of a variety of instruments in which the rate payable on the instrument adjusts periodically to reflect the value (possibly with a premium or discount) of some reference rate of interest. This includes adjustable rate preferred stock, floating rate debt, floating rate notes, and adjustable rate mortgages, among others.

adjustable rate mortgage Known by the acronym *ARM*. Any mortgage contract containing a provision to reset the mortgage coupon rate in response to a change in market rates. The coupon is usually tied to a specific reference rate or index such as the one-year constant maturity Treasury or the eleventh district cost of funds.

adjustable rate note See *floating rate note*.

adjustable rate preferred stock Preferred stock in which the preferred dividend rate adjusts periodically based on some benchmark reference rate.

adjusted strike price A strike price on an option that has been adjusted to preserve the original economics of the option. For example, if an option is written on a stock and the underlying stock splits 2 for 1, then the strike of the option will be adjusted by dividing the original strike by two. The number of options will double, or, alternatively, the number of shares of underlying will double. The new strike price is the adjusted strike price.

adjustment swap See *off-market swap*.

ADRs See *American depositary receipts*.

advance contract See *forward contract*.

advance guarantee Essentially an option, but usually written into some other instrument. See *embedded option*.

advance refunding bonds Bonds issued to refund an outstanding bond issue prior to the date on which the outstanding bonds become due or callable. The proceeds of an advance refunding are held in escrow by a fiduciary and invested in authorized securities until such time as they are used to retire the earlier bond issue.

affected party A counterparty to a swap that has experienced a termination event.

affiliates Holders of greater than 5% of the common stock of a company (i.e., either individuals or corporations).

after market The secondary market for a security after completion of the initial public offering.

after-tax yield A measure of return, stated on a percentage basis, calculated after the payment of taxes. This measure is useful for comparing the returns on investments subject to different tax treatments.

agency cost A term used in corporate finance to describe the fact that directors, officers, and managers of a corporation are agents of the owners (i.e., agents of the shareholders). As such, they are expected to make decisions that will maximize the value of the corporation. However, because the agents might put their own interests, to some degree, ahead of the interests of the owners, the corporation's value may be lower than the maximum attainable value. The difference between the maximum attainable value and the actual market value is called agency cost. The elimination of agency cost has been used to justify leveraged buyouts by management.

agency trades Securities transactions by and between broker-dealers as opposed to stock exchanges or other markets or investors.

agent A person who acts on behalf of another for a fee. The agency relationship involves a fiduciary obligation on the part of the agent to act in the best interest of the principal who is paying the agent's fee.

agreement value method One of three allowable methods for determining damages upon the early termination of a swap. This method is now almost universally employed in swap documentation. The method assesses damages based upon market quotations for obtaining a replacement swap having equivalent terms to the terminated swap.

AIMR See *Association for Investment Management and Research.*

ALCO See *asset/liability management committee.*

algorithm Any process consisting of a well-defined sequence of steps that if followed exactly will lead to the correct numerical solution to a problem, provided that the problem has been correctly specified.

alligator spread See *butterfly spread (options).*

all-in cost The total cost of a financing expressed as an annual percentage rate. In addition to the coupon, all-in cost reflects such things as flotation costs, trustee expenses, and administration expenses. It is useful for comparing the cost of several financing alternatives.

all-or-nothing Any financial instrument that pays either all of some specified value or nothing at all, depending on some specific condition. Such instruments have an option-like component and are constructed from digital options.

all-or-nothing options These are call (put) options that have a payoff equal to the full value of some market price if the value of the underlying at expiration is greater than (less than) the strike price of the option. If not, they pay off nothing. They can be structured to be multi-period, in which case they are all-or-nothing caps or floors. They are constructed from digital options. An example of an all-or-nothing call: If S>X pay S; if S≤ X then pay 0.

alpha (1) In regression analysis, alpha is often used to mean the estimated parameter that represents the intercept term. The estimated parameter representing the slope is called the beta. (2) In portfolio theory, alpha refers to the excess return earned on a security or portfolio relative to what should have been expected given the amount of systematic risk associated with the security or portfolio. In this context it is often called Jensen's alpha. (3) In the U.K., the largest corporations are often referred to as the alpha class of stocks—analogous to Blue Chips in the U.S.

alternative currency option See *dual currency option*.

alternative minimum tax Known by the acronym *AMT*. A U.S. tax levied on individuals who have substantial tax preference items in order to ensure that they incur at least some tax obligation. The AMT must be computed by individuals with certain tax preferences and then compared to the regular income tax. The larger of the two taxes is the tax that must be paid.

alternative options See *better-of options* and *worse-of options*.

Altman z score A numeric value assigned to a corporation that is used to predict the likelihood of the corporation's bankruptcy within a specific period of time. The equation for arriving at the score was obtained via discriminant analysis, through empirical econometric estimation. It uses several financial ratios as inputs. The method has been criticized for (1) lack of a theoretical model, and (2) failure to adjust the input ratios to reflect the accounting elections made by the corporation's management. The method is named for its developer Edward Altman.

American depositary receipts Better known by the acronym *ADRs*. These are securities that represent claims against shares of stock that trade in non-U.S. markets. The foreign securities are purchased and held by a depository institution as custodian. The depository institution then issues depositary receipts against the securities. These trade in the same manner as U.S. stocks. Each ADR gives its holder a pro rata claim on the shares of the foreign

security. The depository institution collects any dividends paid by the underlying stock, converts them to dollars, and then distributes the currency-converted dividend to the ADR holders. Most often, a depositary receipt represents a single foreign stock, but sometimes a number of stocks will be pooled and then depositary receipts will be issued against the pooled securities.

American option An option that can be exercised at any time up to the time of its actual expiration. That is to say, American-type options are continuously exercisable by the option holder. This is in contrast to European-type options, which can be exercised only during a short period of time at the end of their lives.

American terms A method of quoting an exchange rate in terms of the number of dollars one unit of the foreign currency will buy. For example, if the euro is quoted at $1.05000, the quote is in American terms. From the perspective of an American, the quote can also be said to be in *direct terms*. This is in contrast to a quotation in European terms (also called indirect terms) in which the quote is in terms of the number of units of the foreign currency that can be purchased for one dollar.

American window A hybrid between a European-type option and an American-type option. This type of option allows the holder to exercise the option during a limited period of time (the window), which is generally toward the end of the life of the option. The window is longer than the very limited exercise period on a European-type option, but shorter than the entire life of the option as in an American-type option.

amortization (1) The process by which the principal on a loan or the notional principal on a derivative grows progressively smaller with the passage of time because the principal is either repaid (in the case of a loan) or simply reduced (in the case of a derivative). (2) The process by which the premium paid for a bond or other instrument is written down over time. (3) The process by which the value of an intangible asset, such as a patent, is gradually written down for tax purposes.

amortization of premium An annual charge against the premium paid for a bond in excess of its par value.

amortization schedule A schedule that describes how the principal on a loan or a notional contract will be amortized by listing the repayments or reductions of the principal. Such schedules usually also depict the interest payments and the total payments (principal and interest combined).

amortizing See *amortizing debt.*

amortizing cap A cap option on which the notional principal amortizes.

amortizing collar A collar option (see *collar*) on which the notional principal amortizes.

amortizing debt Any form of debt in which the principal balance is repaid gradually over the term of the loan.

amortizing loan A loan that is paid off in equal periodic payments. The payments are applied to principal and interest in varying portions over the life of the loan. The typical example is a home mortgage loan.

amortizing option Any type of option on which the notional principal (i.e., the quantity of underlying) gets smaller over time.

amortizing swap Any swap in which the notional principal amortizes over the tenor of the swap. Thus, interest exchanges are made on a progressively smaller notional principal.

AMT See *alternative minimum tax.*

analytic valuation methods Methods of valuing options or other derivative instruments that rely on the rigorous derivation of a formula (i.e., an equation). The derivation requires a clear enumeration of the relevant assumptions and then the careful derivation of the formula from these assumptions. It is not always possible to derive an analytical solution to a valuation problem, in which case, numeric valuation methods are employed. The famed Black-Scholes-Merton model was the first successful attempt at deriving analytical models for valuing options.

anchors Frequently priced benchmark bonds that are used to price infrequently traded bonds through a matrix pricing approach. For example, all other things being equal, if a two-year anchor bond is at 96 and a four-year anchor bond is at 98, then a non-trading three-year bond is worth 97. Note that this description is an oversimplification because a bond can have many different features including coupon rates. Matrix pricing is one way to mark non-trading bonds to values approximating the market values the bonds would have if the bonds did trade.

and interest The normal way in which bond prices are quoted in the United States. Accrued interest is not included in the price quote and thus the bond buyer pays the bond seller the agreed price and any accrued interest. This contrasts with quotes on a flat basis that do include accrued interest.

announced deals Publicly announced efforts to make acquisitions, engage in mergers, and achieve other forms of business combinations, in contrast to rumors of planned deals.

annual yield A yield that assumes one compounding per year. Also known as an effective annual yield.

annualization See *annualizing*.

annualizing Also known as *annualization*. The conversion of a percentage return earned over any holding period to its annual equivalent. The conversion generates an effective annual rate. Suppose that over some period of time T, the cumulative total return was R. Then the effective annual rate R_e can be found as follows: $R_e = (1 + R)^{1/T} - 1$.

annuity A series of equal-sized payments made at equal intervals in time. Many cash flow streams take the form of annuities. For example, the monthly payments on a level-payment fixed rate mortgage or the coupon payments on a fixed-rate bond would both represent annuities.

annuity bond An amortizing bond that makes equal-sized payments at regular intervals over the life of the bond such that each payment includes both interest and principal. By maturity, the full principal has been repaid so that no bullet principal payment is due at the end of the life of the bond. The amortization process is analogous to that of a conventional mortgage.

annuity note See *annuity bond*.

anticipatory hedge Any hedge that is put on in anticipation of a later cash position. The purpose is to lock in the price prior to taking the actual cash position.

anti-crash warrant A call-like warrant written on an index in which the strike price is equal to the smaller of the value of the index at issuance or the value of the index at a specific time in the future. Essentially, we have to look back to see which index value was the lowest in order to set the strike. See *look-back options* for a more general description of instruments with look-back features.

anti-takeover amendments Amendments to a corporate charter or corporate by-laws designed to place obstacles in the way of would-be acquirers. These include such things as supermajority voting requirements.

appraised value A fair market value assigned to an asset by an independent appraiser experienced at determining fair market values. Often important for assessing the value of an asset to be used as collateral on a loan and for calculating gains/losses on a merger when purchase accounting is used to account for the transaction. Appraised values are intended to be indicative of fair market value.

appreciating swap See *accreting notional swap*.

APT See *arbitrage pricing theory*.

arbitrage Simultaneously transacting in two or more markets in order to earn a profit from a price discrepancy between the two markets. The arbitrage can be across markets separated by space (geographical or spatial arbitrage), across time (temporal arbitrage), across tax rates (tax arbitrage), or across the structural components of the assets traded. In its purest form, arbitrage is risk free and requires no investment of the arbitrageur's own capital. Real world arbitrage, however, is rarely completely risk free and often requires considerable capital for infrastructure.

arbitrage free A situation in which an arbitrageur cannot make a profit because the two instruments are not mispriced relative to one another. Sometimes understood to mean an efficient market. Alternatively, the absence of arbitrage opportunities.

arbitrage pricing theory Known by the acronym *APT*. A model for estimating security returns, particularly for stocks, that is based on systematic risk factors. These factors are captured by factor-replicating portfolios. The method represents a generalization of the capital asset pricing model (CAPM) and makes use of a statistical technique called factor analysis.

arbitrage profit A profit earned by exploiting a discrepancy between the pricing of an asset in two different markets. See *arbitrage* for more detail.

arbitrageur Also spelled "arbitrager." One who engages in arbitrage.

ARCH model See *autoregressive conditional heteroscedasticity model*.

arithmetic average annual return An average formed by dividing the sum of successive annual percentage returns on an investment by the number of years. This form of calculating an average annual return can be very misleading, particularly when the annual returns are volatile. For example, if the annual returns on an investment for the last four years were +20%, –20%, +16% and +40%, the arithmetic average annual return would be 14%. A more reliable measure is the *geometric average annual return*. See *geometric average annual return* for comparison.

ARM See *adjustable rate mortgage*.

ARPS See *auction rate preferred stock*.

arrangement fee A fee charged by an agent for arranging a financial transaction. Analogous to a *commission*. Sometimes called a *structuring fee* if financial engineering is involved.

arrearage The amount of any past due obligations, such as interest on bonds or dividends on preferred stock.

arrears An obligation to make a payment at the end of a payment period. This is the normal practice, for example, in the bond markets where the coupon interest is paid at the end of the coupon period.

arrears swap A swap in which one set of payments is based on an observation made at the end of the relevant period by looking back. Total return swaps are typically structured as in-arrears swaps but not all in-arrears swaps are based on a total return.

ascending yield curve See *upward sloping yield curve*.

Asian option See *average rate option* and *average strike option*.

ask Also known as an *offer price* and as an *asked price*. This is the price at which a dealer will sell an asset. In contrast, a *bid price* is the price at which a dealer will buy the asset.

asked price See *ask*.

assessed value The value placed on property by an assessor for purposes of levying taxes. Assessed values can differ significantly from true market values or appraised value and are not, necessarily, meant to be indicative of market value.

assessment ratio The ratio of the assessed value of real estate or other property to its true market value.

asset allocation The process of dividing investment funds among different asset classes. Asset classes can be defined broadly, such as stocks and bonds, or narrowly, such as investment grade corporate bonds, Treasury bonds, high-yield bonds, and so forth. See *strategic asset allocation* and *tactical asset allocation*.

asset allocation swap Any of a variety of swap structures that are intended to effect an asset allocation strategy. For example, an equity swap in which the equity leg pays the higher of the total return on two equity indexes.

asset class A group of assets that share some general characteristic. For example, real estate makes up an asset class, common stocks of U.S. corporations make up an asset class, and U.S. bonds make up an asset class. Asset classes can be broadly or narrowly defined. For example, a broad asset class can be subdivided into numerous subclasses.

asset swap Any swap written to transform the cash flow characteristics of an asset in order to replicate the cash flow characteristics of another asset. The combination of the original asset together with the swap often constitutes a synthetic instrument. Also used to describe a package consisting of a bond and a pay-fixed/receive-floating interest rate swap, which has the effect of replicating a floating rate note.

asset-backed commercial paper Commercial paper backed by specific assets of its issuer. Asset-backing of commercial paper allows poorer quality corporations to utilize the commercial paper market. This is in contrast to most commercial paper, which is unsecured and issued by high quality issuers. See also *credit-supported commercial paper*.

asset-backed securities Known by the acronym *ABS*. These are bond and note issues collateralized by a cash flow stream that can be associated with almost any well-defined source (e.g., credit card receivables, auto loan receivables, etc.). Mortgage-backed securities are now viewed as a subset of the asset-backed securities market. The process of packaging a pool of claims on a cash flow stream into a security is often called *securitization*. Generally, a corporation holding assets that represent claims to future cash flows transfers ownership of those assets to a backruptcy-remote, special-purpose vehicle, which then issues bonds collateralized by those assets. Various techniques can be used to enhance the credit quality of the ABS.

asset/liability management The management of assets and/or liabilities in such a way as to match cash flows, currency denominations, durations, or maturities of assets and liabilities in order to manage exposure to price risks (i.e., interest rate risk and exchange rate risk).

asset/liability management committee Usually abbreviated *ALCO*. Groups of individuals at banks and other financial institutions with broad authority to manage the risks taken on by those institutions.

asset-or-nothing options Options that pay off the full market value of an asset if the option is in-the-money at expiry and nothing if the option is out-of-the-money at expiry. These options are also known as *all-or-nothing options*. See also *all-or-nothing options*.

assignment (1) The transfer of one's rights and obligations under a contract to another party. (2) The notice to an option writer that the option holder has elected to exercise the option.

Association for Investment Management and Research Known by the acronym *AIMR*. A professional body that promulgates guidelines, disclosure requirements, return calculations, and performance presentation standards for persons involved in the investment management field.

asymmetric margining Any situation in which one party to a contract is required to tender more margin (i.e., collateral) than the other party to the contract either because the contract has an asymmetric payoff (as in the case of an option) or because the creditworthiness of the parties differ.

as-you-like-it option Also known as a *chooser option*. See *chooser option*.

at-market swaps Swaps written with a swap coupon (i.e., fixed rate) that reflects current market conditions. That is, the fixed rate leg has the same present value as the floating rate leg. These are also called *par swaps*, and they contrast with *high coupon swaps* and *low coupon swaps*, which are written off market.

at-the-close Also called *on-the-close*. Orders to buy or sell an asset during the period of time that constitutes the market's official closing period. Orders filled during this period must be filled at a price that falls within the *closing range*.

at-the-money A situation in which an option's strike price and the current market price of the underlying asset are the same, thus there is no intrinsic value. Also sometimes used to describe an asset trading at its par value, such as an interest rate swap whose fixed rate reflects current market conditions.

at-the-open Also called *on-the-open*. Orders to buy or sell an asset during the

period of time that constitutes the market's official opening period. Orders filled during this period must be filled at a price that falls within the *opening range*.

auction calendar The calendar schedule for the regular auction of Treasury securities.

auction rate preferred stock Often referred to by the acronym *ARPS*. Preferred stock in which the coupon rate periodically resets, most often once every 49 days, based on the outcome of a Dutch auction. The rate is usually subject to a cap and the instrument is often putable. The instrument goes under a variety of labels each representing a trademark of a financial institution.

authorized shares The number of shares of common stock a corporation has been authorized by its charter to sell. However, just because the corporate charter authorizes the sale of shares does not mean that the corporation must issue the shares or that it can do so without registering the shares with the SEC.

autocorrelation A situation in which a series of successive observations on a random variable (i.e., a time series) are correlated with, and therefore partially or wholly dependent upon, one another. In such a situation, the successive values generated provide some aid in predicting the future values that will be generated. Many statistical techniques are predicated on the assumption that time series are not autocorrelated. Autocorrelation is also known as *serial correlation*.

automatic exercise A policy on the part of a clearing member of an option's exchange by which the clearing member will always exercise an option on behalf of the option's owner if the option is in-the-money by a preset amount at expiry. The purpose is to prevent options that are in-the-money from expiring worthless because of the option holder's inattention.

autoregressive conditional heteroscedasticity model Known as an *ARCH model*. A statistical process for estimating the parameters of a relationship among variables where the process models the value of the dependent variable as a function of the time-varying properties of the error terms.

average life A measure of the average length of time it will take, or is expected to take, to recover the principal on a debt security. Unlike duration, average life is calculated with respect to principal only and does not discount the principal payments in the averaging process. Often used as an alternative to maturity on amortizing instruments.

average price option Similar to an average rate option, except that the average price of the underlying asset, rather than the average reference rate, is compared to the option's strike price. See *average rate option.*

average rate option An interest rate or exchange rate option that pays off by comparing the average underlying reference rate (calculated based on a series of discrete observations on the reference rate over the life of the option) to the strike price of the option. Such options can be calls or puts. Average rate options are one type of *Asian option.* For example, a call version of such an option might have a payoff given by $max[R_{avg} - X, 0]$ where R_{avg} represents the simple average of a number of observations on the reference rate over some period of time, and X denotes the option's strike rate.

average strike option An option that pays off based on comparing the spot price of the underlying at settlement to the average spot price of the underlying over the life of the option. The average spot price serves as the strike of the option, thus the strike is floating over the life of the option. Such options can be calls or puts. For the call variety, the payoff would be given by $max [S_T - S_{avg}, 0]$ where S_T denotes the spot price at option expiry, and S_{avg} denotes the simple average of the spot price over the life of the option based on a number of observations (such as daily closing prices).

B

baby bond A bond having a face value (i.e., par value) of less than $1,000.

back months Derivatives contracts such as futures and options that have delivery dates or expiration dates that are far forward from the present. This is in contrast to the *front month,* which is the month closest to delivery or expiry. The term *far month* is often used to mean the same thing as back month

and the term *near month* is often used to mean the same thing as front month.

back office In the banking industry, a reference to the various operational functions necessary to support the front office or revenue generating activities. Typical back office functions include payment processing, trade clearing and settlement, information technology support, legal and accounting support, confirmation generation, trade matching, and so forth.

back stub period The last payment period on a floating rate instrument (i.e., an instrument on which the rate periodically resets) if the length of that last payment period is different from that of the other payment periods. These instruments include interest rate swaps and floating rate notes. The back stub period, if there is one, is usually shorter than the other periods. There may also be a shorter first payment period, which would be called a *front stub period*.

back testing A process by which a trading methodology or other algorithm is tested against historic data to evaluate its usefulness. Often used to test value-at-risk models.

back-end load A load or sales charge paid when something is sold. The term is most often used to refer to sales charges imposed when shares of a mutual fund are sold. See *load* for a discussion of the different types of sales charges.

back-end set swap A swap in which the floating rate is observed at the end of the period and applied to the prior period. On a LIBOR-based swap, LIBOR would be observed at the end of the coupon period and then applied retroactively back to the beginning of the period. Also known as an *in-arrears swap*.

back-to-back loans A loan arrangement involving two distinct loans between the same parties. In the first loan, Party 1 is the lender and Party 2 is the borrower. In the second loan, Party 2 is the lender and Party 1 is the borrower. Back-to-back loans predate swaps and are the predecessor of swaps. They were first used to circumvent restrictions on capital movements.

back-to-back swaps Two swaps involving the same counterparty such that for that counterparty the swaps are in the opposite direction. For example, suppose that Party A is a swap dealer, Party B is a corporation, and Party C is a subsidiary of Party B. Suppose that Party C needs a swap to convert the character of a debt issuance. The dealer, however, is not comfortable with Party C's credit and won't do the swap with C. But the dealer is willing to do the swap with Party B. The dealer does a swap with B and then B does an offsetting swap with C. C now has the swap it needs, and B has back-to-back swaps.

backward induction Also known as a *roll back*. Any lattice (tree) methodology that starts with possible future values and discounts the values backward through the tree. At each node in the tree, the values are combined. As the process progresses, the tree narrows until the present value is ascertained. This method can be used to value a bond having embedded optionality from a tree of potential short rates. This is useful for determining a bond's option adjusted spread.

backwardation A situation in which the current spot price of an asset is higher than the current price of a futures contract written on that asset. This is in contrast to contango in which the futures price is higher than the spot price. See *contango* for contrast.

balance sheet An important financial statement prepared in accordance with generally accepted accounting principles (GAAP) that lists all of a corporation's assets at their book values and separately lists all of a corporation's liabilities and the owners' equity at their book values. These statements reflect the values as of a specific date. In recent years, there has been a movement toward changing the method of calculation to focus more on market values and less on book values. Balance sheets are sometimes called *statements of financial position*. The term "balance sheet" stems from the fact that the book value of assets must equal the book value of liabilities and equity.

balloon (1) A fixed-rate mortgage that is scheduled to return the entire principal outstanding, or some large portion thereof, in a lump sum on a date prior to the time the mortgage would be fully amortized. (2) A bond issuance scheduled to return a large portion of the principal on some date prior to maturity. Debt service funds (a type of sinking fund) are often associated with such bonds to assure that sufficient funds will be available to meet the balloon obligation.

balloon payment The payment of the entire principal outstanding on a balloon mortgage or the payment of a substantial portion of the principal on a bond issuance.

band (1) An agreed-upon range over which the exchange rate between two currencies can move before government intervention is required. (2) Another name for a collar. See *collar*.

banded swap See *collar swap*.

bank basis See *bank discount basis*.

bank discount basis Also known as *bank basis* and as *discount basis*. The routinely used convention for quoting yields on Treasury bills and commercial paper. The yield is stated using an actual/360 day count convention with the assumption that the instrument is discounted from its face value by the amount of the interest. See also *bank discount yield*.

bank discount yield Also known as *discount basis*. A measure used to express the yield on certain non-coupon-bearing securities, such as T-bills, that always sell at a discount from face value.

Bank for International Settlements Known by the acronym *BIS*. An organization involving the central banks of many countries that is principally concerned with settling payments among nations.

bank guarantee Any guarantee by a bank on behalf of a customer such that the bank's credit replaces the customer's credit with respect to a specific transaction. Letters of credit are a form of a bank guarantee.

banker's acceptance A money market instrument created as a consequence of commercial transactions. Essentially, a bank letter of credit is issued to support a commercial transaction. When the transaction is complete, the letter of credit is stamped accepted and becomes payable at face value at a specific point in the future. Until that time, it is marketable and trades at a discount from its face value.

Banking Act of 1933 More popularly known as the *Glass-Steagall Act*. While this legislation had a number of important provisions, it is best known as the legislation that divided the financial services industry into three distinct industries: investment banking, commercial banking, and insurance. The act limited a financial institution's activities to one of these three arenas and greatly shaped the evolution of the U.S. financial services industry. The Financial Services Act of 1999 repealed or modified many of the provisions of Glass-Steagall.

bankruptcy (1) Technically, a situation in which the value of a firm's liabilities exceeds the value of the firm's assets so that the firm has negative equity. However, because a balance sheet is usually prepared using book values, technical bankruptcy does not necessarily imply that a formal declaration of bankruptcy will occur. (2) A declaration of bankruptcy is a declaration that a corporation is unable to satisfy its liabilities because it has inadequate assets and/or income and usually leads a corporation to seek protection from creditors under various provisions of the bankruptcy code.

bankruptcy remote entity An entity created to serve as the issuer of structured financial instruments (such as asset-backed securities). The bankruptcy remote entity is usually a special purpose vehicle and is a subsidiary of another entity that seeks to pool and sell assets. Such special purpose vehicles are structured to have a very low probability of bankruptcy, even if the parent should go bankrupt.

BANs See *bond anticipation notes*.

barbell portfolio A portfolio of bonds that is concentrated in two securities, one with a relatively long duration and one with a relatively short duration. Both positions are held long or both positions are held short, so that the duration of the portfolio is a weighted average of the two extreme durations.

barrier options Options that are triggered when an underlying asset price crosses a given price level, called the *barrier price*. Barrier options are path dependent. There are two general types: knock-in and knock-out. When the spot price crosses the barrier price, knock-in options are activated and knock-out options are extinguished. Barrier options are also known as *trigger options* and *limit options*.

barrier price The barrier price specified in a barrier option that causes the option to knock in or knock out. See *barrier options*.

base currency See *functional currency*.

baseball option A knock-out barrier option that knocks out if the barrier price is touched or crossed three times. The option knocks out upon the third touch. The term derives from the game of baseball in which three strikes make an out.

baseline instrument Also know as a *benchmark* instrument. An instrument selected to serve as the benchmark to which other instruments are compared. In hedging strategies, the benchmark instrument functions as a kind of common denominator for a portfolio. That is, the positions within the portfolio are each converted to their risk equivalents in terms of the benchmark. They can then be aggregated to determine the overall risk of the portfolio.

basic See *plain vanilla*.

basic swap See *plain vanilla*.

basis (1) Most generally, the difference between two prices or rates. More narrowly, the difference between the spot price (or rate) of the underlying asset and a futures price (or rate) on the underlying asset. When a futures hedge is placed, the hedger trades price risk for basis risk. See *basis risk*. See also *quality basis, locational basis,* and *time basis*. (2) The adjusted cost of a capital asset for purposes of calculating capital gains and losses. See *cost basis*.

basis point A measure of interest rate changes or differences. A single basis point is 0.01% so that it takes 100 basis points to make 1 percentage point. Interest rate spreads are most often quoted in basis points. Often abbreviated bps and, in market jargon, pronounced "bips" or "beeps."

basis rate swaps See *basis swaps*.

basis risk The potential for changes in a basis. It is measured as the standard deviation of the basis. The basis is the difference between two prices, most often a spot price and a futures price. Basis risk is a function of the degree of correlation between the two prices. When a commercial interest hedges, it essentially exchanges price risk for basis risk. In the case of hedging a position in a commodity (including financial instruments) with futures contracts, the basis risk can be ascertained from the following relationship:

$$\sigma_{basis} = [(1 - \rho) \times 2\sigma^2_{spot}]^{1/2}$$

where σ_{basis} denotes the standard deviation of the basis, ρ denotes the degree of correlation between the spot price and the futures price, and σ^2_{spot} denotes the variance of the spot price. It can be seen that the hedge will be completely effective if the correlation is perfect (i.e., +1). The lower the correlation, the higher the basis risk and, therefore, the less effective the hedge.

basis swaps Contracts to exchange interest payments based on different reference interest rates such as the exchange of LIBOR-based cash flows for Treasury bill rate-based cash flows. That is, they are floating-for-floating swaps in which the two legs pay based on different reference rates. Also known as *basis rate swaps*.

basis trade Any transaction based on the difference between two prices. Such a trade might involve the exchange of a futures contract for the underlying asset (called physicals or actuals). Basis trades are often at the heart of arbitrage strategies.

basket A portfolio containing a specific combination of assets. For example, we could have a currency basket, a stock basket, or a commodity basket.

basket hedging A hedge constructed from a basket of assets (see *basket*) to offset the risk associated with positions in a variety of actuals.

basket options Include *sector options* and *sector warrants* as special cases. Options in which the underlying is a custom-made portfolio of equities, currencies, commodities, or bonds. That is, the option pays off based on a basket of instruments rather than on a single instrument. There is a difference between a basket of options (each written on a single underlying) and an option on a basket of underlyings. A basket option refers to the latter. For example: Suppose three stocks trade for $50, $40, and $90. Call these stocks 1, 2, and 3, respectively. The equally weighted average price of these three stocks is $60. Now suppose we buy an at-the-money call option on an equally weighted basket of these three stocks. The option would pay off at expiry as follows: *max* $[(\frac{1}{3}\Sigma S_i - 60), 0]$.

basket rate A rate formed from a portfolio of rates. A basket rate can be used as the reference rate on a swap.

Basle Accord An agreement in principle reached in December 1987 by the Basle Supervisors Committee that redefined bank capital requirements (i.e., regulatory capital). Subsequent work by the committee led to progress toward basing regulatory capital on the level of the bank's risk exposure.

Basle Supervisors Committee A group of bank supervisors and regulators that met in Basle, Switzerland, to redefine bank capital and to standardize capital requirements for banks.

BBA See *British Bankers' Association.*

BBAIRS Pronounced "B bears." Refers to British Bankers' Association Interest Rate Swap Documentation.

BDT See *Black-Derman-Toy.*

bear floater A floating rate note whose rate is based on the difference between some multiple of a floating reference rate and a fixed rate. The note allows the investor to leverage up a bet that the reference rate is going to rise. Also known as a *leveraged floater.*

bear hug An effort at a friendly takeover that carries a threat of a hostile takeover if the overture for a friendly takeover is rejected.

bear spread A strategy involving two options of the same class (i.e. they are both calls or both puts) written on the same underlying asset and having the same expiration date. One option is bought and the other option is sold. If the strategy is effected using calls, you would buy the higher strike call and write (i.e., sell) the lower strike call. The payoff profile has the characteristic that the trader profits up to a preset amount if the underlying's price falls and loses up to a preset amount if the underlying's price rises. See *vertical spread.*

bear swap A swap in which the notional principal amortizes more rapidly if the swap's reference rate rises. This benefits the fixed rate receiver, who is able to reinvest at a higher rate.

bearer bond A negotiable bond whose title rests with the bearer. That is, it is presumed that the bearer of the bond is the rightful owner of the bond. This is in contrast to registered bonds in which ownership is continuously tracked. Bearer bonds were the standard form of bonds many years ago, but registered bonds are far more common today.

bearish Describes a person who believes that a particular asset or group of assets will fall in value. One who is bearish is inclined to sell the asset. This is in contrast to one who is bullish and believes the value of an asset will rise. With respect to interest rates, a bear believes that rates will rise thereby implying that bond prices will fall.

benchmark An instrument, index, or rate that will serve as a basis of comparison or from which an observation will be taken for purposes of setting a rate on a floating rate instrument. In the latter context, it is often called a *reference asset, reference index,* or *reference rate.* Benchmark portfolios, such as stock indexes and bond indexes, are also known as *normal portfolios.*

benefit of carry A situation in which the cost of carry on a futures contract or other position is negative so that the benefit of carry accrues to the arbitrager. This situation arises when the income earned from holding a security (e.g., coupon payments in the case of bonds, and dividend payments in the case of stock) exceeds the cost of financing the position.

Bermudan option Any option that is exercisable on discrete dates spread out over the option's life, but not exercisable between those dates. This is in contrast to American options, which are exercisable at any time, and in contrast to European options, which are exercisable only during a limited exercise period at the end of the option's life. Bermudan options are also called *mid-Atlantic options* and *quasi-American options.* These terms are all intended to convey the idea that the exercise period is somewhere between that normally associated with an American-type option and that normally associated with a European-type option (i.e., Bermuda is between America and Europe).

best efforts A type of underwriting in which the issuer will receive the proceeds from an issuance of securities only to the degree that the issuance is successful. That is, the underwriting syndicate does not guarantee that all of the securities can or will be sold at the offering price and does not guarantee to the issuer that the issuer will receive the full amount of the *proceeds to the issuer*. In such an underwriting, the issuer bears the risk of a failed offering. For contrast, see *firm commitment*.

beta See *beta coefficient*.

beta coefficient A measure of the systematic risk associated with a single stock or a portfolio of stocks. Systematic risk is measured relative to the market. Most often, the market is taken to be the S&P 500 stock index. The beta of a security is computed as the covariance of the excess returns on the security and the excess returns on the market divided by the variance of the excess returns on the market. Excess return is the difference between the return on the stock (or the market) and the return on the risk-free rate.

better-of options Also known as *alternative options*, but this latter term can also include worse-of options. An option that pays off based on the better performing of two or more assets or indexes. For example, the holder of a better-of call on the S&P 500 and the Nikkei 225 would receive the total return on the better performing of the two indexes or pay the least worst performing of the two indexes should they both produce a negative total return. The payoff function for such options would be given by $max[S_1, S_2, S_3, ..., S_n]$, where $max[\ ]$ denotes the max function

and S_i denotes the value of the ith underlying at the time of the option's expiration. Closely related are worse-of options, which pay the worst performing of several assets or indexes. Better-of options fall within a broader category of options called *rainbow options*. Other types of rainbow options include *outperformance options* and *max-min options*. See these for their distinguishing features.

BEY See *bond equivalent yield*.

bid Also called *bid price*. The price quoted by a dealer at which he will buy an asset. This is in contrast to the dealer's offer price, which is the price at which he will sell an asset. The term can also be applied to interest rate contracts to refer to an interest rate at which the dealer will buy the instrument.

bid price See *bid*.

bid-ask spread Also called *bid-offer spread*. The difference between the bid price and the ask price for any marketed instrument. In dealer markets, the bid-ask spread is the dominant source of the dealer's income. In some markets, this is called the *pay-receive spread*.

bid-offer spread See *bid-ask spread*.

bifurcation The division of some aspect of an instrument into two parts. For example, we can bifurcate risks or cash flows. A bifurcation of risks might involve separating the credit risk from the market risk. A bifurcation of cash flows might involve separating a mortgage payment into its interest and principal components and directing those cash flows to different investors. The term is sometimes used with respect to analytical processes that have been broken into two distinct parts.

Big Bang A reference to the rapid deregulation of the financial services industry in the United Kingdom during the latter half of the 1980s.

big figure See *handle*.

bilateral netting The netting of cash flows (i.e., payments) between two parties. If Party A is set to pay $1,000 to Party B and Party B is set to pay $900 to Party A, then the payments can be netted so that Party A simply pays $100 to Party B. Netting reduces the need for liquidity and the settlement risk. See also *multilateral netting*.

bin (1) As the term is used by the International Securities Exchange (a U.S.–based option exchange), the group of stocks for which an exchange market maker has the right to make markets in options. At the start of the exchange, each bin consisted of 60 stocks. Thus, each market maker had the right to make markets in call and put options on the 60 stocks in his bin. Each bin has 1 primary market maker and 10 competitive market makers. At the launch of the exchange there were 10 bins. (2) See *bucket*.

binary accrual note An accrual note that pays one of two fixed rates. The higher rate is paid if a specific reference rate stays within a designated range and the lower fixed rate is paid if the reference rate is outside the range. Most often, the higher rate is paid for each day that the reference rate is within the range and the lower rate is paid for each day the reference rate is outside the range. See *accrual note* for more detail.

binary LIBOR note A type of binary accrual note in which the reference rate is LIBOR. Generally, if LIBOR is within the designated range, the note pays LIBOR plus a premium; if LIBOR is outside the range, the note pays nothing. See also *binary accrual note* and *range floater*.

binary options See *digital options*.

binary swap A swap in which the floating-rate leg pays at a spread over the reference rate if the reference rate is within a designated range on the setting date and pays a lower rate (often zero) if the reference rate is outside the designated range on the setting date. The fixed rate is paid regardless. The spread over the reference rate when the reference rate is within the range may be viewed as compensation for the risk that the reference rate may move out of the range.

binary tree A model of the future where each progression leads to two possible states. Such a tree is also called a *binomial tree*. Binary trees can be recombining (so that each progression leads to a recombining of values) or non-recombining. In a recombining binary tree, the number of terminal states is given by T+1. In a non-recombining binary tree the number of terminal states is given by 2^T, where T denotes the number of progressions (time periods). Recombining binary trees are a special case of a broader set of models called *lattice models* and are often used to value options and instruments with embedded options.

binomial option pricing model A widely used numerical approach to valuing an option first developed and published by John Cox, Stephen Ross, and Mark Rubinstein. The model divides the life of an option into some number of discrete intervals. With the passage of each interval, the price of the underlying asset can either rise to one and only one new higher value or decline to one and only one new lower value. The values are depicted as the nodes of a binary tree.

binomial tree See *binary tree*.

BIS See *Bank for International Settlements*.

bivariate normal distribution A multivariate distribution involving two random variables both of which are normally distributed with some degree of correlation between them.

black box (1) A reference to an analytical engine employed by traders and others by way of preprogrammed software. The term "black box" is often taken to mean that the analytics employed are proprietary and hence not available to the user or that the analytics and code are beyond the user's ability to comprehend. (2) A group of assets that are used to collateralize a trust and provide a revenue stream to the owners of the trust's units but in which the specific collateral is not identified to the unit holders.

Black-Derman-Toy Known by its initials *BDT*. An interest rate option valuation model that makes use of a binary interest rate tree and employs the entire term structure of interest rates.

Black's approximation A method developed by Fischer Black for calculating the approximate value of a call option on a dividend-paying stock. This is in contrast to the *Black-Scholes model*, which assumes that the underlying stock does not pay dividends.

Black's model A model developed by Fischer Black to value options on futures contracts. It is an extension of the *Black-Scholes model*.

Black-Scholes model The first complete analytical model to value options. It

was developed in 1969 by Fischer Black and Myron Scholes, with assistance from Robert Merton, and published in 1973. As with all option pricing models, the model makes specific assumptions and requires specific inputs. The primary inputs include the strike price, the current spot price of the underlying, an estimate of the volatility of the price of the underlying asset, the risk-free rate of interest, and the time to expiry, measured in years. The model is often called the *Black-Scholes-Merton model*.

Black-Scholes-Merton model See *Black-Scholes model*.

blended index A weighted average of several indexes. For example, an index that consists of 40% S&P 500 and 60% Nikkei 225. In other words, it is a customized index of indexes. See also *rainbow*.

blended index swap A swap in which at least one leg pays off based on the total return on a blended index. These are often equity based (blended index equity swaps) but could just as easily be linked to any asset class or to different asset classes.

blended VaR Also known as *composite VaR*. An estimate of a firm's Value-at-Risk formed by a weighted average of different VaR estimates including parametric VaR (also known as variance-covariance VaR), historic VaR, and simulated VaR (also known as Monte Carlo VaR). See also *value-at-risk*.

block As the term is used with respect to stock transactions, a transaction involving 10,000 or more shares.

block trade A trade involving a block of stock.

blow out bid A bid price to buy some asset where the bid price is significantly above the price of the last trade or previous bid. Blow out bids generally occur when an aggressive buyer is trying to purchase a large quantity of the asset over a very short period of time, as in the case of a tender offer for stock.

blue-sky laws A reference to state securities laws, as opposed to federal securities laws, within the United States. The term is most often used to refer to state registration requirements for the sale of new securities.

board of trade (1) A designated futures exchange. (2) The term is sometimes used to refer to a chamber of commerce or some other form of cooperative trade association. The latter usage is most common in Europe.

boiler plate Standardized contract language for transactions that are routinely done.

boiler room Broker/dealers who employ high pressure sales tactics to sell securities to investors, often targeting naïve investors. The term implies unscrupulous sales practices.

Bond Anticipation Notes Known by the acronym *BANs*. Short-term, interest bearing notes issued by a government in anticipation of a later longer-term bond issuance. The notes are retired from the proceeds of the later bond issuance.

bond basis A convention for quoting the yields on bonds that assumes a specific day-count convention. This may be 30/360 (in the case of corporate bonds, agency bonds, and municipal bonds) or actual/actual (in the case of U.S. Treasury bonds).

bond equivalent yield Often abbreviated *BEY*. Also known as the coupon equivalent yield. A method of calculating and stating the yield on a non-coupon-bearing instrument, such as a T-bill, so that it is directly comparable to the yield on a coupon-bearing instrument. Most often assumes semiannual compounding.

bond indenture The contract that spells out the terms and conditions associated with a publicly traded bond and which defines the relationship between the issuer and the bondholder. Bond indentures contain various clauses, some of which are for the protection of the issuer and some of which are for the protection of the bondholder.

bond index An index formed from a large number of bonds and used as a benchmark for bond performance measurement. Similar in construction and usage to stock indexes.

bond option An option written on a bond. That is, a bond is the underlying asset.

bond rating Also known as a *credit rating*. A measure of the relative likelihood of default associated with a particular bond issuance. Ratings are provided by rating agencies, such as Moody's Investor Services, Standard & Poor's, Fitch, and Duff & Phelps.

bond reconstitution The opposite of stripping a bond of its coupons to create zero coupon bonds. Essentially, one purchases an appropriate collection of zero coupon bonds and repackages them into a conventional coupon-bearing bond.

bond swap Any of a wide variety of strategies that involve the sale of one bond and the purchase of a different bond in order to exploit a view on interest rates, credit spreads, the shape of the yield curve, and so forth. Must be distinguished from derivative swaps (i.e., notional principal swaps), which do not involve the purchase or sale of real bonds. In the U.K, the term *switch* is used to mean a bond swap.

bond value Usually used in reference to a convertible bonds that has value both as a bond and as an option on a given quantity of the underlying equity. Essentially, the bond value is the value of the convertible stripped of the option component. That is, one focuses on the value of the bond component alone. If the convertible trades for less than its bond value, an arbitrage opportunity should exist.

bond warrant An option on a bond. See also *bond option*.

bond with attached warrants See *warrants*.

book (1) Market slang meaning that a transaction giving rise to a position is recorded among the institution's assets and/or liabilities. (2) Market slang that refers to an institution's portfolio of some specific asset type such as a swap book, a foreign exchange book, or an options book.

book entry Refers to ownership of a financial instrument in which ownership is evidenced by a notation on the record-keeping agent's books (or, in modern usage, computer data files). Ownership of such a financial instrument is transferred via a computer entry. This is in contrast to bearer instruments in which ownership is evidenced by the possession of a physical certificate.

book runner The lead manager in a securities underwriting. The term derives from the fact that the lead underwriter is charged with "running the books" on the issuance including providing an accurate accounting to the issuer and to the other members of the underwriting syndicate.

booking a swap Also known as *positioning a swap*. When a swap dealer enters a swap, the swap becomes part of the dealer's book or portfolio.

bookout See *cancellation*.

bootstrapping An iterative numerical procedure to determine the spot zero rate curve implied by conventional coupon-bearing, usually Treasury, bonds. Essentially, the procedure allows one to sequentially extract the arbitrage-free, longer-term spot zero rates from the set of shorter-term spot zero rates and observable prices on coupon bonds. The methodology can also be used to extract spot zero swap rates from a par swap curve.

borrower One who has borrowed money and thus is indebted to the party who has lent money. Also known as a *debtor*. See *debtor* for more detail.

borrower option A cap option on a forward rate agreement. Essentially, it places an upper limit on the cost of a future borrowing.

Boston option Two distinct meanings: (1) Another name for a *break forward*. See *break forward*. (2) Another name for a *deferred payment option*. See *deferred payment option*.

bottom fisher See *vulture capitalists*.

bought deals A bond issuance in which there is only one underwriter. The term is also used, primarily in the United Kingdom, to mean essentially the same thing as a firm commitment underwriting. In this latter usage, there can be multiple underwriters.

bourse French for a marketplace, such as a stock exchange. Variations of the term are widely used in Europe and elsewhere to mean a marketplace.

boutiques Investment banks that specialize in only one or a few narrow market niches, as opposed to a broader-based full-service investment bank.

box spread A trading strategy consisting of a long synthetic futures position and a short synthetic futures position in the same underlying asset with the synthetic futures having the same expiration date. Each of the two synthetic positions is created from put and call options, but the two sides of the spread are created from put and call options having different strike prices. That is to say, the short futures is created from put and call options having one strike and the long futures is created from put and call options having a different strike price. These strategies originated as a way to put off realizing capital gains to the following tax year.

BP See *basis point.* Often pronounced "bip."

Brady Bond A bond issued by a sovereign government to restructure defaulted commercial debt. These bonds were issued during the 1980s when Latin American countries that had taken out large loans from U.S. banks became incapable of servicing their loans as a consequence of rapidly rising commodity prices. U.S. Secretary of the Treasury James Brady led an effort to restructure this debt into partially collateralized bonds in order to avert wholesale loan defaults by these countries.

break A sudden precipitous drop in the price of an asset such that there is a sharp discontinuity in the price from one price level to another. Sometimes used to refer to a sharp drop in a market overall (such as the stock market break of October 1987).

break forward A forward contract on exchange rates that one party can terminate at a prespecified exchange rate to take advantage of favorable exchange rate changes. Also known as a *cancellable option* and as a *Boston option.* The term Boston option, however, also has another meaning. See *Boston option.*

breakeven Also written break-even. At the most general, a point of indifference between two alternatives. Indifference is understood to be in a monetary sense, not a utility sense.

breakeven (convertibles) Used to describe the time it would take a convertible security to recoup the premium paid over common through its yield pickup. The premium paid over common refers to the convertible's conversion premium. Yield pickup refers to the amount by which a convertible's current yield exceeds the common stock's dividend yield. An easy formula to compute breakeven time is:

$$\text{Breakeven time (in years)} = \frac{\text{conversion premium}/(1 + \text{conversion premium})}{\text{convertible current yield} - \text{common dividend yield}}$$

For example, if a convertible trades with a 20% conversion premium and a 6% current yield, and the common pays a 2% dividend yield, the convertible's breakeven is 4.17 years [(0.2/1.2)/ (0.06 − 0.02)].

breakeven (options) With respect to option-based strategies, breakeven refers to those spot prices the underlying asset would need at the time of the option's expiration so that the strategy results in neither a profit nor a loss to the option holder and the option writer.

break-even time See *breakeven (convertibles)*.

Bretton Woods Agreement A multinational accord that established the post–WorldWar II international monetary system for participating nations. The accord served as the basis for the international monetary system until the system broke down in the early 1970s.

bridge financing See *bridge loan*.

bridge loan A loan made to bridge a time gap. The term is often used in the context of acquisitions, particularly leveraged buyouts. In such situations, a start up corporation owned by a small group of investors might obtain a bridge loan to finance an acquisition. Once complete, the corporation will float a bond and use the proceeds to pay off the bridge loan.

British Bankers' Association Known by the acronym *BBA*. A London-based trade association that deals with matters of common interest to member banks. In recent years, the BBA has dealt extensively with standardization of instrument documentation including swaps and forward rate agreements.

broad-based index A large group of assets whose values are combined to produce a single value that is viewed as representative of an entire market.

broker An individual, acting in the capacity of an agent for another, who executes buy and sell orders for the purchase of financial instruments and who receives fees, called commissions, for his/her services. Unlike dealers, brokers are not principals in the transactions, and, consequently, broking

does not require the maintenance of inventory and does not entail price risk.

broker loan rate The rate of interest charged by a securities firm to a client when the securities firm lends money to the client for the purpose of purchasing securities. The securities purchases are used as collateral on the loan.

brokering See *broking*.

broking The business of brokers. Also sometimes called *brokering*. See *broker*.

Brownian motion A random process that describes the behavior of certain random variables as they move through time. This process is often employed in financial modeling to describe the evolution of prices over time. When applied to prices, Brownian motion assumes that the change from one time period to the next is unrelated to either the level of the prices or the past series of price changes. That is, each price change is independent of prior price changes and the volatility of the price changes is constant.

bucket A term that refers to lumping together things that share some common characteristic. For example, cash flow buckets would include all cash flows that occur within a common time interval; risk buckets would include all risks having a common original. Also known as a *bin*.

bucket cash flow The sum of all cash flows that occur during any specified time period.

bucket DV01 The dollar value of a basis point for a swap dealer's entire bucket cash flow. See also *bucket*, *bucket cash flow*, and *DV01*.

bucket shop Broker/dealers who engage in shady trading practices with the result that their customers are defrauded or, at the very least, exploited in ways that are banned by the NASD.

building a book Preselling securities prior to the securities' actual issuance in order to assure that the securities can be moved very quickly once the issuance occurs.

bulge bracket A reference to the largest, most prestigious, investment banks. The name derives from the fact that these investment banks are most often the lead underwriters of securities offerings. The lead underwriters' names are usually printed larger and bolder on the tombstone and on the prospectus associated with the offering and, hence, "bulge" off the page. The bulge bracket is also known as the *special bracket*.

bull and bear notes These are securities that are created by tranching other instruments, such as a fixed rate note, so that one tranche pays a floating rate that moves in the same direction as the reference rate while the other tranche pays a floating rate that moves in the opposite direction of the reference rate. The bull floater is the one that moves inversely with the reference rate and the bear floater is the one that moves directly with the reference rate.

bull spread A strategy involving two options of the same class (i.e. they are both calls or both puts) written on the same underlying asset, and having the same expiration date. One option is bought and the other is sold. When calls are used, the trader would buy the lower strike option and write (i.e., sell) the higher strike option. The payoff profile has the characteristic that the holder profits up to a preset amount if the underlying's price rises and loses up to a preset amount if the underlying's price falls. See also *vertical spread*.

bulldogs Bonds sold by non-British issuers to British investors in the United Kingdom and which are denominated in pounds sterling. Analogous to *Yankee bonds* sold in the United States.

bullet The mid-duration bond in a butterfly hedge.

bullet transaction A banking term that describes a loan in which the principal is repaid in a single transaction upon maturity of the instrument. See also *nonamortizing debt*.

bullish Describes a person who believes that a particular asset or group of assets will rise in value. One who is bullish is inclined to buy the asset. This is in contrast to one who is bearish. When used in respect to interest rates, a bullish individual is one who believes interest rates will decline (because bond prices will rise if interest rates decline).

business-judgment rule A rule that allows corporate decision makers to do what they think is best for the corporation, and, by so doing, immunizes them from liability. Under this rule, so long as the decision was a business decision, taken in good faith, without any conflict of interest that might breach the duty of loyalty, courts are unlikely to find a breach of the duty of care.

busted convertible A convertible bond in which the underlying stock's price is so low that the convertible bond will behave like a straight bond. That is, the embedded option has little value.

butterfly hedge A dollar neutral and duration neutral strategy involving a position in a mid-duration bond, one with a longer duration, and one with a shorter duration. See *butterfly spread (bonds)*.

butterfly shift Describes a situation in which a nonparallel shift in an already humped yield curve results in a change in the degree of the yield curve's "humpedness."

butterfly spread (bonds) A bond strategy involving three similar bonds with different durations. The bond with the long duration and the bond with the short duration are purchased (sold) and the bond with the mid duration is sold (purchased). The strategy is designed to exploit bond mispricings while controlling for interest rate risk.

butterfly spread (options) Also known as an *alligator spread*. An option strategy involving four options of the same class with the same expiration date, but with three different strike prices. Two of the options have the same strike price that is between the strike prices of the other two. The two middle strikes are sold and the two end strikes are purchased. The reverse of this strategy is called a *reverse butterfly* or a *sandwich spread*.

buy-back See *cancellation*.

buy-down The up-front sum that will be received (paid) by a swap dealer for writing an off-market swap with itself as the receiver (payer) of the fixed rate when the swap requires a coupon below current market.

buy-up The up-front sum that must be paid (received) by a swap dealer for writing an off-market swap with itself as receiver (payer) of the fixed rate when the swap requires a coupon above current market.

cabinet trade A transaction in a stock or bond that has very little trading volume.

cable A reference to the exchange rate between the British pound sterling and the U.S. dollar. The term stems from the transmission of exchange rate information between the United Kingdom and the United States through the transatlantic cable.

calculation agent (1) The party designated to calculate the value of an index or rate in the event that that index or rate is not obtainable through normal market mechanics. (2) The party responsible for computing the periodic settlement amount on a derivatives contract or other financial instrument.

calculation date The date specified as such for the calculation of the cash settlement amount on an interest-rate or exchange-rate contract. If the calculation and settlement dates differ, the calculation date will precede the settlement date.

calendar spread (options) See *horizontal spread*.

calibration (1) A process of fine-tuning a valuation model to eliminate biases in valuations caused by nonlinearities or other anomalies. (2) A method for extracting implied volatilities from traded option prices.

call (bond) The act of exercising a call option embedded in a callable bond such that the bondholder is forced to redeem the bond for the bond's call price prior to the bond's maturity date. Call features can range from very simple to very complex. Some call features allow a bond to be called on one and only one date. Others allow a bond to be called on any one of several discrete dates. Still others allow a bond to be called at any time after a specific date.

call (option) See *call option*.

call date The first date that a callable debt instrument or a callable derivative instrument can be called by the party holding the right to call the instrument.

call date (DECS) Certain DECS can be called prior to maturity with the initial call price set at a small premium to the issue price. Typically, the call price declines to the issue price at maturity. The higher the common's trading level above the call price, the greater the probability that it will be called for redemption prior to maturity. See *DECS*.

call loan A loan that can be called by the lender at any time.

call market A market where buy orders and sell orders are matched in batches at designated times of the day. This is in contrast to a *continuous auction market* in which orders are filled (i.e., trades made) as they are received. See *continuous auction market* for contrast.

call money rate The rate of interest that banks charge securities firms when the banks lend money to securities firms. The loans are generally collateralized by securities and are callable. See also *call loan*.

call option An option that grants the holder the right to buy a specified number of units of the underlying asset from the option writer for a specific period of time (called the time to expiry)

at a specific price (called the strike price). Often just called a *call*.

call price The price that the issuer of a callable bond or other callable instrument must pay the holder of that instrument in the event the issuer chooses to call the instrument. The call price is specified in the bond's indenture.

call protection Provisions in a bond indenture that place restrictions on the issuer's right to call the bond. Often refers to a period of time after issuance during which the issuer cannot call the bond.

call provision A provision in a bond indenture or derivative contract that grants a party (usually the issuer) the right to call the instrument. See *call (bond)*.

call risk The risk, borne by the holder of a callable instrument, that the party holding the right to call the instrument will choose to do so. Consider a bond. The holder of a callable bond runs the risk that the issuer will choose to call the bond under the bond's call provisions. The issuer's incentive to do so rises as interest rates decline. Thus, the bond is most likely to be called if prevailing market rates of interest are below the coupon rate of the bond. If called, the bondholder gets its money back sooner than planned and is forced to reinvest at a lower rate.

call swaption See *receiver's swaption*.

callable bond Any bond that can be called by the issuer on or after the bond's call date. That is, the bond issuer has retained a call option permitting the issuer to demand that the bond be returned on or after the call date. If called, the issuer pays the bondholder the bond's call price (analogous to a *strike price*).

callable swap A swap that may be terminated prior to its scheduled maturity at the discretion of the fixed-rate payer. Sometimes called a *cancellable swap* and a *collapsible swap*, though these terms may be applied equally to *putable swaps*, which allow the floating-rate payer to terminate the swap early.

called away The transfer of a position in the underlying from the writer of a call option on the underlying to the holder of the call option on the underlying as a consequence of an exercise of the option. Would also apply to callable bonds. See *assignment*.

called bond A bond in which the issuer has exercised the call provision. Once the payment date has passed, the called bond ceases to accrue interest. It is therefore in the interest of the bondholder to redeem the bond once it has been called.

cancellable forward A forward contract in which one party has the right to terminate the contract upon payment of a prespecified price.

cancellable option See *break forward*.

cancellable swap See *callable swap* and *putable swap*.

cancellation In swaps, an agreement between the two counterparties to terminate the swap, usually accompanied by a termination payment by one party to the other that reflects the replacement cost of the swap. Also known as a *buy-back*, a *bookout*, and as a *close-out sale*.

cap (1) A multi-period option that resembles a strip of single-period call options. The most common type is an interest rate cap that pays off on each settlement date based on the market value of a reference rate and a specified contract rate. The individual single-period call option components are called *caplets*. (2) A provision within a floating rate instrument that places a ceiling on the floating rate. (3) A contract that limits the amount the interest rate on a floating rate loan can increase, either annually or over the life of the loan. Often incorporated into adjustable rate mortgages and structured securities.

cap rate The strike rate set into an interest rate cap option (or other cap option) that is used to determine the payoffs on the option. For example, the payoff on a LIBOR cap option would be given by Payoff = $max[L - X, 0]$, where L denotes the LIBOR rate prevailing on the contract's settlement date, and X is the cap rate or strike rate.

capacity Two common usages: (1) The power or legal authority to enter into a binding contract. (2) Sufficient cash flow to meet credit obligations.

capital (banking) An important tool of bank regulation and safety. Consists of long-term debt and equity and protects depositors by acting as a cushion against losses. Referred to as *regulatory capital*.

capital (corporate) In corporate finance, the term capital refers to the source of a corporation's financing. Capital consists of debt and equity. For accounting purposes, capital is measured in terms of book value and excludes short-term debt (i.e., current liabilities). For many financial purposes, capital is measured in terms of market value and does include short-term debt.

capital asset pricing model A model of expected return on a security based on the expected return associated with the broad market, the risk level of the security relative to the broad market (i.e., systematic risk), and the risk-free rate of interest. The risk is usually measured as the security's beta coefficient. The equation of the capital asset pricing model is as follows:

$$r_x = (\mu_m - r_f) \times \beta_x + r_f$$

where r_x denotes the required rate of return on the stock of corporation X, μ_m represents the expected rate of return on the broad market, r_f denotes the risk-free rate of interest, and β_x denotes the beta coefficient of the stock of corporation X relative to the broad market. See *beta coefficient* for method of computation.

capital gains/losses The difference between the sale price of an asset and the cost basis of that asset. If positive, the difference represents a capital gain. If negative, the difference represents a capital loss. *Cost basis* refers to the original purchase price of the asset adjusted for any subsequent investments in the asset or any depreciation applied to the asset. Cost basis is often referred to more simply as the *basis*, but the term basis has other meanings as well.

capital market instruments Equity and debt instruments having a maturity of one year or more.

capital markets The markets for intermediate- and long-term debt capital (i.e., notes and bonds) and for equity capital (i.e., stock). Includes both the primary and the secondary markets. The primary markets are made by investment banks and commercial banks, and the secondary markets are made by brokers/dealers.

capital markets group A division, department, or designated group within an investment bank or commercial bank whose function is to assist clients in meeting their financing needs through the issuance of debt and equity securities.

capital structure The percentage breakdown of a corporation's capital into that portion which represents debt and that portion which represents equity. For example, we might describe a corporation's capital structure as 60% debt and 40% equity.

capitalization The term can refer to either or both equity capital and debt capital. A corporation's equity capitalization is the number of shares of common stock outstanding multiplied by the current market price of the stock. Debt capitalization is calculated in a similar fashion.

capitalization rate The discount rate that equates the future cash flows associated with a capital instrument (i.e., a bond or stock) with the current market price of that capital instrument.

capitalization weighting Also known as *value weighting*. A method of computing a stock or a bond index that gives more weight to the securities with greater capitalization and less weight to the securities with lesser capitalization. This method is used, for example, in computing the S&P 500 index.

caplet One of the components of a strip of call options that collectively make up a cap option. In other words, each call component is called a caplet.

capped call A call option that has a maximum payoff. For example, the payoff function at expiry would look something like this:

$$payoff = max[max[S - X, 0], M]$$

where S is the spot price at expiry, X is the option's strike price, and M is the maximum payoff.

capped floater A floating rate note with a contractual upper limit on the floating rate.

capped swap A fixed-for-floating swap with a contractual upper limit on the floating rate. Such structures can be decomposed into a fixed-for-floating swap and a separate cap option. See also *rate-capped swap*.

CAPS See *convertible adjustable preferred stock*.

caption An option on a cap option. The caption purchaser has the right to enter a specific interest-rate cap option at a set price for a specified period of time. A caption is useful if the need for a cap option at a later date is not certain at the present time. By entering into the caption now, we can lock in the terms of the cap for an up-front premium (for the caption). If we later choose to exercise the caption, we pay the caption's strike price (which is the premium to acquire the underlying cap).

caput An option on a put option. The caput purchaser has the right to enter a specific put option by paying the caput's strike price (which is the premium to acquire the underlying put). This is a form of compound option (i.e., an option on an option).

carried interest An entitlement to a share of a business's profit for services rendered to the business, often called *sweat equity*.

carrying charge market A situation in which the futures (or forward) price for a commodity is higher than the current spot price of the commodity. A market in this state is often said to be in *contango*. See *contango*. For contrast, see *benefit of carry* and *backwardation*.

carve-out A process by which a corporation creates a subsidiary corporation and then transfers certain assets or operations of the parent to the subsidiary. The subsidiary is then a going concern and is sold by the parent to another corporation or to the public through a public offering. Carve-outs are one vehicle by which a corporation can dispose of assets or operations that no longer fit into its long-term strategic plan or need to be shed for legal reasons.

cash dividend A dividend paid by a corporation in the form of a cash payout to each shareholder where the sum paid is fixed per share and each shareholder receives a payment based on the number of shares he owns. Cash dividends are distinct from stock dividends, which are dividends on common stock that take the form of additional shares of stock.

cash flow (1) When used in the context of investment assets, the cash payments received as a consequence of holding the investment asset are called cash flows. (2) When used in the context of corporate finance there are several subtypes. Most commonly, the corporation's cash flow is calculated as the corporation's net income plus any non-cash expenses that might have been deducted in arriving at net income. Non-cash expenses include such things as depreciation, depletion, and amortization of intangible assets.

cash flow mapping A decomposition of the cash flows associated with a financial instrument or portfolio of financial instruments in which each cash flow is placed into a specific maturity bucket. This is useful for ascertaining the level of risk associated with an instrument or with a portfolio of instruments.

cash flow matching See *dedicated portfolio*.

cash flow stream The series of cash flows associated with a debt instrument, a swap, or any other financial instrument.

cash flow swap A swap that involves the exchange of an irregular series of cash flows.

cash market Also called the *spot market*. A market for the immediate delivery of an asset. The term "immediate" is interpreted in the context of the normal settlement period in the market. For example, in commodities, cash market transactions usually settle in two business days; in the United States, common stock transactions usually settle in three business days; Treasury bonds usually settle in one business day; and currencies usually settle in two business days. Thus, immediate settlement is understood to be one day in some markets, two days in other markets, and three days in still other markets.

cash position A position in any asset, including a financial instrument, with the exception of a position in a derivative instrument, unless the derivative instrument is itself the underlying asset for another derivative instrument. In the latter case, the position in the derivative instrument can itself be regarded as a cash position.

cash settlement (1) In securities trading, a transaction made for immediate settlement and payment, also known as same-day settlement. (2) In futures and option trading, the term refers to contracts that do not provide for physical delivery of the underlying asset. Instead, contracts are settled in cash on a final settlement date using a mark-to-market procedure.

cash-and-carry synthetics Strategies that involve the creation of synthetic risk-free assets (e.g., synthetic T-bills)

by combining instruments in which the market risks are completely offsetting so that the end result is equivalent to a riskless instrument. Cash-and-carry strategies are employed when, due to inefficiencies in the market, the synthetic risk-free instrument generates a higher rate of return than a real risk-free instrument. For example, one could create a synthetic T-bill by purchasing the stocks that make up the S&P 500 index (an index basket) and then selling an S&P 500 stock index futures contract. The two positions, together, replicate a risk-free asset.

cash-callable A bond that may not be called if the refunding will be achieved by issuing lower-cost debt, but may be called if the refunding will be achieved with cash from other sources.

cash-index arbitrage Most often used to describe the act of buying or selling a basket of stocks that mimics a stock index (called a proxy portfolio) and then selling or buying a futures contract on the same index. This is done when the futures contracts are mispriced relative to the underlying stocks. The goal is to earn a riskless profit by either (1) holding the two positions until the futures contract cash settles, or (2) taking advantage of a market movement to unwind the positions at a profit. The strategy is often called *program trading*, but this term has a broader meaning as well. Cash-index arbitrage is quantitatively intense, requiring the rapid examination of thousands of potential portfolios in the search for an exploitable opportunity. Also known as *index arbitrage*.

cash-on-cash return Also known as *current yield*. See *current yield*.

cash-or-nothing options Options that payoff either a fixed contractual amount at expiry or nothing depending upon whether they are in-the-money or out-of-the-money at expiry, respectively. Cash-or-nothing options can be calls or puts. They are created from digital options and resemble, but are different from, all-or-nothing options.

cash-settled options Option contracts that are cash settled on the basis of the value of the underlying asset on the expiration date. Cash-settled options are usually of the European type, but need not be. Most OTC options are cash settled.

CAT derivatives See *catastrophe derivatives*.

catastrophe derivatives Often call *CAT derivatives*. These include catastrophe futures, options, and swaps. CAT derivatives are designed to be used to hedge risks faced by casualty insurance companies and others with an exposure to cataclysmic events such as hurricanes, earthquakes, and so forth.

catastrophe risks Often known in the trade as *cat risks*. The risk of a significant financial loss due to some form of catastrophe such as fire, flood, earthquake, and so forth. These are significant risks to the sellers of catastrophe insurance. In recent years, catastrophe derivatives have been developed that can be used to transfer this risk from those who would ordinarily bear it to those more willing to do so. See *catastrophe derivatives*.

CBO See *collateralized bond obligation*.

CBOE See *Chicago Board Options Exchange*.

CBOT See *Chicago Board of Trade*.

CD See *certificate of deposit*.

ceiling Another name for a cap. See *cap*.

ceiling rate The contract rate on an interest-rate cap that serves as the cap's strike price. Also called the *cap rate* and the *contract rate*. The term *contract rate*, however, can be used to mean a rate specified in any contract.

central bank The central monetary authority of a nation responsible for making monetary policy and overseeing the banking industry. A central bank may be a governmental agency or, as in the United States, a quasi-governmental agency. In the United States, the central bank is the Federal Reserve.

central limit theorem A theorem in statistics which says that the distribution of a random variable X, defined as the sum of a number of draws on another random variable Y, will converge to a normal distribution irrespective of the type of distribution that Y has, provided that all the draws on Y have the same distribution (though it need not be normal). This theorem is frequently appealed to in statistical work in order to justify certain assumptions. Unfortunately, it is frequently misapplied.

certificate of deposit Known by the acronym *CD*. A large denomination negotiable certificate issued by a depository institution, such as a bank or thrift, that evidences a deposit. The certificate may be interest bearing or discounted. If interest bearing, the interest rate may be fixed or floating. Because they are negotiable, CDs are often referred to as negotiable certificates of deposit to distinguish them from small denomination nonnegotiable certificates of deposit purchased by retail investors.

ceteris paribus A Latin term meaning "all other things being equal."

cetes Mexican government Treasury bills.

CFTC See *Commodity Futures Trading Commission*.

chameleon option An option that can change from a call to a put or from a put to a call if certain conditions are satisfied. Generally, the conditions necessary for the change to occur are for the spot price to rise above or fall below some preset level.

charm A second order option Greek that measures the change in an option's delta associated with the passage of time.

cheapest-to-deliver Certain futures contracts allow for the delivery of any one of several underlying assets. Treasury bond futures are the best example of this. Bond futures allow for the delivery of any Treasury bond meeting certain criteria. Each deliverable instrument has an associated *conversion factor* to adjust for the fact that the different bonds have different terms (i.e., different coupons and different maturities). Nevertheless, one bond will, generally, still be less costly to acquire and deliver than any of the others. Such a bond is called the cheapest-to-deliver, or the *CTD*. Importantly, which bond is the CTD can change.

cherry picking A practice in bankruptcy proceedings by which the bankruptcy judge may enforce contracts that are in-the-money to the bankrupt corporation while at the same time abrogating contracts that are out-of-the money for the bankrupt corporation. Master swap agreements, which govern all swaps between the same counterparties, are generally written in such a fashion as to prevent cherry picking.

Chicago Board of Trade Known by the acronym *CBOT* (sometimes by the acronym *CBT*). The oldest futures exchange in the United States, it started as a cash market in grains in the first half of the nineteenth century. Futures trading in grains began in the 1860s. The CBOT has since expanded to trade a wide variety of futures including financial futures.

Chicago Board Options Exchange Known by the acronym *CBOE*, which is pronounced "see-bow." The oldest and largest options exchange in the United States, it opened in 1973 as a subsidiary of the Chicago Board of Trade to provide an organized exchange for the trading of listed stock options.

Chicago Mercantile Exchange Known by the acronym *CME*. Also known by its nickname "the Merc." A leading futures exchange located in the city of Chicago. Originally an agricultural exchange, it now trades many non-agricultural commodities as well. A division, The International Monetary Market (IMM), trades various types of financial futures, including currency futures and Eurodollar futures.

Chinese wall Investment banking jargon to mean that two groups within the same bank are not allowed to speak to one another with respect to certain subjects. This is to prevent conflicts of interest. For example, the investment banking division, whose clients are corporate issuers, is generally not permitted to speak with the research department—which works for sales and trading—because sales and trading's clients are the investors. Thus the two groups within the bank serve distinct client groups whose interests are diametrically opposed. The Chinese wall is intended to prevent abuses of client relationships. When it is necessary to exchange information, the groups will generally consult the bank's legal department to obtain permission to "go over the wall."

choice swap A swap that allows the floating-rate receiver to receive its choice of the reference rate value prevailing at either the beginning or the end of the swap coupon period.

Cholesky decomposition A process of obtaining random samples from a multivariate normal distribution that takes into consideration the degrees of correlation among the different variables. This process has value in simulation and multivariate option valuation.

chooser option A type of exotic option that specifies two strike prices (one a call strike and the other a put strike), a choice date, and an expiration date. The option is not specified, initially, to be a call or a put. Instead, the holder of the option elects on the choice date to specify the option as a call or a put. Once specified, the choice is irrevocable. If a call is specified, the call strike becomes the option's strike price. If a put is specified, the put strike becomes the option's strike price. Once specified, the option will pay off on the expiration date in the same way as a standard option. Note that if the call strike and the put strike are the same *and* if the choice date is the same as the expiration date, then the chooser option is identical to a straddle. If the call strike is higher than the put strike and the choice date is the same as the expiration date, then the chooser option is identical to a strangle. Also called *as-you-like-it options* and sometimes *you choose options*.

churning An unethical practice employed by some broker/dealers having discretionary trading authority over customer accounts in which they engage in excessive trading in order to reap commissions. Churning is an illegal practice but often difficult to distinguish from legitimate investment activity.

circus swap A combination involving a fixed-for-floating interest-rate swap and a fixed-for-floating currency swap in which both floating rate sides are LIBOR based. The combination of these two swaps results in a fixed-for-fixed or floating-for-floating currency swap.

class life In the depreciation of assets under the modified accelerated cost recovery method of depreciation (i.e., MACRS), the number of years that have been assigned to a particular class of assets for depreciation purposes. Class lives include 3-year property, 5-year property, 7-year property, and so forth. See *modified accelerated cost recovery system*.

class of options All of the calls written on the same underlying asset, irrespective of their expiry date and their strike price, represent the call class of options for that underlying. Similarly, all of the puts written on the same underlying asset, irrespective of their expiry and their strike price, represent the put class of options on that underlying. Thus, each underlying has two classes of options.

clean price The standard convention for quoting the bid and offer prices for bonds in which the price quote does not include accrued interest. Thus, the bond buyer pays the clean price plus the accrued interest. This is in contrast to a *dirty price*, which is the sum of the clean price and accrued interest. The dirty price is also known as the *full price*.

clearing association See *clearinghouse*.

clearing corporation See *clearinghouse*.

clearing firm A firm that clears financial transactions for other firms in the industry. Clearing firms are usually members of clearinghouses and are sometimes called *clearing members*.

clearing margin Margin posted with a clearinghouse by a clearing member.

clearing member See *clearing firm*.

clearinghouse (1) An organization that tracks, matches, and guarantees transactions in futures and options. Clearinghouses are the key to the financial integrity of futures and options exchanges and eliminate the need for traders to know whom their counterparties are. Also known as a *clearing association* and, if so organized, as a *clearing corporation*. (2) An organization that acts as a custodian for bearer securities in international markets.

cliquet option See *ratchet option*.

CLO See *collateralized loan obligation*.

close (1) A transaction that offsets an existing position and, thereby, closes out the position. (2) The last trade made during a designated trading session is often called the close.

closed form solution An analytical solution to a valuation problem. The term is often used in reference to option valuation models that take the form of equations (e.g., the *Black-Scholes model*).

closed-end investment company An investment company that does not stand ready to buy and sell its own shares at their net asset value. In such a structure, the shares trade in the secondary market in the same manner as the shares of any publicly held corporation. As such, the shares can trade at a premium to, or at a discount from, their net asset value. This is in contrast to open-end investment companies, often called mutual funds. See also *mutual funds*.

closeout netting A form of netting in OTC derivative transactions, such as swaps transactions, that becomes effective in the event that a default provision is triggered or some other form of termination event occurs.

close-out sale See *cancellation*.

closing date The date on which a transaction is completed including the final payment for, and legal conveyance of, the property. The term is often used in real estate transactions, but can be applied in other contexts as well.

closing period An officially designated period of time just prior to the close of an exchange. It may last from one minute to about fifteen minutes, as prescribed by the exchange. Often used in the context of futures markets.

closing range A range of prices (i.e., high and low) for an asset trading on an exchange (often futures contracts) that occurs during a narrow period of time called the closing period. Any trade made during the *closing period* should have been made at a price that falls within the closing range.

closing trade Also called an offsetting trade. A trade that closes an existing position by taking an offsetting position equal to but opposite that of the existing position.

CME See *Chicago Mercantile Exchange*.

CMO See *collateralized mortgage obligation*.

CMO swap A swap in which the amortization of the notional principal is linked to the amortization of a specific CMO issuance. Such structures are often used to transform the cash flow characteristics of a CMO.

CMS See *constant maturity swap.*

CMT Acronym for *constant maturity Treasury.* A reference to sampling of the yield on a specific (unchanging) maturity Treasury instrument on specific reset dates in order to set the floating rate for a floating-rate instrument. *See constant maturity Treasury.*

CMT swap A swap in which the reference rate for the floating leg of the swap is a specific maturity on the Treasury yield curve. For example, suppose that the swap has a tenor of five years and the reference rate is the two-year CMT. Then, every six months for five years we would observe the yield on the two-year on-the-run Treasury note for purposes of setting the floating rate on the swap for the next six months. Note that there is no connection between the tenor of the swap and the particular maturity of the Treasury chosen as the reference rate. The other leg of the swap is usually fixed. Two CMT swaps can be used to create a yield curve swap. See *yield curve swap.*

CMT-LIBOR differential notes A medium term note that pays the difference between the yield on a constant maturity Treasury (such as the 10-year Treasury) and a specific LIBOR rate such as the three-month LIBOR rate, plus some fixed spread (e.g., 150 basis points).

coefficient of determination An important statistical measure equal to the square of the correlation coefficient. Often used as a measure of hedge effectiveness in which case it measures the percentage of the variation in the price of a cash position explained by the variation in the price of the hedging instrument. Can be obtained as the R^2 from a simple linear regression.

coefficient of variation A measure that attempts to incorporate expected investment return (measured as the mean rate of return) and the investment risk (measured as the standard deviation of the rate of return) into a single number. The coefficient of variation, or CV, is calculated as the standard deviation divided by the mean. The argument is that the lower the CV the less the risk per unit of return. This measure is seriously flawed as a tool for comparing alternative investments.

COFI See *cost of funds index.*

COFI swap Any swap in which the reference rate is a cost of funds index.

collapsible swap See *callable swap.*

collar A combination of a cap (or call) option and a floor (or put) option in which the cap is sold and the floor is purchased. The cap has a higher strike than the floor. Collars can be written on interest rates, on stock prices, on exchange rates, etc. An interest rate collar can be combined with a floating rate note to create a collared floater. The premiums of the collar's combination of options at least partially offset each other. That is, the cap that is sold results in the receipt of a premium and the floor that is purchased results in the payment of a premium. If the two premiums are exactly offsetting, the structure is sometimes called a *zero-cost collar.* Collars have a variety of other names including *min-max structure, floor-ceiling agreement,* and *band.*

collar bond A bond with a floating coupon tied to some benchmark rate but which also has both an upper limit (i.e., cap) and a lower limit (i.e., floor) on the rate it pays. Together, the cap and the floor make up a collar. If the cap and floor are close together, the bond is sometimes called a *min-max bond.*

collar swap A swap in which the floating rate leg has a collar on it such that it will not pay more than some specified upper limit nor less than some specified lower limit. Also known as a *min-max swap* and a *banded swap*. These swaps are created by combining a plain vanilla swap with a collar. See *collar*.

collared floater A floating rate note that has both an upper limit (called a cap or a ceiling) and a lower limit (called a floor) to the floating rate. See *collar*.

collateral Something of value pledged by a borrower to a lender as backing for a debt obligation or derivative transaction in order to improve the creditworthiness of the borrower or counterparty.

collateral agreement Part of a loan or other agreement intended to address credit risk issues by providing for collateralization of the obligation. See *collateral*.

collateral trust bond A bond secured by personal property such as securities or inventory.

collateralized bond obligation More popularly known by the acronym *CBO*. These are securities that have been collateralized by a pool of bonds. Certain tranches bear more credit risk than others with the result that a pool of poorly rated bonds can give rise to at least some tranches that have a relatively good rating. Additionally, such instruments often employ credit derivatives to enhance the credit quality of the tranches.

collateralized loan obligation More popularly known by the acronym *CLO*. Similar to collateralized bond obligations (CBOs) but CLOs use loans as the collateral rather than bonds. See *collateralized bond obligation*.

collateralized mortgage obligation Commonly known as a *CMO*. A bond backed by a pool of whole mortgages or by mortgage passthrough certificates. Such bonds are issued in several distinct tranches. Ordinarily, interest flows to all tranches but principal flows only to the fastest-pay tranche. A wide variety of structures is possible including *interest only* and *principal only* tranches. These instruments were first created to better manage the prepayment risk associated with mortgages and to create instruments with shorter average lives than the mortgages from which they were created in an effort to broaden the secondary market for mortgages.

collateralized security Any security that has been collateralized by assets. When the term is applied to structured finance, it includes CMOs, ABS, CBOs, and CLOs.

collateralized swap Any swap in which one or both of the swap counterparties is required to post collateral in an effort to mitigate credit risk. Such swaps may call for a fixed amount of collateral to be provided by the poorer credit to the better credit, or the swap may require collateral in proportion to the amount by which the swap is out-of-the-money.

color A third order option Greek that measures the amount by which the option's gamma will change as a consequence of the passage of time.

comanager An investment bank that joins the lead manager and takes a major role in distributing securities in an underwritten offering. The comanagers share the management fee portion of the gross spread.

combination matching An asset-liability management approach that combines the dedicated portfolio approach (i.e., cash flow matching) with the immunization approach (i.e., duration matching). Generally, the durations of the asset portfolio and the liability portfolio are matched and the cash flows are matched for the first few years (often five), but not beyond. See *dedicated portfolio, immunization,* and *horizon matching.*

combinations Options trading strategies that involve both calls and puts at the same time. The more common combinations are *straddles, strangles, strips,* and *straps.*

combined seasoned offerings Sometimes called a *piggyback offering.* A public offering of securities that is partly a secondary seasoned offering and partly a primary seasoned offering. See *secondary seasoned offering* and *primary seasoned offering.*

commercial paper Short-term corporate debt instruments often used as part of a rollover strategy to obtain long-term financing at a lower cost. Often called paper and sometimes called *CP.* Commericial paper may be placed with investors either directly by the corporate issuer or through commercial paper dealers. Commercial paper rarely has a maturity longer than 270 days.

commission A fee paid by a principal to an agent for the agent's services in executing a transaction on behalf of the principal.

commission house brokers See *floor brokers.*

Committee on Uniform Security Identification Procedures (CUSIP) A group sponsored by the American Banker's Association to develop standardized procedures for the unambiguous identification of securities in order to avoid confusion regarding what is being

bought and what is being sold in securities transactions. Today, each security issue is assigned a unique CUSIP number. All shares of the same stock will have the same CUSIP number as will all bonds issued as part of the same bond issuance.

commodities Staple items such as wool, sugar, soybeans, pork, copper, gold, and other agricultural or industrial products that are traded on a commodity exchange.

commoditizing The transformation of a custom-made product, originally designed for a specific client with specific needs, into an off-the-shelf product marketed to a wider audience. In the process, the product is transformed from a low volume, high margin product into a high volume, low margin product.

commodity currency In the context of foreign exchange, the currency that is being bought or sold and which is priced in terms of another currency, which is called the *terms currency.* For example, if one wanted to buy 100,000 euros and the euro was priced at $1.0200, then the euro is the commodity currency and the dollar is the terms currency. Of course, which currency is the commodity currency and which is the terms currency is relative, because any exchange rate can be stated with either currency serving as the commodity currency.

Commodity Futures Trading Commission Known by the acronym *CFTC.* The agency of the U.S. government responsible for oversight and regulation of the futures industry. The CFTC was created in 1974 by the Commodity Futures Trading Act and its authority was extended by the Futures Trading Act of 1978.

commodity price risk The price risk associated with holding a position in commodities or an anticipated position in commodities.

commodity swaps Swaps that are structured to convert floating prices for commodities to fixed prices, or vice versa. These swaps have a similar structure to interest-rate swaps but are based on fixed commodity prices and floating commodity prices rather than on fixed interest rates and floating interest rates. Such swaps enable commodity producers and commodity users to manage their commodity price risks.

common stock The financial claims on a corporation held by the owners of the corporation. Each share of common stock represents a pro rata claim on the residual value of the corporation. By residual value, we mean the value that remains after the claims of all creditors and other forms of equity holders, such as preferred stock holders, have been satisfied. In some countries, known as *ordinaries.*

companion bonds Also known as *support bonds.* Tranches of a CMO that have greater cash flow uncertainty than other tranches of the CMO. The latter would include planned amortization class bonds (PACs). The greater certainty of the cash flows on PACs comes from shifting the uncertainty to companion bonds.

company-specific risk Another name for *unsystematic risk.* This is risk that is diminished by diversifying an equity portfolio. See *unsystematic risk.*

comparative advantage A situation in which one country (or corporation) can produce a good (or engage in a borrowing) at less cost than another country (or corporation) in the special sense that it must sacrifice less of an alternative good to achieve production. The term is associated with both the theory of comparative advantage used to explain trading between nations and the theory of relative advantage to explain the existence of the swaps market.

competitive bidding (1) A process in which parties bid for securities and the securities are awarded first to the parties bidding the highest price, then to the parties bidding the next highest price, and so forth until all of the issuance has been awarded. (2) In an underwriting, the bidding by competing underwriting syndicates for the right to underwrite a security issuance.

complement rule An arbitrage argument that says that if two exotic options are both held, they would replicate the behavior of a standard option. Therefore, together they have the same value as the standard option. For example, a knock-in call and a knock-out call, written on the same underlying with the same expiry, the same strike, and the same barrier price, should behave together like a standard call option.

complex options Options in which the strike price of the option can change due to changes in factors other than the price of the underlying. Options in which the strike periodically steps up or down would be an example.

composite hedge A hedge consisting of more that one hedging instrument. For example, a corporate bond dealer might hedge a large position in a 15-year corporate bond partly in a 20-year T-bond futures contract and partly in a 10-year T-note futures contract.

composite VaR Composite value-at-risk. See *blended VaR.*

compound interest Interest earned on interest.

compound option An option written on another option such that the exercise of the first option results in the acquisition of the underlying option.

compression risk Closely related to call risk on callable bonds and prepayment risk on mortgages and mortgage backed securities. The potential for a loss of value from a decline in yields such that the decline in yields leads to the exercise of call options and prepayment options embedded in debt instruments. The result can be that the instrument behaves like a short-dated instrument despite its long maturity.

concave utility functions Often assumed in economic analysis because such functions possess properties that are consistent with fundamental economic tenets concerning consumer and investor behavior. A concave utility function expresses the relationship between utility (i.e., economic satisfaction) and the level of wealth. That is U = f(W). In a concave utility function, the first derivative of the function is positive but the second derivative is negative. This is equivalent to saying that utility is monotonically increasing in wealth, thereby satisfying the law of insatiability; and marginal utility diminishes as wealth increases, thereby satisfying the law of diminishing marginal utility.

concavity The opposite of convexity. A value diagram that is concave relative to the underlying value driver. Concavity is usually associated with options such that a normally convex value diagram for a bond may have regions of negative convexity (i.e., concavity) due to the presence of embedded options.

concentrated equity positions Large stock positions that are difficult to liquidate by traditional means and often represent a significant portion of an individual's net worth.

conditional probability A probability that is conditional upon something else happening or not happening.

condor A type of option spread involving four options of the same class (i.e., all are calls or all are puts), all having the same expiration date. The options differ in their strike prices. The two middle strike options are sold and the two end strike options are purchased. For example, suppose that we have four March calls on XYZ. These options have the following strikes: 90, 95, 100, and 105. In a condor we would sell the 95 and the 100 strikes and we would buy the 90 and the 105 strikes. Condors get their name from the shape of their profit diagrams. Butterfly spreads have a sharp point in the center; the center peak is flattened in a condor (the condor is a species of bird whose head droops while it flies).

conduit A vehicle that passes through cash flows. For example, mutual funds hold stock and pass the dividends received and the capital gains earned through to the beneficial owners of the shares of the mutual fund. This entitles the mutual funds to *conduit tax treatment,* which basically means that they are not taxed on their income provided they pass most of it on to the owners. The owners are taxed on the income. Conduit tax treatment is intended to avoid double taxation of income.

conduit tax treatment Passthrough tax treatment predicated on the fact that the conduit is merely a vehicle to pass income from its source to its rightful recipient. As long as the income is passed through, there is no reason to tax the conduit.

confidence channel A continuum of confidence intervals for the outcomes of an investment portfolio (measured as cumulative total return) at some given confidence level over a continuum of investment horizons. For example, we might be interested in the 90% confidence channel for an investor with a five-year horizon. Then, for each point in the future out to five years, we compute the 90% confidence interval. Each interval has an upper and a lower limit. We connect the upper limit values over the investment horizon to get an upper bound for the channel and the lower limit values to get the lower bound for the channel. We might also draw a line representing the mean outcomes over the horizon.

confidence interval The range of values centered around the mean that captures a specified percentage of the outcomes from a stochastic process. For example, if a random variable has a mean of 30, we might be interested in knowing the range of values centered at 30 that captures 90% of the total possible outcomes. Calculating a confidence interval requires knowledge of the nature of the random variable's distribution and the parameters associated with the random variable. In the case of the normal distribution, there are only two relevant parameters—the mean and the standard deviation.

confidence level The number of times out of 100 that a stochastic process will generate an outcome in a prescribed range. Expressed as a percentage. For example, if a random variable would take on a value between 10 and 50 eighty percent of the time, then we can be eighty percent confident (the eighty percent confidence level) that a randomly selected draw on the variable will lie in the range 10 to 50.

confirmation A written statement transmitted by mail, telex, fax, or e-mail, detailing the relevant economic terms involved in a transaction. The transaction is usually initiated via phone conversations or an internet-based communication.

conflict of interest A situation in which an agent's interests conflict with the interests of the agent's client or in which the interests of two of the agent's clients are in conflict. When a conflict of interest arises, agents are often required to recluse themselves from the situation by terminating or suspending the relationship until such time as the conflict is resolved. Within financial institutions, where the interests of clients will likely conflict, the financial institution employs procedures and processes to protect each of the clients. These procedures and processes are referred to as a Chinese wall. See *Chinese wall.*

conglomerates Companies that have business interests across a range of unrelated products and services often through subsidiary holdings.

consol bonds Perpetual bonds issued by the British government. These bonds pay fixed rates of interest but have no maturity date and hence are never redeemed. These bonds were first issued to consolidate the British government's war debts, which gave rise to the nickname consols.

consolidation The formation of a single new company from the combination of two pre-existing companies in which neither of the two original companies survives.

constant maturity swap Often referred to by the acronym *CMS.* A swap in which a floating payment is determined by periodic reference to the par swap rate for a swap of a constant tenor. Similar to a constant maturity Treasury swap but the swap curve is used in lieu of the Treasury yield curve.

constant maturity Treasury Often referred to by the acronym *CMT*. A reference to repeated observations on the yield of a specific-maturity Treasury security. For example, if every six months we observe the yield on the on-the-run five-year Treasury note, that would represent a constant maturity Treasury.

constant maturity Treasury swap Also known as a *CMT swap*. A swap in which a floating payment is determined by reference to the prevailing yield on an on-the-run Treasury bond of a specified and unchanging maturity. For example, a five-year CMT swap with a tenor of two years and making semiannual payments would require observation of the yield on the five-year Treasury note at the inception of the swap and would pay this rate at the end of six months. At the time of the first payment, an observation would be made on the yield of the new five-year Treasury note for purposes of determining the next payment. This process would be repeated a total of four times. The other leg of the swap could be fixed or floating.

constant prepayment rate Often indicated by the acronym *CPR*. In mortgage analytics, a constant annual percentage of the outstanding principal balance on a mortgage or mortgage portfolio assumed to be prepaid each year. Actual prepayments can differ significantly from the CPR.

constructive sales Investors often have a powerful tax incentive not to sell a position in a security that has appreciated in value despite the fact that they no longer wish to hold the position, either because the risk is too concentrated or because they no longer view the security as a good investment. Financial engineers have devised a variety of instruments and strategies to produce an outcome that is economically equivalent to a sale without an actual sale of the security taking place. This is most often accomplished using equity swaps or a combination of options. In order to reduce taxpayers' ability to avoid capital gains taxes via these strategies, the U.S. Congress passed constructive sales rules that, essentially, treat a structure or strategy designed to be economically equivalent to a sale as though a sale had actually taken place.

contagion effect The tendency for a crisis in one asset class or geographic region to spread to other asset classes or geographic regions. For example, a crisis in the bond markets in one country could spread to other markets in that same country or to bond markets in other countries.

contango The opposite of *backwardation*. That is, the current price for future delivery (i.e., the futures price) is higher than the current spot price of the underlying asset. Contango is typical in a carrying charge market. The term is sometimes defined as a situation in which a commodity's futures price is greater than its expected future spot price. See also *carrying charge market*.

contingent orders An order entered with a broker to buy or sell one asset where the order is contingent upon some other order also being filled. For example, we might have an order to buy one futures contract and sell another futures contract where each transaction is contingent upon the other transaction also being done. This is commonly the case in a spread strategy and often the case in roll hedging.

contingent premium cap A contingent premium option in which the option is a cap. See *contingent premium option*.

contingent premium option An option in which the purchaser does not pay the premium up front. Instead, if the option is in-the-money at expiration, the option holder pays the full premium. If the option is out-of-the-money at expiration, the holder does not have to pay any premium. The premium on contingent premium options is higher than the premium on conventional options.

contingent premium swap option A contingent premium option in which the option takes the form of a swaption (i.e., an option on a swap). See *contingent premium option*.

contingent swap A swap agreement that becomes effective if and only if a specified event occurs. Any of a variety of events could be specified, such as a business merger, or a price or an interest rate rising (or falling) to a certain level.

contingent takedown option An option to buy a security, often a bond. These options are usually issued to the original purchasers of the security as sweeteners (i.e., to make the issue more attractive). The option grants the original purchaser of the security the right to buy additional units of the security on specified terms. Similar to a warrant to buy stock and often called a *bond warrant*.

continuous auction market Any market in which orders to buy and orders to sell are channeled upon receipt to an exchange for immediate execution at currently prevailing and ever-changing prices. This is in contrast to a call market system in which buy orders and sell orders are aggregated for some period of time and then matched in batches at designated times of the day.

continuous compounding A system of compounding interest in which the compounding occurs continuously. That is, with each instant of time, interest is earned. During the following instant of time, interest is earned on the interest that was earned during the prior instant of time. When rates of interest or percentage changes in value are measured in this way, they possess useful mathematical properties that rates stated with any other compounding frequency lack. For this reason, percentage changes in most advanced analytical work are measured as continuously compounded rates.

continuous market In theory, a market that has infinite depth and liquidity and in which price changes are infinitesimally small. Thus, to get from any one price to any other price, the asset must trade at every price in between. Continuous markets are also assumed to be always open. Many modeling exercises are based on the premise that the markets are continuous, which is a necessary precondition for dynamic hedging strategies. In practice, no market is truly continuous. Markets may be approximately continuous if they are liquid and price changes are small.

continuous time The idea that time flows like a river and is not divided into natural intervals. The calculus on which many valuation models are developed assumes continuous time. This was the approach that Black, Scholes, and Merton took in developing the first complete closed form option valuation model. Continuous time modeling contrasts with discrete time modeling, which assumes that time can be divided into discrete intervals (e.g., years, months, weeks, days, hours, minutes, etc.). As discrete time intervals are divided into ever smaller time increments, discrete time models become more like continuous time models. In fact, the results of the two approaches converge as the discrete time intervals become infinitesimally small.

contract for difference Often called a *difference contract* or a *diff contract*. These are contracts, whether forwards, futures, or options, that pay off based on the difference between two prices or rates.

contract rate The fixed rate of interest (or fixed exchange rate) that serves as the basis of a cash settlement on a forward contract or an option contract. In the case of an option, this rate is often called a strike rate. On a forward, the cash settlement will be the difference between the reference rate and the contract rate.

contraction (1) In the context of corporate restructuring, the downsizing of a corporation. This can be accomplished through divestitures, spin offs, or carve-outs. (2) In macroeconomics, a reference to negative economic growth as measured by a shrinkage in gross domestic product (GDP). If it goes on for a sufficient period of time, it is called a recession. (3) The shortening of the average life of a mortgage portfolio as a consequence of a decline in interest rates, which triggers refinancings.

contraction risk The risk that when interest rates fall, large numbers of homeowners may refinance their mortgage loans.

control stock Any stock of an issuer (including registered and unregistered shares) that is owned by an affiliate of the issuer (i.e., an officer, a director, or other person who, through stock ownership or otherwise, controls the management policies of the issuer). Rule 144 of the Securities Act of 1933 places the following restrictions on the sale of such stock: (1) Current public information on the issuer must be available.

(2) No minimum holding period is allowed. (3) The number of shares that may be sold by a holder within a three-month period is subject to volume limitations equal to the greater of 1% of the shares of the same class outstanding or the average weekly trading volume (averaged over the prior four calendar weeks). All Rule 144 sales of securities of the same class (restricted or nonrestricted) by or on behalf of the owner and certain persons related to the owner must be aggregated. (4) Sales must be made by the owner to a market maker in the stock or by a broker on behalf of the owner to purchase in unsolicited agency transactions and (5) Form 144 Notice of Sale must be filed with the SEC and the principal exchange (if any) for the stock no later than the day on which the sell order is entered.

convenience yield The value that accrues to the holder of a position in a cash asset, as opposed to the holder of a futures contract on the asset. This concept was rather abstract until the introduction of stock index futures and bond futures. The holder of cash stocks receives dividends and the holder of cash bonds accrues interest. Stock index futures and bond futures holders derive no such benefits.

conventional mortgages Also known as *level payment mortgages*. Mortgages having a fixed term and a fixed coupon rate with all payments of equal size. While the payments are of equal size, the interest component gets smaller and the principal component gets larger with each payment.

convergence The tendency of certain things to come together. These may include a convergence of ideas, a convergence of market prices, or a convergence of the values generated by valuation models. For example, in the futures markets, a futures price should converge to the spot price of the underlying asset as the futures contract approaches its delivery date. This is a consequence of a gradual reduction in the cost of carry. As a second example, the values generated by a discrete time binomial option pricing model should converge to the values generated by analytical models as discrete time is divided into very small increments.

conversion arbitrage Any strategy that seeks to combine (or to disassemble) instruments having one set of investment characteristics in order to obtain one or more instruments having a different set of investment characteristics. The resultant instruments are often described as synthetic. Such strategies are executed in order to exploit a pricing discrepancy between the real and the synthetic securities.

conversion factors A set of multiplicative factors published by the Chicago Board of Trade to equalize the values of the different Treasury bonds and notes that can be delivered on Treasury bond and Treasury note futures contracts.

conversion option The option embedded in a convertible bond allowing the bondholder to convert the bond into a specified number of shares of the issuer's common stock. The number of shares that the bond may be converted into is called the *conversion ratio*.

conversion premium The premium over conversion value at which a convertible trades. For example, a $100 convertible with a $50 conversion value has a 100% conversion premium. Conversion premium is one measure of a convertible's equity sensitivity. The lower the conversion premium, the higher the equity sensitivity. Conversely, the higher the conversion premium, the lower the convertible's sensitivity to common stock movements.

conversion price The price of common stock above which, at maturity, a holder of a convertible security should convert the security into common stock rather than accept the security's redemption value. If the common stock trades below the conversion price at maturity, the holder should accept the redemption value. If the common stock trades above the conversion price, the convertible is in-the money. The conversion price is computed by dividing the convertible's par value by its conversion ratio. Therefore, a $1,000 face value convertible bond that converts into 50 shares has a $20 conversion price. Remember, corporate bond prices are quoted as a percentage of par so care must be taken to express the bond price in actual dollars to compute the conversion price.

conversion ratio The number of shares of common stock received upon conversion of a convertible security. A convertible security can be converted at any time, in most cases, into the number of shares of common stock given by the conversion ratio.

conversion value The value of common stock represented by each convertible. Conversion value is computed by multiplying the price of the underlying common stock by the conversion ratio. With regard to convertible bonds, divide the conversion value by 10 as bond prices are quoted in 100s and not in 1,000s.

convertible adjustable preferred stock Sometimes referred to by the acronym *CAPS*. A form of convertible preferred stock in which the preferred stock is convertible on a dividend payment date to the number of shares of common stock having a market value equal to the par value of the preferred. For example, suppose that the preferred has a par value of $100 and on a dividend payment date the common is trading at $40 a share. Then, on that date, one share of preferred is convertible into 2.5 shares of common. It is clear from this structure that the conversion ratio (i.e., the number of shares of common that can be obtained from one share of preferred) is variable. This is the distinguishing feature of this form of preferred stock.

convertible bond Long-term debt instruments that are not secured by collateral and that are convertible into other assets of the issuer, usually common stock. See also *convertible debt.* Convertible bonds and *convertible preferred stock* together make up a category of securities called *convertibles* or *convertible securities.*

convertible debt A debt instrument that is convertible into some other asset of the issuer—usually common stock. The most common type is the convertible bond.

convertible from fixed to floating A debt instrument in which the holder can convert the instrument's fixed coupon into a floating coupon under preset terms.

convertible from floating to fixed A debt instrument in which the holder can convert the instrument's floating coupon into a fixed coupon under preset terms.

convertible into equity A financial instrument that is convertible into some number of shares of the issuer's equity.

convertible preferred stock Preferred stock that is convertible into a specified number of shares of common stock at

the option of the holder of the convertible preferred stock.

convertible securities Any security, such as a convertible bond or convertible preferred stock, that is convertible into some other security, usually common stock of the issuer.

convertibles See *convertible securities.*

convex tax function A tax function is a graphic depiction of the relationship between a corporation's (or individual's) net income before taxes and the total income tax liability. The net income before taxes is usually plotted on the horizontal axis and the tax liability is plotted on the vertical axis. The tax function is said to be convex if the tax liability rises at an accelerating rate as net income rises. This is equivalent to saying that the effective tax rate rises as net income before taxes rises. When a corporation has a convex tax function, which is the usual case, hedging price exposures to reduce the volatility of income has the beneficial side effect of reducing the average annual tax burden.

convexity An important interest rate risk measure used in conjunction with a fixed income instrument's duration. Essentially, convexity measures the rate at which the instrument's duration is changing as the instrument's yield changes. Mathematically, it is the second derivative of the instrument's price with respect to its yield divided by the instrument's price. The concept of convexity in the fixed income markets is analogous to the concept of gamma in the options markets.

convexity adjustment Used to mean an adjustment to correct for convexity bias. However, the term *convexity bias* has several meanings with the result that the term convexity adjustment has several meanings. See *convexity bias.*

convexity bias The term has several meanings. (1) In the context of bond pricing, the convexity of the price/yield function causes duration to overestimate the amount by which the bond's price will change for a given change in yield. This overestimate is often called convexity bias. (2) In the context of Eurodollar futures, the LIBOR rates implied by Eurodollar futures are biased upward because the profit function of a Eurodollar futures contract is perfectly linear with respect to LIBOR, while a true forward contract on LIBOR displays convexity. As a result, a short position in a forward contract that is hedged in Eurodollar futures gives rise to a straddle-like option. The value of this straddle-like option is a function of the degree of convexity of the forward contract and the volatility of LIBOR. The value of the option is the degree of the bias, which is often called convexity bias. (3) In a binomial approach to calculating an option adjusted spread (OAS) on a bond, the expected present value from the two forward short rates that can evolve from the current forward short rate (i.e., the two values at the next time period are obtained from the single value this time period) will not give rise to the same present value as the current forward short rate due to a convexity bias. The model must be calibrated to eliminate the convexity bias.

core business risks Those risks faced by a business that are peculiar to the business concerned. Such risks include production risks, market share, useful outcomes from research and development, and so on.

corporate credit spread risk The risk that the cost of financing a corporation will change due to changed perceptions about the issuer's credit quality.

corporate finance desk The group within an investment bank responsible for maintaining the investment bank's relationships with its corporate clients. The group advises the corporate clients on such matters as the sale of debt and equity securities, risk management, and mergers and acquisitions.

corpus From Latin for "body." Refers to the principal on a loan, bond, or note. The term is most often used in legal contexts.

correlation coefficient Often called *correlation*. A widely used statistic that measures the degree of linear relationship between two random variables. The correlation coefficient must lie in the range of –1 to +1. The correlation coefficient is found by dividing the covariance of the two random variables by the product of the two random variables' individual standard deviations. Correlations play a critical role in portfolio construction and risk management. Indeed, the effectiveness of a hedge can be ascertained from the degree of correlation between the spot price of the cash position to be hedged and the price of the hedge instrument. The higher the correlation, the more effective the hedge will be.

correlation risk The risk that the correlation between two positions will suddenly change. For example, portfolio diversification aims at reducing risk by holding positions that have relatively low correlations with one another. If the correlations suddenly rise, the overall riskiness of the portfolio rises. In a hedging context, if two positions represent hedges for one another, then a high degree of correlation is desirable because the positions will be held on opposite sides of the market (i.e., one long and one short). A sudden drop in correlation would then result in an increase in overall risk. See *correlation co-efficient*.

correspondents Financial institutions that clear trades for other financial institutions. For example, all brokerage firms execute trades on behalf of clients, but not all brokerage firms clear trades. Those that execute but do not clear are called *introducing brokers*. Those that clear for introducing brokers are called *correspondents*.

corridor The term corridor has a number of meanings, all referring to positions in derivatives. One of these is a collar on a swap created using two swaptions.

corridor swap A swap in which the floating leg accrues interest only on those days when the reference rate lies within a specified range. Similar in concept to a *range floater*.

cost basis The cost, after adjusting for depreciation and/or improvement, of a capital asset for purposes of calculating a capital gain or loss upon the sale of the asset. Often called the *accounting basis* or simply the *basis*. The latter term has a variety of other meanings as well.

cost of a hedge The difference between the expected profit on an unhedged cash position and the expected profit on the cash position when hedged. The cost, defined this way, can be positive, negative, or zero. Importantly, this definition overlooks some important benefits of hedging such as the potential for tax savings and the ability to operate on a larger scale with the same capital base.

cost of capital The cost incurred by a corporation in obtaining the debt capital and the equity capital it needs to finance its activities. The cost of debt capital is always lower than the cost of equity capital for two reasons: (1) The

interest paid on debt is tax deductible for the corporation while the dividends paid to equity holders are not tax deductible. (2) The equity holders' claims on the corporation are subordinate to the debt holders' claims and, hence, holding equity is more risky. The overall cost of capital to a corporation is a weighted average of the after-tax costs of the two components of capital (i.e., debt and equity).

cost of carry The cost of carrying a position over a period of time. This includes not only all explicit costs but also such implicit costs as the opportunity cost of money (if not included among the explicit costs).

cost of funds index Usually abbreviated *COFI*. Any of several indexes of the cost of funds to financial institutions calculated as weighted averages of the monthly interest cost of liabilities. More widely quoted COFIs are often used as benchmarks that serve as the reference rate for interest rate swaps and some variable rate debt instruments. For example, the 11th district cost of funds index is one of the more widely used.

counterparty (1) A principal in a swap or other financial transaction, as opposed to an agent such as a broker. (2) The party taking the other side of a financial contract.

counterparty risk The risk faced by one counterparty to a derivative contract that the other counterparty will default on its obligations thereby causing loss to the first counterparty. In some derivatives, counterparty risk is one way (i.e., options in which the full premium is paid up front), but in others (i.e., swaps) it is two way.

country risk Also known as *political risk* and *sovereign risk*. The risk of loss, due to political developments or other sovereign-related causes, on contracts involving cross-border cash flows. Historical practice has been to manage this risk by limiting exposure by country. For example, a bank might make loans to corporations in Country X and might place a limit on the exposure to any one corporation in Country X, but it would simultaneously place a limit on overall lending (i.e., aggregate lending) to corporations domiciled in Country X.

coupon (1) The periodic interest payment on a debt instrument. (2) The periodic interest payment on the fixed-rate side of an interest rate or currency swap.

coupon bonds Bonds that pay periodic interest. The periodic payment is called the coupon. The term is generally used to refer to bonds that pay a fixed coupon.

coupon leverage Some debt instruments leverage up the effects of a change in interest rates, particularly for inverse floating rate instruments. For example, suppose that a particular issuer could sell a five-year fixed rate note at par if it pays a coupon of 7.5%. It could also sell a five-year floating rate note if it pays LIBOR (L). Suppose now that the issuer offers an inverse floating rate note paying a coupon of 22.5% – 2 × LIBOR. Thus, if LIBOR is 7.5%, the instrument pays 7.5%. If LIBOR rises 1%, the coupon declines by 2%. If LIBOR declines by 1%, the coupon rises by 2%. The leveraging up of the coupon is called coupon leverage.

coupon rate (1) The fixed rate of interest on a debt instrument. (2) The fixed rate of interest on the fixed-rate side of a swap. (3) The floating rate on a floating rate note is often referred to as a floating coupon.

coupon stripping The act of separating the claims for coupon payments on a bond from the bond itself so that each coupon payment is an obligation in its own right. The act of removing the coupons from the bond creates a collection of zero coupon bonds and is called stripping. Treasury bonds were first stripped of their coupons in 1977 by Merrill Lynch to create the first form of Treasury-based zero coupon bonds called Treasury Investment Growth Receipts or TIGRs. Today, Treasurys can be stripped through the Fed wire system to create generic zeros called STRIPS.

coupon swap A plain vanilla fixed-for-floating interest rate swap.

covariance A measure of the degree to which two random variables move in the same or opposite direction with respect to one another. In other words, if two random variables generally move in the same direction, they would be said to have positive covariance. If they tend to move in opposite directions, they would be said to have negative covariance. Covariance is measured as the expected value of the products of the deviations of two random variables from their respective means. A variance is a special case of a covariance. See *variance-covariance matrix.*

covenants Clauses in a bond indenture that place restrictions on the issuer's activities, or which provide protections for the bondholder or the issuer. Can also refer to clauses within a derivatives contract having a similarly restrictive nature.

cover (1) In the context of short sales of securities, the return of borrowed securities used for a short sale. (2) In bidding on auctioned securities, the spread between the winning bid and the next highest bid.

covered call A situation in which the writer of a call option owns the underlying asset on which the option is written. Thus, if the option is exercised, the option writer can deliver the underlying without having to purchase it.

covered interest arbitrage A strategy requiring the borrowing of funds in one currency for lending in another currency with two simultaneous foreign exchange transactions (one spot and one forward) to remove the exchange rate risk. These strategies are undertaken when the difference between the interest rates in the money markets is out of line with the difference between the forward foreign exchange rate and the spot foreign exchange rate. This type of covered interest arbitrage results in an equilibrium state known as *interest rate parity*.

CPR See *constant prepayment rate*.

crack spread The potential for profit to an oil refiner from the difference between the prices of refined products made from oil and the price of the crude oil from which these products are made.

crack swap/option A swap or option contract in which the reference rate is linked in some manner to the crack spread. See *crack spread*.

credit arbitrage The derivation of profit (or, equivalently, cost savings) by exploiting differences in borrowing costs for different credit borrowers. Credit arbitrage is often used as an explanation for the use of swaps to reduce corporate borrowing costs.

credit derivative An over-the-counter, usually off–balance sheet, instrument that makes payments based on some specified credit-related measure or event. For example, some swaps and

options pay off if and only if some credit event, such as a default, occurs; other swaps and options pay off based on the difference between the yields on instruments with dissimilar credit ratings. This difference in yields is called a *credit spread*. Credit derivatives were first developed in the early 1990s as an outgrowth of total return swaps and options, but the real growth of the market did not begin until the second half of the 1990s.

credit enhancement Any of a variety of measures that improve the creditworthiness of a bond, loan, or swap. These may include guarantees from third parties, overcollateralization, reserve funds, and special purpose vehicles that are bankruptcy remote.

credit event Any credit-related condition specified as a credit event by the counterparties to a financial instrument. Credit events will almost always include extreme conditions, such as a default on a required payment, but may include less extreme conditions such as a downgrade of some reference asset. A credit event triggers the termination of most over-the-counter derivatives.

credit exposure The potential for a financial loss to result from the inability of a counterparty to a financial transaction to fulfill its obligations. In the case of a loan or bond, credit exposure represents the potential for a loss of the principal. In a swap, credit exposure has two components: current exposure—representing the current mark-to-market value of the position; and potential exposure—representing future changes in the mark-to-market value of the position. Credit exposure is also called *credit risk*.

credit facility Any lending arrangement (including both the party willing to provide capital and the mechanics of the lending and collateralization processes) that is in place and can be drawn upon if needed.

credit quality A measure of default risk associated with an issuer of an obligation or investment contract. Credit ratings assigned by Moody's Investor Services and Standard & Poor's (S&P) are widely used measures of an issue's credit quality. Companies with the highest credit quality receive AAA ratings from both agencies. Companies in default, on the other hand, are rated D.

credit rating A rating of a debt issue or loan, or the rating of a corporation's or an individual's creditworthiness. When the term is applied to bonds, it is often called a bond rating. See *bond rating*.

credit risk The possibility of default by a counterparty to a transaction and the financial loss to the other counterparty that would result. See also *credit exposure*.

credit risk equivalent Part of the bank capital guidelines adopted by the Federal Reserve in 1989. Determined by marking off–balance sheet positions to their market values and then adding a prescribed add-on factor. The guidelines grew out of the Basle Capital Accord.

credit risk premium The portion of a debt instrument's yield that reflects compensation to the lender for bearing credit risk. Not necessarily the same thing as a credit spread. A credit risk premium is the difference between the yield on the credit-risky instrument and the credit-risk-free instrument, all other things being equal. A credit spread is the difference between the yields on two instruments, both of which might be credit-risky. If one of the instruments is credit-risk free, then the credit risk premium and the credit

spread are the same. Credit risk premiums are measured in basis points.

credit spread The difference between the yield on a bond in one credit group (e.g., AA corporate) with some specific maturity and the yield on a bond in a different credit group (usually a Treasury) having the same maturity. Sometimes called a *quality spread*. The term credit spread is a bit of a misnomer because the credit spread can be partially explained by differences other than credit quality—such as differences in the taxability of income generated and differences in liquidity.

credit spread forward Similar to a credit spread swap but pays off only once. See *credit spread* and *credit spread swap*.

credit spread option A type of credit derivative. Can be a call or a put. If a call, an option that pays off if the credit spread between two bonds exceeds a fixed spread (i.e., the strike) at the time of the option's expiration. If a put, an option that pays off if the credit spread between two bonds is less than a fixed spread (i.e., the strike) at the time of the option's expiration. See *credit spread*.

credit spread swap A type of credit derivative. A swap in which one counterparty pays a fixed amount (i.e., a fixed credit spread) to the other on each of the swap's settlement dates while the second counterparty pays the first a variable amount based on the actual credit spread between two instruments on those same dates. The actual size of the net payment made will be determined by the difference between the fixed spread and the floating spread, and by the size of the notional principal on the contract.

credit swaps A broad subgroup of credit derivatives that includes *credit spread swaps*, *total return swaps*, and *de-*

fault swaps. See these specific types for details.

credit transition matrix A table or matrix showing the probability that an entity with any given credit rating will move to any one of a number of other credit ratings within specific periods of time. Such matrices are constructed from historical data and do not usually take into consideration the specific characteristics of a particular entity.

credit watch A warning by a credit rating agency, such as Standard & Poor's or Moody's Investor Services, with respect to a specific bond issuance, that a credit rating change is imminent.

creditor One who is owed money by another. The creditor relationship usually arises as a consequence of lending money, but it may arise in other ways as well. Also called a *lend*er and an *obligee*.

credit-risk transference The use of an instrument such as a credit swap, or other vehicle, to transfer credit risk from one party to another party without transferring title to the source of the credit risk.

credit-supported commercial paper Commercial paper issued by poorer quality or less well-known corporations in which the issuer has obtained credit backing from a better quality or better-known entity.

creditworthiness A reference to the likelihood that a party to a contract will default on its obligations. The greater the likelihood of default, the less creditworthy the party.

cross When a broker is handling the buy side and the sell side of a transaction in a security, such as a New York Stock Exchange listed stock, the broker will make the transaction (the cross) at a price set by the specialist in the security. This is to ensure that both parties get a fair price on the transaction and to eliminate the potential for a conflict of interest.

cross currency swap A swap similar to an interest rate swap but in which one leg pays a fixed rate denominated in one currency (and paid on notional principal in that currency) while the other leg pays a floating rate denominated in a different currency (and paid on notional principal in that currency). Such swaps are also called *currency swaps* and *currency coupon swaps*.

cross default A provision in a financial contract (such as a swap) that states that a default on any other obligation of the party will be treated as though it were a default on the financial contract. These clauses are intended to prevent selective defaults that would favor one creditor over another.

cross hedge A hedge employing contracts written on an underlying instrument that differs in a meaningful way from the instrument that is the subject of the hedge. For example, if an airline hedges its exposure to the spot price of jet fuel in crude oil futures, that would be a cross hedge. This is in contrast to a *direct hedge*, in which the hedge contracts are written on an underlying that matches in all respects the subject position.

cross rate An exchange rate for two currencies implied by the exchange rates for each of those currencies relative to some other currency. For example, the exchange rate between dollars and sterling and the exchange rate between dollars and yen together imply the exchange rate between sterling and yen. This implied rate is the cross rate.

crowd The group of traders who gather around a trading pit.

crush spread The difference between the prices of the products created from crushing soybeans (soybean meal and soybean oil) and the price of the soybeans themselves. This represents the source of profit for soybean processors.

CTD See *cheapest-to-deliver*.

cumulative A feature common with preferred stock that requires any unpaid preferred dividends to accrue such that they must be paid prior to any dividend payments to common shareholders. A similar feature is often included with income bonds, which are bonds that pay interest only to the extent earned. The unpaid residual is sometimes cumulative.

cumulative density function A function that provides the total probability of achieving an outcome for a random variable ranging from the lowest possible value for the random variable up to any specific value of interest. For example, we might ask what is the probability that some interest rate (such as six-month LIBOR) will be 5% or less one year from today. Cumulative density functions are derived from probability density functions. They are also known as *cumulative probability functions*.

cumulative probability function See *cumulative density function*.

cumulative total return The total return on an investment, including both the income generated and the capital appreciation, expressed as a percentage and measured over the length of the holding period. For example, if an investment of $100 has grown to $300 over a period of six years, the cumulative total return is 200%.

currency The money issued by a government or the government's central bank and which is recognized as the legal tender of the country. Examples would include the American dollar, Japan's yen, and Mexico's peso. In some cases, a group of nations may employ a common currency. The European Union's European monetary unit (euro) is the best example of this.

currency change dual currency bond A variant of the dual currency bond in which the coupons are paid first in one currency and then in another, alternating according to a prescribed pattern. The coupon rate in each currency is fixed.

currency coupon swap See *cross currency swap*.

currency denomination The currency in which a financial instrument or cash flow is denominated. For example, a bond may have its principal and interest denominated in dollars. In this case, it can be described as a dollar-pay bond. Some instruments employ more than one currency. For example, see *dual currency bond*.

currency futures Futures contracts written on currencies. Each contract covers a specific number of units of the foreign currency. In the United States, currency futures prices are stated in American terms. For example, $1.0200 per euro. See *American terms*.

currency markets Also known as *foreign exchange markets, FOREX markets*, and *FX markets*. These are the markets in which the world's currencies are exchanged. With the exception of futures markets in currencies, the currency markets are dealer markets made, for the most part, by banks.

currency matching An asset/liability management technique applied to multi-currency balance sheets. Involves the matching of the currency character of assets and liabilities.

currency option An option, either call or put, written on an exchange rate. For example, a call option on the euro/dollar exchange rate with a strike exchange rate of $1.05 would pay off, at expiry, the sum $max[S - \$1.05, 0] \times NP$, where the S denotes the spot exchange rate at expiry, NP denotes the notional principal in euros, and max denotes the max function (i.e., the larger of the numbers in brackets). Also known as *FX options*.

currency overlay management The delegation of the management of the exchange rate risk associated with either an international asset portfolio or a multinational business operation to parties other than those responsible for the management of the portfolio or the business. The goal is to allow each party to concentrate on what it does best.

currency risk Also known as *exchange rate risk*. The risk of a financial loss due to a change in the value of one or more currencies. For example, a U.S. investor who holds a portfolio of Japanese stocks may be viewed as both long the stocks and long the yen. If the value of the yen declines, relative to the value of the dollar, the investor would suffer a loss even if there were no change in the yen prices of the stocks he holds.

currency swap An agreement between two parties for the exchange of a future series of interest and principal payments in which one party pays in one currency and the other party pays in a different currency. The exchange rate is fixed over the life of the swap. See also *cross currency swap*. Currency swaps may involve fixed-for-floating pay-ments, fixed-for-fixed payments, or floating-for-floating payments.

current yield A measure of the current income from a debt instrument obtained by dividing the annual coupon payment by the current market price of the bond. It is expressed as a percentage. This measure can be misleading because it fails to consider the discount or premium associated with the bond. This is not the "yield" that is referred to when people speak of a bond's yield. Also known as *cash-on-cash return*.

currents See *on-the-run*.

curtailment The prepayment of a portion of the principal balance on a mortgage loan but not the full prepayment of the principal. The full repayment of the principal would result in the termination of the mortgage loan; a curtailment does not.

curve risk A measure of interest rate risk that focuses on the potential for gain/loss resulting from changes in the yields for specific maturities along the yield curve. That is, it asks how sensitive a portfolio's value is to changes in specific yields, all other things being equal. This is useful when one is concerned about the possibility of the yield curve twisting.

CUSIP An acronym for *Committee on Uniform Securities Identification Procedures*. This system assigns a unique nine-digit code to each security issuance making it easy to identify different securities and avoid mistakes in the purchase, sale, transfer, and settlement of securities.

custodial fees Fees charged by custodians of securities and custodians of collateral for the safekeeping of the securities or collateral.

custodian A person or institution that holds securities in safekeeping for another.

customized benchmarks Benchmarks that are customized to serve the purposes of a specific user. For example, a mutual fund whose asset allocation requires that 40% of the fund's assets be held in bonds and 60% be held in stock might require a customized benchmark consisting of 40% Lehman bond index and 60% S&P 500 index. The fund's performance can then be measured against the customized benchmark.

cylinder The purchase of a put option and the simultaneous sale of a call option having a higher strike price than that of the put. Both options are written on the same underlying asset with the same expiration date. When these two option positions are overlayed on an existing long position in the underlying, the result is a collar. See *collar, zero-cost collar,* and *range forward* for related structures.

daily limit The maximum amount by which the price of a security, a futures, or an option can change over the course of a single day, relative to the prior day's close. Some markets impose daily limits and other markets do not. Daily limits have several purposes: One is to prevent prices from moving too far too fast with the result that they outrun a clearinghouse's ability to secure additional margin from traders. Another is to give markets a chance to settle down when they are overly volatile. Also known as a *daily limit move.*

daily limit move See *daily limit.*

daily settlement The process of settling futures contracts at the end of each day by moving variation margin from the day's losers to the day's winners. Also known as *marking-to-market.* See *mark-to-market.*

date sensitivity risk Refers to the risk (to a derivatives dealer) associated with running a derivatives portfolio from mismatches in floating-rate reset dates on the two sides of its derivatives book. For example, suppose that a swap dealer is paying LIBOR on one swap and receiving LIBOR on another swap. The floating rates are offsetting, but the reset dates might not match. Date sensitivity is an unsystematic form of risk. Consequently, as a portfolio of swaps gets larger, the holder of the portfolio becomes progressively less sensitive to this form of risk.

dated date The date that a security, such as a bond, begins to accrue interest. If the date is not an anniversary date of the coupon payment date, then the bond will have a short or long first coupon. See also *front stub period.*

day count The method of counting days over which interest accrues relative to the number of days assumed to be in a year. There are three main conventions. See *actual/actual, actual/360,* and *30/360.*

day order An order to buy or sell an asset which is good for a single trading session (originally, the trading day). If the order is not filled by the end of the trading session, the order will automatically be cancelled. This is in contrast to an *open order,* which is good until the trader who placed it explicitly cancels it.

day trade A position that is taken and closed out within a single trading day.

day trader One who limits his trading activity to day trades.

de facto Existing in fact even if not explicitly declared. The term is often used in contrast to *de jure,* which means explicitly declared. Both terms are often used in conjunction with federal government guarantees on the debt of federal agencies. Some debt has a *de jure* (explicit) guarantee; other debt is best viewed as having a *de facto* (implicit) guarantee.

de jure Explicitly declared in law. Most often used in conjunction with bonds that carry an explicit guarantee of another party (e.g., the federal government). This is in contrast to a *de facto* guarantee, which is not explicitly stated, but nevertheless assumed to exist. See *de facto* for more detail and contrast.

dealer One who acts as a principal in the business of buying and selling securities or other financial instruments for purposes of earning the difference between the bid and offer prices. Effective dealing requires the maintenance of inventory, which can be long or short, and this exposes the dealer to some price risk. Financing the inventory and managing the price risk are the two most important challenges for a dealer. Dealing contrasts with *broking.* Brokers act as agents, not as principals, in an effort to earn commissions. See *broking* for contrast.

dealer paper Also called *dealer-placed paper.* Commercial paper that is distributed through the agency of a commercial paper dealer. This is in contrast to directly placed paper, which is commercial paper distributed directly by the issuer to investors.

dealer-placed paper See *dealer paper.*

dealing Also called *market making.* The act of being a dealer. See *dealer.*

debentures In the United States, an unsecured debt security of a corporation. This is in contrast to mortgage bonds, which are collateralized by real property of the issuer. Debentures, mortgage bonds, and related instruments are collectively called bonds. Debentures often have a hierarchical structure in terms of the strength of their holders' claims on the issuer. For example, senior debenture holders' claims come before subordinated debenture holders' claims.

debt exchangeable for common stock Known by the acronym *DECS,* but the same acronym is used for dividend enhanced convertible stock (a similar product). All three terms are trademarks of Salomon Smith Barney. Debt exchangeable for common stock is a type of equity-linked note. Essentially, these instruments are convertible at maturity into common stock. Therefore, they have some equity-like characteristics, but they pay a coupon that is higher than the dividend on the underlying common stock.

debt markets Also referred to as credit markets. The markets for the borrowing and lending of money. The debt markets include the markets for short-term debt (money markets) as well as the market for long-term debt (bonds) and include both privately placed and publicly traded debt. The intermediate- and long-term public debt markets (i.e., the bond market) are a subset of the capital markets.

debt service fund A fund established to accumulate resources for the eventual retirement of principal and interest on a long-term debt obligation. These were formerly called sinking funds, but the term sinking fund now has broader meaning. A debt service fund is today viewed as one type of sinking fund.

debt warrant An option on a bond or other debt instrument.

debt-for-equity swap The use of an equity issuance by a firm to buy back some or all of its outstanding debt (or vice versa). The purpose may be to alter the capital structure of the firm (i.e., leverage up or leverage down) or to take advantage of some accounting or tax opportunity. May involve a direct exchange of debt for equity in a corporation.

debtor One who owes money to another. The opposite of a creditor. The debtor-creditor relationship usually arises as a consequence of a borrowing but can arise in other ways as well. When it arises out of a borrowing, the debtor can be called a *borrower*. Also known as an *obligor*, but this term has a broader meaning as well. See also *obligor*.

debtor-in-possession A company that has filed for bankruptcy protection and is allowed to continue to operate under the supervision of a court.

declining call schedule A stepped call structure in a bond in which each call date has a lower call price than the one before. In such structures, the call price gradually declines to par.

deconstructing a security The process of segregating the components of a financial instrument into discrete economic categories (e.g., a convertible bond consists of a straight bond and an equity option with a floating strike; a

Treasury security has principal and interest components; common stock can have appreciation and dividend components). Also called *stripping* and *bifurcating*. See *bifurcation*.

DECS See *dividend enhanced convertible stock*. See also *debt exchangeable for common stock*. Both of these instruments use the acronym DECS.

dedicated balance sheet See *dedicated portfolio*.

dedicated portfolio An asset/liability management technique that seeks to structure an asset portfolio in such a fashion as to generate cash inflows that precisely match the cash outflows on the entity's liabilities. Sometimes the term *dedicated balance sheet* is used to describe the overall balance sheet of such an entity.

deductible The amount of an insured loss that must be borne by the insured before the insurance takes effect. This concept applies to options in the same way as to health or other insurance policies. For example, a put option with a strike price of $70 per share on a stock that is currently trading at $73 per share has a built-in deductible amount of $3 per share.

deep discount bonds Bonds that are trading at a substantial discount from their face value.

deep-in-the-money options (1) In an economic sense, options that are in-the-money by a substantial amount. That is, they have substantial intrinsic value. Many option pricing models provide accurate valuations for options at-the-money or near-the-money but fail to provide accurate valuation for options deep-in-the-money or deep-out-of-the-money. (2) In a tax sense, any option that is in-the-money by more than another option that is in-the-money. For example, if a call option has a strike of 45, the next higher strike is 50, and the underlying is trading at $51, then the 50-strike call is near-the-money and the 45-strike call is deep-in-the-money. Note that an option can be deep-in-the-money from a tax perspective but not deep-in-the-money from an economic perspective, or vice versa.

deep-out-of-the-money options Analogous to deep-in the-money options, but with the option *out-of*, rather than *in*, the money. See *deep-in-the-money options*.

default The failure to pay interest or principal when due on a loan or debt security.

default losses Losses suffered by a holder of debt securities as a consequence of defaults on the part of issuers of those securities. Default losses will be equal to par less the recovery rate.

default rates (1) The weighted percentage of the bonds or other debt instruments in a portfolio to default over the course of one year. (2) Measures of the historical tendency of bonds of given ratings to default within specific periods of time. When used in this way, the term should be interpreted to mean anticipatory default rates. For example, if one were to look at all BBB-rated bonds and found that of all BBB-rated bonds, about 2% will default within one year, then the one-year default rate on BBB-rated bonds would be 2%. This would not imply that holders of BBB-rated bonds can expect to lose 2% of their investment in the first year. The actual loss will be a function of the default rate and the *recovery rate*. The recovery rate is the percentage of the bond's par value that is eventually re-

covered following a default. See also *recovery rate* and *bond rating*.

default risk (1) The risk that a party to a contract will fail to make a payment when required to do so. Usually associated with insolvency or bankruptcy. When used in this way, the term is synonymous with credit risk. (2) In swap banking, the term is used more broadly to describe the risk of an event of default. An event of default can mean any credit event that triggers the default provisions of the swap. This can be any credit-related event that the swap counterparties agree to and can fall far short of failure to pay interest or principal on time. (3) In swap banking, the term is sometimes used to describe a swap bank's exposure from the combination of credit risk and market risk.

default swap A type of credit swap in which one leg pays a fixed sum periodically and the other side pays nothing unless one of a specified list of credit events occurs. Most often, the specified credit event is a default on a particular reference credit. For example, a hedge fund might buy a corporate bond. There is the risk that the corporate bond might default so the hedge fund purchases a default swap in which the bond is the reference credit. On the swap, the hedge fund pays its counterparty (i.e., a credit swap dealer) a fixed sum annually, say 1.20%. This is paid on an amount of notional principal equal to the par value of the reference credit held by the hedge fund. If the reference credit (i.e., the bond) defaults, then the dealer pays the hedge fund a sum of money determined by a previously agreed-upon formula. Most often, this will be the difference between the par value of the bond and the recovery rate following the default. Essentially, the default swap dealer was selling credit protection. Default swaps can be one-way default swaps, as is the one above, or they can be two-way default swaps in which each counterparty is selling credit protection to the other but on different reference credits.

defaulting party A counterparty to a swap or other bilateral financial transaction that has experienced any credit-event listed under "events of default."

defeasance The purchase of bonds of high quality, usually U.S. Treasury bonds, in such quantity as to provide sufficient cash flow from these bonds (in the form of interest and principal payments) to fully meet the purchaser's obligations on its own debt issues. If the high-quality bonds purchased are irrevocably pledged to satisfy the purchaser's own debt obligations, both the high-quality bonds purchased and the purchaser's own debt obligations can be removed from the purchaser's balance sheet. Defeasance is a tactic used by municipalities and corporations to remove constraints on their activities enumerated in the indentures associated with their own debt issuances. The debt obligations of the defeasing party that have been fully collateralized in this way are said to be *defeased* or escrowed.

defeased See *defeasance*.

deferred coupon bonds Bonds that do not pay interest for some extended period of time. This includes bonds that pay no interest until maturity (called zero coupon bonds) and bonds that defer payment for a period of time and then begin to pay regular coupon interest (called accretion bonds). Deferred coupon bonds are a subset of a wider group of instruments called deferred-pay securities. See *zero coupon bonds, accretion bonds,* and *deferred-pay securities*.

deferred delivery A contract delivery schedule that involves a period of time longer than that customary for cash market transactions. Both futures and forward contracts involve deferred delivery.

deferred payment option An option that allows early exercise (i.e., American-type) to lock in the prevailing intrinsic value but which when exercised is not settled immediately. Instead, the value is carried to the end of the option's life and settled then. Also known as a *Boston option* (although the term Boston option has other meanings as well) and a *deferred payout option*. Sometimes called a *deferred-payment American option*. Such options are more often puts than calls and are often found embedded in other instruments.

deferred payout option See *deferred payment option*.

deferred rate-setting swap See *delayed rate-setting swap*.

deferred serial bonds Serial bonds in which the first installment does not fall due for at least two years from the date of issue. See *serial bond*.

deferred swap See *forward swap*.

deferred-pay securities Securities that defer the cash payment of interest or dividends for some period of time in order to allow the issuer to preserve cash for that period. They include both *deferred coupon bonds,* such as zero coupon instruments, and *payment-in-kind* instruments (*PIKs*).

deferred-payment American option See *deferred payment option*.

deferred-start option An option that is purchased before its life actually begins. One might elect to buy such an option because she believes she will need the option later and finds the current pricing attractive.

deferred-strike option An option on which the strike is not set at the time it is written, but is set later based on a formula specified in the option. For example, the strike might be set equal to the spot price of the underlying at expiry. Deferred strikes are often included in various types of lookback options.

defined benefit plan A type of retirement program in which the employer has guaranteed its employees a specific benefit upon retirement. The amount of the benefit is usually tied to the employees' salary during the final year or an average of the last several years of service. This is in contrast to a *defined contribution plan*. See *defined contribution plan* for contrast.

defined contribution plan A type of retirement program in which an employer's annual contribution to the plan is set by contract. The beneficiary of the plan generally has some control over where the proceeds are invested. The employer/sponsor of the plan makes no guarantee of the level of benefits that will be afforded by the plan upon the employees' retirement. This is in contrast to *a defined benefit plan*. See *defined benefit plan* for contrast.

delayed cap A floating rate debt instrument that has a cap (i.e., upper limit) on the floating rate, but the cap does not take effect until sometime after the issuance of the instrument.

delayed LIBOR-reset swap An interest rate swap in which the floating rate is LIBOR and in which LIBOR is observed and paid at the end of the coupon period, as opposed to the normal case in which LIBOR is observed at the beginning of the coupon period and then

paid at the end. Also known as a *LIBOR in arrears swap*, or a *back-end set swap*.

delayed rate-setting swap Also called a *deferred rate-setting swap*. A fixed-for-floating interest-rate swap in which the swap commences immediately but the swap coupon is not set until later. Such swaps will, generally, state the formula that will be employed when the coupon is set. For example, suppose that a client asked a swap dealer for its current quote (swap coupon) on a three-year interest rate swap. The client would be the fixed-rate payer. Suppose that the quote is given as the three-year T-note rate plus 60 basis points. The delayed rate-setting swap might specify that the client has the right to set the swap coupon any time the client wants for six-months from the swap's effective date, but when the client sets the coupon, the coupon will be set at the three-year T-note rate plus 70 basis points.

delivery date The date that a futures contract is scheduled to deliver if the futures contract is deliverable. Not all futures are deliverable. Those that are not are cash settled and the delivery date would then be called a *final settlement* date.

delivery month The month when a futures or option contract is due to deliver or settle. Contracts are distinguished from one another by their delivery month. For example, we would say June gold to distinguish a June-delivery gold futures contract from a September-delivery gold futures contract, which would be called September gold.

delivery options On a deliverable derivative instrument, such as a futures contract, one party may have the right to choose the delivery instrument or the delivery location. In the case of futures contracts, delivery options always belong to the short. The best example of this is Treasury bond futures. The short has the right to deliver any of a large number of different Treasury bonds on the contract and can be expected to deliver whichever one is the cheapest for him to deliver.

delivery risk Also called *settlement risk.* The risk that is created by the differences between market settlement hours, which may result in exchanges of interest and/or principal and/or securities at different times or even on different days. The first paying party is exposed to the risk that the later paying party will default after the first paying party has made its required payment or delivery but before the later paying party has made its payment or delivery. Various devices can be used to mitigate delivery risk. For example, we can limit the sizes of exchanges on a single day, or we can employ a third party to receive both sides of the transaction before passing the payments through.

delta The amount by which the value of an option would change relative to a small change in the value of the underlying asset. For example, a delta of $0.40 means that the value of the option (i.e., the fair option premium) would change by $0.40 as a consequence of $1 change in the value of the underlying asset. Note that the delta is the partial derivative of the option valuation function with respect to the price of the underlying. Delta is one of a number of risk measures that collectively make up the option's *Greeks.*

delta hedging Refers to a risk management strategy used by option dealers and others. Essentially, the option dealer holds a position in options on a specific underlying. In the aggregate, these options expose the dealer to *delta risk.* That is, the overall option book has a positive or negative delta so that a

change in the underlying's price will cause a gain or loss on the option book. The dealer takes an offsetting position in the underlying, which always has a delta of one. The result is that the combination of the option book and the offsetting position in the underlying has a delta of zero. This is called *delta neutral.*

delta neutral When an option book has been fully and correctly hedged with respect to delta risk, it is said to be delta neutral, which means the value of the option book will not change if the market price of the underlying asset changes. See *delta* and *delta hedging.*

delta risk The risk of a loss due to a positive or negative delta. See *delta.*

denomination (1) The minimum incremental face amount of a security, such as a bond, that can be traded. In the case of most bonds, this is $1,000, but it may be larger or smaller. Price quotes should not be confused with denominations. For example, prices of bonds are usually quoted as a percentage of par, which can be interpret as the price per $100 of par value. However, the denomination of the bond would ordinarily be $1,000. (2) The face amount of a bond held by a bondholder, but not necessarily the minimum tradable amount. (3) The currency in which a security's price or coupon is stated, sometimes called *currency denomination.*

depletion The write-down of the value of land as a consequence of the extraction of the mineral content from the land. Similar in concept to depreciation but only applicable to natural resource–containing assets.

Depository Institutions Deregulation and Monetary Control Act of 1980 This legislation began a major deregulation of the commercial banking industry and set the stage for the eventual demise of much of the Glass-Steagall Act.

derivative (1) A financial instrument that derives its value from a more basic financial instrument. For example, an option on a stock (a basic form of derivative) derives its value from the underlying stock. Derivatives can be used to either increase or decrease risk. (2) A generic term to describe a wide variety of financial instruments ranging from standardized, exchange-listed products to custom-made, over-the-counter instruments whose values depend on, or are derived from, the price or value of one or more underlying assets, including indexes, exchange rates, interest rates, or commodity prices. Derivative instruments are the elemental building blocks of structured products. Elemental derivative instruments fall into two categories: forward-based, such as forward contracts, futures, and swaps; and option-based, including put and call equity options, caps, floors, interest rate, currency, and exotic options.

descending yield curve See *inverted yield curve*.

deterministic models Models that place a value on future cash flows where both the size and the timing of said cash flows are known in advance with certainty. This is in contrast to *stochastic models* in which future cash flows are uncertain with respect to size, timing, or both.

diagonal spread A spread in options that is simultaneously vertical and horizontal. See *vertical spread* and *horizontal spread*.

diff contract See *contract for difference*.

diff swap See *differential swap*.

difference contract See *contract for difference*.

differential swap An interest rate swap in which one leg is referenced to a floating rate in a different currency but paid on notional principal denominated in the same currency as the other leg. For example, a floating-for-floating interest rate swap in which one leg pays dollar LIBOR and the other leg pays yen LIBOR, but both rates are paid on notional principal in dollars. On the surface, these swaps resemble currency swaps, but they are not. Because dollar LIBOR and yen LIBOR are not equal, a differential must be added to, or deducted from, one side to equate the values of the two legs of the swap. It is from this differential that the swap derives its name. Also known as a *diff swap*.

diffs See *euro-rate differential futures*.

digital options Options that pay off the sum of 1 or 0 depending on whether they are in-the-money or out-of-the-money, respectively, at expiration. They are usually of the European-type and are also known as *binary options*. Digital options are building blocks used to construct other instruments such as all-or-nothing options and range floaters. See *all-or-nothing options*. Sometimes, the terms all-or-nothing option and digital option are used synonymously, in which case a digital option can be interpreted as an option that pays off only one of two possible values, but not necessarily 1 or 0.

direct hedge A hedge in which the hedge contracts are written on an underlying that exactly matches the subject of the hedge (usually a cash position). This is in contrast to a *cross hedge*, in which there is something meaningfully different between the cash position that is the subject of the hedge and the underlyings on the hedge contracts. See *cross hedge* for contrast.

direct paper See *directly placed paper*.

direct terms See *American terms* (currency quotation convention).

directly placed paper Also known as *direct paper*. Commercial paper that is sold to (i.e., placed with) investors directly by the issuing corporation. This is most common with finance companies that are regular issuers of commercial paper. It contrasts with dealer paper, which is distributed through the agency of commercial paper dealers.

director A person appointed or elected to manage and direct the affairs of a corporation. A director has a fiduciary duty to the corporation and to its shareholders.

dirty price Also known as the *full price*. This is the present value of a bond including the value of any accrued interest. This is in contrast to the *clean price,* which does not include accrued interest. Dealers quoting bond prices generally quote clean prices.

discontinuance of index calculation A contract document provision that provides for an alternative method of index calculation if the primary calculator of the index fails to update the index values or if the cash securities underlying the index cease to trade. This sort of provision is important when a financial instrument's value or payoff is a function of some published index.

discount basis See *bank discount basis*.

discount bond A bond selling below its par (face) value. This will generally be the case when a bond's yield to maturity is higher than its coupon rate. Certain bonds, such as zero coupon bonds, will always trade at a discount from par.

discount factor A multiple used to discount the value of a future cash flow to the present value of that cash flow. The discount factor is obtained from a discount rate and the number of years before the cash flow will be received. The multiple is given by $(1 + k)^{-T}$ where k is the discount rate and T is the number of years before the cash flow will be received. The discount factor will be a number less than 1.

discount margin The spread to the reference rate on a floating-rate instrument that discounts the floating-rate instrument to its actual market price. For example, suppose that a floating rate note that pays six-month LIBOR and which is reset every six months is trading at 97. Some number of basis points would have to be added to LIBOR in order to discount the instrument's market price to 97. This number is the discount margin. Discount margins may arise because of a change in the creditworthiness of the issuer.

discount swap A swap in which the fixed rate is set below the at-market rate at the time the swap is written with the difference made up by a balloon payment at some future point, usually maturity.

discounting The process of calculating the present value of cash flows to be received at future points in time.

discretionary account A brokerage account in which the account representative has discretionary authority to make trades on behalf of the account owner.

discriminant analysis A multivariate forecasting technique often used to determine which financial ratios or combination of financial ratios is most reliable for predicting business failure.

distribution syndicate The collection of investment banks that participate in the underwriting of a security issuance (called the underwriting syndicate) together with the broker/dealers who make up the selling group. Together, these two groups comprise the distribution syndicate.

disutility A loss of utility (i.e., negative utility). The term is often associated with risk aversion. That is, investors get negative utility from risk. If risk rises, utility declines. Utility is a term used in economics to describe the satisfaction that comes from the consumption of goods and services, but can also be applied to the satisfaction that comes from holding an investment portfolio. In the latter case, expected return generates positive utility and risk generates negative utility.

diversifiable risk See *unsystematic risk.*

diversification The act of spreading investable funds among the securities of different issuers, such as the stocks of different corporations, and/or spreading funds among different classes of investment assets such as stocks, bonds, real estate, and commodities. The latter activity is often called *asset allocation.* See *asset allocation.* Diversification reduces the risk associated with holding investment assets, relative to investing all of the available funds in a single asset. Specifically, diversification reduces a type of risk called *unsystematic risk.*

divestiture The sale by a corporation of some of its assets, divisions, or subsidiaries to other corporations or to investor groups.

dividend A payment made to the owners of common stock of a corporation

by the corporation. The dividend may be in the form of a cash payment, called a *cash dividend,* or in the form of additional shares of the stock, called a *stock dividend.*

dividend declaration date The day that the Board of Directors of a corporation announces the amount of the dividend to be paid, the date the dividend is to be paid, and the holder-of-record date.

dividend enhanced convertible stock A type of preferred stock, known by the acronym *DECS.* These securities are convertible into common stock of the issuer and pay a dividend that is higher than the yield on the common into which they are convertible. The instrument is structured to allow partial participation in the upside on the underlying stock (i.e., price appreciation), but full participation in the downside (i.e., price depreciation). This risk of loss is mitigated by the higher-than-market dividend. For a more general type of instrument, see *equity-linked notes.*

dividend yield The annualized dollar dividend on a stock divided by the current market price of the stock. Similar to the current yield on a bond. This measure does not reflect the expected rate of return on a stock as it does not include expected appreciation in the stock's market value. Indeed, many profitable corporations, such as Cisco Systems and Microsoft, have long had policies of not paying any dividend at all. Thus their dividend yields would be zero.

dividend yield risk Risk of changes in stock dividend rates. This risk is difficult to hedge but is usually a marginal risk (i.e., not a very important risk).

dollar bond Also known as a *dollar-pay bond*. A bond denominated in U.S. dollars, as opposed to some other currency.

dollar convexity The product of a fixed income security's convexity and its dirty price (that is, Dollar Convexity = Convexity × Dirty Price). Dirty price is the full price of the security including accrued interest.

dollar duration The product of a fixed income security's modified duration and its dirty price (that is, Dollar Duration = Modified Duration × Dirty Price). Dirty price is the full price of the security including accrued interest.

dollar pay A term used to describe any instrument or the component of any instrument that pays in dollars. The term is most often used when the currency in which payments will be made is not clear from the context or when an instrument has multiple currency components.

dollar value of a basis point Often denoted *DV01*. The dollar amount by which the market value of a $100 par value bond would change if the bond's yield changes by exactly 1 basis point. It is obtainable from a bond's full price (the full price is the sum of the bond's quoted price plus any accrued interest), the bond's modified duration, and a single basis point as follows: DV01 = $D_M \times P \times 0.0001$ where D_M is the bond's modified duration, P is the full price, and 0.0001 is a single basis point. DV01s are also called *present value of a basis point* and *price value of a basis point*. Note, some users define a DV01 on a par value other than $100.

dollar-pay bond See *dollar bond*.

dollar-weighted rate of return A measure of return on an investment portfolio that explicitly takes into consideration both the size and the timing of a sequence of purchases. This measure is computed in the same manner as a rate of return, and is most useful when an investment has been acquired in stages over a period of time.

domestic issue A debt or equity instrument sold in the country in which the issuer is domiciled.

double exempt A reference to municipal bonds that are exempt from both federal and state income taxes, as opposed to some bonds that might be exempt from one but not the other.

double-barrelled bond Also known as *dually secured bonds*. These are tax-exempt revenue bonds that are backed by two or more revenue sources, as opposed to one revenue source.

down tick A price change to the downside.

down-and-in option A type of barrier option that is activated if the spot price declines sufficiently to cross a specific barrier price set below the spot price prevailing at the time the option is written. Such crossing must occur before a specified date to be relevant. See *barrier options*. Such options can be calls (down-and-in-calls) or puts (down-and-in puts). They are also known as *knock-in options*, but this latter term also includes up-and-in options.

down-and-out option A type of barrier option that automatically terminates (extinguishes) without value if the spot price crosses a specified barrier price set below the spot price prevailing at the time the option is written. Such a crossing must occur before a specified date to be relevant. See *barrier options*. Such options can be calls (down-and-out calls) or puts (down-and-out-puts). They are also known as *knock-out op-*

tions, but this latter term also includes up-and-out options.

downgrade The lowering of the credit rating on a debt obligation.

downgrade trigger A clause in a contract, particularly a derivative contract, that states that the contract will terminate or some other substantive change will occur if a specific reference credit's rating falls below a preset level.

downside risk Focuses on only negative deviations from an expected outcome, as opposed to the more general type of risk that includes any deviation, either positive or negative, from an expected outcome. Closely related are the notions of *shortfall risk,* which is the risk of achieving an outcome below some target level, and *value-at-risk,* which is the maximum amount that might be lost at some level of confidence over some risk horizon.

downward sloping yield curve See *inverted yield curve.*

drift rate The average rate of increase or decrease, generally stated on an annual basis, that a particular stochastic variable is expected to experience.

drop-lock A floating rate note that pays a sum linked to a reference rate but which suddenly becomes a fixed rate if the reference rate drops below some preset trigger level. The coupon then remains fixed for the remainder of the note's life.

dropping tickets Brokers transmitting customers' orders electronically to a syndicate desk.

dual currency bond A bond on which the principal payments are made in one currency and the interest (coupon) payments are made in a different currency.

There are a number of types. Some simply specify one currency for the coupon payments and another for the principal payments. Others provide either the issuer or the investor with an option to elect the currency of payment. See *option currency bond.*

dual currency option Also known as an *alternative currency option.* An option that allows its holder to buy (or sell) either of two currencies, each having its own strike price.

dual currency swap Another name for a fixed-for-fixed currency swap (i.e., a currency swap in which both legs pay fixed rates but on different currencies). The fixed rates are individually set based on market conditions in the currency, so that the rates, while both fixed, are usually different.

dual strike option An option that employs one strike price for part of the option's life and a different strike price for the remainder of the option's life. Such options must be exercisable prior to the resetting of the option's strike price for the dual strike feature to be meaningful.

dual syndication The use of two separate syndicates to distribute a security issuance. One syndicate distributes the security within the domestic market and the other syndicate distributes the securities in the international markets.

dual trading The practice on some exchanges of allowing members to trade in the capacity of floor brokers (i.e., trading for others to earn commissions) and floor traders (i.e., trading for themselves) during the same trading session. It has been argued by some that this practice creates opportunities for the abuse of customers but it has also been argued that this practice helps maintain market liquidity.

dually secured bond See *double-barrelled bond*.

due diligence An investigative process undertaken to verify information that has been provided and to uncover any and all material information of a financial and legal nature pertaining to the offering of securities. The process culminates in meetings held among the comanagers of the underwriting to review and confirm the acceptability of all material matters related to the issuance.

duet bond A type of bond sometimes seen in the Eurobond market in which the bond pays a coupon equal to the difference between two amounts specified in different currencies. For example, a bond might pay 14% in dollars on a fixed number of dollars less 7% in yen on a fixed number of yen. This is equivalent to being long two units of a dollar-pay bond and short one-unit of a yen-pay bond. These bonds are a variant of the dual currency bond.

duration A measure developed by Frederick Macaulay and published in 1938. It is often defined as a weighted average of the time to maturity of the cash flows associated with a fixed income instrument, where the weights are formed from the present value of each cash flow relative to the sum of the present values of all of the cash flows. It is considered a measure of interest rate risk and is measured in years. It is also known as *Macaulay duration* to distinguish it from modified duration. Note that the term duration is often used to mean modified duration, which is different from duration. See also *modified duration*.

duration matching Matching the modified durations of assets to the modified durations of liabilities. Duration matching is one component of an immunized balance sheet. Widely used by financial institutions in an effort to manage interest rate risk. See *immunized portfolios*.

duration neutral (1) A situation in which a bond trading strategy has a duration of zero on a net-net basis. (2) A balance sheet in which the dollar duration of the assets exactly equals the dollar duration of the liabilities.

duration-based hedging model A hedging model used to obtain hedge ratios from the ratio of the dollar duration of the cash instrument and the dollar duration of the hedging instrument. Unless adjusted for differences in yield changes for the two securities, the model implicitly assumes that all changes in all yield curves take the form of mutual parallel shifts.

duty of loyalty The legal duty of a fiduciary to act for the exclusive benefit of those whose money is being managed—not for the benefit of the fiduciary personally or for any other party.

DVOI See *dollar value of a basis point*.

dynamic asset allocation See *synthetic options*.

dynamic asset replication An active strategy involving the periodic adjustment of the sizes of positions held in one or more instruments in order to replicate the market behavior of some other instrument. Often, the term is used to describe portfolio insurance strategies that are achieved through dynamic asset allocation.

dynamic hedging (1) A risk management strategy that involves changing the number of units of the hedge instrument employed in response to, or in anticipation of, market events. For example, selling stock index futures in order to protect stock portfolios from adverse price movements, thus eliminating market risk without incurring stock transaction fees, which are higher than for futures instruments, and without losing dividend cash flows from the stocks themselves. (2) In the context of managing an option portfolio, periodically revising the size of the hedge in order to keep the portfolio delta neutral.

early exercise The exercise of an option prior to the option's expiration date.

earnest money An early term for the money or securities posted as collateral in futures trading. Now more commonly called *margin*. See *margin* in the context of futures.

earnings per share Usually abbreviated *EPS*. A company's net income after taxes divided by the number of shares of common stock outstanding. Can be calculated on either a diluted or non-diluted basis. When calculated on a diluted basis, the number of potential additional shares that would result from the exercise of stock options that the corporation has distributed plus any shares that would result from the conversion of convertible securities is added to the number of shares technically outstanding.

economic value added Usually abbreviated *EVA*. A measure of the dollar surplus value created by an investment or a portfolio of investments. It is computed by taking the excess return as a percentage (calculated as the difference between the rate of return on capital invested less the cost of that capital) and multiplying by the amount of capital invested.

economies of scale Any production situation, including the provision of financial services, in which the cost per unit produced decreases as the number of units produced increases. Per unit cost should not be confused with total cost. The latter will rise directly with the quantity produced irrespective of the behavior of per unit costs.

effective annual percentage cost (1) Any financial cost expressed on a percentage basis as an effective annual rate. Very useful for comparing alternative financing methods. (2) Often used to convert the one-time premium paid up front for multi-period options in order to re-express the cost of these options on a basis that is more easily understood.

effective convexity Also known as *option adjusted convexity*. A measure of a bond's convexity that takes into consideration the convexities of options embedded within the bond. If no options are present, then effective convexity is identical to convexity.

effective date Also known as the *value date*. The date that a financial instrument, such as a swap, begins to accrue interest (i.e., takes value).

effective duration Also known as *option adjusted duration*. A measure of a bond's interest rate risk that takes into consideration the durations of the options embedded within the bond. If no options are present, the effective duration is identical to the modified duration. Effective durations are more reliable than modified durations for bonds with embedded optionality.

effective margin As the term is used with respect to floating rate securities, the average number of basis points over the reference rate that the holder can expect to earn over the life of the security.

effective tax rate A percentage calculated as the total tax liability, based on a corporation's tax books, divided by the corporation's net income before taxes, based on its GAAP books. For example, if taxable income and income taxes are $100 million and $20 million, respectively, based on the corporation's tax books; and taxable income and income taxes are $150 million and $35 million, respectively, based on the corporation's GAAP books, then the corporation's effective tax rate is 13.3%.

efficiency of a hedge The degree of risk reduction provided by a hedge relative to the cost of the hedge. Measured with the aid of the correlation between the spot price of the cash position to be hedged and the price of the hedging instrument. Related to, but not quite the same as, *hedge effectiveness.* For example, if hedge instrument #1 has a 0.84 correlation with the cash position and hedge instrument #2 has a 0.84 correlation with the hedge instrument, then they are equally effective. Now suppose that hedge instrument #1 has a cost of $0.002 per unit hedged and hedge instrument #2 has a cost of $0.003 per unit hedged. Then hedge instrument #1 is the more efficient.

efficient frontier The set of portfolios, usually stock portfolios, that have the highest rates of returns for any given level of risk. Return is measured as the expected (or mean) rate of return and risk is measured (most often) as either the variance or the standard deviation of the rate of return. The efficient frontier is a subset of the *minimum variance set.* The efficient frontier is also known

as the *efficient set* and the *efficient loci* and is sometimes called the *Markowitz efficient frontier.*

efficient hedge A hedge that achieves a given level of risk reduction at minimum cost.

efficient loci See *efficient frontier.*

efficient markets hypothesis A theory that holds that all competitive markets price assets correctly in the sense that, at any given point in time, the market price accurately reflects the relevance of all available information. The theory was first formally put forward by Eugene Fama in 1970, but others had alluded to the underlying premise much earlier.

efficient set See *efficient frontier.*

elections (accounting) As used in accounting, *elections* are choices as to how to treat revenues, expenses, assets, and liabilities for purposes of recording these items when the accounting rules allow for more than one treatment. GAAP and/or tax rules often allow for more than one treatment. For example, a capitalized asset can be depreciated using an accelerated form of depreciation or a straight-line form of depreciation; inventory cost can be calculated on a "first in first out" or a "last in first out" basis. Elections can significantly affect a corporation's accounting profits, tax obligations, and cash flow.

ELKS A trademark of Salomon Smith Barney. See *equity-linked securities.*

embedded option An option contained within another security such as a bond (e.g., callable bonds) or a swap (e.g., capped swap). Home mortgages usually include an embedded option allowing the homeowner to prepay the principal in whole or in part at any time without any penalty. The presence of embedded options greatly complicates the valuation of a security.

emerging markets Securities markets of economies that are at an early stage of economic development within a capitalist market framework. Such markets are often characterized by one or more of the following: limits on foreign ownership, limited investor protections, and the potential for currency inconvertibility.

Employee Retirement Income Security Act of 1974 Known by the acronym *ERISA*. This legislation regulates private pension funds. It established responsibilities for corporations providing pension plans for their employees in such matters as funding their obligations, investing in the corporation's own securities, and vesting. It also established the Pension Benefit Guarantee Corporation.

end user In the context of swaps and other OTC derivatives, any counterparty other than a derivatives dealer. The end user can be a corporation, a municipality, a federal agency, a bank, an investment company, a pension fund, or even a sovereign government. The key point is that the end user is using the derivative for speculation, hedging, or arbitrage as opposed to making markets in derivative instruments in order to earn a bid-offer spread.

enhanced indexing Also known as *indexing plus*. The management of a portfolio such that the stated goal is to approximate the performance of a benchmark index while at the same time trying to outperform the index. Such a strategy is in contrast to simple indexing wherein the goal is to replicate the performance of the index. En-

hanced indexing necessarily involves more risk than simple indexing.

environmental risks Risks to which a business is exposed and over which it has no direct control, such as price risks. Examples of other environmental risks faced by a typical business include such things as changes in tax law and changes in customer demographics.

EPS See *earnings per share*.

equity kicker An equity interest in a company given to persons or institutions that provide some service to the company in lieu, or partially in lieu, of monetary compensation. Equity kickers are sometimes provided in exchange for capital raising activities.

equity market Most often used to mean the market for publicly traded equity securities (i.e., the stock market). But, the term can be used to include both the private and the public equity markets. The public equity market is a subset of the capital markets.

equity return risk The price risk associated with holding a portfolio of equity securities.

equity swap See *equity-linked swap*.

equity warrant An option to buy the stock of a corporation and which is usually issued by the corporation on whose stock it is written. Warrants are often attached to a bond as a sweetener in order to sell the bond with a lower coupon rate. Warrants tend to have considerably longer maturities at issue than do call options.

equity-linked notes Debt securities in which the coupon or the final redemption of principal is linked to the performance of some equity benchmark, such as the S&P 500. Such instruments are often principal protected so that the investor is guaranteed to get back the principal invested in full, but may not get any interest. The latter are sometimes described as *principal-protected equity-linked notes*.

equity-linked securities Known by the acronym *ELKS*. Both the name and the acronym are trademarks of Salomon Smith Barney. These are one of many proprietary versions of equity-linked notes. See *equity-linked notes*.

Equity-linked swap Any notional principal swap in which the cash flows on at least one leg of the swap are linked to the total return on a single stock, a stock index, or some combination thereof. Also known as an *equity swap*. Not to be confused with a debt-for-equity swap, which involves the real, as opposed to notional, exchange of debt for equity.

equivalent positions Two positions which are equivalent in some way. They may be equivalent with respect to all of their characteristics or to just certain of their characteristics, such as risk. In the latter case, positions are often said to be *risk equivalent*.

equivalent taxable yield A measure often computed for tax-exempt securities that indicates what the yield on a taxable security would have to be to yield an equivalent after-tax return. For example, a tax-exempt bond yielding 6% would have an equivalent taxable yield of 10% for an investor in a 40% tax bracket.

ERA See *exchange rate agreement*.

ERISA See *Employee Retirement Income Security Act of 1974*.

escalating swap Similar to an *accreting notional swap*. See *accreting notional swap*.

escrowed bonds Debt issued by an entity that has been defeased through the purchase of very high quality bonds, usually Treasury bonds. Essentially, an entity that has issued bonds purchases Treasury bonds in sufficient quantity so that the cash flows from the Treasurys exactly match the entity's obligations on its own debt. The cash flows on the Treasurys are then pledged irrevocably to meet the cash flows on the entity's own debt. The entity's own bonds are then called *escrowed bonds*. See *defeasance*.

Eurobond A bond sold outside of the country of the issuer but denominated in the currency of the country of the issuer.

Eurobond market Any market for Eurobonds.

Eurocurrency A currency unit held on deposit at a bank outside of the country of the currency unit's issue. Eurodollars are the largest sector of the market.

Eurodollar bonds Dollar-denominated bonds and bond-like instruments sold outside the United States.

Eurodollar conventions The rules stipulated to quote rates on Eurodollar deposits (LIBOR).

Eurodollar deposit A dollar deposit held in a bank outside the United States. These deposits are lent by the banks that hold them to other banks at what is called the London interbank offered rate, or LIBOR.

Eurodollar futures Futures contracts on Eurodollars were first introduced by the Chicago Mercantile Exchange in 1982. They represent futures contracts on Eurodollar deposits. In actuality, they are futures contracts on the rate of interest on Eurodollar deposits. This rate is called LIBOR.

Eurodollar futures strip A position in multiple Eurodollar futures with sequential delivery dates. For example, if you were long a March ED futures, a June ED futures, and a September ED futures, they would, collectively, make up a Eurodollar futures strip. Sometimes, called a *Eurostrip*. Eurodollar futures strips can be used to hedge a floating rate instrument (such as an FRA or the floating leg of a swap), or they can be used to place bets on the future shape of the LIBOR forward curve.

Eurodollars Dollars held on deposit at a bank outside the United States. See *Eurodollar deposit*.

European option An option that can be exercised only during a limited exercise period at the very end of the option's life. This is in contrast to an American-type option, which can be exercised at any time. The terms European and American are derived from the regions in which these options first appeared, but the terms no longer have any geographic meaning.

euro-rate differential futures Known as *diffs*. Futures contracts traded on the Chicago Mercantile Exchange that are structured to allow a U.S.-based firm to hedge non-dollar money market rates.

Eurostrip Also known as a *Eurodollar futures strip*. Successive Eurodollar futures contracts are strung together in a series to replicate some other instrument or to hedge a LIBOR-based risk exposure.

Euroyen bonds Bonds denominated in yen and traded outside Japan.

EVA See *economic value added*.

event of default An event that is indicative of a credit problem. In the context of swaps, occurrences that constitute events of default are specified in the swap documentation. The occurrence of such an event terminates all swaps governed by the same master agreement between the parties.

exchange of borrowings The simplest form of a currency swap in which each counterparty to the swap obtains funds from third-party lenders and then exchanges the funds so obtained. The term was used to describe early currency swaps. It is rarely used today.

exchange option An option to exchange one asset for another asset.

exchange rate Also called *foreign exchange rate*. The price of a unit of one currency stated in terms of units of another currency. The currency in which the rate is quoted is sometimes called the *terms currency* and the currency that is being bought or sold is sometimes called the *commodity currency*. For example, if a euro is currently worth $1.02, then the euro is the commodity currency and the U.S. dollar is the terms currency. Exchange rates can be quoted for the immediate exchange of the currencies (called a *spot exchange rate*) or for the future exchange of the currencies (called a *forward exchange rate*).

exchange rate agreement A derivative contract that cash settles for the difference between some future spot exchange rate and the exchange rate specified in the contract. For example:

$$\text{Payoff} = [S_T - X] \times NP$$

where S_T denotes the spot exchange rate at some future point in time T, X denotes the exchange rate written into the contract (contract rate), and NP is the notional principal. Often abbreviated *ERA*.

exchangeable bonds A bond in which the holder has the option to convert from a fixed rate to a floating rate or from a floating rate to a fixed rate during prespecified periods of time.

exchange-rate differentials The differences between spot and forward (or forward and forward) exchange rates for the same currencies. The forward exchange rate can be at either a premium or a discount to the spot exchange rate.

exchange-rate options Also known as *currency options*. Options on which the underlying asset's price takes the form of an exchange rate. Such options can be single period (i.e., calls and puts) or multi-period in nature (i.e., caps and floors).

exchange-rate risk The risk that a future spot exchange rate will deviate from the currently quoted forward exchange rate for that date. Any party holding a long or short position in a foreign currency or holding a position in assets and/or liabilities denominated in a foreign currency has an exchange rate exposure.

exchanges A membership association organized to provide a marketplace for purchasers and sellers of securities. Examples include the New York Stock Exchange, the Chicago Board of Trade, and the Chicago Board Options Exchange. Traditionally, exchanges provided a physical floor where buyers and sellers (or their representatives) could meet to conduct business. In recent years, exchanges have moved increasingly (and often reluctantly) toward screen-based trading with no need for a physical floor. In February 2000, the Securities and Exchange Commission approved the application of the International Securities Exchange (ISE) to operate as the first entirely screen-based options exchange in the United States.

exchange-traded contracts Standardized derivatives that trade on designated futures and options exchanges, as opposed to custom-made derivatives that trade over-the-counter.

ex-dividend date The date that the price of a stock is lowered at the opening of the market by the amount of the next dividend to be paid. In the United States, presently, the ex-dividend date precedes the holder-of-record date by two business days.

executive stock options Options issued to the management of a corporation by the corporation on its own stock. Such options are often issued to better align the interests of management and the shareholders. Often called *incentive stock options*.

exercise date Sometimes used to mean the same thing as an *expiration date*, particularly for European-type options.

exercise price See *strike price*.

exercising (an option) The act of giving notice to the clearinghouse (or other party) of one's decision to exercise one's rights under an option contract. The result is that the underlying asset is transferred from one party to the contract to the other party to the contract and payment for the underlying is transferred in the opposite direction. American-style options can be exercised at any time before expiration. European-style options can be exercised only at the time of their expiration.

exit plan A financial plan to stop losses once they begin to occur, before they can grow so large as to exceed the comfortable limits of an organization.

exit strategy A plan by some or all of the founders of a company to liquidate their equity interest in the company once certain goals have been achieved. Exit strategies might involve taking the company public or selling the company to an existing corporation.

exotic options Also called *nonstandard options* and sometimes called *second generation* or *third generation options.* Any option having terms—including strike price, underlying asset price, expiration conditions, expiration date, exercise conditions, payoffs, and so forth—that differ from standard calls and puts. Generally, such instruments have unique, custom-made terms. Such options usually trade over-the-counter and are usually, but not always, European type.

expansions Any activity that results in the enlargement of a business. This might include expanding the existing activities (such as opening more outlets), acquiring competitors, or merging with other businesses.

expectations theory A theory of the term structure of interest rates which implies that longer-term interest rates are simply unbiased reflections of the market's expectation of sequential future short term rates of interest. The theory is cast in terms of spot (i.e., zero coupon) rates and forward short rates of interest, but can easily be extended to coupon yields (i.e., yields on coupon-bearing bonds). The theory implies that there is no premium built into longer-term interest rates to reflect a greater

level of interest rate risk. Thus, the theory is a risk-neutral theory. The typical upward slope to the yield curve cannot, then, be explained by a risk premium and must be explained by anticipated future rates of inflation, which are reflected in the forward interest rates. The theory is known also as the *pure expectations theory* and the *unbiased expectations theory.*

expiration date The end of an option or warrant's term. If not exercised by the end of its term, both put and call options expire worthless. Also known as an *exercise date.*

exploding option See *one touch all-or-nothing.*

exposure The amount of risk one is exposed to. Often used to mean the maximum amount of loss that could occur if a counterparty defaulted.

extendable bonds Bonds in which the holder of the bond (bondholder) has the right to extend the life of the bond, usually on the same terms as the original bond, for an additional period of time. Also refers to bonds in which there is both an embedded call option and an embedded put option having the same strike price. If neither side exercises, the bond's life continues beyond the option expiration date. This latter case is often called a *retractable bond.*

extendable reset A feature found in some high yield bonds that requires the coupon be reset at one or more future points in time so that the bond will trade at a preset price. The resetting will reflect the level of interest rates at the time and the credit spread as dictated by the market.

extendable swap A fixed-for-floating interest-rate swap in which one counterparty has the right to extend the swap beyond its scheduled maturity date. More generally, any swap in which one of the counterparties has the right to extend the life of the swap beyond its maturity date on the same terms as the original swap.

extension risk Risk that, when interest rates increase, homeowners will hold on to their lower-interest loans longer so that prepayments will decrease. This causes a mortgage portfolio's average life to extend beyond what was ex-

pected, which, in turn, causes the lives of any mortgage-backed securities derived from the underlying pool to have their average lives lengthen.

extinguishable option An option in which the holder's right to exercise terminates if the spot price of the underlying crosses a prespecified level. Also known as *knock-out options*. There are a number of types, all of which are a subset of a broader family of options called *barrier options*. See *barrier options*.

face value The value appearing on the face of the certificate of a fixed-income security (such as a bond, note, or mortgage) that represents the amount due upon maturity of the security. It is also known as the par value and usually, but not always, represents the price paid for the instrument when originally sold by the issuer.

factor analysis A statistical methodology to find a relatively small number of variables (factors) that explain most of the variation in some other, correlated, variable. Similar to principal component analysis. The analysis does not, itself, identify the factors. Factor analysis is the statistical methodology that underlies arbitrage pricing theory, which has been used to obtain better estimates of the required return on individual securities than can be obtained from the capital asset pricing model.

fair value (1) The value of a security based upon a valuation model believed to capture the essence of the economic factors that determine value. Alternatively, the equilibrating price between demand and supply. The latter should

equal the former if an asset market is an efficient pricing mechanism. (2) The value placed on an asset by an independent expert appraiser, in which case it can be called appraised value. See *appraised value*.

fairness opinion A written document provided by a qualified independent appraiser as to the value of assets or securities for purposes of judging the "fairness" of a financial transaction.

fallen angels High yield, or speculative grade, bonds that have a low credit rating but which had an investment-grade credit rating at the time of issuance. This is distinct from other high yield bonds that were issued with a speculative grade rating or without any rating at all.

FAS 133 A long-awaited and controversial statement by the Federal Accounting Standards Board that spells out criteria for accounting for financial derivatives, particularly with respect to the accounting for, and the treatment of, hedges.

FASB See *Financial Accounting Standards Board*.

fastest-pay tranche The tranche on a collateralized mortgage obligation (CMO) that is presently scheduled to receive principal. Most tranches of a CMO receive regular interest payments, but only one tranche at a time receives principal payments. These principal payments pay down the principal balance of the tranche. Once fully paid down, the tranche is retired and the principal flows are redirected to the next tranche. For this reason, whichever tranche is currently receiving principal is the fastest-pay tranche. See also *collateralized mortgage obligation*.

FCM See *futures commission merchant*.

Fed A reference to the Federal Reserve System.

Federal Home Loan Mortgage Corporation Usually abbreviated *FHLMC*. One of several federally sponsored corporations that sell securities backed by pools of mortgages. The FHLMC guarantees the ultimate payment of principal and the timely payment of interest on its mortgage passthrough certificates. Known by its nickname Freddie Mac.

Federal National Mortgage Association Usually abbreviated *FNMA*. One of several federally sponsored corporations that sell securities backed by pools of mortgages. The FNMA guarantees the timely payment of interest and principal on its mortgage passthrough certificates. Presently owned entirely by private stockholders. Known by its nickname Fannie Mae.

Federal Reserve An entity created by the Federal Reserve Act of 1913 to make monetary policy. The Federal Reserve, known by its nickname *the Fed*, is overseen by a seven-member Board of Governors. The Federal Reserve System, is the de facto central bank of the United States, though its individual components, the twelve Federal Reserve District banks, are quasi-private institutions. The Fed is responsible for making monetary policy, overseeing the regulation of the banking system, facilitating payment mechanisms (e.g., check clearing, electronic funds transfers, etc.), regulating the use of margin in securities transactions, managing liquidity, and, on occasion, interacting in the foreign exchange markets to manipulate the value of currencies.

FHLMC See *Federal Home Loan Mortgage Corporation*.

fiduciary A person responsible for investing his or her company's money or the money of others. Fiduciaries have a duty to act exclusively for the benefit of those they represent.

fiduciary obligation An obligation to act in the best interest of another.

final settlement The date on which cash-settled futures are marked-to-market using the spot price of the underlying as the final settlement price. On this date, the contracts cease to exist. This is in contrast to the daily mark-to-market, which is based on the settlement price of the futures contract for the day.

Financial Accounting Standards Board Known by the acronym *FASB*. An independent body recognized by both the SEC and Congress as having an authoritative role in setting accounting standards in the United States. The FASB periodically issues statements of guidance on accounting matters called Financial Accounting Statements (FAS). These statements form a large part of what are known as generally accepted accounting principles (GAAP).

financial engineering The use of financial instruments, such as derivatives, to obtain a desired mix of risk and return characteristics. More broadly, the application of financial technology to solve financial problems and exploit financial opportunities. Sometimes used more narrowly to mean financial risk management. The essential feature of financial engineering is that it uses innovation and financial technology to engineer structures (including solutions to problems).

financial engineers Persons who engage in financial engineering activities as their principal occupation. Sometimes defined more narrowly as those who engage in structured product origination activities. Often taken to include financial economists (including academicians) who contribute to the development of financial engineering technology (i.e., valuation methodologies, risk management methodologies, basic research, etc.).

financial futures Futures contracts written on financial instruments or financial indexes of any sort. This is in contrast to futures written on commodities. Financial futures include currency futures, stock index futures, and various types of interest rate futures.

financial intermediary A financial institution that stands between two end users of the intermediary's products. In the traditional context, one user is represented on the asset side and the other is represented on the liabilities side of the intermediary's balance sheet. For example, a bank that takes deposits from investors (liabilities side of the bank's balance sheet) and then lends them in the bank's name to borrowers (asset side of the bank's balance sheet) would constitute a financial intermediary. In the context of swaps and other off–balance sheet derivatives, the classic balance sheet view of an intermediary is somewhat obscured. In this case, a dealer, such as a swap dealer, may be seen as intermediating between two end users.

Financial Services Act of 1999 This legislation was passed by Congress to explicitly repeal many provisions of the Glass-Steagall Act (i.e., the Banking Act of 1933). Since the early 1980s, the provisions of the Glass-Steagall Act had been eroding as the Federal Reserve and other regulatory bodies chipped away at its many restrictions. The Financial Services Act of 1999 finally enacted into law what was happening around the edges anyway.

finite difference method A method of solving a finite difference equation that has applicability in solving for the value of certain derivative contracts, particularly options.

firm commitment A type of underwriting commitment in which the underwriting syndicate guarantees an issuer that all of its securities will be sold and that the issuer will receive the full amount of the *proceeds to the issuer* associated with the sale of the securities at the offering price, less the gross spread. In such an underwriting, the underwriting syndicate bears the risk of a failed offering. For contrast, see *best efforts*.

fiscal agent An entity, usually a commercial bank or investment bank, that has been designated by the government to act for it or for one of its agencies in any of a variety of financial transactions including the sale of federal agency securities. The Federal Reserve Bank of New York acts as the fiscal agent in the sale of Treasury securities.

Fisher Equation An equation that relates nominal rates of interest to required real rates of interest and expected or anticipated rates of inflation. Named for Irving Fisher, its originator. In this context, the term nominal means the observed rate in the market place. For example, suppose that lenders require a real rate of return on their money (i.e., a net increase in their purchasing power) of 3% a year. At the same time, the would-be lenders anticipate a 2% rate of inflation. In such a scenario, the nominal rate of interest would be 5%.

$$\text{That is } r_{nominal} = r_{real} + i_{anticipated}.$$

fitted yield curve A hypothetical yield curve formed by fitting a smooth curve through many points representing the yields associated with bonds of different maturities. The maturities are plotted on the horizontal axis and the yields are plotted on the vertical axis. There are a number of different curve-fitting techniques that can be used to fit a smooth curve. The most commonly employed is a *piecemeal cubic spline*. A fitted yield curve is in contrast to a linearly interpolated yield curve.

fixed coupon A coupon rate (interest rate) on a bond that is invariant from one coupon period to another. This is in contrast to a floating coupon. The term "coupon" stems from the now antiquated practice of clipping a coupon from a bond and sending it to the paying agent in order to collect the interest due.

fixed income security Any security that meets one or more of the following tests: (1) pays a fixed sum periodically; (2) pays a fixed sum at maturity; (3) pays a formula-determined amount periodically; or (4) pays a formula-determined amount at maturity. The term fixed income security stems from the first of these four tests, which was the principal form for many decades.

Most fixed income securities are debt instruments, but preferred stock also satisfies the tests above. Common stock does not satisfy any of the tests and is not, therefore, a fixed income security.

fixed interest rate An annual percentage rate that does not change and is paid on some principal or notional principal at designated intervals. Such intervals may be more or less frequent than yearly.

fixed price A price that does not change over the life of an instrument or contract. The term is understood to include fixed rates of interest.

fixed-for-floating interest-rate swap A swap in which one counterparty pays a floating rate of interest while the other counterparty pays a fixed rate of interest. This is the most common type of swap.

fixed-rate payer An individual, corporation, or other entity that pays a fixed rate of interest on a financial instrument such as an interest rate swap or a fixed rate bond. Can also be spelled "fixed-rate payor."

fixing date The date on which the reference rate is observed for purposes of calculating the cash payment due on a multi-period interest-rate option such as a rate cap or rate floor. Also known as the *reset date*.

flat (1) Without premium or discount. As in a floating rate of interest that is set equal to a reference rate, such as LIBOR, without adding or deducting any basis points. (2) A bond quotation that includes accrued interest. This is in contrast to a bond quotation that does not include the interest, called *and interest*. See *and interest*.

flat volatility Usually used to mean that the same volatility was used to value each of the component caplets that collectively make up a cap option.

flat yield curve A situation in which the yield curve (i.e., the graphic depiction of the relationship between the yields on bonds and the maturities of those bonds) is flat or approximately so. See also *yield curve*.

flex options Options introduced by the American Stock Exchange that allow the purchaser or writer some flexibility with respect to setting the parameters of the option. These include the strike price, the expiration date, and so forth.

float (1) Money tied up in the payment process. For example, if one party (the payer) writes a check to another party (the payee), it will take some time before the check clears the payer's bank. Until that time, the money appears in both the payer's and the payee's accounts. This money is called the float. (2) The number of outstanding shares of stock that are available for trading (i.e., not restricted or subject to lock-up agreements).

floater (1) A shortened name for floating rate note (see *floating rate note*), (2) A type of CMO tranche whose return will decrease as the reference interest rates (such as LIBOR) fall and increase as the reference interest rate rises.

floating coupon A coupon rate (interest rate) on a bond that is periodically reset to some reference rate to ensure that the bond's coupon always reflects the market rate of interest. This is in contrast to a fixed coupon.

floating interest rate A rate of interest that periodically resets to reflect market conditions. This is in contrast to a fixed

rate of interest, which stays the same over the life of the instrument.

floating price The floating price paid on a fixed-for-floating or floating-for-floating swap or on a floating-price cash market transaction. In the case of an interest rate or currency swap, the term is synonymous with floating rate.

floating rate note A debt instrument that pays a floating rate of interest such that the rate periodically resets based on some benchmark reference rate of interest. The rate resets on the designated reset dates and each reset is ordinarily applicable to the immediately following coupon period. Also called a *floater* and an *FRN*.

floating-for-floating interest-rate swap An interest rate swap in which both counterparties pay a floating rate of interest but these are tied to different reference rates. Called a *basis swap* if the floating rates are tied to short-term money market rates, such as LIBOR. Some floating-for-floating interest-rate swaps, such *as yield curve swaps,* are tied to long-term reference rates such as specific points on a Treasury yield curve. See *basis swaps* and *yield curve swaps.*

floating-rate CDs Certificates of deposit on which the interest rate is periodically reset to reflect changing market conditions. Such CDs generally have a longer maturity than fixed rate CDs.

floating-rate debt Also known as *adjustable rate debt* and *variable rate debt.* Any form of debt on which the interest rate is periodically reset to reflect changing market conditions. Such resets usually involve reference to some benchmark rate of interest, such as prime, LIBOR, or a COFI.

floating-rate payer An individual, corporation, or other entity that pays a floating rate of interest on a financial instrument such as an interest rate swap or a floating rate note. Can also be spelled "floating-rate payor."

FLOATS See *municipal floating-rate bonds*.

floor An instrument that consists of a strip of put options on some underlying asset, each of which has the same strike price (or strike rate) and which have sequential settlement dates. Thus, it is a multi-period option with each payoff given by the payoff function for a put option: Payoff = max[X – S, 0] × NP. Thus, the option pays off on each settlement date if and only if the spot price or reference rate is below the strike price or strike rate on a fixing date. See also *interest rate floor*. Floors are often embedded in floating rate instruments to guarantee some minimum return each period. For example, they are sometimes found embedded in floating rate notes and in interest rate swaps.

floor brokers Persons who are members of an exchange or who lease seats on an exchange in order to transact in financial instruments on behalf of others in exchange for commissions. They are more properly called *commission house brokers*.

floor rate The rate that serves the function of a strike rate in an interest rate floor option or a foreign currency floor option. A floor is a multi-period put option and the floor rate is the constant strike rate.

floor traders Persons who are members of an exchange or who lease seats on an exchange in order to transact for themselves and avoid paying commissions to others. Such persons are more correctly called *registered traders*, but are known in market slang as *locals*.

floor-ceiling agreements See *collar*.

floorlet One of the component options that collectively constitute a floor option. A floorlet, as a component of a floor, is analogous to a caplet, a component of a cap option. A floorlet is a type of put option. See *caplet* for contrast.

flotation costs The direct and indirect costs borne by the issuer of a security that are associated with selling a new issue. The flotation costs include all costs other than the coupon rate that will be paid on the issue. The flotation costs include legal fees, underwriting fees, printing fees, registration fees, and so forth.

flotions Options written on floor options. That is, these are single period options (i.e., calls and puts) written on multi-period floor options. The flotion gives its holder the right, but not the obligation, to enter into a floor option on preset terms for a given period of time. If exercised, the flotion results in the creation of a floor option.

FNMA See *Federal National Mortgage Association*.

Follow-on offering See *seasoned public offering*.

Foreign currency options Also called *exchange rate options* or *currency options*. An option in which the underlying is an exchange rate.

foreign exchange markets See *currency markets*.

foreign exchange rate The rate, stated in terms of one currency, at which two currencies can be exchanged. For example, if the foreign exchange rate of euros for dollars is $1.0200, it would imply that one euro can be bought for $1.0200. See *exchange rate* for further discussion and other references.

foreign exchange risk The risk that the value of a position in a foreign currency or the value of an asset and/or a liability denominated in a foreign currency will change adversely as a consequence of a change in an exchange rate, relative to the party's functional currency. See also *currency risk*.

foreign issue A debt or equity instrument trading in a country different than the issuer's country of domicile. See *Yankee bonds, bulldogs,* and *samurai bonds* as examples.

FOREX markets See *currency markets*.

formula method One of three methods for determining damages upon the early termination of a swap. No longer widely used.

forward band A collar in which the premium paid on the cap (floor) is exactly equal to the premium received on the floor (cap). Also known as a *zero-cost collar*. See *collar* and *zero-cost collar*.

forward contract Also known as an *advance contract*. An agreement requiring the delivery of a certain quantity of a currency or other asset by a specified date in the future at a price agreed upon at the time of contracting. Such contracts are privately negotiated in the over-the-counter derivatives market and as such are distinguished from more standardized contracts for later delivery traded on futures exchanges.

forward discount The difference between a forward rate and a spot rate when the forward rate is below the spot rate.

forward exchange agreement Often abbreviated *FXA*. A type of cash-settled forward agreement used to hedge changes in exchange rate changes. For example, such an agreement will pay a sum at maturity given by the difference between the exchange rate at the contract's maturity and the exchange rate prevailing at the contract's inception. See also *exchange rate agreement*.

forward exchange rate A current rate of exchange for an exchange of currencies scheduled to take place at a later date. Also called a *forward rate,* but the latter term can also refer to a forward interest rate. There are multiple forward exchange rates for any two currencies, each associated with a different scheduled exchange date.

forward premium The difference between a forward rate and a spot rate when the forward rate is above the spot rate. This is in contrast to a *forward discount*. See *forward discount* for contrast.

forward rate (1) With respect to interest rates, a rate of interest expected to prevail at some point in the future. Often used to mean a *forward short rate,* which is the rate of interest expected to prevail on a one-period instrument at some point in the future. These rates can be derived, or inferred, from rates prevailing on other instruments. (2) With respect to exchange rates, a rate of exchange prevailing now for the exchange of currencies at a later date.

forward rate agreement Commonly known as an *FRA*. An interest-rate forward contract written on a notional principal and cash settled on the basis of the difference between the fixed contract rate and the value of the reference interest rate on the settlement date. The resultant settlement value is discounted to adjust for an up-front settlement. Settlement amount = discounted value of

$[S_T - X] \times NP$, where S_T is the spot value of the reference interest rate on the fixing date, X is the contract rate, and NP is the notional principal.

forward short rates See *forward rates*.

forward start option An option that is written with a later start date and written such that, at its start date, it will be at-the-money. That is, the option premium is set at the time the option is written, but the strike price is not set until the later start date. On the option's start date, the strike is set to the spot price prevailing on that date.

forward start swap Another name for a *forward swap*. See *forward swap*.

forward swap Also called a *deferred swap* and sometimes called a *forward start swap*. A fixed-for-floating interest-rate swap in which the swap coupon is set at the outset but the start of the swap is delayed.

fourth market A reference to direct institution-to-institution trading of securities. That is, the sale of securities by one institutional investor to another institutional investor that bypasses the broker/dealer community.

FRA See *forward rate agreement*.

FRABBA terms Standard terms for forward rate agreements established by the British Bankers' Association and used on many interbank FRAs.

fraption An option written on a forward rate agreement (FRA). Such an option allows the holder to enter into an FRA on prespecified terms should the fraption holder elect to exercise the fraption.

fraudulent conveyance The transfer of ownership in a business for purposes of defrauding creditors.

FRN See *floating rate note*.

front month The closest delivery or exercise month for exchange traded futures or options. The term *near month* is often used to mean the same thing. This is in contrast to the *back months*, which are the delivery or exercise months more forward than the front month. The term far months is often used to mean the same thing as back months.

front running Also known as *trading ahead of the client*. An illegal practice in which a party responsible for filling an order on behalf of a client buys or sells the asset in advance of filling the client's order based on the knowledge that the client's order is about to be executed and that the client's order is likely to move the market.

front stub period A first coupon period on a floating rate instrument that is shorter than a normal full coupon period. See also *back stub period*.

front-end fee A fee paid up front for the origination of a swap or other derivative instrument. Front-end fees have largely disappeared and are imposed today only when the swap or similar instrument involves some special financial engineering. Front-end fees are also imposed when the swap involves some option-like feature. In these cases the fee is best viewed as an option premium.

front-end load A load or sales charge imposed when something is purchased. The term is most often used in the context of the sales charges levied on the purchase of mutual fund shares. See *load* for a discussion of the different types of loads.

full faith and credit A pledge by a government's taxing jurisdiction to repay its debt obligation from whatever sources it may legally employ. The term is usually used in connection with bond issuances.

full price See *dirty price*.

full service Financial institutions that provide such a wide range of financial services that they can provide almost any service a client might desire. This is in contrast to boutiques, which limit themselves to providing a few specialty services.

fully registered A security whose ownership is recorded by a registrar in the name of the holder or his nominee. Transfer of ownership requires the signature of the registered owner.

functional currency The currency in which an entity keeps its accounting books. This is usually its domestic currency, but in some cases may not be. Also known as the *base currency*.

fundamental analysis A method of determining whether an asset is undervalued or overvalued in the market place by ascertaining, through a process of discounting the asset's likely future cash flows to their present value or a similar process, the fair market value of the asset and then comparing this fair value to the asset's current market price.

future value The value of a present sum of money at a future date, based on an appropriate interest rate and the number of years until that future date. The future value, assuming annual compounding of interest, is given by $FV = P \times (1 + r)^T$, where FV is the future value, P is the present sum of money, r is the interest rate, and T is the number of years into the future.

futures See *futures contract*.

futures commission merchant Known as an *FCM*. A firm providing brokerage services in the futures markets.

futures contract Also know as a *futures*, sometimes called a *future*. Standardized contracts for deferred delivery (or cash settlement) of commodities and financial instruments. Always traded on a designated futures exchange and, in the United States, regulated by the Commodity Futures Trading Commission. These contracts are marked-to-market daily based on settlement prices. The mark-to-market results in the transfer of variation margin from the day's losers to the day's winners. These contracts are guaranteed by a clearinghouse, which eliminates any need for the contracting parties to know their counterparty, since the counterparty becomes the clearinghouse.

futures exchange An exchange that trades futures contracts. In the United States, to be a futures exchange, a market must be designated as such by the Commodity Futures Trading Commission. Highly standardized futures contracts are traded on these exchanges using a dual auction, open outcry system.

Futures Exchange Act of 1974 In 1974 the U.S. Congress passed the Commodity Futures Trading Commission Act. This legislation created the Commodity Futures Trading Commission (CFTC) to regulate the futures industry. Prior to the passage of this act, futures trading was regulated by the Commodity Exchange Authority (CEA), a division of the Department of Agriculture.

futures option An option in which the underlying is a futures contract. If the option is exercised, the underlying futures contract will be delivered. Futures options trade on the same futures exchanges as the underlying futures contracts.

futures price The current price of a specific futures contract. For a futures price to have meaning, one must specify the underlying and the delivery date. For example, one might say "June silver on the COMEX is trading at $4.21." This would mean the price today of silver for delivery in June on the exchange known as the COMEX is $4.21 per ounce.

futures series All futures contracts having identical terms (including the same delivery month) and trading on the same exchange constitute a series. Because they have identical terms, all such contracts are fungible.

futures strip A series of futures contracts with successive delivery (settlement) months. Most often used to refer to a series of interest-rate futures such as Eurodollar futures. For example, a sequence consisting of the March ED contract, the June ED contract, and the September ED contract would constitute a strip. See also *Eurostrip*.

FX markets See *currency markets*.

FX options See *currency options*.

FXA See *forward exchange agreement*.

GAAP Acronym for *Generally Accepted Accounting Principles*. The set of accounting principals to which public corporations are expected to conform in the preparation and presentation of their financial statements to their shareholders.

GAAP books A corporation's financial statements prepared in accordance with generally accepted accounting principles. These can differ from a corporation's financial statements as prepared for filing with the taxing jurisdictions. The latter are called *tax books*.

GAINS A Goldman Sachs trademark for a type of *partial strip*. See *partial strips*.

gamma One of several measures of the risks associated with options that are collectively known as the option *Greeks*. The gamma is the rate of change in an option's delta with respect to changes in the market value of the underlying asset. This is equivalent to the second derivative of the option's valuation function with respect to the price of the underlying. Essentially, a gamma measures the rate of change in the option's delta. See *delta*.

gamma neutral Describes an option book (e.g., a portfolio of options) on a specific underlying asset that has an overall gamma of zero. In this context, the book includes any hedges that were put on to achieve the zero-gamma objective.

gamma risk A type of risk that option market makers are exposed to as a consequence of a positive or negative gamma. If the market maker's option book has a positive or negative (i.e., nonzero) gamma and there is a change in the price of the underlying, the market maker will experience some gain or loss even if the option book's delta is zero.

GARCH model A statistical model used to forecast volatility where the underlying variable may exhibit mean reversion. GARCH stands for Generalized Autoregressive Conditional Heteroscedasticity.

Gaussian distribution See *normal distribution*.

GDRs See *global depositary receipts*.

general collateral Describes a repurchase agreement (repo) in which the borrower can supply any Treasury security as collateral (as opposed to a specific Treasury security). See *repurchase agreement*.

general obligation bonds Government bonds, including municipal bonds, which are backed by the full faith and credit of the issuing authority. This is in contrast to *revenue bonds*, which are backed only by the specific revenue source. See *revenue bonds* for contrast.

generalized autoregressive conditional heteroscedasticity See *GARCH model*.

generalized Weiner process A stochastic process in which the changes in the variable over short periods of time are normally distributed with a mean and a variance that are proportional to the length of time involved. These stochastic processes are widely used to model price evolution over time and, hence, form the basis for many stochastic valuation models.

Generally Accepted Accounting Principles Known by the acronym *GAAP*. The generally accepted rules of accounting as promulgated by the Federal Accounting Standards Board (FASB) and other recognized authorities.

generic See *plain vanilla*.

generic swap Also known as a *plain vanilla swap* and a *basic swap*. The simplest or most standard form of a given type of swap. A swap in which the first counterparty pays the second a fixed rate or price on some quantity of notionals and the second counterparty pays the first a floating rate or price on the same quantity of notionals. See *plain vanilla swap*.

geographic arbitrage Also known as *spatial arbitrage*. The buying of an asset in one market and the simultaneous selling of the asset in another market in order to exploit a price discrepancy between the two markets. In order to be profitable, the difference between the two prices must be greater than the sum of the transaction, transportation, and financing costs.

geometric average Found by taking the nth root of the product of n numbers. For example, to find the geometric average of the numbers 5, 8, and 3, do the following:

$$(5 \times 8 \times 3)^{1/3}.$$

geometric average annual return An average formed by taking the geometric average of successive annual percentage returns on an investment. This form of calculating an average annual return is more reliable than the arithmetic average annual return because the geometric average reflects the effects of compounding while the arithmetic average does not. For example, if the annual returns on an investment for the last four years were +20%, −20%, +16%, and +40%, the geometric average annual return would be 11.7%, while the arithmetic average would be 14%. The calculation of a geometric average annual rate of return requires that we add the number "1" to each annual rate and then deduct the number "1" from the final result. Specifically, the equation for obtaining a geometric average annual rate of return (GA) from a series of annual returns over N years is given by:

$$GA = [(1 + r_1) \times (1 + r_2) \times ... \times (1 + r_N)]^{1/N} - 1$$

See *arithmetic average annual return* for comparison.

geometric Brownian motion Describes a stochastic process in which the natural logarithm of a random variable follows a generalized Weiner process. See *generalized Weiner process*.

GIC See *guaranteed investment contract*.

gilts Sovereign bonds of the British government. These are analogous to Treasury bonds in the United States.

Glass-Steagall Act See *Banking Act of 1933*.

global depositary receipts Known by the acronym *GDRs*. These are the European counterpart to American depositary receipts. Unlike ADRs, where the underlying securities are held by banks, in GDRs the underlying securities are held by specialized European depositories. See *American depositary receipts* for more detail on the general structure.

global hedging See *macro hedging*.

global investing Investing in securities of both domestic and nondomestic entities. For example, an American investor investing in the securities of both U.S. and non-U.S. issuers would be engaged in global investing. This is distinct from *international investing* which is limited to investing in securities of nondomestic issuers. The term global investing is often taken to mean investing in the securities of a large number of countries including one's own country, whereas international investing could be interpreted very narrowly as involving securities of a single country other than one's own country.

globalization The increasing tendency for national borders to be irrelevant to the financial markets.

GLOBEX A trading system developed through a collaborative effort of the Chicago Mercantile Exchange, the Chicago Board of Trade, and Reuters to trade futures contracts electronically. Its primary purpose when developed was for after-hours trading.

GNMA See *Government National Mortgage Association*.

GNP See *gross national product*.

golden handcuffs Components of an employment contract that make it financially advantageous for an employee to remain with the firm. For example, a profit-sharing plan might vest over a period of time. By leaving the firm, the employee would forfeit that portion of the profit sharing not yet vested.

golden parachutes Large, contractually guaranteed payments to senior management in the event that the corporation for which they work is taken over or bought out.

good-til-cancelled Known by the acronym *GTC*. See *open order*.

Government National Mortgage Association Known by the acronym *GNMA*. A wholly-owned and sponsored corporation of the U.S. government that guarantees mortgages which are insured by the Federal Housing Authority or guaranteed by the Veterans Administration. These mortgages, which are assumable, are pooled for subsequent issue of pass-through certificates. Commonly known by its nickname Ginnie Mae.

government securities dealer Any dealer in U.S. government securities such as Treasury securities. The term would include both the primary dealers and the non-primary dealers.

governments Also called *govies*. Securities issued by the United States government. Sometimes the term means only U.S. Treasury securities; at other times it means both Treasury securities and agency securities. The latter are debt issues of U.S. agencies and federally sponsored corporations.

govies See *governments.*

grace period (1) A period of time built into an amortization schedule of a debt instrument during which none of the principal amortizes. (2) A period of time during which a late payment on an obligation will not incur a penalty.

graduated payment mortgage Sometimes referred to as a *GPM*. Any fixed-rate mortgage schedule in which the mortgage payments get larger at designated points in time. Most often, the payments on such mortgages periodically reset to a new level and then remain constant at that new level for some period of time before resetting again. After some period of time, usually five years, the payment is fixed for the remainder of the term of the mortgage. GPMs typically experience negative amortization in the early years because the early-year payments are insufficient to cover the interest due. The difference between the interest due and the scheduled payment is then added

to the principal, thereby resulting in the negative amortization.

graduated rate coupon Also known as a *multiple coupon*. These are bonds in which the coupon on each payment date is preset at issuance, but in which not all the coupon payments are the same. Most often, these increase or "step up" at some point.

grantor A person who sells (i.e., writes) an option. The term *grantor* is more common in Europe than in the United States. The term *writer* is preferred in the United States. See also *writer.*

grantor trust A contractual arrangement that provides a legal "container" into which a variety of assets can be deposited and resold in smaller economic units to investors that might otherwise be unable to participate in certain types of markets (e.g., oil, other commodities, or currencies). Publicly offered trusts are regulated under the Investment Company Act of 1940, but private trust transactions are generally unregulated.

grave dancers See *vulture capitalists.*

Greeks A general term that describes the risk measures associated with options and with instruments containing embedded options. The term derives from the fact that the risk measures are named for letters of the Greek alphabet. The principal Greeks include *delta, gamma, vega, rho,* and *theta.* See these terms individually for a precise meaning of each.

Green Shoe option See *overallotment option.*

greenmail A combination of a *targeted block repurchase* and a *standstill agreement.* Essentially, a corporation's board agrees to have the corporation buy all of the stock held by a hostile shareholder who is threatening to take control of the corporation (this is the targeted block repurchase component). The stock is purchased at a price that is above the current market price. In exchange for the premium paid for the stock, the owner of the targeted block signs an agreement not to purchase stock in the corporation for a specific period of time (this is the standstill agreement component).

gross national product The term is usually abbreviated *GNP*. The total market value of all goods and services produced for final consumption in the course of a single year.

gross negative fair value The total of the fair values on all contracts on which a party owes money to counterparties without any netting against those contracts on which the party would be owed money by counterparties. Thus, this value represents the largest loss that the entity could cause its counterparties if it defaulted. This calculation is often done on swap portfolios. For example, suppose that a corporation is a party to three interest rate swaps. The first has a mark-to-market value of −$2.4 million, the second has a mark-to-market value of +$1.3 million, and the third has a mark-to-market value of −$3.1 million swaps. Thus, the corporation would owe money in the event of a default on swaps 1 and 3. The gross negative fair value is the sum of mark-to-market values of swaps 1 and 3, or −$5.5 million.

gross positive fair value The total of the fair values on all contracts on which a party is owed money by other counterparties without any netting against those contracts on which the party would owe money to other counterparties. Thus, this value represents the largest loss that the entity could incur if its counterparties defaulted. This cal-culation is often done on swap portfolios. For example, suppose that a corporation is a party to three interest rate swaps. The first has a mark-to-market value of +$2.4 million, the second has a mark-to-market value of +$1.3 million, and the third has a mark-to-market value of −$3.1 million swaps. Thus, the corporation is owed money in the event of a default on swaps 1 and 2. The gross positive fair value is then the sum of mark-to-market values of swaps 1 and 2, or −$3.7 million.

gross spread The difference between the offering price of publicly offered securities and the proceeds paid to the issuer of the securities by the underwriters. The underwriters and selling group earn the gross spread as compensation for their underwriting (i.e., risk taking) and distribution (i.e., selling) services. The gross spread typically ranges from one to eight percentage points, depending on the type of security being sold and the size of the offering. The gross spread is divided into a management fee, an underwriting fee, and a sales credit. These components are typically 20–25%, 20–25%, and 50–60% of the gross spread, respectively. The gross spread is known also as the *underwriting spread* and the *underwriting discount*.

Group of Thirty Also called *G30*. An international panel representing industry, government, and academia and supported by the major financial institutions participating in the global financial markets. Its purpose is to develop and recommend best practices and principles in conduct of the markets, particularly the over-the-counter derivatives markets. In July 1993, the group issued a document entitled *Derivatives: Practices and Principles*, and in December 1994 it released the results of a follow-up survey on the extent to which its recommendations had been implemented.

growing equity mortgage The purest form of a graduate payment mortgage in which each mortgage payment is larger than the last by some percentage amount or some absolute amount. The term has also been used to describe other mortgage structures.

GTC Acronym for *good-til-cancelled*. See *open order*.

guaranteed bonds Bonds that are secured by a guarantee provided by another entity. Most often, such a bond is issued by a subsidiary corporation and guaranteed by a parent corporation. In some cases, a bond may be guaranteed by the Federal government. In other cases, a bond may have a guarantee from a bond-insurer.

guaranteed investment contract Known by the acronym *GIC*. A pension/insurance type contract that guarantees a fixed stream of income to the contract holder for some period of time.

Hammersmith and Fulham A borough (local governmental region) of Britain. The governing council of this borough engaged in a large number of interest rate swaps in the late 1980s with a number of swap dealers in an effort to speculate on the direction of interest rates. The speculation resulted in large losses to the borough, following which the courts ruled that the council did not have the legal authority to enter into the contracts on behalf of the borough, thereby rendering the contracts null and void. As a consequence, the dealer banks suffered large losses. This case was important because it demonstrated the legal risk faced by dealers and the importance of determining whether the party authorizing a derivatives contract has the legal capacity to contract on behalf of the entity that he or she claims to represent.

handle The integer part of a security's price when that price is stated as a percentage. For example, if a security is trading at $97\,^{14}/_{32}$, the handle would be 97. Sometimes called the *big figure*.

hard call protection A period of time following issuance during which a call-able security cannot be called for any reason. That is, the convertible security cannot be called prior to its hard call date and the holder of the security is said to have hard call protection. This is generally very important when the security is also convertible. Convertible securities typically pay a higher yield than common. Therefore, the greater the length of call protection, the greater the income pickup over common.

Heath-Jarrow-Morton model A widely used, interest rate option valuation model that derives the entire forward rate curve at each iteration. The model is multi-factor and can be simulated using Monte Carlo methods. The model is named for its creators: David Heath, Robert Jarrow, and Andrew Morton.

hedge Can be used as either a verb or a noun. As a verb, the act of taking a position in an instrument, usually a derivative, in order to offset the risk associated with a position in another instrument, usually a cash position. As a noun, a position in an instrument that offsets the risk associated with a position in another instrument.

hedge accounting The practice of deferring gains and losses on instruments held as hedges until the losses and gains on the positions being hedged are realized. In other words, an accounting treatment that allows us to look at the hedge position as though it were inseparable from the position being hedged with gains and losses on the two positions recognized jointly at the time the gains or losses on the hedged position are realized. Hedge account rules are now described by FAS 133.

hedge effectiveness The degree to which a hedge offsets the price risk associated with a cash position or an anticipated cash position. Hedge effectiveness is most often measured with the aid of the correlation coefficient, which measures the degree of correlation between the price of the cash position (i.e., the spot price) and the price of the hedge instrument. The greater the degree of hedge effectiveness, the lower the basis risk. See *basis risk* for more detail.

hedge efficiency The degree to which a hedge provides risk reduction per unit of cost.

hedge fund A private investment partnership typically open to only wealthy individuals and/or qualified institutional investors. The partnership is run by a general partner who oversees the investment activities of the fund. Such funds have considerable latitude in their investment strategies and will take both long and short positions, use significant leverage, and often take positions in derivative financial instruments. The term "hedge fund" is widely regarded as a misnomer because the term would seem to imply little risk, while in fact, hedge funds often take considerable risk.

hedge optimality In the language of economics, the degree to which a hedge maximizes the hedger's economic utility. In lay terms, an effort to determine the best hedge given the trade-off between risk reduction and cost.

hedge ratio The number of units of a hedge instrument that must be held, per unit of the cash position held, in order to minimize the overall portfolio variance (i.e., the variance of value of the cash position and hedge combined).

hedging The act of calculating the proper size of a hedge and then taking a position of that size in an appropriate hedge instrument for the purpose of offsetting the risk associated with a cash position. A hedge can be taken in any of a variety of derivative instruments (including forwards, futures, swaps, listed options, and over-the-counter options) or in a different cash instrument. Importantly, a derivative dealer will often hedge its derivatives book in another type of derivative, and can hedge its derivative book in a cash position. The latter is the reverse of the usual description of hedging, but is no less accurate. Hedging is undertaken to achieve net risk reduction.

herd instinct The buying or selling of securities for no other reason than others are doing it. The term describes the tendency to feel safe if one is doing the same thing as everyone else is doing. It is often used in a derogatory manner. Recent developments in behavioral finance have placed greater emphasis on the biological foundations of the herd instinct.

high coupon swap This swap is written with a swap coupon (fixed rate) that is above market. When a high coupon swap is written, the party receiving the above market coupon will pay a front end fee equal to the present value of the difference between the high coupon and the at-market coupon. This is in contrast to a *low coupon swap*. See also *off-market swap*.

high net worth A reference to individuals having a net worth (i.e., the difference between the value of their assets and the value of their liabilities) beyond some specified level. Many brokerage firms target high net worth investors, particularly when marketing more highly engineered financial products. Unfortunately, there is no consensus as to the net worth threshold necessary to qualify for high net worth status.

high yield bonds Also known as *junk bonds* and *speculative grade bonds*. These are bonds that have either a speculative grade rating or no rating at all. The former are usually bonds that were issued with investment grade ratings but deteriorated until they became speculative grade. These are sometimes called *fallen angels*. The latter are bonds for which no rating was obtained, often because of insufficient history. They are often issued to finance various forms of M&A activity, particularly leveraged buyouts, and are sold in private placements. These are nicknamed *rising stars*.

highly leveraged transaction Sometimes represented by the acronym *HTL*. A transaction, usually involving a portfolio of bank loans, that is sold to an investor using considerable leverage in the purchase. Such transactions are often made by hedge funds. If credit risk is present, the investor might mitigate the credit risk using credit derivatives.

historic vol See *historic volatility*.

historic volatility Often called *historic vol*. Volatility is usually measured as the standard deviation of the percentage price change, where the percentage price change is measured on an annual basis and under the assumption of continuous compounding. Historic volatility is the price volatility of an asset calculated from historic data. It is therefore an ex post measure (i.e., backward looking.) This is in contrast to an implied volatility. See *implied volatility*. Volatilities are a critical input in the valuation of both options and instruments containing embedded options.

historical simulation Simulating possible future outcomes for a random variable from past behavior of that same random variable. The method assumes that the stochastic properties of the random variable will be the same in the future as in the past. The method is sometimes used to generate historical value-at-risk. See *historical value-at-risk*.

historical value-at-risk One of several methods used to calculate a value-at-risk measure. Value-at-risk, or VaR, is a measure of the maximum financial loss that might occur as a consequence of changes in market prices over some risk horizon at some level of confidence. Historical VaR is generated via historical simulation.

holder (1) The buyer of an option contract, often said to be long, (2) The owner of any security (e.g., a bondholder).

holder-of-record date Also called the *record date*. The date on which a person must be a legal owner of stock in order to be entitled to receive a dividend paid by the corporation. There is a lag between the time an individual purchases a stock and the time that the individual becomes the legal owner of the stock. In the United States, this is presently three business days. Thus, an individual must buy a stock at least three business days prior to the holder-of-record date to be a holder of record on the holder-of-record date.

holding companies Corporations that hold large equity interests in other corporations. Holding corporations are sometimes formed to circumvent laws prohibiting a single corporation from engaging in more than one of several distinct lines of business. They can also serve to insulate the parent company from financial calamities incurred by the subsidiaries.

holding period The length of time that a position in an investment is held and, consequently, the length of time over which the return on the investment is measured.

holding period return The percentage return earned from holding an investment over the entire holding period. Also known as *cumulative total return.*

horizon An expected holding period, as in *investment horizon,* or a period of time over which a risk exposure is going to be experienced or measured, as in *risk horizon.*

horizon matching Also known as *combination matching.* Involves both immunization of a balance sheet and cash flow matching for the early years. See *combination matching.*

horizontal bear spread A horizontal spread in options in which the position holder is long the near month and short the back month. See also *horizontal spread.*

horizontal bull spread A horizontal spread in options in which the position holder is long the back month and short the front month. See also *horizontal spread.*

horizontal merger A merger between two companies within the same niche of the same industry. For example, the merger of two oil refiners or the merger of two hotel chains would both be horizontal mergers.

horizontal spread Also known as a *calendar spread* and a *time spread.* An option position involving simultaneous long and short positions in options of the same class (i.e., both are calls or both are puts) and written on the same underlying asset. Both options have the same strike price but they have different expiration dates.

hostile takeover The attempt by one corporation (i.e., the acquirer) to take over another corporation (i.e., the target) in which the target corporation perceives the effort as hostile. In such situations, it is usually expected that the acquiring firm's management is not seeking an understanding with the management of the target firm in an effort to win the target's cooperation in the acquisition. Also, in such cases, the acquirer will usually replace the target's senior management should the takeover be successful.

HTL See *highly leveraged transaction.*

humped yield curve A situation in which the yield curve rises with maturity for some period but declines with maturity thereafter. That is, the yield curve rises and then falls over the maturity spectrum.

hybrid securities Securities that have characteristics of more than one asset class. Convertible bonds were one of the earliest hybrid securities because they have the risk/return characteristics of both debt and equity. Various types of structured securities, including equity-linked notes, are more recent manifestations of hybrid securities. Some hybrid securities have characteristics of as many as three different asset classes (e.g., debt, equity, and commodity).

hypothecation The pledging of property to secure a loan. Hypothecation does not transfer title to the lender but does encumber the property such that it cannot be sold. In the event of a default, the right to sell the hypothecated property is transferred to the lender. Hypothecation is also employed in the securities market on margined securities purchases.

ICON See *index currency options.*

illiquid Difficult to buy or sell without making a very significant price concession. Liquidity is often measured by the size of the bid-ask spread and/or by the size of the market at both the bid and offer prices.

IMM Acronym for *International Monetary Market.*

IMM settlement dates The settlement dates of IMM Eurodollar futures contracts are the third Wednesday of the specified month. IMM denotes the International Monetary Market, a division of the Chicago Mercantile Exchange. These dates are often used as settlement dates on forward rate agreements and swap contracts.

IMM swaps Swaps that are priced off the IMM's Eurodollar futures strip and which use IMM settlement dates.

immediate pay Bonds that pay their coupon at the beginning of each payment period, as opposed to the usual case wherein bonds pay their coupon at the end of each payment period.

immunization An approach to managing the interest rate risk inherent in some businesses by focusing on the durations of the corporation's assets and liabilities. As such, it is a form of asset/liability management that works by matching the overall duration of the asset side of the balance sheet to the overall duration of the liability side of the balance sheet. More advanced approaches to immunization will match the convexities of the assets and liabilities in addition to matching the durations of the assets and the liabilities. All references here to duration refer to modified duration.

immunized portfolios Asset portfolios held by an entity, such as a pension fund, that have been structured to have the same overall duration as the overall duration of the same entity's liabilities. See *immunization.*

implied distribution A statistical distribution for the future spot price of some asset that has been deduced or inferred from the prices of a set of options written on that asset. That is, it is a distribution that is consistent with the observed prices of the options.

implied repo rate A financing rate that equates the fair value of a futures contract to the current market value of the underlying. Most often used in the context of bond futures and stock index futures. It is extracted from an arbitrage-free cost of carry model. Essentially, if the implied repo rate differs from the actual repo rate, an arbitrage opportunity exists (ignoring transaction costs). Repo refers to a repurchase agreement. The repo rate is the borrowing rate on a collateralized repo transaction. The implied repo rate is what this rate would have to be for no arbitrage opportunity to exist.

implied volatility An estimate of the future volatility of some asset's price where said volatility is measured as the standard deviation of the annual percentage change in the price of the asset when the percentage changes are measured under the assumption of continuous compounding. These estimates are called implied volatilities because future volatility is not currently observable and, hence, must be inferred from the prices of options trading on the asset. See also *historic volatility* and *volatility.*

in-arrears swaps See *back-end set swaps.*

incentive stock options See *executive stock options.*

income bond A bond which pays coupon interest provided that the bond issuer has sufficient income, as defined in the bond indenture. If the issuer has insufficient income, the issuer does not have to pay the interest due and the failure to pay does not constitute default. The interest on such bonds is usually cumulative. See *cumulative.*

indemnification method One of three methods for assessing damages upon the early termination of a swap. No longer widely used.

indenture Also known as a *trust deed.* An indenture is the contractual relationship between a bond issuer and the bondholders. It spells out the details of the relationship between the parties including such things as collateral, cou-

pon, call provisions, call protection, and so forth.

index A cross-section of some asset class that is constructed to serve as a general guide to overall market performance and which is often used as a benchmark against which a portfolio manager's performance can be compared.

index amortizing swap Any swap whose notional principal amortizes based on the successive values of some index, often an interest rate. For example, as the reference interest rate declines, the rate of amortization of the notional principal usually accelerates; as the reference interest rate rises, the rate of amortization of the notional principal usually decelerates. Such swap structures are often used to hedge amortizing debt portfolios where there are embedded prepayment options (such as in most mortgages). Also known as an *indexed principal swap.*

index- and asset-linked notes Debt securities that offer investors principal preservation (i.e., return of the principal investment at maturity) and potential capital appreciation (called a kicker) linked to the movement of an index or other asset (e.g., equity, a commodity, or an exchange rate).

index arbitrage See *cash-index arbitrage.*

index currency option Sometimes abbreviated *ICON.* A type of *option currency bond* issued by the Long-Term Credit Bank of Japan in1985. See *option currency bond.*

index futures A futures contract written on an index of some sort. The most common type is stock index futures, but the concept is general enough to be applied to a bond index, a currency index, a real estate index, and so forth. Such futures are always cash settled.

index option An option contract written on an index of some sort. The most common type is stock index options, but the concept is general enough to be applied to a bond index, a currency index, a real estate index, and so forth. Such options are always cash settled.

indexed principal swap See *index amortizing swap.*

indexing Any investment strategy designed to generate returns that mirror some benchmark index. Such strategies are usually largely passive in nature. However, some enhanced indexing strategies may be more active in nature.

indexing plus See *enhanced indexing.*

index-linked notes See *index- and asset-linked notes.*

indicative swap pricing schedule Industry term used to describe the quoted price schedule for the swaps in which a swap dealer makes a market. The term "indicative" is meant to imply that these rate quotes apply to plain vanilla swaps and that a number of assumptions should be made. For example, indicative prices assume that the counterparty is a best credit. Actual pricing may vary depending on the terms of the swap, the creditworthiness of a counterparty, and other factors. Thus, indicative pricing is meant to mean that the pricing is only a general indication of the prices at which the dealer will enter swaps. The actual price will probably deviate from the indicative pricing.

individual retirement account See *IRA.*

inefficient hedges Any hedge such that another hedge exists that either offers the same level of risk reduction at less cost or has the same cost and is more effective.

inflation-indexed bonds Inflation-indexed bonds and notes are structured so that the coupon payment, the principal, or both the coupon payment and the principal change in such a manner as to compensate the bondholder for changes in some price index. For example, on the U.S. Treasury's inflation-indexed bonds and notes, the coupon rate is fixed but the principal increases or decreases to reflect the rate of inflation during the prior period. The fixed coupon rate is then applied to the larger (or smaller) principal. By this process, the investor achieves considerable protection from a loss of purchasing power due to inflation. While not often described as such, inflation-indexed bonds and notes can be viewed as a combination of a plain vanilla fixed rate bond and a macroeconomic derivative in which the macroeconomic index is a specified rate of inflation, such as the CPI.

INFLOS See *municipal floating-rate bonds.*

informationally efficient Prices that accurately reflect the value of all available information. Closely associated with the efficient markets hypothesis. See *efficient markets hypothesis* for further discussion.

initial margin Also called *original margin.* The amount of margin that a trader must have in his margin account in order to take a position. Once a position has been taken, the trader must keep the margin above a certain level called the maintenance level. The maintenance level is below the initial level. See *margin* and *maintenance margin.*

initial public offering More commonly known by the acronym *IPO.* The first issuance of common stock to the general public following registration of the securities with the Securities and Exchange Commission. The offering of the registered stock transforms the private corporation into a public corporation and subjects it to the disclosure requirements and regulatory oversight of the SEC.

inside barriers The most common form of barrier options. Inside barriers are barrier options in which the same asset's price serves as both the underlying asset's price and the option's barrier (i.e., trigger) price. This is in contrast to an *outside barrier* in which the asset whose price is used as the trigger is different from the underlying asset. See *barrier options* for more detail and *outside barrier* for contrast.

inside debt Loan debt, as opposed to bond debt, in which the lender has access to proprietary information about the borrower. That is, the lender requires the borrower to provide information that is considered confidential by the borrower. The lender is expected to maintain the confidentiality of such information.

inside market Prices at which dealers will trade securities with one another, as opposed to prices offered to the general public. Also known as an *interdealer market*.

institutional investors Large investors that represent various types of institutions including such entities as insurance companies, pension funds, mutual funds, hedge funds, large endowments, and so forth. This investor class is distinguished from individual investors as a class. Individual investors make up the retail investor market.

insurable risk Any risk such that the risk exposures of those who bear the risk are not highly correlated with one another. Such risks can be insured against. Examples of insurable risks include the financial consequences of death (life insurance), fraud, fire, liability, and so forth. This is distinct from noninsurable risks, such as price risk, in which the exposures of all parties having a similar risk are very highly correlated. These latter risks can be hedged, though not insured in the usual sense.

insurance A contract that transfers a financial risk from one party to another in exchange for an up-front fee called a *premium*.

insured bonds Bonds for which a guarantee has been purchased by the issuer from a third-party insurer in order to improve the credit quality of the bond issue.

intangible assets Assets that are not of a physical nature but which nevertheless have value. These include such things as copyrights, patents, licenses to operate, and goodwill.

interbank swaps Swaps between two swap dealers.

intercommodity spreads Buying a futures contract on one commodity, such as soybeans, and selling futures contracts on other commodities, such as soybean oil and/or soybean meal, in order to profit from a perceived aberration in the pricing of the commodities. Intercommodity spreads are a type of intermarket spread.

interdealer market See *inside market*.

interest The cost of borrowing money. Compensation for the use or forbearance of money.

interest differential (1) In a swap, the difference between the amount of interest

Counterparty 1 must pay Counterparty 2 and the amount Counterparty 2 must pay Counterparty 1. (2) The rate differential between the rates on two different instruments having the same maturity. In this context, the preferred term is "interest-rate differential." (3) The rate differential between instruments of the same maturity but denominated in different currencies.

interest only See *interest-only strip*.

interest rate and currency exchange agreement A multicurrency, standard form agreement first published by the ISDA in 1987. Designed to serve as a master swap agreement.

interest rate cap Also called a *rate cap* and, sometimes, just a *cap*. Multi-period cash-settled options on interest rates. The cap purchaser receives a cash payment whenever the reference rate exceeds the ceiling rate (also called the *cap rate* and sometimes called the *contract rate*) on a fixing date. Such instruments may be viewed as a portfolio of simpler call options. When viewed this way, the individual components are called *caplets*. See also *cap*.

interest rate collar Also called a *collar*. A combination of an interest rate cap and an interest rate floor such that a cap is sold and a floor is purchased, or vice versa. When used in conjunction with a floating rate instrument, the effect is to place upper and lower bounds on the cost of funds if borrowing or on the return if investing.

interest rate floor A multi-period interest-rate option that provides a cash payment to the holder of the option whenever the reference rate is below the floor rate (also called the *floor* and sometimes the *contract rate*) on a fixing date.

interest rate futures Futures on debt instruments or interest rates. The value of an interest rate futures contract moves inversely with changes in the level of interest rates. Examples include Treasury bond futures and Eurodollar futures.

interest rate guarantee An option on a forward rate agreement. Also known as a *fraption*. See *fraption*.

interest rate option An option in which the underlying asset is a debt security or an interest rate. For example, an option on LIBOR. Such options can be single period or multi-period in nature. The former include calls and puts and the latter include caps and floors. All of these options can also be written on underlyings other than interest rates.

interest rate parity A relationship between the nominal interest rates in two countries and the spot and forward exchange rates for those two countries' currencies. Interest rate parity is a consequence of covered interest arbitrage. In brief, parity implies that the difference between two currencies' forward and spot exchange rates is fully explained by the difference between the interest rates in those countries. Interest rate parity exists when profitable arbitrage is not possible. See also *covered interest arbitrage*.

interest rate risk (1) The risk that a future interest rate will deviate from its expected value. (2) The price risk associated with holding a fixed-rate debt instrument as a result of fluctuations in the instrument's yield. This risk is most often measured by means of the instrument's modified duration and related measures.

interest rate sensitivity A measure of the sensitivity of a fixed income security's price to changes in the level of interest rates. Usually measured with the aid of modified duration.

interest rate spread The difference between the interest rate received on an entity's assets and the interest rate paid on its liabilities. For certain financial institutions, the interest rate spread is the principal source for deriving profit.

interest rate swap An agreement between two parties to engage in a series of interest payment exchanges on the same notional principal denominated in the same currency. In the simplest form, one counterparty pays a fixed rate of interest and the other counterparty pays a floating rate of interest. The fixed rate is called the *swap coupon* and the floating rate is called the *reference rate*.

interest rate swap master agreement A contractual agreement that spells out the terms on all swaps written between the same two counterparties. As such, these are master swap agreements. Standardized agreements are promulgated by both the International Swaps and Derivatives Association (ISDA) and the British Bankers' Association (BBA).

interest-only strip Usually abbreviated *IO*. Also known as an *interest-only tranche*. A tranche of a passthrough security, such as a CMO, which gives the holder the right to receive a portion of every interest payment, but not a portion of the principal payments.

interest-only tranche See *interest-only strip*.

intermarket front running The purchase of instruments or assets in one market (such as futures or options) based on knowledge of a client's order in another market. This involves trading ahead of the client in the related market in anticipation that the client's order will move the market. Such behavior is always unethical and often illegal.

intermarket spreads The act of going long in a contract in one market and short in a contract in a different market because one believes that the difference between the two prices will narrow or widen. Such strategies can involve bonds, futures, or equities. Depending on the instruments used to do the spreading, also known as *sector spreads* and sometimes as *intercommodity spreads*.

intermediation Standing between two parties. The term is often used to describe the activities of banks in which they intermediate between the providers of capital and the users of capital.

internal rate of return Usually abbreviated *IRR*. The discount rate that equates the sum of the present values of the cash flows associated with an investment to the initial cost of the investment. This is equivalent to the discount rate that makes the net present value of the investment exactly zero.

International Association of Financial Engineers Known by the acronym *IAFE*. A professional society of practitioners and academicians engaged in various aspects of financial engineering. The society serves as a networking, research, and information exchange organization. The IAFE is headquartered in New York City.

international investing Investing in securities that are issued by nondomestic entities. For example, an American investor investing in stocks and bonds issued exclusively by non-U.S. entities would constitute international investing. This is somewhat different from global investing which includes investment in issues of both international and domestic entities.

International Monetary Market Known by the acronym *IMM*. A subsidiary of the Chicago Mercantile Exchange, the IMM is a major market in the United States for currency futures, interest rate futures, and stock index futures.

International Swaps and Derivatives Association Known by the acronym *ISDA*. Originally known as the International Swap Dealers Association. ISDA is a New York–based trade association that deals with matters of common interest to member derivative dealers. This organization took a leading role in developing standardized documentation for over-the-counter derivatives contracts.

in-the-money In the case of a call option, a situation in which the spot price of the underlying asset is higher than the strike price of the option. In the case of a put option, a situation in which the spot price of the underlying asset is lower than the strike price of the option. The term is also used to describe swaps. A swap is said to be in-the-money for a counterparty if it has a positive mark-to-market value for that counterparty. It would be out-of-the-money for the other counterparty to the swap.

intramarket spreads A strategy involving a long position in one contract and a short position in another contract within the same overall market. For example, if futures are used, an intramarket spread might involve going long a June delivery contract and short a September delivery contract on the same underlying asset.

intrinsic value (1) A component of an option's value. It is the greater of the amount by which an option is in-the-money or zero. If the option is of the American type, this represents the value that could be captured if the option were exercised immediately. (2) The term is sometimes used in other contexts to refer to the value below which an instrument's price should not fall (because if it did an arbitrage opportunity would arise).

introducing brokers Securities firms that do not clear trades but which instead depend upon the services of clearing firms to complete the clearing and settlement operations associated with their transactions. The clearing firms are called *correspondents.*

inverse floater (1) A type of structured note in which the interest rate fluctuates inversely with the direction of some reference rate of interest; (2) A type of CMO tranche whose return will increase as the index interest rate (such as LIBOR) falls and decrease as it rises.

inverted market A market in which the normal relationships, in the sense that they exist most of the time, are inverted. For example, if it is normal for the futures prices on an underlying asset to be progressively higher the further forward one looks, but instead one finds the futures prices progressively lower, the market would be said to be inverted.

inverted yield curve Also known as a *descending yield curve* and as a *downward sloping yield curve.* This is a situation in which debt instruments with shorter maturities are yielding more than longer maturity debt instruments having otherwise similar terms. This is in contrast to an upward sloping yield curve, which has been, historically, the prevalent type. See *upward sloping yield curve.*

investment advisor A person who manages the investment assets of another in exchange for a fee.

Investment Advisors Act of 1940 This legislation extended the SEC's regulatory and supervisory authority to persons and entities that provide investment management services and related advisory services.

investment banking Narrowly defined: the process and activities associated with assisting corporations in raising capital via the issuance of debt and equity securities. More broadly defined: the collection of services and related activities provided by investment banks to their corporate clients and understood to include raising capital, assisting in financial risk management, advising in mergers and acquisitions, advising on capital structure issues, and so forth.

Investment Company Act of 1940 (as amended) This legislation is often called the "40s Act." Among its requirements: open-end investment companies (mutual funds) and closed-end investment companies must register with the SEC; investment companies must provide prospectuses to potential investors; and companies are required to have outside directors on their boards.

investment grade bond Any bond that has been rated as such by a rating agency. In the case of Moody's Investor Services, these would be ratings of Baa or better. In the case of Standard & Poor's, these would be ratings of BBB or better.

investment horizon The length of time until the planned use of the proceeds from the liquidation of an investment portfolio. This liquidation might be for the purpose of meeting living expenses or for the purpose of revising the asset allocation scheme. For example, a 35-year old plans to retire at age 60, at which time he would liquidate his portfolio and re-position his wealth for his retirement years; he has an investment horizon of 25 years. When the investment horizon is limited to the length of time until the investment strategy will be revised, it is sometimes called a *planning horizon.*

investment premium The premium over investment value at which a convertible security trades. The lower a convertible's investment premium, the better its price support. Busted convertibles typically trade at low investment premiums and possess little equity sensitivity. At the other extreme, equity-sensitive convertibles trade at high investment premiums and possess little price support. See also *investment value.*

investment value The value of a convertible security below which its price should not fall regardless of a decline in the value of the underlying common stock. This is the value that the instrument would have absent the conversion privilege. For example, a convertible bond has some minimum value based on its value as a straight bond. This is a function of its coupon, maturity, and the yields of comparable-risk straight bonds. When the convertible security is a convertible bond, the investment value is often called the convertible's *bond value.*

investor A person (or an institution) who holds an asset in order to enhance his financial position. Also sometimes called a *holder.*

invoice price The amount that the long must pay the short when a Treasury bond is delivered by the short to the long on a Treasury bond futures contract. This includes a sum determined by the futures price and the conversion factor but also includes any accrued interest on the bond.

IO See *interest-only strip*.

IPO See *initial public offering*.

IRA Acronym for *individual retirement account*. An important innovation adopted by Congress to encourage individuals to save for their retirement by granting preferential tax treatment to income generated from these accounts and, in some cases, to the funds contributed to the accounts.

IRR See *internal rate of return*.

irredeemable gilts A type of British government bond that has no specific maturity date but which can be called by the government with three months' notice after a specified date has passed.

ISDA See *International Swaps and Derivatives Association*.

issuance As a verb, the process of issuing new securities. As a noun, an issue of securities. See also *issue*.

issuance costs Also known as *flotation costs*. The incidental costs associated with an issuance of securities. Includes all costs other than the contractual coupon or dividend payment. See *flotation costs*.

issue Also called an *issuance*. The full set of securities issued as part of the same securities offering.

issued shares The number of shares of common stock that a corporation has distributed. This can be equal to, but not more than, the authorized shares. It includes shares that have been distributed but later repurchased by the corporation. Repurchased shares are called *treasury stock*.

issuer An entity that has issued securities.

Ito process An Ito process is a type of generalized Wiener process where the drift rate and volatility of the process may be a function of the stochastic variable and time. Geometric Brownian motion is a particular version of an Ito process that is often used to describe the evolution of security prices and, at times, interest rates. Here security price changes are random, prices are lognormally distributed, returns are normally distributed, and uncertainty regarding future price changes increase at a decreasing rate. Geometric Brownian motion underlies the seminal Black-Scholes-Merton option pricing model. Thus an Ito process is a model used to describe how prices change through time and has appealing economic properties.

Ito's lemma Ito's lemma is a famous mathematical result derived by the Japanese mathematician K. Ito in 1951. Loosely speaking, it can be regarded as the chain rule of stochastic calculus. In finance, Ito lemma's is often used to derive the stochastic process followed by the price of a derivative security. For example, if the underlying asset follows geometric Brownian motion, then Ito's lemma demonstrates that a derivative security whose price is a function of the underlying asset's price and time also follows geometric Brownian motion. Indeed, the two securities would exhibit the same source of risk, implying that an appropriate mix of the two securities could eliminate risk. It is this seminal result that led to the development of the Black-Scholes-Merton model as well as many modern hedging theories and applications.

joint venture An entity established, and owned, by two or more companies in order to facilitate the achievement of some shared objective. Joint ventures usually have limited goals and limited lives and fall short of a merger of the enterprises that established them. For example, several automobile companies might establish a joint venture for the purpose of developing a more fuel-efficient automobile engine. Once this goal is accomplished, the companies share the resultant technology but the venture itself terminates.

junk bonds Also known by the preferred term *high yield bonds*. This category of bonds includes two broad groups: those with speculative grade ratings and those bonds with no ratings at all. See *high yield bonds* for more detail.

kappa Kappa is an alternative name for the option Greek known as *vega*. See *vega*.

key rate durations Measures of the sensitivity of a bond's price to specific points (key rates) along the Treasury spot curve such as the 2-year, the 5-year, the 10-year, and the 30-year. The sensitivity at each point is measured assuming that the other key rates have not changed and the rates between the key rate of interest and the next key rate have changed linearly.

knock-in options A type of barrier option that is activated if the spot price crosses a prespecified level, or barrier, before a specific date. Includes both *down-and-in* and *up-and-in options*. See also *barrier options*.

knock-out options A type of barrier option that is extinguished if the spot price crosses a prespecified level, or barrier, before a specific date. Includes both *down-and-out* and *up-and-out* options. See also *barrier options*.

kurtosis The fourth moment of a statistical distribution that focuses on the tails. It is a measure of the fatness of the tails of the distribution. See also *leptokurtosis*.

ladder A bond investment strategy in which bonds are purchased and held with sequential maturity dates. For example, an investor with $100,000 to invest might place 10% in bonds maturing in 1 year, 10% in bonds maturing in 2 years, and so on out to 10 years. As each bond matures, the investor rolls the redemption proceeds into a new bond at the end of the ladder (i.e., 10 years in this case). The investor can live off the coupons collected on all the bonds without ever touching the principal. The ladder strategy is self maintaining and limits exposure to interest rate risk. Ladders can be constructed using zero coupon bonds instead of coupon-bearing bonds.

ladder options A type of exotic option that locks in a specific payoff if the underlying's price crosses a specified level, called a "rung." When the option is initiated, it can be structured to have any number of rungs so that there can be multiple rungs in the same ladder option. As each rung is sequentially crossed, the option locks in higher payoffs.

lambda Lambda is an alternative name for the option Greek known as *vega*. See *vega*.

large caps Corporations having a large equity capitalization. The amount of equity capital necessary for a corporation to qualify as a large cap is somewhat arbitrary. See also *capitalization* for a discussion of how capitalization is measured.

law of one price An equilibrium relationship that is enforced by arbitrage. The law states that the prices of the same commodity offered in two different markets should never differ by more than the cost of transporting the commodity between the two markets (after adjusting for the exchange rate between the two markets if the prices are denominated in different currencies). Violations of the law of one price can indicate barriers to trade.

LBO See *leveraged buyout*.

lead underwriter The investment bank selected to manage an underwriting and oversee the activities of the underwriting syndicate. The lead underwriter is also known as the *manager* or *book runner*. If two or more investment banks share the role of lead underwriter, as is sometimes the case, the lead underwriters are called *comanagers*.

LEAN See *LIBOR-enhanced accrual note*.

LEAPS Derived from the term *long-term equity anticipation securities*. These are options on individual stocks and stock indexes having a much longer term to expiry at the time of their creation than do standard equity options. This term is often three years.

legal risk (1) The risk that a contract (such as a financial derivative contract) will not be enforceable. (2) Risks associated with customer suitability for certain types of investments, compliance with securities regulations, disclosure materials, copyrights, and so forth.

legs (futures) In a spread trade involving futures, a trader is long one delivery month and short a different delivery month. Each contract is called a leg of the spread. The spread can be put on as a unit or by "legging into it" one leg at a time.

legs (swaps) Also called *sides*. The fixed and floating sides of a swap. The fixed rate side is called the fixed rate leg and the floating rate side is called the floating rate leg.

lender One who has lent money to another. Also known as a *creditor* and as an *obligee*. The latter term, however, has a broader meaning implying one to whom another has an obligation.

lender option A put option written on a forward rate agreement (FRA).

leptokurtosis A situation in which the tails of a statistical distribution are fatter than they should be. That is, there is greater probability of an occurrence in the tails than would be expected under the assumed distribution.

letter of credit Known by the acronym *LOC*. A bank lending facility that guarantees to lend funds to the holder of the LOC for some period of time. LOCs are widely used to guarantee payment on purchases of goods, as collateral on commercial paper when issued by less than the best credit corporations, and to meet margin requirements on futures contracts.

level-payment fixed-rate mortgage A conventional fixed rate mortgage in which the principal amortizes over the life of the mortgage in such a fashion that each payment (usually made monthly) is identical. The earliest payments are mostly interest and the later payments are mostly principal, but the total payment is the same each period. Also known as *level payment mortgages* and *conventional mortgages*.

Level-payment mortgage See *level-payment fixed-rate mortgage*.

level-payment swap A swap that is amortizing but has been structured so that the fixed rate payments are the same size over the life of the swap. This is accomplished by making the interest payments smaller than they would otherwise be at the swap's outset but larger than they would otherwise be toward the end of the swap's life. Essentially, the fixed rate payments are first calculated as though the notional principal amortizes over the life of the swap. This gives rise to fixed payments that get progressively smaller (because they are interest only). The present value of this series of payments is then calculated. Next, a series of level payments is calculated that has the same present value as the declining payments. The level payments are then used in lieu of the declining payments.

leverage (1) The ratio of the amount of value represented by an investment to the amount of money actually invested. With a high level of leverage, one experiences large gains or losses as though a much larger amount were invested. Leverage can increase the risk of large losses just as it increases the opportunity for large gains. (2) In investment finance, the use of any instrument or mechanism to magnify potential returns with concomitant magnification of financial risk. The use of futures, options, and securities purchased on margin all provide leverage. (3) In corporate finance, the use of debt in the capital structure or fixed cost in the operations of the corporation constitutes leverage.

leveraged buyout Known by the acronym *LBO*. LBOs involve the acquisition of a corporation by investors using largely, if not entirely, borrowed money. The borrowed money is the source of the leverage. While the methodology varies from one LBO to another, in a typical scenario, a group of investors forms a holding company for purposes of acquiring a target firm. They arrange bridge financing that is used to make a tender offer for the target's stock. Once a controlling interest in the target has been acquired, the minority shareholders are paid off based on fairness opinions obtained from independent appraisers. The holding corporation then issues high-yield bonds to pay off the bridge loan. At this point, the LBO is complete. It is usually followed by taking the corporation private, slashing costs, disposing of some assets, and paying down the high yield debt. At some point later, the corporation may go public again in a secondary initial public offering, which affords the buyout investors the opportunity to cash out.

leveraged floater A floating rate note in which the payoff has been levered up by multiplying the reference rate by some factor and then deducting a fixed rate. For example, suppose that a plain vanilla floating rate note would pay LIBOR and that, over the life of the note, the average value of LIBOR is expected to be 5.50%. A leveraged floater, using a leverage multiplier of 2, would pay off (2 × LIBOR) − 5.50%. Leveraged floaters often have an embedded option so that the payoff cannot be negative. Also known as a *bear floater*. See *bear floater*.

leveraged swaps A type of swap in which the floating leg pays a multiple of the reference rate set on the fixing date. A variety of constructs can achieve the same result. The fixed rate leg must be set at the same multiple to preserve the equivalence of the present values of the two legs of the swap. Such a contract can allow the counterparties to achieve the outcome associated with a large notional principal while using a smaller notional principal. Sometimes called a *levered swap*. Note, the leverage multiplier can be more than one or less than one.

Levered swap See *leveraged swap*.

LIBID The *London Interbank Bid Rate*. This is the rate at which a bank will borrow Eurodollar deposits. It is not widely used as a reference rate.

LIBOR An acronym for *London Interbank Offered Rate*. The interest rate a large international bank with an excellent credit rating is quoting to lend Eurocurrency deposits. For example, dollar LIBOR would be the offered rate on Eurodollar deposits. LIBOR is quoted for different currencies and for different deposit terms. This rate is widely used as the reference rate for setting the floating rate on floating rate instruments including floating rate notes and interest rate swaps. It is also the rate at which Eurodollar futures settle on their final settlement date. Note, for purposes of settling derivatives contracts, the LIBOR is usually an average of the rates quoted by a number of banks.

LIBOR curve The LIBOR zero-coupon interest rate curve that relates the LIBOR interest rate to the term of the LIBOR-based lending. This curve can be extracted from a par swap yield curve via the bootstrapping methodology. The result is an implied LIBOR curve.

LIBOR flat LIBOR quoted without any premium or discount.

LIBOR in-arrears swap See *in-arrears swap*.

LIBOR-enhanced accrual note Known by the acronym *LEAN*. This is a type of range floater in which the reference rate is LIBOR. See *range floater* for more detail.

LIMEAN This is an average of LIBOR and LIBID. See *LIBOR* and *LIBID*.

limit move In certain markets, particularly futures markets, the futures price might be subject to a daily price-change limit. That is, the price is not permitted to change—either up or down—by more than the preset limit. Once the price moves by the limit amount, the market shuts down until traders are willing to trade within the allowable daily range or until the market opens again the next day. In some countries, individual stocks are subject to daily limit moves.

limit options See *barrier options*.

limit order An order to buy or sell an asset or security in which the buyer or seller specifies a price. The order may be filled at the limit price or at a better price, but not at a worse price. That is, on a buy limit order, the order may not be filled at a higher price. On a sell limit order, the order may not be filled at a lower price. This is in contrast to a *market order*.

LIMOS A Merrill Lynch trademarked version of *partial strips*. See *partial strips*.

linear As used in mathematics, any functional relationship between two variables in which the relationship graphs as a straight line. In a multivariate context, this may take the form of a plane or a hyperplane.

linear contracts Any derivative financial instrument whose payoff profile or profit diagram graphs as a straight line, with respect to the underlying price that drives profit and loss on the contract. Linear contracts include futures, forwards, and swaps, but exclude options—which are nonlinear.

liquidity A reference to the ease, and the price concession required, to buy and sell assets. The easier to buy and sell and the smaller the bid-offer spread (which represents the price concession) the more liquid the market for the asset is.

liquidity preference theory See *liquidity premium theory*.

liquidity premium The amount by which a forward short rate exceeds the expected future spot short rate. It is difficult, if not impossible, to measure a liquidity premium with precision. Some theories of interest rate term structure maintain that no such premium exists.

liquidity premium theory A theory of interest rate term structure that holds that the shape of the yield curve is explained by a risk premium demanded by investors. This theory implies that forward short rates are higher than expected future spot short rates. The longer the maturity of the instrument, the larger the risk premium demanded. This is one of several theories to explain the normal upward slope to the yield curve. In contrast, the expectations theory implies that forward rates equal expected future spot short rates. The liquidity premium theory is also known as the *liquidity preference theory*.

liquidity risk A type of market risk arising from a low level of trading volume. In such a situation, the difference between the bid price and the offer price can be very large. This can make it difficult and costly to execute a hedge and/or to offset a position. It is possible for a liquid market to suddenly become quite illiquid with negative consequences for those who need to transact quickly.

listed option Any option traded on an organized exchange and having standardized terms. Often referred to as *standard options*. This is in contrast to options that trade over-the-counter and whose terms are fully negotiable.

load A sales charge associated with the purchase or sale of equity interests in a mutual fund. If charged upon the purchase, the load is called a *front-end load*. If charged upon the sale, the load is called a *back-end load*. This is contrast to a *no load* structure in which there are no sales charges on either the purchase or the sale of equity interests.

loan-to-value Often abbreviated *LTV*. The ratio of the value of a loan to the market value of the collateral used to secure the loan. This is an important measure in any secured financing, including mortgages.

LOC See *letter of credit*.

local currency return The return on an investment measured in terms of the currency in which the investment is denominated. For example, a bond denominated in yen would produce an annual total return in yen. This return is the local currency return. For a foreign holder of the yen-denominated bond, return to the investor is a function of both the local currency return and the change in the exchange rate between the yen and the investor's domestic currency.

Locals See *floor traders*.

locational basis The difference between two prices attributable to the cost of moving the commodity the distance between the two markets. For example, cash wheat prices in North Dakota might be different from wheat futures prices in Chicago in part because the demand/supply conditions in North Dakota differ from the demand/supply conditions in Chicago. Normally, arbitrage will pull prices together but only to the extent that the price difference exceeds the transportation cost. See also *basis*.

lognormal distribution A type of asymmetric statistical distribution believed to describe, at least approximately, the future values of many financial variables, such as asset prices. If a random variable, denoted X, has a lognormal distribution, then a new random variable, denoted Y, such that Y is formed by taking the natural logarithm of X, has a normal distribution. Under a very common set of assumptions, asset prices would be expected to possess lognormal distributions. However, empirical evidence indicates that asset distributions often deviate somewhat from a true lognormal distribution. Nevertheless, lognormal distributions are widely assumed for purposes of valuing derivatives, particularly options.

London interbank bid rate See *LIBID*.

London interbank mean rate See *LIMEAN*.

London interbank offered rate See *LIBOR*.

long A party is said to be *long* an instrument when he or she owns the instrument. Alternatively, an individual has a long position (sometimes an implied long position) if he or she would benefit from a rise in the price of the instrument. Generally, buying the instrument establishes a long position unless the purchase offsets an existing short position. See *short* for contrast.

long an option Describes the position of the holder (purchaser) of an option.

long a swap The floating-rate receiver (who is also the fixed-rate payer) on an interest rate swap. This is in contrast to being short a swap. See also *short a swap*.

long bond A reference to the most recently issued 30-year Treasury bond. The yield on the long bond serves as an important benchmark for long-term interest rates and is watched very closing by the markets. Only the on-the-run 30-year Treasury is referred to as the long bond.

long hedge A hedge involving a long position in some derivative instrument.

long vega A position, usually involving options, such that any increase in the implied volatility of the underlying asset will generate a profit. Vega refers to one of the option Greeks (see *vega*). See *long volatility*.

long volatility Also called *long vol*. An option position that is structured to produce a profit should the markets perceive an increase in the future volatility of the underlying asset's price. Also called *long vega*.

long-dated forwards Foreign exchange forward contracts with a maturity greater than one year.

long-dated swaps Swaps with long tenors (i.e., maturities). Sometimes understood to be swaps with tenors too long to be priced off Eurodollar futures.

long-term equity anticipation securities Known by the derived term *LEAPS*. See *LEAPS*.

lookback options Any of a group of options in which the calculation of the payoff at expiry involves looking back over the path that the underlying asset's price took in reaching its terminal value. On some lookback options, the option's strike is set based on the highest or lowest value that the underlying's price achieved over the option's life. On others, the strike is fixed but the payoff is calculated based on the difference between the highest (or lowest) value the price of the underlying achieved and the fixed strike price of the option.

lot A unit of measure representing the standard trading size for a particular market. For example, in the stock market a *round lot* is 100 shares. An *odd lot* is anything less than 100 shares.

low coupon swap A swap written with a swap coupon (fixed rate) that is below market. When a low coupon swap is written, the party paying the below-market coupon will pay a front-end fee equal to the present value of the difference between the at-market coupon and the below-market coupon. This contrasts with a *high coupon swap*. See also *off-market swap*.

lowest call price With respect to *PERCS*: The call price at maturity or the cap price. If the PERCS trades above the call price at maturity, the PERCS will be called for redemption and the PERCS holder will receive the call price in cash or common. With respect to an *ELKS*: The holders receive in cash the lesser of the call price or the value of one share of common stock.

LTV See *loan-to-value*.

Macaulay duration A weighted average of the time to payment of a security's cash flows. The weights are calculated as the ratios of the present value of each cash flow to the sum of the present values of all the cash flows. Macaulay's duration was the original duration measure and was published in 1938. It was, and continues to be, an important interest rate risk measure but is generally inferior to modified duration. Modified duration can be obtained from Macaulay's duration. Today, when people refer to duration they may be referring to Macaulay's duration, modified duration, or effective duration. See also *modified duration* and *effective duration* for comparison.

macro hedging A hedge taken to offset the residual risk between a firm's assets and liabilities. Unlike a micro hedge, macro hedges are not identified with a specific asset or liability. For example, a firm may have some interest rate sensitive assets and some interest rate sensitive liabilities. To some degree these sensitivities are offsetting. These risks are netted to arrive at the residual risk. Macro hedging targets the aggregate residual risk. Often called *global hedging*.

macroeconomic options Also known as *macro options*. Options in which the reference index is a macroeconomic variable or index. These options can be written as either single period or multiperiod options. They can be linked to a level of economic activity, such as GDP, or to a price index such as the CPI. See also *macroeconomic swaps*. Macroeconomic options can be used to hedge exposures to macroeconomic forms of risk such as business cycle risk and purchasing power risk.

macroeconomic swaps Also known as *macro swaps*. Swaps on which at least one leg is pegged either to a macroeconomic variable or index such as GDP growth or to a broad price index such as the CPI. That is, one leg might pay a rate based on the macroeconomic index and the other leg might pay a fixed sum. Such swaps can be used to hedge business cycle risk and purchasing power risk. See *swap* for more detail on swap structures in general.

MACRS See *modified accelerated cost recovery system*.

maintenance margin The minimum margin level that must be maintained by the holders of certain types of financial instruments, such as futures. The maintenance margin is set below the *initial margin* necessary to establish a position. If the trader's margin falls below the maintenance level, he or she must bring the margin up to the initial margin level or close out the position.

making a market See *market making*.

management fee (1) Part of the gross spread on an underwriting. The management fee is split among the comanagers on a negotiated basis, often equally, but in some cases with a higher portion of the split going to one firm or another, depending on placement capability or as a sweetener to join the underwriting. (2) Fees paid to investment advisors for the management of investment portfolios.

manager (1) One who is responsible for overseeing and coordinating activities. (2) The lead underwriter in an underwriting of securities.

mapping The decomposition of a securities portfolio or a derivatives portfolio into time buckets. Mapping exists in a number of forms, including cash flow mapping, duration mapping, and so forth. For example, in cash flow mapping, all cash flows occurring during the same bucket interval are combined as though they occur at exactly the same time. Cash inflows and cash outflows are partially offsetting.

margin (1) In securities trading (stocks and bonds), refers to the portion of the purchase price paid in cash by the purchasing principal (with the remainder of the purchase price borrowed). (2) In futures trading, refers to a required performance bond tendered by each party to a futures contract. The margin on futures is a small percentage of the contract's notional value. In this context, margin serves as collateral and is sometimes called *earnest money*. Margin can be tendered in the form of cash or securities. (3) The difference between two values, sometimes expressed as a ratio (e.g., profit margins, net interest margins, etc.).

margin call A customer notification by a broker/dealer or commission merchant that additional margin must be tendered by the customer in order to continue to carry positions in the account. Margin calls most often occur as a consequence of the daily mark-to-market process. That is, the daily mark-to-market has resulted in a loss of margin so that the remaining margin is insufficient to carry the positions currently held. A margin call may also be triggered by a periodic revaluation of securities used as margin collateral.

margin requirements The minimum amount of cash or other assets a brokerage firm requires in a margin account to permit particular investments.

market consensus (1) The market price of an asset represents the market's consensus opinion of the relevance of all information available to market participants. If one subscribes to the efficient markets hypothesis, then the market consensus represents a better estimate of the asset's value than does the opinion of any single market participant. (2) An average of opinions obtained via a survey of specific market operatives concerning an asset price, whether an asset should be bought or sold, or the future value of an economic indicator.

market disruption events A clause in a financial contract that limits or cancels exercise rights if liquidity in certain cash or futures markets fails to exist.

market maker Also known as a *dealer*. A party that makes a market in an instrument by offering to both buy and sell the instrument. The market maker profits from the difference between its bid and offer prices.

market making Acting as a dealer in a security or other instrument. See *market maker*. Also called *making a market*.

market order An order to buy or sell at the best available price. A market order to buy would be executed at the current offer price. A market order to sell would be executed at the current bid price. Except under unusual market conditions, market orders can always be filled immediately. This is in contrast to a *limit order.*

market risk The risk that an asset (or an instrument such as a derivatives contract) will decrease in value with changes in market conditions, such as changes in interest and currency rates or fluctuations in equity and commodity prices. Also known as *price risk.*

market segmentation theory See *segmented markets theory.*

market value of an option See *option premium.*

marketability Sometimes used to mean the same thing as liquidity. Can be used to mean an inability to buy or sell an asset because of contractual encumbrances or legal restrictions. Thus, a security can be liquid (in that others are willing to buy or sell it) but nonmarketable. Examples include contractual provisions among the equity holders in private businesses, restricted stock held by insiders of a corporation, or stock subject to lock-up agreements.

marking-to-market See *mark-to-market.*

marking-to-model The act of calculating the value of a position based on the value implied by a model because market prices are not observable. This has inherent risks, the most important of which is model risk. See *model risk.* Marking-to-model contrasts with marking-to-market.

Markov process A stochastic process in which the change in the value of a random variable in the next period does not in any way depend on either the current level of prices or the past history of prices. Many stochastic processes are Markovian in nature. When a stochastic process does not satisfy the Markov process criteria, it is sometimes referred to as non-Markovian.

Markowitz efficient frontier See *efficient frontier*.

mark-to-market (1) In futures, the practice of periodically adjusting a margin account by adding or subtracting funds based on changes in the market value of the contracts held. (2) In other markets, such as swaps, dealers employ the practice to measure profits and losses and risk exposures on their portfolios. Also known as *marking-to market*.

martingale A stochastic process that exhibits no directional bias (i.e., no drift). The term is often used interchangeably with the term *random walk*.

master agreement An agreement that governs all transactions between the same two counterparties.

master swap agreement A document written in such a fashion that its terms govern all swap activity between the same counterparties. Each new swap is viewed as a supplement to the master agreement.

matador bonds Bonds sold in Spain to Spanish investors by non-Spanish issuers. Analogous to Yankee bonds but applicable to Spain.

matched needs When two end users have identical, but mirror image, needs and so can satisfy each other's requirements by entering into a mutually beneficial relationship.

matched swaps A pair of swaps that have identical but mirror image provisions.

matrix pricing A process for pricing a bond (or other financial instrument) by developing a list of its characteristics (i.e., type of issuer, rating, coupon, call/put features, etc.) and comparing those characteristics to other bonds having similar characteristics. From the pricing of the other bonds, a value for the subject bond can be inferred. This pricing method is most often used when the subject bond is not traded and a mark-to-market value is required for determining profit and loss, managing risk, or some other purpose.

maturity The length of time from the present until a financial instrument is scheduled to be redeemed or to terminate. In the case of some derivatives, the term *tenor* is used in lieu of the term maturity.

maturity date The specific date when a financial instrument is scheduled to mature. In some contracts this is called a *termination date, delivery date*, or *final settlement date*.

maturity sectors A grouping of bonds into sectors based on their maturity. There are essentially four sectors: money market (generally out to 1 year), short term (1–5 years), intermediate term (5–12 years), and long term (more than 12 years). These designations are somewhat arbitrary.

maturity spread The difference between the yield on a bond having one maturity and an otherwise equivalent bond having a different maturity. Both bonds must come from a homogeneous grouping of bonds (e.g., both must be Treasurys or both must be AAA-rated corporates, etc.). For example, if a 30-year Treasury bond were yielding

6.47% and a 10-year Treasury note were yielding 5.90%, then the 30–10 maturity spread would be 57 basis points. This sort of spread is distinct from a credit spread, which is the difference between the yields on two bonds drawn from different classes of bonds (e.g., one might be a corporate and the other a Treasury).

max function A mathematical function that selects the highest value from a set of values. It contrasts with the min function, which selects the smallest value from a set of values. Max and min functions have important roles in calculating option payoffs.

maximum annualized yield to maturity The annualized rate of return earned on a PERCS or an ELKS if the underlying common stock trades above the call price at maturity. The rate of return includes the income earned on the security as well as any capital gain or loss.

max-min options Also known as *maximum options* and *minimum options*. There are two related types for each class of options (i.e., there are *max calls* and *min calls* and there are *max puts* and *min puts*.) In these options, there are several underlying assets, each of which has its own strike price. The option pays off based on the better-performing asset's strike price. The payoff for a max call is given by $max[max[S_1 - X_1, S_2 - X_2, ..., S_N - X_N], 0]$, the payoff for a min call would be $max[min[S_1 - X_1, S_2 - X_2, ..., S_N - X_N], 0]$, the payoff for a max put would be $max[max[X_1 - S_1, X_2 - S_2, ..., X_N - S_N], 0]$, and the payoff for a min put would be given by $max[min[X_1 - S_1, X_2 - S_2, ..., X_N - S_N], 0]$.

MBS Acronym for mortgage-backed security. See *mortgage-backed security*.

mean A statistical measure of central tendency. To obtain the value, multiply the values a random variable might take on by their respective probabilities and then sum all the products. The mean is the value to which a simple average tends upon repeated sampling from the same distribution.

mean reversion The tendency of certain financial variables, such as interest rates, to revert back to their long-run average values. When a variable is characterized by mean reversion, there is a departure from a pure random walk. That is, with each successive movement away from the long-run average, the likelihood increases that the next movement will be toward the average.

mean reverting Variables that exhibit mean reversion. See *mean reversion*.

medium term note Often denoted by the acronym *MTN*. A corporate debt instrument having several maturity ranges varying from nine months to 30 years. Their distinguishing characteristic is that they are continuously offered to investors by an agent of the issuer. Thus, they are a subset of the continuously offered market. Medium term notes are registered with the SEC under Rule 415 (shelf registration). Because they can have very long maturities, the term "medium term note" is a misnomer.

micro hedge A hedge taken to offset the risk associated with a specifically identified cash position. Contrasts with a *macro hedge*.

mid caps Corporations having an equity capitalization too small to qualify as a large cap but too large to qualify as a small cap. The amount of equity capital necessary for a corporation to qualify as a mid cap is somewhat arbitrary. See also *capitalization*.

mid-Atlantic options See *quasi-American options*.

mid-market An average of the bid and offer prices.

mid-rate An average of a pay rate (bid) and a receive rate (offer). For example, an interest rate swap dealer will quote one swap coupon (i.e., fixed rate) if the dealer will be the receiver of the fixed rate payments and a different swap coupon if the dealer will be the payer of the fixed rate payments. The average of these two rates is the dealer's mid-rate.

minimum variance set A set made up of those portfolios that have the lowest variance for a given level of expected return. The efficient frontier is a subset of the minimum variance set and consists of portfolios such that for any given variance the curve reflects the portfolio that has the maximum expected return. The curves of these two sets are different. The minimum variance set is parabolic while the efficient frontier is concave. See *efficient frontier* for contrast.

Ministry of Finance The government agency that regulates the financial markets and financial market participants in Japan. The Ministry of Finance, often abbreviated *MOF*, encompasses many of the functions associated with the Treasury Department, the Federal Reserve, the SEC, and the CFTC in the United States.

min-max bond See *collar bond*.

min-max structure See *collar*.

min-max swap Also called a *collar swap*. A fixed-for-floating interest-rate swap in which the floating-rate side is bounded between an upper and a lower limit. Sometimes called a *banded swap*.

mismatch risk The risk to a dealer from failing to precisely match the provisions of the various transactions in book. For example, a swap dealer might enter a pair of nearly matched swaps. On one the dealer is the fixed rate payer and on the other the dealer is the fixed rate receiver. One or more of the terms might be mismatched such as the reference rate on the floating rate leg, the payment frequency, the payment dates, the reset dates, and so forth. This sort of mismatching gives rise to a type of market risk called mismatch risk. Some forms of mismatch risk are unsystematic in nature and tend to diversify away. Others have to be hedged.

model A stylized representation of reality designed to reduce reality to its fundamental components in order to aid understanding. In the context of valuation models, analytical models are equations that have been derived, based on a set of initial assumptions, to value an instrument; numeric models take the form of processes (such as algorithms) that lead to a valuation.

model risk The risk that an asset has been valued using the wrong model or the right model with the wrong parameters. Model risk is a major concern for financial institutions that cannot mark their positions to market on a daily basis because the prices necessary to do so are not observable. In these situations, positions will often be marked to the value implied by the model. This is called *marking-to-model*. Should the model be inappropriate for the assets being valued, the valuations assigned could be seriously in error.

modified accelerated cost recovery system Known by the acronym *MACRS*. The principal method of accelerated depreciation of capital assets employed in the United States. This method replaced its predecessor, the accelerated cost recovery system. Under MACRS, each asset is assigned a class life (not the same as useful life). For each class life, a specific percentage of the original cost can be depreciated each year. Generally, the early years have a higher depreciable percentage than do the later years. This is in contrast to the alternative *straight-line method of depreciation,* in which the percentage of original cost allowable as depreciation is the same each year.

modified duration A measure of a fixed income security's interest rate sensitivity. This measure was published by John Hicks in 1939 and is sometimes called Hick's duration. Modified duration is a better measure of interest rate sensitivity than is Macaulay's duration (which is usually just called duration). It may be defined as the ratio of the percentage change in a bond's price to the change in the yield on the bond that caused the bond's price to change. Unlike Macaulay's duration, modified duration is not measured in years, though people often do add the word "years" in error.

$$\text{modified duration} = \frac{\text{Macaulay duration}}{(1 + \text{periodic rate})}$$

where the periodic rate is the annual discount rate (or yield) divided by the number of assumed compoundings.

moments The parameters of a statistical distribution. The first moment is the mean and the second moment is the variance. Other moments include skewness (third moment) and kurtosis (fourth moment).

monetizing an option Corporations often own options without realizing it. Such options are often implicit components of contracts or some other aspect of their commercial activity. These options have value but are often overlooked or ignored with the result that they are allowed to expire worthless. If these options are recognized, mirror image options can be sold to a derivatives dealer allowing the corporation to convert its options to cash. This process is called monetizing embedded options.

monetizing collar A zero-cost collar transaction combined with a margin loan. The proceeds to the investor are typically greater than on a conventional margin loan. A monetizing collar allows an investor to take most of the value out of a position without closing out the position. This may be done for tax reasons or to unlock the cash tied up in a position that cannot be sold due to lock-up agreements or other restrictions.

monetizing equity swap An investor makes payments to a counterparty that represent the cash flows on an equity position. The equity position usually represents restricted stock or a concentrated equity position. In exchange, the counterparty pays the investor the cash flows associated with another asset or a diversified index. The combination of the original equity position and the swap has the economic effect of being equivalent to a sale of the equity position and the reinvestment in another asset, while at the same time allowing the investor to retain stock ownership and voting rights.

money market instruments Debt instruments having a maturity of less than one year. These instruments include such things as Treasury bills, certificates of deposit, commercial paper, repurchase agreements, and most Eurodollar deposits.

money market mutual funds Mutual funds that invest exclusively in money market instruments having very little interest rate risk. Such funds usually attempt to maintain a net asset value (NAV) of $1 per share.

money market yield Also known as money market basis and yield basis. A method of calculating the yield on certain money market instruments. When applied to U.S. dollar interest rates, the method uses an actual/360 day count convention. For example, if a 182-day CD in the amount of $1 million were quoted at 5.85%, the CD would pay interest at maturity calculated as follows:

Interest = $182/360 \times 5.85\% \times \$1$ million

This interest would be payable upon maturity.

Monte Carlo simulation See *simulation (Monte Carlo)*.

Moody's Investor Services Often called Moody's. One of two dominant firms in the bond rating business. This firm is a subsidiary of Dun & Bradstreet.

mortgage A debt instrument secured by real property. Real property includes land and buildings.

mortgage bonds Bonds secured or collateralized by real property.

mortgage coupon rate See *mortgage rate.*

mortgage derivative A financial instrument that derives its value from mortgage pools, such as mortgage-backed passthrough securities or collateralized mortgage obligations.

mortgage originators Financial institutions that work with individuals in need of financing for home purchases. The mortgage originator performs the credit investigation, writes a mortgage loan agreement, and provides the money to the mortgagors. The signed mortgage document is evidence of the indebtedness and might be retained by the mortgage originator as an investment or sold by the mortgage originator to another institution possibly for pooling and securitization.

mortgage pool A group of mortgages having similar terms that have been pooled for the purpose of creating pass-through securities or other types of mortgage-backed securities such as collateralized mortgage obligations.

mortgage rate The contractual rate of interest on a mortgage obligation. Also known as the *mortgage coupon rate.*

mortgage revenue bonds Revenue bonds on which the revenue to meet the bond's interest and principal payments comes from mortgage payments or rental payments from governmental housing projects.

mortgage servicers Institutions that service mortgages. Servicing a mortgage means collecting and processing the mortgage payments, sending dunning letters when mortgage payments are not made on time, bringing foreclosure proceedings if necessary, and handling other incidental activities associated with routine mortgage payment processing including escrowing real estate taxes. For providing these services, the mortgage servicer earns servicing fees. Mortgage servicing was once inextricably linked to ownership of the mortgage. However, with the development of mortgage pooling and securitization, mortgage servicing rights have become separable from mortgage ownership.

mortgage servicing rights The right to service a mortgage. See *mortgage servicers.*

mortgage swaps Any of a variety of interest rate swaps on which the cash flows are structured to mimic the cash flows on a mortgage portfolio. The critical feature of such swaps is the method of notional principal amortization.

mortgage-backed security Know by the acronym *MBS*. Any security backed by the cash flow stream generated by a pool of mortgages. The simplest types are passthrough certificates on mortgage pools, which represent pro rata claims on the cash flows of the pool. More complex forms include collateralized mortgage obligations, which involve parsing the cash flows in such a way as to form tranches, each having characteristics different from the other tranches.

mortgagee The lender in a mortgage contract.

mortgagor The borrower in a mortgage contract.

MSRB See *Municipal Securities Rulemaking Board*.

MTN Acronym for *medium term note*.

multi-index option An option that is written on more than one underlying and which pays off based on the better performing of the various underlyings. This is similar to an *outperformance option*.

multilateral netting Any cash flow netting arrangement that allows for the netting of cash flows among more than two counterparties. For example, if A owes B $3 and B owes C $2 and C owes A $4, this nets to counterparty C paying $1 to A and $1 to B. Netting reduces the need for liquidity and the need to set aside cash to meet cash outflows. As such, it allows the counterparties to keep cash working and helps to offset settlement risks.

multi-period options Any cash-settled option that has a series of successive settlement dates. On each settlement date, the option behaves as though it were a single-period option. The two main types of multi-period options are caps and floors. Caps are equivalent to a series of sequentially expiring call options, and floors are equivalent to a series of sequentially expiring put options. See *cap* and *floor*.

multiple coupon See *graduated rate coupon*.

municipal floating-rate bonds Municipal floating-rate bonds are municipal securities that pay a floating rate of interest that periodically resets based upon some reference rate. Closely related are municipal inverse floating-rate bonds, which pay a coupon tied to the same reference rate but structured so that the coupon on the bond moves in the opposite direction of the reference rate. A fixed rate bond can be decomposed into a combination of a floater and an inverse-floater. Many investment banks have developed proprietary floating rate and inverse floating rate municipal bond products. These products are known by their acronyms. Examples include Goldman Sach's floaters called PARS (periodic auction reset securities) and inverse floaters called INFLOS; Merrill Lynch's floaters called FLOATS and inverse floaters called RITES (residual interest tax-exempt securities); and Lehman Brothers' floaters called RIBS (residual interest bonds) and inverse floaters called SAVRS (select auction variable-rate securities).

municipal inverse-floating rate bonds See *municipal floating-rate bonds*.

Municipal Securities Rulemaking Board Known by the acronym *MSRB*. A regulatory body established under the Securities Exchange Act of 1934, as later amended, to regulate dealers, brokers, and others involved in the marketing of municipal securities. It is subject to oversight by the SEC.

municipal strip obligation Zero coupon bonds created by stripping off the coupon payments on municipal bonds in the same way that Treasury-based zero coupon bonds are created by stripping off the coupons on Treasury bonds. Municipal strip obligations can have the added benefit of generating tax-exempt interest income.

mutual fund A regulated investment company organized for the purpose of investing a pool of capital contributed by individual investors. The investors, in turn, own equity interests in the investment company. The net asset value of the investment company is allocated to each investor in proportion to his or her equity interest in the company. Equity interests in the mutual fund may be evidenced by common stock or by partnership interests, depending upon the form of legal organization. When an investment company is organized as an open end investment company, the investment company is called a mutual fund. An open end investment company is one that will sell new shares to investors and buy shares back from investors at any time at the then prevailing net asset value. See also *closed end investment company, load,* and *no load.*

naked When a financial position is not hedged. This implies that the holder of the position is at risk for a loss of value from an unfavorable market movement. The term is most often used in conjunction with derivatives positions. See *naked option writing.*

naked option writing Writing an option without an offsetting position in the underlying with the result that an adverse change in the price of the underlying results in a loss of value on the option without an offsetting gain on the underlying. If the option is exercised, the option writer will need to either acquire or dispose of the underlying in the cash market. This is in contrast to covered option writing in which the option writer holds a position in the underlying that can be used to satisfy the obligation should the option be exercised.

naked position See *naked.*

natural hedge The tendency for the market risks arising out of routine commercial transactions to be partially offsetting. For example, a corporate bond dealer who makes markets in many corporate bonds may find himself long some bonds and simultaneously short other bonds. The different bonds each expose the bond dealer to interest rate risk, but the interest rate risk associated with the long positions and the interest rate risk associated with the short positions are partially offsetting and are, therefore, natural hedges for one another.

NAV See *net asset value.*

near month See *front month.*

nearby In futures or options, the contract next to deliver or expire. Also called the *near month* and sometimes called the *front month.*

negative amortization Any amortization schedule in which the principal or, in the case of swaps and related instruments, the notional principal increases from the initial level for at least some period of time. Some instruments experience a period of negative amortization followed by amortization.

negative convexity A situation in which the convexity of a bond is negative, as opposed to the normal positive convexity. Such situations are caused by embedded options within the bond. Callable bonds and prepayable mortgages typically have regions of negative convexity.

negotiated sale The sale of a security in which the terms of the sale are negotiated between the issuer and the purchaser without subjecting the offering to competitive bidding.

net asset value Usually denoted by the acronym *NAV*. The pro rata share of the asset value (less liabilities) on any pooled investment vehicle such as a mutual fund. That is to say, we take the market value of all of the assets of the mutual fund, subtract the market value of all of the mutual fund's liabilities, and then divide this difference by the number of shares of the fund outstanding. The result is the per share net asset value.

netting (1) Standard practice in swap documentation requiring that only the payment differentials on swaps be exchanged with the higher-paying party making payment of this difference to the lower-paying party. (2) Under a master agreement, all payments between the same parties may be netted even when they involve payments on different instruments. (3) The reduction of risk exposures by netting under a master agreement.

new issue The first offering of a security.

new product risks Risks arising from errors made in structuring a new product or incorrect assumptions about the underlying asset or market.

Newton-Raphson method An interactive procedure for solving for points in nonlinear relationships that is more efficient than a simple binomial search in that it will lead to a solution with fewer iterations. The procedure is based on the error and the slope at each iteration.

Nikkei 225 The most widely quoted Japanese stock index. Computed as a price-weighted index of 225 stocks that trade on the Tokyo Stock Exchange. Often used as a benchmark on equity-linked swaps.

no action letter A letter issued by the staff of the SEC stating that the staff will not recommend to the Commission that the SEC take action with respect to a specific transaction. Such letters are generated in response to a request by one or both of the transaction's parties in order to remove regulatory risk from the transaction. The issuance of a no action letter signifies that the SEC will not object to the transaction, thereby reducing or eliminating regulatory risk.

no arbitrage opportunity A situation in which an arbitrageur cannot earn a risk-free profit. The assumption of no arbitrage opportunity is widely used in valuation models to determine the theoretically fair values of instruments (particularly options).

no load Usually refers to the absence of a sales charge in conjunction with the purchase or sale of equity interests in a mutual fund.

node In a lattice model, the value that a variable might have at a given point in time. See *binomial option pricing model*.

nonamortizing See *nonamortizing debt*.

nonamortizing debt A debt obligation in which the full principal is repaid in a single transaction upon maturity of the debt with no repayments of principal prior to maturity. This is in contrast to amortizing debt in which the principal is repaid in installments. Debt that is nonamortizing is often said to have a bullet principal repayment. See *bullet transaction*.

noncallable bond A bond that is not callable.

noncallable/nonputable convertible bond A convertible bond that is neither callable nor putable.

noncumulative In reference to dividends on preferred stock and coupons on bonds, if payments are missed they are not carried forward. This is in contrast to preferred stock and bonds that are cumulative. See *cumulative*.

nondividend paying stock Stock that does not pay a dividend. Certain stock option pricing models are predicated on the assumption that the underlying stock does not pay dividends.

noninvestment grade A situation in which a debt instrument has a credit rating below that necessary to qualify as investment grade. Such instruments are often described as *speculative grade bonds*. See *speculative grade bonds, high yield bonds,* and *junk bonds*.

non–path dependent options Also known as *path independent options*. Options whose final payoff at expiry is not dependent upon the price path that the underlying asset's price took in arriv-ing at its value on the expiry date. Examples of non–path dependent options are simple calls and puts. These options are in contrast to *path dependent options*, whose values at expiry do depend on the price path taken by the underlying asset.

non-putable bond A bond that is not putable.

non-standard options See *exotic options*.

nonstationary A situation in which the parameters of a model change over time.

nonsystematic risk See *unsystematic risk*.

normal backwardation A situation in which a futures price is below the expected future spot price. See also *backwardation*.

normal distribution A type of statistical distribution, often called a "bell curve" because of its shape, that accurately describes many stochastic processes. Normal distributions are continuous and symmetric. They are fully described by just two parameters: their mean and their variance, which represent the first two *moments* of the distribution. Normal distributions are sometimes known as *Gaussian distributions*, after their discoverer.

normal market In the context of futures, a situation in which futures prices are higher the further forward the delivery date. This term is a bit antiquated because it would not describe a normal market for certain financial futures, particularly Eurodollar futures. It developed in the context of storable commodity futures.

normal portfolio See *benchmark*.

normal yield curve A yield curve that is upward sloping. Also called an *upward sloping yield curve* or an *ascending yield curve*.

note futures Futures contracts on Treasury notes. There are several varieties, but they all have the same general structure.

notice In the context of callable bonds, the amount of time that an issuer must give a bondholder from the time the call is announced until the call is effective. This is usually between 30 and 45 days for a floating rate note and between 45 and 90 days for a fixed rate bond.

notice of sale A legal notice announcing the terms and conditions of a bond sale.

notional IOs A tranche of CMOs that receives only the excess coupon interest resulting from the overcollateralization of the issue. See also *interest only* and *principal-only securities*.

notional principal The amount of principal on which the interest is calculated on a swap or related instrument, including FRAs and interest rate options. In the case of interest rate swaps, FRAs, and interest rate options, the principal is purely "notional" in that exchanges of principal never take place.

notionals The quantity of underlying on a derivative instrument where said underlying is not, usually, deliverable. The notionals serve as the basis for either calculating the final cash settlement or computing the sequential cash flows in the case of a multi-period instrument such as a swap. For example, an interest rate swap will pay a floating rate of interest on one leg and a fixed rate of interest on the other leg. These rates are stated as annual percentages. The percentages are translated into actual dollar amounts to be exchanged by multiplying by the contract's notional principal.

novation The replacement of a contract or a group of contracts with a single new contract.

numeric procedures Also known as numeric methods. Any of a variety of methodologies for arriving at an approximate value for a financial instrument (usually derivative contracts) by way of an iterative process having a finite number of steps. These methods are most useful when an analytical formula has not been derived or cannot be derived.

numeric valuation methods Models to value assets where such models rely on numeric procedures rather than analytically derived equations. See *numeric procedures*.

OAS See *option adjusted spread*.

OAS analysis See *option adjusted spread analysis*.

obligation A duty imposed by either law or contract.

obligee One to whom another owes an obligation under a contract. This would include the right to receive cash flows on a financial instrument.

obligor One who is obligated to perform a duty under a contract. This would include the obligation to make payments on a financial instrument.

OCC (1) In the context of option markets, refers to the *Options Clearing Corporation.* (2) In the context of the banking industry, refers to the *Office of the Comptroller of the Currency.*

odd lot As used with respect to stock transactions, any transaction involving less than 100 shares of stock. See also *round lot.*

OECD See *Organization of Economic Cooperation and Development.*

off–balance sheet A position with potential financial consequences that does not appear on either the asset side or the liabilities side of a balance sheet.

offer price See *ask.*

Offering price The price at which the securities that make up a security issuance are offered for sale by the underwriters.

Office of the Comptroller of the Currency A governmental body responsible for chartering and overseeing federally chartered banks (called national banks).

official statement A legal document that describes the issuer and the terms of a municipal debt issue and which summarizes all relevant salient features of the underlying documents and agreements that support the issue. Analogous in some degree to a *prospectus.*

off-market coupon A coupon on a swap or other instruments that deviates from currently prevailing market conditions. This is in contrast to an at-market coupon, which reflects current market conditions.

off-market swap A swap that has a coupon that deviates from currently prevailing market conditions for newly written swaps. If written off market, the swap will usually involve a *buy up* or a *buy down.* That is, a sum will be paid up front by one of the two counterparties to the other of the two counterparties to have the swap written with a coupon that deviates from that applicable on an at-market swap, but with the same floating rate that would be used on an at-market swap.

offshore Outside of a particular country's geographic and jurisdictional boundaries.

offshore market A market for securities or other instruments that is located outside of a particular country's geographic and jurisdictional boundaries. As such, said country has no authority to regulate the offshore market unless authority to do so has been granted by international treaty.

off-the-run Those U.S. Treasury securities that are not the most recent issues for their respective maturities.

one touch all-or-nothing An all-or-nothing option which pays off if the spot price of the underlying crosses a specified barrier prior to a specific date. See also *exploding option* and *all-or-nothing options.*

one-way collared floater See *ratchet floater.*

on-the-close See *at-the-close.*

On-the-open See *at-the-open.*

on-the-run Those U.S. Treasury securities that are the most recent issues for their respective maturities. The term is also used more narrowly to refer to the most recently issued Treasury securities of specific maturities, most notably the

2-year, the 5-year, the 10-year, and the 30-year. Also called the *currents*.

open interest The number of futures or option contracts outstanding of a given series at a given point in time. It is a single count of either the long positions or the short positions, but not both as that would represent a double counting.

open order An order to buy or sell an asset. The order is good until the person who placed it specifically directs that it be cancelled. Also known as a *good-til-cancelled* order or a *GTC*. Such orders will automatically cancel if the asset involved ceases to exist (e.g., a futures contract delivers, an option expires, a bond matures, etc.). Some commission houses have a policy of terminating unfilled open orders after some period of time (e.g., six months) or if the market price deviates from the price specified in the order by more than some percentage. An open order is in contrast to a *day order*.

open position A position in a financial instrument that has not been closed or offset by another transaction.

open-end investment company Commonly referred to as a mutual fund. An investment company that stands ready to issue new shares or buy back outstanding shares at the net asset value of those shares. See *mutual fund*.

opening range The highest and lowest prices at which a security or futures contract trades during the limited opening period following the beginning of trading for the day. All orders to be filled at-the-open should be filled within the opening range.

opening trade A trade that creates a position in a financial instrument or security. This is in contrast to a trade that

closes or terminates an existing position.

operational risk The risk that loss will occur due to an operational failure of some sort including inadequate management and oversight.

optimal hedge The hedge that maximizes the hedger's utility. The term is sometimes used to mean the variance-minimizing hedge.

optimal portfolio The portfolio among many portfolios that maximizes an investor's utility.

optimization A process that leads to the optimal solution to a problem. By optimal solution, we mean better—in some sense—than any other solution. In the context of portfolio management, optimization refers to an algorithm that identifies the portfolios that have the highest rate of return for any given level of risk.

option Any contact or provision of a contract that grants its holder the right, but not the obligation, to do something. Such a right can have considerable value. Options are also known by the terms *rights, warrants,* and *privileges*. Financial options involve the right, but not the obligation, to buy or sell something at a set price for a fixed period of time. See *call option* (call) and *put option* (put) for descriptions of specific types.

option adjusted convexity See *effective convexity*.

option adjusted duration See *effective duration*.

option adjusted spread The number of basis points which, when added to a calibrated binomial tree of risk-free short rates, results in a bond valuation that precisely matches the observed price of the bond in the marketplace. One important use for an option adjusted spread is to determine the incremental return on a risky bond having embedded options relative to the return on a risk-free benchmark bond, such as a Treasury bond. This incremental return is then compared to the incremental credit risk to determine if the risk/return tradeoff is appropriate.

option adjusted spread analysis Also known as *OAS analysis*. The process and associated analytics involved in deriving, interpreting, and using an option adjusted spread. This involves building a model to determine a fixed spread, stated in basis points, over a binomial tree of calibrated risk-free short rates such that when the cash flows on the bond are sequentially discounted backward through the tree, the sum of the present values is equal to the observed market price of the bond. The analytics involve deriving the binomial tree of risk-free short rates, calibrating the tree, calculating the spread, and then using the spread to value the embedded option and determine the bond's effective duration.

option adjusted yield The yield that discounts the future cash flows on a bond to the bond's current market price after adjusting for the value of any embedded options.

option class Refers to either the calls or the puts, but not both. That is, all of the call options written on the same underlying irrespective of the expiration date and strike price would represent the call class. Similarly, all of the put options written on the same underlying irrespective of the expiration date and strike price would represent the put class.

option cost See *option premium*.

option currency bond A type of dual-currency bond in which either the investor or the issuer has the right to choose which currency in which to denominate the payments.

option dated forward contract Also known as an *option forward*. A forward contract on foreign exchange containing an option with respect to the date of the currency exchange.

option forward See *option dated forward contract*.

option free Any instrument that does not contain any embedded options, such as an option-free bond.

option grantor See *option writer*.

option holder Also called the option purchaser. The owner of an option. The holder is said to be "long the option."

option on futures Options written on futures contracts. If the option is exercised, the futures contract is the delivered instrument.

option on physicals Any option written directly on some underlying asset, particularly commodities, as opposed to an option written on a futures contract that itself is written on an underlying asset.

option premium The price paid by an option purchaser to an option writer for the valuable right which an option conveys. The option premium is often described as consisting of two parts: intrinsic value and time value. Intrinsic value represents the value that could be captured if the option were to be exercised immediately. Time value represents the potential for the option to acquire more intrinsic value before it expires.

option pricing models Models developed to value options. Some models are analytical in nature and take the form of a derived equation. Others are numerical in nature and take the form of an iterative process that leads to an unambiguous solution. See also *analytic valuation methods* and *numeric valuation methods*.

option series All of the options of a particular option class that share the same expiration date and the same strike price. All such options would be fungible making it possible to liquidate a position in an option by taking an offsetting position in another option of the same series.

option writer Also known as an *option grantor.* The party who grants an option by selling the option instrument. The option writer is said to be "short the option." The option writer receives an option premium from the option purchaser as consideration for the valuable right that the option conveys. If the option is exchange traded, the option writer will be required to post margin to guarantee later performance should the option holder choose to exercise the option.

Options Clearing Corporation Also known by the acronym *OCC.* Should not be confused with the Office of the Comptroller of the Currency, which also uses the acronym OCC. The clearinghouse for all listed stock options and most commodity options traded in the United States.

ordinaries Equivalent to *common stock.* The term "ordinaries" is used in some countries to mean the same thing that common stock means in the United States.

ordinary annuity An annuity is a series of *N* equal-sized payments that are spread out equidistant in time. An ordinary annuity is an annuity in which the first payment will be made precisely one period from the present and the last payment will be made *N* periods from the present. This is in contrast to an *annuity due,* in which the first payment is due immediately, the second payment is due one period from the present, and the last payment is due *N* − *1* periods from the present.

Organization of Economic Cooperation and Development An organization of European states for mutual economic cooperation and gain.

Original margin See *initial margin.*

original-issue high-yield bonds Bonds that were rated less than investment grade or had no rating at the time of issue. This is in contrast to bonds that were rated investment grade at the time of issue but whose rating deteriorated over time until they were no longer investment grade. See also *high yield bonds.*

origination points Fees paid up front for the origination of a mortgage loan or other type of loan. Each point is a percentage point and is paid on the loan principal.

OTC See *over-the-counter.*

OTC options Privately negotiated and often tailor-made options that trade over-the-counter. They range from simple calls and puts to very exotic structures.

out-of-the-money (1) In the case of a call option, a situation in which the spot price of the underlying asset is below the strike price of the option. In the case of a put option, a situation in which the spot price of the underlying asset is above the strike price of the option.

Out-of-the-money options have no intrinsic value, but may have time value. (2) In the case of a swap, a situation in which the mark-to-market value of the swap is negative for the counterparty, in which case it would be in-the-money for the other counterparty. See, for contrast, *in-the-money*.

outperformance option An option that pays off the amount by which one asset or index outperforms another asset or index if the difference between them is positive and pays off zero otherwise. For example, an investor might purchase an outperformance option on the S&P and Nikkie, such that the option pays off either the difference between the total returns on these two indexes or zero. The payoff function would be given by $max[S_1 - S_2, 0]$. Outperformance options are one of several types of *rainbow options*. Other types of rainbow options include *better-of, worse-of,* and *max-min options*. See each of these types for details.

outright Another name for an outright forward. See *outright forward*.

outright forward A foreign exchange forward contract. That is, a contract for the later exchange of two currencies.

outside barrier A barrier option in which the asset whose price serves as the trigger price for the option is different from the asset that serves as the option's underlying asset. For example, suppose that the barrier option is an up-and-in on gold. The barrier's trigger is tied to the price of oil. That is, if the price of oil rises above the trigger, then the option on gold comes into existence. Outside barriers are relatively rare compared to inside barriers, which use the same asset for the underlying and the trigger. See *barrier options* for additional discussion.

outside debt Debt instruments, such as bonds, in which the lender (i.e., bondholder) does not have access to non-public (i.e., confidential) information about the borrower. This is in contrast to *inside debt,* which usually takes the form of bank loans, in which the lender does have access to nonpublic information.

outstanding shares All of the shares of common stock that a corporation has issued (i.e., distributed) less any shares that the corporation has repurchased. Repurchased shares are called *treasury stock*. Thus the number of shares outstanding is the difference between the number of shares issued and the number of shares of treasury stock.

overallotment option Also known in market slang as the *Green Shoe option*. A clause in an underwriting agreement that allows the underwriters to go back to the issuer for additional securities, usually up to a maximum of from 15% to 20% of the planned issuance, in the event that the demand for the securities leads to an oversale of the issuance. The additional securities are purchased from the issuer at the offering price. The term "green shoe option" derives from the fact that this clause was first employed in an offering of securities by the Green Shoe Company.

overcollateralization A situation in which the value of the collateral used to secure a loan or back a security exceeds the value of the loan itself.

overnight money Funds that are lent on an overnight basis. That is, the money is lent from the close of business one day to the opening of business the next day. The two most common forms are Fed funds and overnight repos.

overnight repo A repurchase agreement that provides for a secured lending for a period of one business day.

over-the-counter Known more commonly by the acronym *OTC*. A dealer market in which transactions take place via telephone, telex, and other electronic forms of communication as opposed to trading on the floor of an exchange. At least one of the counterparties to the transaction is a dealer. In an exchange transaction, neither the buyer nor the seller is likely to be a dealer. Some stocks, most bonds, and all OTC derivatives trade in over-the-counter markets.

P/E ratio See *price-to-earnings ratio.*

PA An abbreviation for percent annual, meaning an annual rate of interest compounded annually.

PAC bonds See *planned amortization class bonds.*

package Any derivative that is constructed from a portfolio of plain vanilla call or put options, but which may have other components, such as the underlying asset itself, included as part of the portfolio. This would include such things as caps (which are portfolios of calls) and floors (which are portfolios of puts).

PAM See *pledged account mortgage.*

par The face value of a bond used to calculate the size of periodic coupon payments or the face value of preferred stock used to calculate the periodic dividend payments. In the case of a bond, par is usually equal to the bond's principal.

par bond A bond trading at its par value. This is in contrast to a bond trading above its par value, called a *premium bond,* and a bond trading below its par value, called a *discount bond.*

par swap Also known as an *at-market swap.* A swap in which the swap coupon is set to reflect current market conditions. Of course, while a swap may be written at par, it will move away from par as market conditions change. Once market conditions have changed, the swap will be in-the-money for one counterparty and out-of-the-money for the other counterparty.

par swap curve Also called a *swap curve,* a *swap yield curve,* and a *par swap yield curve.* This is a plot of the fixed coupons on par (i.e., at-market) swaps of different maturities plotted against their maturities. It is constructed in the same way as any other yield curve. Such curves employ the swap mid-rate (i.e., the midpoint between the dealer's bid rate and offer rate).

par swap yield curve See *par swap curve.*

par value Also known as *redemption value* and as *face value,* although these terms can have different meanings in different contexts. Generally, the face value of a bond or a share of preferred stock. When used in this way, the par value is stated per bond or per share. In the case of a bond, the par value is often $1,000, but can be more or less. The term is also used to describe the par value of an entire issuance. For example, a bond issuance might have a par value of $10 million, but is sold in the form of 10,000 individual $1,000–par value bonds. In the case of bonds, the par value is what the investor can expect to receive upon redemption at maturity. The size of the periodic coupon payment is computed by multiplying the coupon rate by the bond's par value and then dividing by the number of coupon payments in a year. Preferred stock generally has no maturity date; therefore, the stock's par value is used as the basis for computing the preferred stock dividend.

par yield The coupon rate on a bond necessary for the bond to sell at par. That is, its coupon rate and its yield are the same.

parallel loans An arrangement in which two corporations agree to make loans to each other's subsidiaries. The parallel loan is a precursor of the modern swap and has a purpose similar to a currency swap. The structure of parallel loans, however, is generally considered inferior to that of swaps because it embodies considerably greater counterparty risk in the absence of a legally binding right of set off agreement.

parallel shift A shift in an interest rate curve (i.e., a yield curve, a spot curve, or a forward curve) that is everywhere parallel. That is, the curve shifts in the same direction by the same number of basis points everywhere along its surface.

PARS See *municipal floating-rate bonds*.

partial strips These are bonds that have a zero-like property for some period but then behave like coupon bonds after that period. That is to say, for a certain period of time, usually up to a call date, they are like zero coupon bonds, but after the call date (assuming they

are not called) they behave like a coupon-bearing instrument. They are a type of *step-up bond*. Merrill Lynch has issued such bonds under the trademark LIMOS and Goldman Sachs has issued them under the trademark GAINS.

participating cap An interest-rate cap in which the purchaser pays a reduced premium in exchange for forgoing an agreed-upon portion of the amount by which the cap is in-the-money on the fixing date.

participating forward Also known as a *profit-sharing forward* and as a *ratio forward*. A forward contract with a built-in floor to protect the buyer of the forward contract from an excessively adverse price movement. The payoff on such an instrument would have the following functional form: Payoff = $(S - X)$ + Max$[F - S, 0]$, where S denotes the reference rate or spot price, X denotes the contract rate, and F denotes the floor's strike rate or price. For the protection afforded by the floor, the buyer of the forward would normally be expected to pay the seller an option premium. But, in a participating forward, the premium is waived in exchange for the buyer agreeing to pay the seller a percentage of any gain on the contract. The percentage paid is called the seller's participation rate. There is a trade-off between the level of the floor and the seller's participation rate. Suppose that a participating forward is written with a contract rate (X) of $20 and a floor rate of $15. Now, suppose that on the fixing date, the reference rate is $12. The contract would pay off $(12 - 20)$ + Max$[15 - 12, 0]$ = -5. Thus, instead of losing $8, as would have happened had this been a plain vanilla forward, the buyer loses only $5. There is no gain on this contract, so the contract holder does not pay anything to the seller for the option. These structures are similar to, but not the same as, a range forward.

participating option An option on which the purchaser pays a reduced premium in exchange for forgoing a portion of the amount by which the option is in-the-money at expiry. The term is more general than participating cap, which refers only to cap options with a participating feature. Also known as a *profit-share option*.

participating swaption A type of participating option in which the option is a swaption. See *swaption* and *participating option*.

passive strategies Investment strategies that are intended to replicate the risk/return performance of some benchmark. The degree of success of the portfolio manager is judged by how closely his portfolio tracks the benchmark in terms of both the rate of return and the degree of correlation. The key parameters for judging performance are obtained from a regression of the periodic returns on the portfolio against the periodic returns on the benchmark. The parameters are the regression slope (should be close to 1) and the R-2 (should be close to 1).

passthrough certificates Also known as *participation certificates*. Single class mortgage-backed securities that represent a pro rata claim on a pool of whole mortgages. Thus, both the interest component and the principal component of payments on mortgages in the pool pass through to the passthrough certificate holders. Principal prepayments, if any, also pass through. See also *passthrough securities*.

passthrough investor An individual or institution that invests in passthrough certificates.

passthrough rate The rate of interest paid on passthrough certificates. This rate is equal to the mortgage rate less the servicing agent's fee and the guarantor's fee (if any). For example, suppose that the mortgages in the pool carry a mortgage coupon of 6.90%. Suppose that the servicing agent keeps 45 basis points for its servicing function and the guarantor of the pool receives 5 basis points (this is analogous to an insurance premium). Then, the passthrough holders receive a passthrough rate of 6.40% (i.e., 6.90% − 0.45% − 0.05%).

passthrough securities Financial instruments that are collateralized by a pool of mortgages. Individual mortgagors make payments on their mortgages to the mortgage-pool servicer, and the payments are passed through on a pro rata basis to the security holders.

path dependent options Options on which the final payoff at expiry is dependent upon the price path taken by the underlying asset over the life of the option. Examples of path dependent options include Asian options (also called average rate options), which pay off based on an average of the spot price over the life of the option, and lookback options, which pay off based on the highest or lowest price the underlying asset achieved over the life of the option.

path independent options See *non–path dependent options*.

payer's swaption A option that grants its holder the right to enter into a swap as fixed-rate payer and floating-rate receiver. The swap would have a preset coupon rate (i.e., fixed rate). Also known as a *put swaption*. See also *swaption*.

payment dates The dates on which the counterparties to a swap, or other contract, exchange contractually mandated payments.

payment-in-kind Often denoted by the acronym *PIK*. This refers to any financial instrument that pays additional units of itself in lieu of cash. A dividend on common stock that takes the form of additional shares of stock or coupon payments on a bond that take the form of additional units of the bond are examples of payments-in kind.

payoff The cash flow (i.e., value) realized by an investor in a derivative at the end of the derivative instrument's life or on one of its settlement dates. The term can also be used to describe the gain or loss from holding any financial instrument (not just derivatives) for any period of time or as part of any investment strategy.

payoff profile A visual depiction, by way of a graph, of the profits (and losses) associated with a position in a financial instrument. For some instruments, the payoff profiles are linear. For other instruments such as options, they are nonlinear.

pay-receive spread Also called a *bid-ask spread*. The difference between a derivatives dealer's receive rate and pay rate on generic swaps or forwards of a given tenor. In the case of a swap, the dealer's receive rate is the fixed rate coupon that the counterparty would pay the dealer in exchange for receiving LIBOR. The dealer's pay rate is the swap coupon the dealer would pay a counterparty in exchange for receiving LIBOR. The amount by which the dealer's receive rate exceeds the dealer's pay rate is the source of the swap dealer's profit.

pension fund A fund set up, typically by corporations or unions, to pay pension benefits to employees after they retire.

per unit pricing The accepted practice of quoting the prices of financial instruments on a per unit basis irrespective of the number of units of the asset actually covered by the contract. For example, a standard exchange-listed stock option covers 100 shares of the underlying stock. But, the option premium (bid and ask) is quoted per share covered. Thus, a quoted option premium of $6 means $600.

PERCS See *Preferred Equity Redemption Cumulative Stock*. Both terms are trademarks of Morgan Stanley Dean Witter.

perfect negative correlation A perfectly linear, but inverse, relationship between two variables such that a change in one variable allows one to predict the change in the other perfectly. However, the two variables move in opposite directions. See also *perfect positive correlation* and *correlation coefficient*.

perfect positive correlation A perfectly linear and direct relationship between two variables such that a change in one variable allows one to predict the change in the other perfectly. The two variables move in the same direction. See also *perfect negative correlation* and *correlation coefficient*.

perfect swap See *actual rate swap*.

perfectly correlated A perfect linear relationship (either positive or negative) between two variables. See also *correlation coefficient*.

periodic rate-setting swap A swap in which the floating rate is set based on an average of the values of the reference rate since the last payment, as opposed to the usual practice of setting the floating rate at the beginning (or end) of the period based on a single observation on the reference rate. This is a common practice on commodity swaps. Also known as a *periodic resetting swap*.

Periodic resetting swap See *periodic rate-setting swap*.

persistence The tendency of a state to continue without change. The term is sometimes used with respect to either the shape of the yield curve or the term structure of volatility. In the former case, persistence would imply that the current shape of the yield curve would persist irrespective of what the forward rates suggest.

physicals See *actuals*.

piecemeal cubic spline A method of fitting a curve to data that breaks the data up into several subsets, each subset representing a range of values for the independent variable. (This is the piecemeal component). A curve is then fit to each subset of data using a cubic function. (This is the cubic component). The curve that is fit to each subset of the data is forced to begin at the same point that the prior curve ended. (This is the spline component.). The piecemeal cubic spline approach is one of the most common approaches to fitting a yield curve to yield/maturity data. For example, the yields of noncallable Treasury bonds (including both on-the-run and off-the-run Treasuries) are plotted against their respective maturities. The maturities are then divided into short-term, intermediate-term, and long-term. A cubic function is then fit to each subset and the ends of the curves are splined to form one continuous fitted benchmark yield curve.

piggyback offering See *combined seasoned offering*.

PIK See *payment-in-kind*.

plain vanilla Also called *generic* or *basic*. The simplest form of a financial instrument. Often associated with the first manifestation of an instrument (e.g., a plain vanilla swap). Sometimes referred to as *vanilla*.

plain vanilla swap A swap having the most common generic terms. For example, a plain vanilla USD interest rate swap would be a nonamortizing swap making semiannual payments in which one counterparty pays a fixed rate and the other counterparty pays a floating rate. The reference rate for the floating leg would be six-month LIBOR.

planned amortization class bonds Known by the acronym *PAC bonds*. These are specially crafted tranches of CMOs structured so that the principal amortizes according to a preset schedule irrespective of how the principal on the underlying mortgage collateral prepays. Greater stability is created by having another class of bonds, called *support bonds* or *companion bonds,* that absorb some of the principal pre-payments on the mortgage pool. Thus, the greater certainty of the timing of the cash flows on the PACs is achieved via greater uncertainty on the timing of the cash flows on the support bonds.

planning horizon The length of time before an investment strategy will be reconsidered. See *investment horizon*.

pledged account mortgage Known by the acronym *PAM*. A mortgage contract requiring a separate time deposit account dedicated to making a portion of each mortgage payment. The draw from the pledged account augments the payment made by the mortgagors. As a consequence, the monthly payment made by the mortgagors is lower than on a conventional mortgage.

PO See *principal only*.

points A point usually means one percentage point when talking about fixed income securities but is also used to mean $1 when talking about equity securities. A point should not be confused with a *basis point*, which means 0.01%. The term *points* is often used to describe the origination fee associated with a mortgage, where the fee is stated as a percentage of the mortgage principal. See also *origination points*.

political risk A form of country risk. Essentially the risk that counterparties to financial transactions will default because of political upheaval in a country, such as a change in policy toward external parties or the overthrow of a government. The government may prohibit entities within its jurisdiction from fulfilling their obligations to their counterparties in other countries. See *country risk*.

population variance See *variance*.

pop-up option Another name for up-and-in options. See *barrier options, up-and-in options*, and *knock-in options*.

portfolio The collection of all positions in all assets, whether long or short, held by an individual or an institution. We often focus more narrowly on the portfolios held by individuals or departments within an institution. Such portfolios are often called, in market jargon, *books*. For example, each corporate bond dealer has a bond book, each option dealer has an options book, and so forth. The term can also be used to describe the collection of assets on a corporation's balance sheet (asset portfolio) as distinct from the collection of liabilities on the corporation's balance sheet (liability portfolio).

portfolio immunization An asset/liability management strategy that seeks to select assets in such a fashion as to minimize the difference in interest-rate sensitivities between assets and liabilities. This is typically done by matching the duration of the asset portfolio to the duration of the liability portfolio.

portfolio insurance The use of options, or trading strategies that replicate the behavior of options, to protect the value of assets. Portfolio insurance that uses active trading to replicate options is often called *dynamic hedging*. A form of portfolio insurance, in which stock index futures were the traded asset, was widely used to protect the value of equity portfolios in the latter half of the 1980s. This strategy received some of the blame for the sharp drop in equity prices that occurred in October 1987.

portfolio theory The body of scientific theory that describes the relationship between the risk and the expected return associated with a portfolio of securities or other assets. Modern portfolio theory began with the work of Harry Markowitz and was later extended by other researchers including William Sharpe, James Tobin, and Stephen Ross, among others. Modern portfolio theory most often defines expected return as the mean annual rate of return associated with the portfolio and measures the risk as either the standard deviation of this rate of return or, alternatively, the beta coefficient of the portfolio measured relative to some benchmark.

position limit The limit to the size of a position in a specific instrument that may be held by a single individual or firm or by a group of individuals or firms acting in concert. Position limits are imposed to prevent individuals from manipulating the market price in a noncompetitive fashion.

position risk The market risk, credit risk, or other exposure to a specific securities holding or book of holdings by a firm through its trading desk.

positioning a swap Also called *booking a swap*. The taking of a position in a swap by a swap dealer. This contrasts with a broker that acts as an agent in a swap and does not take the swap on its own books.

positive cash flow collar A collar that results in a positive cash flow to the end user. This will occur if the premium paid for (received from) the cap portion of the collar is less (more) than the premium received from (paid for) the floor portion of the collar. This is in contrast to a zero cost collar, on which the two premiums are the same and therefore fully offsetting. See also *collar* and *zero cost collar*.

positive convexity A reference to the curvature found in the price/yield function on a straight bond. That is, if the price of a straight bond is plotted on the vertical axis and the yield is plotted on the horizontal axis, the curve will be seen to be convex to the origin. This sort of convexity is the normal case in the absence of embedded options. When options are embedded in a bond, the bond will often exhibit regions of negative convexity.

positive yield curve Another name for a normal or upward sloping yield curve. See *normal yield curve*.

Preferred Equity Redemption Cumulative Stock Known by the acronym *PERCS*. Both terms are trademarks of Morgan Stanley Dean Witter. This instrument is one of many proprietary varieties of equity-linked notes. See *equity-linked notes*.

preferred stock A type of equity instrument issued by some corporations. Unlike common stock, preferred stock pays a defined dividend. This may be a fixed percentage of its par value, or it may be floating. In the latter case, the dividend will usually be pegged to some standard reference rate of interest plus a spread. Preferred stock is more like debt than equity.

preliminary prospectus A documented submitted to the Securities and Exchange Commission in preparation for a public offering. The preliminary prospectus contains all material information relevant to the offering. The filing is preliminary because certain information is deliberately left out. Omitted information includes such things as the offering price of the securities and the size of the offering, which are negotiated just prior to the issuance. In market jargon, a preliminary prospectus is often called a *red herring* because the warnings are printed in red ink on the cover page.

premium (1) The difference between a bond's market value and par value when that difference is greater than zero. Bonds exhibiting a premium are often called *premium bonds*. (2) A sum of money paid periodically to an insurance company to keep the insurance policy in force. (3) The price paid for an option or an option-like product. Some instruments, such as structured notes and callable bonds, have embedded options. In these products the premium will usually be embedded within the price of the product and may not be stated explicitly.

premium bonds Bonds trading above their par (face) value. This will generally be the case if the bond's coupon rate is above the bond's yield.

premium-free option See *zero-premium option*.

prepayment A paydown of principal on a mortgage or other debt obligation prior to the principal's scheduled payment. That is, some or all of the principal is paid early thereby reducing the loan balance. Prepayment is possible because many loan agreements allow principal to be prepaid without penalty.

prepayment risk A form of risk borne by investors in certain types of debt instruments. The term is most often applied to investments in mortgages and mortgage-backed securities. Prepayment risk is the risk that the issuer will elect to prepay the principal prior to the scheduled principal payment date(s) thereby forcing the investor to reinvest the amount prepaid. Rational issuers would be expected to prepay when market interest rates drop sufficiently to justify refinancing the underlying mortgage. As a result, the investor receives a lower return on the new investment. The same kind of risk applies to holders of callable bonds, but in this case the risk is usually called *call risk* rather than prepayment risk.

prepayments Repayments of principal on a mortgage or other type of prepayable loan in advance of those prescribed by the amortization schedule.

present value The current value (i.e., the value right now) of a sum of money to be received at some later date. The computation of a present value requires knowledge, or at least an estimate, of a future cash flow and an appropriate rate at which to discount the cash flow. The process is the mathematical inverse of calculating a future value. See also *present value discount factor.*

present value discount factor The present value of one dollar to be received at a later point in time. Must be stated in the context of some given discount rate and some specific point in the future when the money will be received. See also *discount factor.*

present value of a basis point Another name for the dollar value of a basis

point or DV01. See *dollar value of a basis point.*

present value of income pickup In the context of PERCS and ELKS, the present value of the amount by which the yields on PERCS and ELKS exceed the yield on the underlying common stock.

price risk Any financial risk exposure faced by a firm as a consequence of a potential for changes in the market prices of assets and/or liabilities. This includes changes in interest rates, exchange rates, and commodity prices. The term is often used synonymously with *market risk,* but the term market risk can have a broader meaning.

price value of a basis point See *dollar value of a basis point.*

price weighting A method of computing an index, such as a stock index, in which the prices of the securities are simply summed. An adjustment factor is usually required to account for things like stock splits. The Dow Jones Industrial Average and the Nikkei 225 are both computed using a price-weighting methodology.

price-to-earnings ratio Often called a *P/E ratio.* The ratio of a corporation's price per share to its earnings per share. Such ratios can be stated on the basis of the past year's realized earnings (called trailing earnings) or following year's forecasted earnings.

primary dealers Dealers in government securities that have been designated as primary dealers. In the case of Treasury securities, a dealer must be designated as a primary dealer by the Federal Reserve. All other dealers are non-prime dealers. Only primary dealers can submit competitive bids to purchase Treasury securities at the periodic auctions.

primary government securities dealer
Any one of the roughly forty dealers in U.S. Treasury Securities designated by the Federal Reserve to participate in making both the primary and the secondary markets in government securities. These dealers submit competitive bids to purchase Treasury securities at the periodic auctions of these securities. Other parties desiring to submit competitive bids must submit their bids through these primary dealers.

primary market The market in which new issues of securities are initially distributed for sale. For example, the primary market in corporate securities is made, for the most part, by the investment banking community through the underwriting and distribution of securities sold as part of public offerings and the direct sale of corporate debt securities through private placements to qualified investors. In a primary market transaction, the issuer receives the proceeds from the sale, less any fees paid. This is in contrast to secondary market transactions, which involve the transfer of securities from one investor to another investor.

primary seasoned offering Also known as a *follow-on offering*. A public offering of securities by a corporation that has already done an initial public offering (IPO) of its common stock and now wishes to raise additional equity capital by selling additional shares of stock.

prime cap An interest-rate cap in which the reference rate is tied to the prime rate of interest. The prime rate is the rate charged by commercial banks to their best business customers. The prime rate rises and falls as a bank's funding cost rises and falls.

principal The capital or face amount of a debt or other obligation upon which interest accrues.

principal component analysis A statistical process that identifies a small set of variables that explain most of the fluctuation in some other variable. Similar to *factor analysis*.

principle of comparative advantage A well-established theory first developed by David Ricardo in the nineteenth century to explain trade between nations. In brief, the theory holds that, assuming an appropriate exchange rate, both nations will benefit from trade if each concentrates production in that commodity in which it holds a comparative advantage and then trades a portion of its production for a portion of the other nation's production. Refinements of the theory allow for transaction costs. The concept is equally applicable in explaining trade more generally and for explaining the benefits that accrue to the counterparties to a swap. When applied to swaps, comparative advantage is often called relative advantage.

principle of offsetting risks This is an extension of portfolio theory, which states that risk can be reduced if two simultaneous positions are held such that manifestations of the individual risks, which take the form of deviations from expected values, are in opposite directions. This is the principle on which hedging is based.

principal only Also known as a *PO*, and a *principal-only strip*. A tranche of a mortgage passthrough security that gives the holder the right to receive a portion of every principal payment, but not the right to receive any portion of the interest payments. That is, in exchange for the initial investment in the PO, the PO investor is entitled to receive a series of principal payments until the principal has been fully paid. The total amount of principal to be paid is fixed so once fully paid, the PO terminates. If interest rates decline, mortgagors accelerate repayment with the result that the cash flows to the PO holder are accelerated. Cash flows received sooner have greater value than cash flows received later, so PO investors benefit significantly from a decline in mortgage interest rates.

principal-only securities See *principal only*.

principal-only strip See *principal only*.

principal-protected equity-linked notes Equity-linked debt instruments that pay a coupon equaling some fraction of the total return on some benchmark equity index and protect the value of the principal so that the debt holder is assured of getting all of the principal back at maturity. Some earlier versions of equity-linked notes paid a coupon that was equal to some fraction of the total return on some benchmark equity index (e.g., the S&P 500). If the total return on the equity index turned out to be negative for a coupon period, the coupon would be negative. This would be dealt with by reducing the principal. These instruments were not attractive to investors because of the potential loss of principal. The principal-protected feature eliminates this risk.

private equity sale A discounted private sale by a holder of restricted stock to a counterparty who holds the stock until it is freely tradable or otherwise further monetizes it or sells it pursuant to an exemption from registration. Typically, the original holder loses all control and equity ownership in the stock and receives less than 100% of the current market value of the stock, but has no economic risk in the position going forward.

private placements Corporate security issuances that are exempt from registration with the SEC and which can only be sold to qualified investors. Qualified investors include most institutional investors and others who meet specified criteria. Securities sold through private placements are often highly structured and tailor-made to suit the needs of the issuer and the investor, whose needs can be quite different. Private placement eliminates the registration delays associated with public offerings of securities. However, such securities can be resold only to other qualified investors and, as such, are far less liquid than registered securities.

privilege An early term for an *option*. See *option*.

proceeds to the issuer The amount of money to be paid to the issuer of securities by the underwriters upon completion of the distribution. In a firm commitment underwriting, the proceeds to the issuer is a contractual commitment. If the securities are sold at the offering price, then the difference between the gross proceeds from the sale and the proceeds to the issuer is the underwriting spread.

profit diagram A graphic portrayal of the profit from an investment as of a certain point in time under a range of values for the underlying asset. Often drawn to depict the profit potential of option strategies but can be drawn for any instrument. Closely related to profit diagrams are value diagrams, which indicate the value of a position for a range of prices for the underlying. For futures contracts, profit diagrams and value diagrams are the same. For option contracts, however, the value diagram has to shift to reflect the premium paid (or received) from the option's purchase (or sale) before it can be used as the profit diagram. Closely related to profit diagrams are *payoff profiles* and *risk profiles*, terms often used interchangeably.

profit-share option See *participating option*.

profit-sharing forward See *participating forward*.

program trading The buying and selling of baskets of stocks, often as bundles, for purposes of replicating indexes and/or trading baskets of stocks against stock index futures. To find exploitable arbitrage opportunities, thousands of hypothetical baskets of securities must be considered in a very short period of time, necessitating the use of automated algorithms to both find appropriate baskets and generate the trades. See *cash-index arbitrage*.

promised yield See *yield-to-worst*.

promissory note Any of a variety of debt instruments evidenced by a note promising to repay borrowed money together with interest according to a specified repayment schedule.

prospectus A document that describes all of the terms and risks surrounding a public offering of debt or equity and which provides important information concerning the issuer of the securities. A prospectus must be provided to an investor prior to the sale of the securities to the investor.

protective covenants Provisions written into a bond or other debt instrument's indenture to protect the interests of the lender. Protective covenants can include limits on the degree of the borrower's allowable indebtedness, restrictions on the types of business activities in which the borrower might engage, protections from call via a refunding of the debt, and so forth.

protective put A put option purchased for the purpose of protecting the value of a long position in an asset. The put option that is purchased is written on an underlying asset that is the same as, or very similar to, the asset that is held long. For example, an investor might have a long position in IBM stock. If he purchases a put option on IBM stock in order to protect the value of his long position in IBM stock, the put would be said to be a protective put.

provisional call protection Aside from hard call protection, some convertibles also possess provisional call protection. That is, they cannot be called prior to the provisional call date unless the common trades above a certain price, typically from 40% to 50% above the conversion price, for a specified period of time.

prudent-investor rule A rule that requires a fiduciary to discharge his or her duties with the same care, skill, and diligence that a prudent person acting in this capacity under the circumstances then prevailing who is familiar with such matters would use to conduct an enterprise of like character and with like aims.

PSA Acronym for *Public Securities Association*. Also used in reference to principal prepayment assumptions as generated by the Public Securities Association from historical data on mortgage lending.

pseudo-coupon date A date on which a generic bond with similar terms as some reference bond would pay a coupon even though the reference bond will not pay a coupon on that date. Useful for discussing bonds with non-generic terms.

public offerings Securities (e.g., stock and bond) issuances offered for sale to the general public. In the United States, such offerings generally have to be registered with the Securities and Exchange Commission, though there are exceptions. This is in contrast with private placements, which are sold only to qualified investors. See *private placements*.

Public Securities Association Also known by the acronym *PSA*. An industry association whose historic principal prepayment schedules on debt securities, particularly mortgages, are used as benchmarks.

pull-to-par The tendency for a premium bond to gradually lose its premium and for a discount bond to gradually lose its discount as time passes and the bond approaches maturity. Essentially, the bond will be redeemed at maturity for par, so the price and par must converge as the bond approaches maturity.

purchase fund A fund set up by the issuer of a bond to buy bonds whenever the market value falls below some preset level. The purchases are handled by a purchasing agent. These funds are often confused with sinking funds but are not the same thing. Purchase funds are used to buy bonds to support the price whereas sinking funds are used to retire bonds irrespective of the market price.

purchase option An option to buy leased property at the end of, or during, the lease term.

purchasing power parity Often denoted PPP. A relationship that attempts to explain the spot exchange rate between two countries' currencies on the basis of the average price of the average good in each of the two countries. For example, the spot exchange rate of currency X for currency Y (i.e., the number of units of currency X that can be purchased for one unit of currency Y), denoted here $E_{X,Y}$, would, in a frictionless world, be equal to the price index of country X, denoted here I_X, divided by the price index for country Y, denoted here I_Y. That is $E_{X,Y} = I_X \div I_Y$. The empirical evidence supports PPP when measured over very long time periods such as a century, but very significant departures from PPP occur and continue for extended periods, often decades at a time. For this reason, PPP is not widely accepted as a practical guide to spot exchange rates among those who trade over relatively short periods.

purchasing power risk The risk that, upon liquidation, the proceeds from an investment will have less purchasing power than anticipated at the time the investment was made. That is, the risk that inflation will eat away at the real value of an investment. Purchasing power risk is a very real form of risk on bond investments. For example, an investment is made in a bond paying a fixed coupon rate of 7%. At maturity, the bond returns par. Inflation will result in the par value received at maturity having less purchasing power than it did at the time it was originally lent. Structures designed to mitigate purchasing power risk include floating rate notes and inflation indexed bonds.

pure arbitrage Also known as *academic arbitrage*. Defined as simultaneously transacting in two or more markets to earn a profit without taking any risk and without using the arbitrager's own capital. As a practical matter, most real world arbitrage involves at least some modest risk (e.g.,. execution risk, systems risk, model risk, counterparty risk, etc.).

pure discount bonds A term most often used in academic discussions involving fixed income analytics. Refers to zero coupon bonds issued by a sovereign such that they are completely free of default risk.

pure expectations theory See *expectations theory*.

put An option that grants its holder the right to sell the underlying asset to the option writer at the option's strike price for a fixed period of time. Some options provide for the physical delivery of the underlying upon exercise, but others are cash settled for the value that would be captured if exercised. Such options can be used to speculate on the direction of the underlying, to speculate on volatility, to hedge price risks, and in some cases, to hedge credit risk.

put option See *put*.

put price The price paid by the issuer of a putable bond to the holder of the putable bond if the holder elects to put the bond back to the issuer. See *putable bond*.

put swaption See *payer's swaption*.

putable bond A bond containing an embedded option that allows the holder of the bond to put the bond back to the issuer on or after a fixed date, called the put date, at a fixed price called the put price. Also spelled *puttable bond*.

putable swap A fixed-for-floating interest-rate swap in which the floating-rate payer has the right to terminate the swap prior to its scheduled maturity date. This is in contrast to a callable swap in which the fixed-rate payer has the right to terminate the swap early. Also spelled *puttable swap*.

put-call parity A mathematical relationship between call options and put options written on the same underlying and having the same expiration date such that a long position in a put option can by synthesized from a long position in a call option and a short position in the underlying asset. This fundamental relationship provides a means to derive the fair value of a put option from the fair value of a call option, and vice versa. Put-call parity was first identified by Hans Stoll.

puttable bond See *puttable bond*.

puttable swap See *puttable swap*.

PV01 Notation for the present value of a basis point or the price value of a basis point. Also known as the dollar value of a basis point, denoted *DV01*. See *dollar value of a basis point* for a description.

qualified independent underwriter Often denoted *QIU*. A written opinion from a QIU is required under NASD (National Association of Securities Dealers) Schedule E requirements relating to whether the pricing of a structured product that is to be issued is fair to the investor. This requirement relates to potential conflicts of interest which could arise if the issuer and the lead underwriter are affiliated entities. A QIU assures investors that the instrument's offered price is fair relative to other publicly traded instruments and market conditions affecting the asset upon which the structured product is based. The fairness opinion is provided to the lead underwriter and cited in the prospectus supplement.

qualified investor See *accredited investor*.

quality basis The difference between two prices caused by the difference between the quality characteristics of the two goods. For example, the price of one type of wheat (cash wheat) might differ from the price of wheat futures in Chicago in part because the cash wheat might be of one specific variety while the futures contract might require delivery of an altogether different variety of wheat. Quality basis is one component of the overall basis. See also *basis*.

quality option The option implicit in some contracts (such as certain futures contracts) that allows the seller of the contract (the short) to deliver any one of several alternative underlying assets. For example, on a Treasury bond futures, the short has the option of delivering any one of a great many Treasury bonds in lieu of the hypothetical bond on which the contract is written. The seller will, generally, choose to deliver whichever of the underlying bonds can be delivered most cheaply. Also known as a *substitution option*.

quality spread The difference between the borrowing cost of a poorer credit firm and the borrowing cost of a better credit firm for a given type of borrowing, a given interest character, and a given term. Related to, but not quite the same as, a credit spread.

quality spread differential The difference between a quality spread in a fixed-rate market and a quality spread in a floating-rate market. The quality spread differential is considered a measure of the potential gains from engaging in financial swaps. This may, however, overstate the true extent of the gains. The existence of a quality spread differential explains the comparative advantage that can allow all parties to swaps to derive some financial benefit.

quanto A term that applies anytime an instrument pays off in one currency based on a rate earned in another currency, which has the effect of treating the exchange rate as though it were fixed. As a consequence, instruments that are quantoed are often perceived to have built-in exchange rate risk protection.

quantoed option See *quanto*. Quantoed options can be calls or puts, standard options or exotic options. The payoff function for a quantoed call option (per unit of underlying) would be given by the following:

$$\text{Payoff} = \text{FX}_{fixed} \times max[S - X, 0].$$

Where FX_{fixed} denotes a contractually agreed exchange rate for converting the call's payoff, S denotes the spot price at expiry, and X denotes the strike price.

quantoed swap See *quanto*. A swap in which at least one leg pays in a currency other than the functional currency of a counterparty and that counterparty wants exchange rate risk protection. Essentially the swap has a built-in hedge on the exchange rate risk.

quasi-American option An option that allows investors to exercise the right that the option conveys at several distinct times over the option's life but not continuously. Thus, the exercise period is not quite American (American-type options allow for continuous exercise) but not quite European either (European-type options allow for exercise only at the end of the option's life). Also called a *Burmudan option* and a *mid-Atlantic option*.

R

raider An individual or a company that seeks to acquire a target corporation via a hostile takeover. The raider generally makes a tender offer directly to the shareholders of the target firm. See also *acquirer*.

rainbow A blended index of equity returns for indexing the reference rate on an equity swap. The term is also sometimes applied to a variety of exotic options where the underlying represents a weighted average of several different indexes, or a choice of some sort among a number of underlyings. See also *blended index*.

rainbow options Any of a variety of options that pay off based on several underlying assets or indexes. Rainbow is a general term that includes several subtypes including *better-of, worse-of, outperformance,* and *max-min options*. See the specific types for details.

random walk See *martingale*.

range floater A type of structured note in which the instrument pays an enhanced floating rate (usually in the form of a spread to the reference rate) provided that the reference rate stays within some defined range. If the reference rate strays outside the defined range, the range floater pays a substantial discount to the reference rate. For example, a range floater might pay LIBOR + 75 bps when LIBOR is between 4% and 6% but might pay only 75 bps when LIBOR is below 4% or above 6%. Also known as a *range note*. See also *accrual bond* and *LIBOR-enhanced accrual note*.

range forward A forward contract, usually on an exchange rate, that specifies a contract range instead of a contract rate. If, at maturity, the spot rate is within the contract range, the contract pays the prevailing spot rate. If the spot rate is outside the range, the contract pays either the upper or the lower end of the range, depending on whether the spot price exceeds the upper end or falls below the lower end. Such contracts are, essentially, a forward exchange agreement coupled with a call and put option. Also known as a *cylinder* and as a *collar*.

range note See *range floater*.

RAP See *Regulatory Accounting Principles*.

ratchet floater Also called a *one-way collared floater* and a *sticky floater*. A floating rate note with a resettable floor and a periodic cap. The floor rate provides some downside protection. In exchange, the note buyer gives up most of the upside (i.e., he retains the ability for the rate to rise, but only by a small amount such as 25 basis points for each reset). If rates rise, the floor rate can reset to a higher rate but the amount cannot exceed the cap. The floor rate will never be reset to a rate lower than the prior floor rate, just as a ratchet wrench moves in only one direction.

ratchet option This structure is also known as a *cliquet option*. A multiperiod exotic option in which the option's strike for the first period is set equal to the underlying's spot price at the time the option is written. If the option is in-the-money on its first settlement date, the option pays off and the strike is reset to the then prevailing spot rate of the underlying. This happens repeatedly over the life of the option.

rate anticipation swap A type of bond swap (as opposed to a derivative swap). That is, one bond is sold and another bond is purchased in anticipation of a change in interest rates. For example, if interest rates are expected to decline, a portfolio manager might sell short-duration bonds and purchase long-duration bonds because long-duration bonds are more sensitive to changes in interest rates. If rates were expected to rise, the portfolio manager would do the opposite.

rate-capped swap A fixed-for-floating interest rate swap in which the floating-rate side is capped (i.e., cannot rise above a specified level). Can be created as a unit or by combining an interest rate swap with a separate interest rate cap. Also known as a *capped swap*.

rating (1) An expression of an opinion concerning the likelihood that an issuer will default on a specific obligation. The term is most often associated with the debt ratings published by debt rating agencies. (2) An expression of the likely future performance on an equity or other investment asset. For example, equity research departments rate equities as buy (outperform), hold, or sell (underperform).

ratio forward See *participating forward*.

ratio write A situation in which an investor writes call options on stock in less than a 1-to-1 proportion. That is, the option is written on fewer shares than the investor holds. Also called a *variable write*.

Real Estate Mortgage Investment Conduit Known by the acronym *REMIC*. Essentially a CMO in which the entity serving as the trust that passes through the interest and principal payments is treated as a non-taxable entity. The rules for creating non-taxable trust entities were spelled out in the Tax Reform Act of 1986. REMICs are a type of CMO and are usually referred to as CMOs, but not all CMOs are REMICs.

rebalancing The act of periodically adjusting the size of positions within a portfolio. This may be done to maintain cohesiveness with a benchmark or to maintain a particular level of risk. In the context of an options portfolio, it may be done to maintain delta neutrality.

recapitalization (1) The sale of additional debt and/or equity securities to bring new capital into an enterprise. (2) A change in a corporation's capital structure by the sale, buyback, or sale and buyback of debt and/or equity securities.

receiver's swaption An option on a swap in which the option holder has the right to enter into a swap as the fixed-rate receiver and floating-rate payer. The swap has a preset coupon rate (i.e., the fixed rate). Also known as a *call swaption*. See *swaption*.

record date See *holder-of-record date*.

recovery rate The percentage of a bond's principal recovered through legal action, or by other means (often negotiation), following a default on the bond. For example, if a $100 par value bond defaulted and subsequent action led to a settlement for $60, the recovery rate would be 60%. The process of settling claims against a financially impaired corporation is called a *workout*. The recovery rate is the end product of a workout.

redemption (1) Often used to mean the termination of an indebtedness prior to the stated final maturity of the obligation, as through a call, a tender, or an exchange. (2) Can be used to mean the retirement of the obligation at maturity. In this case, it is often referred to as redemption at maturity.

redemption fund An account established for the purpose of periodically depositing funds toward the eventual redemption of a debt obligation. This was the earliest form of a sinking fund but is not the only type of sinking fund today. Also known as a *debt service fund*. See also *sinking fund*.

redemption price The price at which a bond may be redeemed. Often used to describe the price at which a bond may be redeemed prior to maturity. For example, if callable, the bond's redemption price is the call price. If putable, the bond's redemption price is the bond's put price.

reduced cost option Loosely defined to mean any option in which the option's buyer has reduced the premium, relative to the fair premium, through some sort of give-back. The buyer may sell a different option (e.g., a collar) or give up a portion of the gain on the option (e.g., a participating option). When the cost is reduced to zero by the sale of one option having a premium identical to the fair premium of the option purchased, the structure is called a *zero-cost collar*. See *zero-cost collar*.

reference asset In some derivative instruments, such as total return swaps, the derivative pays a floating rate based on the performance of some specific asset. This asset is called the reference asset. If the asset is an index, such as a stock or bond index, then the asset is sometimes called a reference index. In credit derivatives, the reference asset is often called the *reference credit*.

reference credit In credit derivatives, the asset on which the floating rate is based is often called the reference credit. See *reference asset* and *credit derivative*.

reference rate The designated rate (such as six-month LIBOR or three-month T-bill) on any cash-settled interest-rate contract including swaps, forward rate agreements, and interest-rate options. The reference rate is the rate that is observed on the reset date used to calculate the payment to be made on the contract's next settlement date. References rates are usually well-defined benchmarks (e.g., LIBOR, T-bill rates, COFI, etc.).

refinancing See *refunding*.

refunding The process of retiring an existing issue of debt with funds obtained from the sale of a new issue of debt. Also known as a *rollover* and as a *refinancing*.

refunding bonds Bonds issued to refund outstanding bonds. This can take two forms: The refunding bonds can be issued and the funds used to redeem the outstanding bonds, or the refunding bonds can be issued in exchange for the outstanding bonds.

refunding provisions See *refunding restrictions*.

refunding restrictions Also know as *refunding provisions*. These special covenants are often included in the indenture of a callable bond. They specifically prohibit the retirement of a bond by call if the funds used for the call are obtained by issuing a new bond.

regionals See *submajors*.

registered bonds Bonds for which ownership is recorded and tracked by a registrar. Transfer of ownership requires the signature of the registered owners.

registered traders See *floor traders.*

registered with respect to principal only A registered bond in which interest is paid to the party submitting interest coupons. The principal can be paid only to the registered owner. See *registered bonds.*

registration (of securities) The Securities Exchange Act of 1934 requires corporations to register securities with the Securities and Exchange Commission (SEC) before they sell them to the public.

regression analysis Statistical procedures used to fit equations to data. In graphical form, lines, curves, or planes are fit to data. The most used form is linear regression, which fits a straight line to data. This line is the best fit in the sense that it minimizes the sum of squared errors. Various forms of nonlinear regression exist to fit curves to data sets.

regular settlement The normal number of days to the settlement of a financial transaction. For example, in the United States, regular settlement for a corporate security transaction (stock or bond) is three business days. Regular settlement for a Treasury security transaction is one business day.

Regulatory Accounting Principles Sometimes referred to as *RAP.* Accounting principles that are promulgated by the regulatory authority and with which regulated institutions must comply Such principles may differ from both generally accepted accounting principles (GAAP) and tax accounting principles. RAP's purpose is ensuring regulatory compliance as opposed to reporting financial information to shareholders or tax authorities.

regulatory capital Capital that an institution, usually a financial institution such as a bank, is required to maintain in order to be in compliance with the requirements set forth by the institution's regulatory agencies. It may be calculated as a percentage of the institution's risk assets or by some VaR-like risk measure.

reimmunization An adjustment to the positions held in order to bring a formerly immunized balance sheet back to a state of immunization. Reimmunization is often necessitated by changes in some of the positions held, changes in a portfolio's duration caused by the passage of time, or changes in the value of key variables, such as interest rates.

reinvestment rate The rate at which the cash flows generated by a security or a portfolio of securities can be reinvested for future earnings. Because the reinvestment rates may not be knowable in advance, they represent a source of risk, called *reinvestment risk.* See *reinvestment risk.*

reinvestment risk The risk that the general level of interest rates will have changed from some initial level by the time the cash flows from an investment are due to be reinvested. As a consequence, the terminal value from the initial investment and the reinvestments is uncertain.

relative advantage A synonym for *comparative advantage.* The notion that one party may have a borrowing advantage in one market relative to another party even if the first party is at an absolute borrowing disadvantage.

relative performance options Financial instruments that give investors the right to receive the return of one asset or index of assets over and above the return of another asset or index. For example, an option that pays off based on the difference between the total return on IBM stock and the total return on the S&P 500 index. Also called *outperformance options*.

relative quotation A quote on an instrument that is stated in terms of another instrument. In the case of U.S. dollar interest rate swaps, swap dealers usually quote their indicative prices as spreads over Treasury securities of equivalent maturities. For example, if current market conditions dictate a swap coupon on a two-year interest rate swap of 6.30% and at that moment the two-year Treasury note is trading at a yield of 5.80%, then the swap would be quoted as TN + 50 bps (i.e., the two-year Treasury note yield plus 50 basis points). This method of quotation allows dealers to honor their quotes for a longer period of time than they would be able to do if they quoted on an absolute basis. In the case above, the absolute quotation for the swap coupon is 6.30%.

Rembrandt bonds Bonds sold in the Netherlands to Dutch investors by non-Dutch issuers. Analogous to *Yankee bonds*.

REMIC See *Real Estate Mortgage Investment Conduit*.

reoffered yield The yield offered by a bond at the time its original purchasers purchased it.

replacement swap A swap that is entered to replace a swap that is terminated prematurely. Frequently, an end-user of a swap (as opposed to a dealer) will decide to terminate a swap early. The dealer will calculate the mark-to-market value of the swap to be terminated: this

is the cost of a replacement swap. This sum will be paid either by the end user to the dealer or by the dealer to the end user. The swap is then terminated.

repo See *repurchase agreement*.

repo rate The rate of interest paid or received on a repo transaction.

repurchase agreement Also known as a *repo* and as an *RP*. A method of borrowing that involves the sale of a security with the simultaneous agreement to buy it back later at a specific date and price. These agreements are widely used in the securities industry as a means of obtaining relatively inexpensive short-term financing. This is economically equivalent to a collateralized loan. The reverse of this process is called a *reverse*, a *reverse repo*, or a *resale* and is often used to obtain securities for purposes of delivering on short sales.

resale See *reverse repurchase agreement*.

reset The process of periodically observing some benchmark reference rate for the purpose of resetting either the floating rate on a floating rate instrument or the floating rate leg of a swap.

reset dates The scheduled dates for resetting the floating rate of interest on swaps, cap and floor options, and other floating rate instruments.

reset frequency The frequency with which a floating rate will be reset. For example, an instrument might reset semiannually, quarterly, or monthly.

reset options, warrants, and notes A provision in an option, warrant, or index-linked note that allows for the strike price to be moved or reset to the then-current asset or index level to which the instrument is linked.

reset risk The risk to the holder of a floating rate instrument that the rate will reset to a lower rate on a reset date or the risk to the issuer of a floating rate instrument that the rate will reset to a higher rate on a reset date.

restricted list A list of securities that employees of an investment bank are not allowed to trade because the investment bank is handling a transaction on behalf of the issuer of those securities. See also *watch list*.

restricted stock Unregistered stock owned by an affiliate or nonaffiliate that was sold in a private transaction by the issuer or the issuer's affiliate. The sale of restricted stock must meet the following requirements:

(1) Current public information must be available regarding the issuer

(2) A two-year holding period must commence upon the acquisition of the securities from the issuer or the issuer's affiliate in a private transaction. The period commences when the securities are paid in full. One who acquires restricted stock from a nonaffiliate in a private transaction can tack onto the holding period of the nonaffiliate, but one who acquires any stock (restricted or nonrestricted) from an affiliate in a private transaction takes on a new two-year period

(3) The number of shares that may be sold by a holder within a three-month period is subject to volume limitations equal to the greater of 1% of the shares of the same class outstanding or the average weekly trading volume (averaged over the prior four calendar weeks). All Rule 144 sales of securities of the same class by or on behalf of a nonaffiliate owner and certain persons related to the owner must be aggregated, and all Rule 144 sales of securities of the same class by or on behalf of an affiliate owner and certain persons

related to the owner must also be aggregated

(4) Sales must be made by the owner to a market maker in the stock or by a broker on behalf of the owner to purchase in unsolicited agency transactions

(5) Form 144 Notice of Sale must be filed with the SEC and the principal exchange (if any) for the stock no later than the day on which the sell order is entered. [Note: Under certain circumstances for certain holders of restricted stock, the restricted stock becomes unrestricted after a holding period that ranges from one to three years, but volume restrictions may apply.]

restrictive covenants Provisions in a bond indenture that restrict the issuer's rights to engage in certain practices.

restructuring (1) A general term that can include any substantive change in the ownership, financing, or operations of a business, often involving some form of expansion, contraction, or realignment of management. (2) The reworking of debtor's obligations usually involving some write-off of debt on the part of the creditors or a reduction in the rate of interest paid to the creditors in order to avoid a worse calamity such as a declaration of bankruptcy by the debtor.

retail market Any market specifically designed to handle securities transactions of a relatively small size and, hence, geared to the individual investor. Contrasts with the wholesale market designed for large trades among institutional investors.

retractable bonds Bonds and notes that contain both an embedded call option (held by the issuer) and an embedded put option (held by the investor) with the same expiry date and the same strike price. If neither side chooses to exercise its option, the bond continues. These are sometimes called *extendable bonds,* but the latter term can have other meanings.

return on assets Often abbreviated *ROA.* A widely used measure of corporate profitability. ROA is defined as the firm's earnings after taxes (i.e., net income) divided by its total assets, usually measured at book value. It is also known as *return on investment* or *ROI.*

return on investment See *return on assets.*

return on risk-adjusted assets Sometimes abbreviated RORA. A relatively new financial ratio introduced to measure a bank's profitability as a function of its risk-weighted assets. It is defined as the ratio of the firm's net income after taxes to its total risk-weighted assets.

revenue bonds Municipal bonds that pledge the revenue from one or more specific sources to meet the interest and principal payments on the bonds. Examples would include bonds that are serviced from the tolls on a specific road, bridge, or tunnel. These bonds are distinct from *general obligation bonds,* which are secured by the general taxing authority of the issuer. Revenue bonds are generally more risky than general obligation bonds.

reversal The act of switching from a fixed rate basis to a floating rate basis or vice versa, usually in conjunction with a swap.

reverse See *reverse repurchase agreement.*

reverse butterfly Also know as a *sandwich spread.* This is the opposite of a butterfly spread. The two middle strikes are purchased and the two end options are sold. See *butterfly spread.*

reverse inquiry An inquiry with respect to the availability of private placement securities. The term stems from the fact that usually an issuer of securities inquires about the availability of private placement investors. In a reverse inquiry, the investors inquire about the availability of securities for purchase.

reverse repo See *reverse repurchase agreement.*

Reverse repurchase agreement Also known as a *reverse* and a *reverse repo.* Sometimes called a *resale.* The opposite of a repurchase agreement. The purchase of a security with the simultaneous agreement to sell it back later at a specific date and price. Reverse repos are widely used by dealers in securities to acquire securities for short sales. One party's repo is another party's resale.

reverse split This is the reverse of a stock split. A number of shares are combined to form a single new share. This most often happens after a corporation's stock price has fallen to a very low value. For example, 20 shares of stock trading at $0.50 might be converted to a single share trading at $10.

reverse-annuity mortgage A mortgage in which a homeowner with substantial equity in his/her home receives periodic payments from a mortgage lending institution. Each such payment represents a reduction in the homeowner's equity and an increase in the mortgage principal. The mortgage is repaid in whole at a single point in time. These mortgages were designed to allow elderly homeowners with little income to monetize their equity in order to remain in their homes longer.

reversible swap A swap that provides for the fixed-rate payer and the floating-rate payer to reverse roles at some time during the life of the swap.

reversion level The level at which a price or rate that has been rising or falling is likely to reverse direction. This assumes that there is a tendency toward some long-term level. Rates that tend to pull back toward their long-term mean are described as *mean reverting*.

revolving line of credit A credit line that can be drawn upon and repaid repeatedly and which remains good for some period of time provided that it has been properly serviced. A revolving line of credit is one type of revolving credit facility.

rho One of the option Greeks. It is defined as the dollar amount by which the value of an option, or an instrument containing an embedded option, would change if there were a change in the rate of interest.

RIBS See *municipal floating-rate bonds*.

riding the yield curve Also known as *rolling down the yield curve*. A bond trading strategy considered attractive in a steeply upwardly sloped yield curve environment. The investor buys a long-dated bond with a high yield and holds it for a time. With the passage of time, the yield declines (assuming no change in the yield curve) as the maturity shortens, causing the price of the bond to rise. At some point, the now shorter-maturity bond is sold, the proceeds are used to buy a new long-dated bond, and the process is repeated.

right Certain options are known as rights. For example, subscription rights are often just called *rights*. The term *right* can be used more generally to refer to any option. See *option*.

right of assignment A right to transfer one's interest in a contractual relationship without seeking permission of the other party to the contract. Rights of assignment often contain provisions that restrict the types of parties to whom the assignment can be made.

right of set off The right to terminate payments on an obligation upon the failure of another party to make its required payments on a contractually separate obligation.

rights issue Also called a *rights offering*. An issuance of subscription rights to holders of existing securities of a corporation. The rights give them the right to buy the underlying for a fixed period of time at a fixed price.

rights offering See *rights issue*.

rising stars A type of high yield bond. These bonds are distinguished from another class of high yield bonds called *fallen angels*. Simply because they lack credit ratings, rising stars are classified as high yield. On the other hand, fallen angels currently have a poor credit rating but at the time of issue had an investment grade rating. See *high yield bonds* for more discussion.

risk averse A dislike of risk. The risk averse individual suffers a loss of utility (called *disutility*) from the presence of risk. The greater the risk the greater the loss of utility. Risk aversion as a description of rational behavior is a tenet of almost all financial theory.

risk equivalent The number of units of one instrument that has exactly the same amount of a certain type of risk as another instrument. For example, if we were long $5 million of a particular corporate bond, analysis might reveal that this position has exactly the same amount of interest rate risk as a long position in $3 million of a particular Treasury bond. Thus, these two positions would be described as risk equivalent with respect to interest rate risk.

risk free Any position in a financial instrument such that the value of the position as of some specific point in the future (called the investment horizon) is known with certainty. That is, there is no possible chance of a deviation from the expected value. This means the instrument is free of market risk (i.e., price risk), credit risk, sovereign risk, and so forth. Note that the definition of a risk-free asset is inseparable from the length of the holder's investment horizon. For example, a one-year Treasury bill is a risk-free asset to an investor with a one-year investment horizon. But, a one-year Treasury bill is not a risk-free asset to an investor with a two-year investment horizon because the one-year rate is uncertain during the second year.

risk horizon The length of time, measured from the present, until a value will be determined such that a profit or loss will be realized. Alternatively, the period of time before the uncertainty surrounding a profit/loss is eliminated. For example, an airline sells a charter today for a flight that is to be flown 30 days from today. The jet fuel necessary to fly the flight will not be purchased until immediately before the flight is made. The time between selling the charter and buying the fuel creates a risk-horizon of 30 days. The profit remains uncertain until the jet fuel is purchased.

risk management The use of financial engineering technology of various sorts to manage the risks associated with financial positions and exposures. These risks include market risk, credit risk, model risk, legal risk, and other forms of financial risk. On a broader plane, risk management encompasses business risks other than financial risk (e.g.,

system risk, obsolescence risk, patent risk, risk of casualties, etc.).

risk neutral pricing In many valuation models, particularly option valuation models, individuals are assumed to behave as though they were risk neutral with respect to volatility risk (i.e., the volatility of market prices). While this may seem to be at odds with the financial tenet of risk aversion, it is not. The investor can combine two assets that are individually risky, in a volatility sense, and produce a portfolio that is risk-free in a volatility sense. As such, the portfolio should return the risk-free rate. Risk neutral pricing does not imply that individuals are risk neutral with respect to other forms of risk, such as credit risk. Risk neutral pricing in a credit sense would imply that the expected yield on a credit-risky debt instrument (such as a corporate bond) should equal the yield on a credit-risk-free bond (such as a Treasury bond) after allowing for the probability and expected recovery rate of a default.

risk premium A return in excess of the risk-free rate that a security should be expected to provide as compensation for the risk associated with the security.

risk profile A visual depiction, by way of a graph, of the financial consequences (i.e., profit and loss) resulting from a change in an asset's price or the value of some underlying index or rate. Very similar in concept to a profit diagram or payoff profile. The term risk profile applies if the graph focuses on the risk exposure. If it focuses on the expected gain, the term profit diagram applies.

risk As used among risk managers, the risk that the enterprise is exposed to risks that the enterprise has not identified and therefore has failed to manage.

risk-adjusted returns Returns that have been adjusted upwards or downwards to account for a level of risk different from that of some benchmark to which the returns will be compared. The performance of portfolio managers is now most often measured on a risk-adjusted basis. Various measures for risk-adjusting include Sharpe's ratio, Treynor's index, and Jensen's alpha.

risk-free rate The rate of interest on a fixed-rate debt obligation that is completely free of credit risk. In the context of zero coupon bonds, the term means that the bonds are also free of reinvestment risk. Risk-free rates are only risk-free in a reinvestment risk sense if the maturity of the instrument precisely matches the investment horizon. Many people use the one-year T-bill rate as the risk-free rate if the investment horizon is exactly one year. In some applications, a term-repo rate is used as the risk-free rate.

risk-weighted asset Part of the bank capital guidelines adopted by the Federal Reserve in January 1989. Obtained by multiplying the credit risk equivalent by a risk-weighting factor. Some quantity of risk exposure is assigned to all positions, including those that might be off balance sheet.

RITES See *municipal floating-rate bonds*.

ROA See *return on assets*.

roadshows Organized marketing presentations of pending securities offerings made to investors and brokers. The marketing presentation is repeated as the roadshow travels from city to city. Roadshows provide an important opportunity for the investor community to learn about pending initial public offerings.

ROI See *return on investment*.

roll back See *backward induction*.

roll down calls See *roll down options*.

roll down options Term includes both *roll down calls* and *roll down puts*. These are options that start out looking like standard calls and puts, but become barrier options if the underlying price reaches a specified level (the roll down strike).

roll down puts See *roll down options*.

roll point A period in time during which some or all of a stack hedge position is lifted in one delivery or expiration month and re-established in a different delivery or expiration month. See *stack and roll hedging*.

roll risk The chance that money will be lost while a stack hedge is being rolled from one delivery/expiration month to a different delivery/expiration month. This can happen if other traders realize the hedger's strategy and position themselves to profit from it. See *stack and roll hedging*.

roll up calls See *roll up options*.

roll up options Term includes both *roll up calls* and *roll up puts*. These are options that start out looking like standard calls and puts, but become barrier options if the underlying price reaches a specified level (the roll up strike).

roll up puts See *roll up options*.

roller coaster swap Two distinct meanings both used in conjunction with interest rate swaps. (1) Any swap in which the notional principal accretes (i.e., increases) for a period and then amortizes (i.e., decreases) to zero over the remainder of its tenor. (2) Any swap in which the roles of the fixed-rate payer and the floating-rate payer periodically reverse. The term roller coaster swap has two meanings because two swap dealers independently introduced the term at about the same time.

rolling call A feature found in some callable bonds allowing them to be called at any time following a certain date. That is, the call feature is continuously available to the issuer following the call date. This is in contrast to a stepped call. See *stepped call* for contrast.

rolling down the yield curve See *riding the yield curve.*

rollover The issuance of new short-term money market securities to fund the retirement of an existing security. Also known as a *refunding;* however, the term *rollover* is usually used in connection with money market instruments while the term *refunding* is often used in connection with longer term debt.

rollover risk The risk that an issuer of a short-term debt obligation, such as commercial paper or certificates of deposit, will be unable to sell new short-term debt obligations to obtain funds to pay off the existing obligations. Rollover risk can be a manifestation of liquidity risk or credit risk.

ROR The rate of return (including current income and capital appreciation) stated on an annual basis.

round lot As the term is used with respect to stock market transactions, a round lot is a transaction involving 100 shares of stock. See also *odd lot.*

RP See *repurchase agreement.*

Rule 144 Two-year holding period and the trading volume requirements pursuant to SEC Rule 144. Rule 144 is part of the Securities Act of 1933, the main purpose of which is to require SEC registration of securities sold to the public. However, registering stock is time consuming and expensive. For this reason, issuing companies often sell unregistered stock privately and often choose not to register control stock and restricted stock for resale to the public. In the absence of registration, the only practical way for holders to sell control stock or restricted stock is in accordance with the requirements of Rule 144 or in a private transaction. See *control stock* and *restricted stock* for details of these two categories and for the rules applicable to sale.

Rule 145 Stock received in connection with a merger, consolidation, or other reorganization by a person who was an affiliate of the disappearing company (and who does not become an affiliate of the surviving company), or stock acquired from such a person by a nonaffiliate of the issuer in a private transaction. Rule 145 stock is subject to some of the same selling restrictions as Rule 144 stock.

Rule 415 See *shelf registration.*

running a book See *warehousing.*

sa Abbreviation meaning an annual rate of interest compounded semi-annually. Usually denoted by lower case letters as sa or s.a.

sale of deep-in-the-money call options A costless yield enhancement strategy to an investor. The investor sells the option, receives cash, retains control of stock, and avoids immediate taxation. The investor has price protection up to the call's strike price and downside protection equal only to the value of the premium received. The investor's upside price exposure is mitigated by the eventual salability of the stock position, but the investor retains the downside stock price risk.

sales credit Part of the gross spread on the underwriting of a security. The sales credit goes to the retail (i.e., sales and trading) side of each firm involved in the offering, on a pro rata basis (i.e., based on the amount of securities sold by each firm). The broker usually receives from 25% to 50% of the sales credit relating to his or her sales, the balance of which goes to the broker's firm. The higher a broker's production level, the higher the "grid" or percent payout he or she can demand. Sales credits are usually paid to brokers monthly.

sale of stock through a structured equity program Provides public corporations, affiliates, and shareholders with a means to sell large amounts of stock over time in a cost-effective, consistent, and quiet manner. Such sales are conducted through an SEC shelf registration.

salvage value The market value of an asset at the time of its disposition. At one time, U.S. depreciation methods required an estimate of the salvage value, defined as the value of the asset at the end of its useful or economic life. Presently, estimates of future salvage value are not required in calculating depreciation.

SAM See *shared appreciation mortgage.*

samurai bonds Bonds issued by non-Japanese corporations but denominated in yen and sold in Japan to Japanese investors. Analogous to *Yankee bonds.*

sandwich spread See *reverse butterfly.*

SAVRS A trademark of Lehman Brothers. See *municipal floating-rate bonds.*

scale The coupon rates on the different maturities of a serial bond as proposed by the underwriters at the time of sale. See *serial bond.*

scalper A trader who holds positions for only a very short period of time in an effort to capture small movements resulting from uneven order flow. That is, he looks to pick up the bounce between the bid and the offer. The term is often used in the futures markets.

scenario analysis A forecast of possible future outcomes based on a set of assumptions concerning the variables that drive the outcome. Scenario analysis can have a variety of purposes, such as to generate value-at-risk estimates, or used to create a corporation's pro forma financial statements. When used to obtain value-at-risk estimates, a Monte Carlo simulation is usually employed, which may be thought of as the outcome of multiple scenarios.

search costs In the context of brokered transactions, the costs, both direct and indirect, of finding a counterparty with matched needs.

seasonal swaps Any type of swap structured to generate a stream of cash flows that offsets the seasonality of the user's cash flows from its normal business operations. Such a swap can be an effective cash management tool.

seasoned With respect to equity and debt securities, securities that have traded for a sufficiently long enough time that the market has revealed their value. The term is often used with respect to foreign sales of securities. Unregistered securities cannot be sold to American investors, but can be sold outside the United States to non-American investors. However, once sufficient time has elapsed (usually defined to be 90 days), the securities are considered seasoned and may be purchased by U.S. investors.

seasoned pools In the mortgage-backed securities market, a seasoned mortgage pool consists of mortgages that are aged at least 12 months.

seasoned public offerings Any public offering of equity securities by a corporation that has already done an initial public offering. Thus, the offering represents a new issuance of securities but not the first issuance of securities. Seasoned public offerings are relatively easy to price compared to initial public offerings because the market has had time to reveal fair value. The term includes two subtypes: a *primary seasoned offering* and a *secondary seasoned offering*. See *primary seasoned offering* and *secondary seasoned offering* for the distinction.

SEC See *Securities and Exchange Commission*.

second generation options These are also known as *exotic options* and *nonstandard options*. They include all variety of options more complex than, or having terms meaningfully different than, standard call and put options. Examples include barrier options, digital options, outperformance options, chooser options, and so forth. See *exotic options*.

secondary initial public offering Sometimes labeled an *SIPO*. A public offering of securities by a formerly private corporation that had at some point in its history been a public corporation. That is, a public corporation that at one time had done an initial public offering but was then taken private. The corporation now goes public for a second time making its public offering a secondary initial public offering. SIPOs often grow out of earlier leveraged buyouts. See *leveraged buyout*.

secondary market The market in which a security or other instrument trades after its initial issue. The initial issue takes place in the primary market. See *primary market*. The secondary market for equities includes both the listed exchange markets and the OTC dealer markets. The secondary market for bonds, in the United States, is largely an OTC dealer market.

secondary seasoned offering The sale of securities held by a principal (often a founder or venture capitalist) in a corporation to the general public through a public offering process. The proceeds of the offering, after deducting the underwriters' discount, go to the party selling the securities not to the corporation. This is in contrast to a *primary seasoned offering* in which the corporation is the issuer. Secondary seasoned offerings and primary seasoned offerings are often done simultaneously, in which case they are called *combined seasoned offerings*.

sector options A type of basket option in which the basket consists of a group of securities drawn from a particular industry sector, such as an option on a technology index.

sector spreads Spread trades between different market sectors. For example, one might go long a Treasury bond and go short a corporate bond of the same maturity if one believes that the credit spread between the corporate bond and the Treasury bond is going to widen.

Or, one might buy an index product on a large cap index, such as the Dow Jones Industrial Average, and sell an index product on a small cap index if one believes that large cap stocks will outperform small cap stocks.

sector warrants Similar to a sector option, but generally of longer duration. See *sector options*.

securities Marketable financial claims on the issuing entity. These instruments may be in either book entry or bearer form and may or may not be evidenced by certificates. The clearest examples include common stock and bonds of corporations, but other sorts of claims can be deemed securities as well. See also *security*.

Securities Act of 1933 (as amended) This legislation (1) requires full disclosure of all material information before a corporation issues securities, (2) requires an annual audit by an independent auditor, and (3) forbids fraudulent and deceptive practices in the sale of securities. Importantly, the law allows the investor to hold responsible the investment banks that underwrote the securities, as well as the corporation that issued the securities, for failure to fully disclose all material information.

Securities and Exchange Commission Commonly known by the acronym *SEC*. An agency created by Congress in 1934 as part of the Securities Exchange Act of 1934. The SEC promulgates the rules governing securities issuance (primarily stocks, bonds, and options), the operation of securities markets, the activities of investment companies, the activities of investment advisors, and such other matters as might be relevant to primary and secondary securities markets in the United States. The SEC's jurisdiction did not extend to futures contracts. Until 1974, the regulation of

the latter was the responsibility of the Agricultural Department. In 1974, Congress passed the Commodity Exchange Act (CEA), which created the Commodity Futures Trading Commission (CFTC) with responsibility for the regulation of the futures industry. In 1982, Congress amended the CEA and the federal securities laws dividing jurisdiction over options and futures contracts on financial instruments between the CFTC and the SEC. Today, the SEC has regulatory jurisdiction over stock options, currency options, certificates of deposit, and stock indexes, among other securities; and over stock and option exchanges.

Securities Exchange Act of 1934 This legislation created the Securities and Exchange Commission, extended disclosure requirements to secondary market transactions, permitted the SEC to regulate the conduct of exchange broker/dealers, gave the Federal Reserve the power to set margin limits on securities transactions, prohibited fraud and price manipulation in the secondary market, and restricted the use of securities as collateral for bank loans.

Securities Industry Association Known by the acronym *SIA*. A professional society for individuals involved in the securities industry.

securitization The process of monetizing a future cash flow stream by using the stream as backing for a security. Securities created in this way are called *asset-backed securities*. This process can allow the original holder of claims to monetize them in order to use the proceeds for more productive purposes. Securitization usually involves the creation of a *special purpose vehicle* that is bankruptcy remote. The SPV serves as the issuer of the asset-backed securities.

security The term is defined in Section 2 (1) of the Securities Act of 1933 and Section 3 (a) (10) of the Securities Exchange Act of 1934 and generally refers to any note, stock, treasury stock, bond, debenture, certificate of interest, or participation in any profit-sharing agreement or any option transaction entered into on a U.S. national securities exchange.

security market line The equation of the capital asset pricing model. Often referred to by its initials SML. The SML forecasts the expected rate of return on a stock or a portfolio of stocks based on the amount of systematic risk associated with the stock or portfolio of stocks, the expected rate of return on the market, and the risk-free rate of interest. The systematic risk is measured by the stock's beta coefficient. See *capital asset pricing model* and *beta coefficient* for more detail.

segmented markets theory Also known as the segmentation theory. A theory of the term structure of interest rates which explains the shape of the yield curve by the existence of distinct markets for debt of different maturities.

self-regulatory organizations Known by the acronym *SRO*. U.S. public marketplaces that regulate themselves under the auspices of the SEC or other regulatory bodies (i.e., national stock exchange and, in the United States, the NASDAQ). Also includes broader industry groups such as the NASD, the NFA, and the MRMB.

sell offs Any of a variety of strategies employed by a firm to dispose of assets by way of a sale of the assets or a transfer of an ownership interest in the assets. The most common forms of sell offs are *spin offs, divestitures,* and *carve-outs*. Spin offs involve partitioning a corporation's assets and operations into several distinct corporations and then giving ownership interests in each of these spin offs to the owners of the original corporation. Divestitures involve the outright sale for cash, or other consideration, of a corporation's assets, divisions, or subsidiaries. Carve-outs are hybrids between spin offs and divestitures.

selling group members Broker/dealers that participate in the distribution of a new issuance of securities but do not bear the underwriters' liability. They earn sales credits for their role, but they do not share in the other components of the gross spread associated with an underwriting.

semiannual Twice yearly.

semiannual bond basis The standard convention for quoting yields on bonds in countries where the standard practice is for bonds to pay semiannual coupons. In this case, the yield on the bond assumes semiannual compounding.

semiannual pay A debt instrument that pays coupons semiannually.

semiannual rate Any annual rate of interest that is paid in two semiannual installments. Not to be confused with a half-year rate which is a rate of interest stated on a six-month basis. Alternatively stated, a nominal annual rate of interest that assumes two compoundings per year.

senior An obligation, usually a debt obligation, that has a senior claim on the assets of the issuer relative to some other obligation. The latter is said to be subordinated, or junior.

sensitivity analysis Similar to scenario analysis, but used to determine how sensitive an outcome is to changes in the value of one of the driver variables.

Separate Trading of Registered Interest and Principal Securities Known by the acronym *STRIPS*. A Treasury program that allows for the separation of coupons and principal on conventional Treasury notes and bonds having original issue maturities of not less than 10 years. The program allows for the efficient creation of zero coupon Treasuries from conventional Treasuries.

serial bond Any bond issue consisting of two or more blocks with each block having a different maturity. Individual blocks may carry the same or different coupons but are all governed by the same prospectus.

serial correlation See *autocorrelation*.

series (1) With respect to bonds, a subset of a mortgage bond issue sharing common features. (2) With respect to options, all options of the same type, written on the same underlying asset, having the same expiration date and the same strike price. (3) With respect to futures, all futures listed on the same exchange and having the same terms, including the same delivery month.

service payments A generic term sometimes used to describe the periodic payments on a bond or swap.

servicing fees Fees earned for providing various ancillary services in connection with mortgages. Ancillary services include such things as collecting monthly mortgage payments, serving notice of delinquency, collecting real estate taxes for escrow, and bringing foreclosure proceedings when necessary.

servicing rights The contractual right to service a debt obligation and collect the associated servicing fees.

settlement (1) In the context of securities (stocks and bonds), the payment and accompanying transfer of ownership that completes a transaction. (2) In futures, the daily mark-to-market with accompanying transfers of variation margin. (3) In swaps and cash settled options, the payment of the cash due on the settlement date under the terms of the derivative contract.

settlement date Several meanings: (1) In securities trading, the date payment for securities is made and the securities are delivered. (2) In futures trading, the date a cash-settled contract is marked to the spot price or index. (3) In swaps and related trading, the date that the cash payment is due.

settlement price In the context of futures and listed options, the price established by the clearinghouse to be used as the basis of the daily mark-to-market of positions in order to determine the variation margin flows.

settlement risk See *delivery risk*.

shadow book A record of investor orders that is kept by the lead manager during an initial public or private offering of securities. It is built from indications of interest from each co-manager. The shadow book provides information on potential demand that allows for a decision on whether to proceed with the offering and provides some guidance in the pricing of the offering.

shared appreciation mortgage Often denoted by the acronym *SAM*. A mortgage made at a below market interest rate but in which capital appreciation is shared between the homeowner and the mortgage lender.

shareholder A person who owns shares of stock in a corporation. This includes holders of common stock and holders of preferred stock. Shareholders are also called stockholders. Stock represents an ownership interest in a corporation.

shark repellent Any of a number of related defensive strategies designed to thwart hostile corporate takeover attempts.

shelf registration Technically known as *Rule 415.* A method of filing a registration statement with the SEC for the issuance of new publicly offered securities so that the issuance can take place in stages over an extended period of time. This has the following advantages: The issuer is allowed to raise funds through securities sales as financing needs arise. He or she avoids both the additional cost of preparing a new issuance and the extended delays associated with receiving SEC approval. Each use of the shelf registration is called a *takedown.*

short Several meanings: (1) In the context of stocks and bonds, a party who is short has borrowed securities from another party and sold the securities in the hope of buying the securities back at a later date at a lower price. (2) In the context of futures and options, a party is said to be short if he or she has sold a futures contract or written an option contract. This differs from a short position in stocks/bonds in that one does not have to borrow a futures or options contract in order to sell it short.

short a swap The floating-rate payer (who is also the fixed-rate receiver) on an interest rate swap. This is in contrast to being long the swap.

short against the box A situation in which the investor fully monetizes restricted or clean stock, locks in the price, has use of the cash proceeds during the time the position is held, and retains control of the stock. The investor

runs the risk of the borrowed stock being called away, but this risk is mitigated by the deliverability of the stock held as collateral.

short an option The position of an option writer.

short call strategy A short position in a call option. Essentially, a bet that the price of the underlying will decline. Short call positions can be used in conjunction with long positions in the underlying, in which case they are called covered calls. See *covered call.*

short hedge A hedge involving a short position in a derivative instrument.

short option value The value of the call option embedded in a PERCS or an ELKS.

short put strategy A short position in a put option. Essentially a bet that the underlying will rise in value and the option writer will reap the option premium.

short sales (1) With respect to securities, sales of borrowed securities. (2) With respect to options and futures, the creation of a position by way of the sale of the instrument. See *short.*

short sell See *short.*

short vega One who would benefit from a decline in the implied volatility of the prices of the assets that underlie an option portfolio.

short volatility Any position in which the position taker will benefit from a decline in the implied volatility of an asset's price. Most often, this means the party is net short options. When implied volatility declines, the value of options declines. All other things being equal, the holder of a short position will generally benefit from a decline in the value of the option. The effect of volatility on option prices is measured by a metric called *vega*. Hence, short volatility is often referred to as *short vega*.

short-dated swaps Swaps with relatively short tenors.

shortfall risk A measure of the likelihood that the actual return on an investment portfolio will fall below some target level. Shortfall risk is measured in a probabilistic sense. For example, if a target return is 10% for the coming year, its shortfall risk is the probability that the actual return will be less 10%.

shout option An option in which the option holder has the right to lock in a minimum value at one and only one point in time over the option's life. This occurs at a time of the holder's choosing. The option may have greater value at expiry than the minimum value but it cannot have less value. In a sense, shout options combine the features of a variety of other exotic options including lookback options, ladder options, and ratchet options.

SIA See *Securities Industry Association.*

sides (of a swap) With respect to a swap, refers to the fixed-rate paying side and the floating-rate paying side. Also called *legs*.

sigma A Greek letter. Lower case sigma (σ) is often used to symbolize "standard deviation." Because the volatility of an option is measured as the "standard deviation of the annual percentage change continuously compounded," the term sigma is often used to refer to an option's volatility. In the context of option Greeks, it is sometimes used to mean the same things as *vega*. Upper case sigma (Σ) is used to mean a summation.

simple interest A method of calculating interest without compounding. Usually stated on an annual basis. When stated on an annual basis, it is equivalent to the effective annual rate of interest.

simulation (Monte Carlo) A statistical process based on probabilities. Simulation can be used to value certain financial instruments and to derive measures of risk (such as value-at-risk) when an analytical model is neither available nor feasible. Essentially, the analyst describes, in a probabilistic sense, the variables that drive value. Then, by employing a random number generator, the analyst obtains one possible value of the subject variable. For example, the value of the underlying asset's price is one of the drivers of the value of an option on the underlying. The underlying asset price is then a driver variable and the option's value is the subject variable. By repeating this process thousands of times, the analyst obtains a great many possible values for the subject variable. From these values, an expected value can be ascertained. Monte Carlo simulation gets its name from its roots in simulating gaming outcomes.

single monthly mortality Known by the acronym *SMM*. Used in the mortgage markets to mean the percentage of the mortgage balance on a pool of mortgages expected to be prepaid during a single month.

sinker See *sinking fund bond.*

sinking fund (1) A provision written into a debt instrument's indenture requiring the gradual amortization of the instrument either by periodic repurchases of portions of the outstanding issue or by deposits to a trust account. (2) Often used to describe an amortization schedule in which a fixed percentage of the principal is amortized each period.

sinking fund bond Any bond or note having a sinking fund provision. Often called a *sinker*. See *sinking fund*.

SIPO See *secondary initial public offering*.

skewness The third moment of a statistical distribution. Certain distributions are symmetrical, in which case the skewness is zero. Others have a tilt to the right (skewed right) or a tilt to the left (skewed left).

skip-day settlement Any settlement that involves one more day than is considered the regular settlement period. For example, in Treasuries, regular settlement is one business day, so a skip-day settlement would be two business days.

slippage See *transaction costs*.

small caps Corporations having a small equity capitalization. The amount of equity capital necessary for a corporation to qualify as a small cap is somewhat arbitrary. See also *capitalization*.

SMM An acronym for single monthly mortality. See *single monthly mortality*.

sovereign risk The risk that an issuer may be barred by its government from making interest and principal payments on its debt. In the context of swaps, the risk that a counterparty will be barred by its government from fulfilling its swap obligations. Sovereign risk is often likened to credit risk, but this can be misleading. Credit risk is usually regarded as a diversifiable form of risk. Sovereign risk is less easily diversified because the counterparty is likely to experience a similar manifestation of it on all contracts with all counterparties within the jurisdiction of the same sovereign. Thus, sovereign risk should be viewed as distinct from credit risk and managed separately from credit risk.

spatial arbitrage Also known as *geographic arbitrage*. Arbitrage that involves the simultaneous purchase and sale of the same asset trading in markets that are geographically isolated from one another (e.g., the purchase of silver in Chicago and the simultaneous sale of silver in New York in order to exploit a price discrepancy between the two markets).

SPDRs Pronounced "spiders." An acronym for Standard & Poor's Depository Receipts. SPDRs were introduced in 1993 by the American Stock Exchange. They are, essentially, pro rata shares in a portfolio that replicates the Standard & Poor's 500 index. Thus one can trade SPDRs as though one were trading the entire S&P index as a unit. The same concept has been used to trade other indexes.

special bracket See *bulge bracket*.

special purpose vehicle An entity, such as a corporation, set up to provide the legal and business framework for some specific purpose. Sometimes called special purpose corporations. When the purpose is to create an investment product having unique investment characteristics, the special purpose vehicle often takes the form of a Unit Trust. When tax benefits are an important objective, the special purpose vehicle will often take the form of a partnership or a limited liability company (LLC). Special purpose vehicles are often designed to be bankruptcy remote, meaning they have a very low likelihood of experiencing bankruptcy. This is useful if the vehicle will be used to issue securities and the sponsor of the vehicle wants the securities to have an investment grade rating.

specialists A type of exchange member responsible for making an orderly market in a designated security, such as a stock or option. Specialists hold orders from brokers on their order book until the orders can be filled. They make a market in the designated securities by quoting both a bid price and an offer price.

specific collateral As the term is used in the repurchase agreement market, a repo in which the borrower must supply the specific Treasury security requested by the lender. This is most likely to be the case when the lender is planning to use the collateral to make delivery on a short sale of the same security.

speculative grade bonds Included among those bonds often called *high yield* or *junk bonds.* These bonds have a less than investment grade rating but are still not in default. Moody's Investor Services gives these bonds less than a Baa rating. Standard & Poor's gives them less than a BBB rating. All these bonds are known as *non–investment grade.*

speculators Persons who take a position in one or more assets in order to exploit a belief that a price is going to rise or fall, or to exploit a view that some relationship is going to change—such as the shape of a yield curve or the size of a credit spread. Speculation differs from arbitrage in that speculation is risky and arbitrage is designed to be risk-free.

spin offs A process by which a corporation divides itself, along functional or regional lines, into several distinct corporations. The owners of the pre-split corporation then receive shares in each of the post-split corporations. They are then free to (1) retain the shares of the several corporations, (2) keep the shares of some spin-offs and sell the shares of

other spin-offs, or (3) sell the shares of all the spin-offs. Spin-offs are one vehicle by which a corporation can dispose of assets or operations that either no longer fit into its long-term strategic plan or need to be shed for legal reasons. There are two subtypes of spin-offs: *split ups,* in which the original corporation ceases to exist, and *split offs,* in which the original parent continues to exist.

split offs See *spin offs.*

split ups See *spin offs.*

spot (1) Can be used to mean the same thing as actuals (see *actuals*). (2) The price in the spot market. See *spot market.*

spot curve Also called *spot rate curve* and *zero coupon curve.* A depiction of the relationship between spot rates and maturities for zero coupon bonds. This curve is usually drawn with respect to risk-free rates derived from sovereign bonds, such as U.S. Treasury bonds.

spot exchange rate Also known as a *spot rate,* but the latter term can also be used to describe a special type of interest rate. The spot exchange rate is the exchange rate quoted for immediate delivery of a currency. As a practical matter, immediate delivery is understood to be two business days. See also *exchange rate.*

spot interest rates Another name for currently prevailing zero coupon interest rates. Technically correct term is spot zero rates, but most often just called *spot rates.*

spot market The market for the immediate purchase or sale of an asset. Also called the *cash market.* The term "immediate" has to be interpreted within the context of the asset involved. For example, immediate delivery of Treasury securities is one business day, currencies is two business days, and common stocks in the United States is three business days.

spot price The price of an asset in the spot or cash market. In other words, the price of an asset for immediate, as opposed to later, delivery.

spot rate Can be a reference to a spot interest rate or to a spot exchange rate, depending on the context. See *spot interest rate* and *spot exchange rate*.

spot rate curve See *spot curve*.

spot volatilities The volatilities used to price a multi-period option, such as a cap or floor, when each component of the cap (caplet) or of the floor (floorlet) employs a different volatility.

spread Several meanings are defined by the context: (1) The difference between the bid price and the ask price (see *bid-ask spread*). (2) Simultaneous long and short positions in options of the same class but having different expiration months. (3) Simultaneous long and short positions in futures written on the same underlying asset (but different delivery months) or different underlying assets (with the same delivery month). (4) The difference between the offering price and the proceeds to the issuer for a public offering that accrues to an underwriter as compensation for its services (called gross spread). (5) The number of basis points added to the Treasury yield curve to determine the swap coupon on a USD interest rate swap. There are other meanings as well.

spread lock A structure that enables the holder to lock in a specific spread over some benchmark index or rate. For example, a spread lock might lock in a

spread of 50 basis points over some specific Treasury bond for a period of 30 days.

Spread options See *spread-lock options*.

spread-lock options Options written on the spread over some specific benchmark rate or index. Such options allow the holder to lock in a spread if the holder decides to exercise the option. The option holder can allow the option to expire should the spread move more favorably in the market. Also known as *spread options*.

spread-lock swap An interest rate swap in which the holder has the right to set the fixed rate leg at some specific number of basis points above some benchmark rate (usually a specific maturity on the Treasury yield curve) for a period of time, or at a specific point in the future. Such spread-locks are often embedded within a *deferred rate-setting swap* (also known as a *delayed rate-setting swap*).

SRO Acronym for a *self-regulatory organization*. See *self-regulatory organizations*.

stabilizing bid A bid price provided by the lead underwriter in an IPO and intended to stabilize the market during the distribution period. The stabilizing bid helps keep the market price from falling during the distribution period thereby facilitating the sale of the securities.

stack and roll hedging A strategy by which a stack hedge is periodically rolled into the next delivery month. See *stack hedge*.

stack hedge A hedge structure that employs a number of futures contracts of a single delivery month to hedge a series of exposures, each corresponding to a different delivery month. For example, the payments on a floating rate note that pays three-month LIBOR quarterly for three years (a total of 12 payments) could be hedged by the issuer by shorting a large number of Eurodollar futures contracts having just one delivery (settlement) date. As that date draws close, the contracts can be offset and a new hedge established in the next delivery month. This is called a roll. This hedge strategy involves considerable basis risk but has the advantage of keeping the hedge in the more liquid front month contracts. See *strip hedge* for contrast.

stakeholders Anyone having a vested interest of some sort in a business. A corporation's stakeholders include the stockholders, the bondholders, the employees, the corporation's customers, the corporation's vendors, the local government, and the federal government.

Standard & Poor's A corporation in the business of formulating and publishing ratings for bonds and other securities to make it easier for investors to judge credit quality. Standard & Poor's also publishes a number of widely quoted and widely watched stock indexes including the S&P 500 and the S&P 100, among others.

standard basket A composite currency such that the value of one unit of the composite currency equals a weighted average of the values of the basket's several currencies.

standard deviation A statistical measure of dispersion around some central value (i.e., dispersion about the mean). Obtained by taking the positive square root of the variance. A true variance or population variance is obtained in three steps: (1) multiply the squared deviations from the mean by the probabilities

of those deviations occurring; (2) sum these products to find the variance; and (3) the square root of this variance is the standard deviation. See *variance.*

standard form agreements Standardized swap contract documentation first published in 1987 by the International Swap Dealers Association (now known as the International Swaps and Derivatives Association). Published in two forms including the Interest Rate Swap Agreement (U.S. dollar contracts only) and the Interest Rate and Currency Exchange Agreement (multi-currency).

standard options See *standardized options.*

standardized options Often used to describe the simplest types of plain vanilla options (i.e., calls and puts). Sometimes used to mean exchange-traded options that are guaranteed by the Options Clearing Corporation (OCC) and therefore free of counterparty risk. This is in contrast to OTC options and warrants. The latter involve some risk that the writer of the option will default and expose the purchaser to counterparty risk.

standstill agreement A contract between a corporation and an individual (or between a corporation and another corporation) in which the latter agrees to refrain from some specific activity for some period of time. Standstill agreements are often coupled with *targeted block repurchases* to terminate a threatened acquisition. Essentially, the corporation agrees to buy back a block of stock that the would-be acquirer has amassed. This buyback takes place at a price above the market price. In return, the would-be acquirer signs a standstill agreement in which it agrees not to purchase the corporation's stock again for some number of years. When a standstill agreement is used together with a targeted block repurchase, the combination is often called *greenmail*.

standstill yield to maturity The annualized rate of return earned on a PERCS, ELKS, or DECS if the underlying common stock's price is unchanged at maturity. The higher the standstill yield to maturity, the better the risk/reward of a PERCS or ELKS relative to owning the underlying common stock.

state Usually a reference to a particular interest rate environment, but can be used in a more general context to mean any given state of the world (e.g., exchange rates, interest rates, employment rates, etc.).

static hedge A hedge that does not have to be changed once it is in place. That is, the position can be held to its planned maturity without changing the quantity of the hedge instrument. This is in contrast to dynamic hedging, which requires periodic adjustments to the size of the hedge to achieve the desired outcome. See *dynamic hedging* for contrast.

static replication The replication of one instrument (the target instrument) by combining several other instruments in a portfolio such that the portfolio will continuously behave exactly like the target instrument without any periodical adjustments to the portfolio's components. This is in contrast to dynamic replication, which requires continuous monitoring and adjusting of the sizes of the portfolio components in order to maintain equivalence with the target instrument.

static spread A measure of the risk premium on a corporate bond relative to Treasury bonds. It is computed by finding the fixed number of basis points that must be added to each spot rate on the Treasury spot rate curve such that

the present value of the corporate bond is equal to its market price. This is less sophisticated than an option-adjusted spread, but more sophisticated than a simple credit spread.

step-down bond (1) Bonds in which the coupon rate is high at first and later steps down to a lower level. (2) Floating rate notes that pay a spread over the reference rate. The spread decreases in a prespecified fashion. For example, the floating coupon might pay LIBOR + 75 bps for the first two years and then step down to LIBOR + 50 bps. In such structures, there can be a number of steps down.

step-down swap Two distinct meanings: (1) An interest rate swap in which the swap coupon (fixed rate) periodically steps down to a new lower level. The other leg is usually LIBOR. (2) A swap in which the notional principal gets smaller at preset points in time or in response to the occurrence of specified events.

stepped call A feature in a callable bond that allows for the bond to be called only on coupon payment dates. This is in contrast to a *rolling call*. Usually with stepped-call bonds, the bond cannot be called during a period of call protection following issuance. See *rolling call* for contrast.

stepped coupon bond A serial bond in which the coupon rate changes annually for all outstanding bonds rather than being uniform over the life of each maturity component within the serial structure.

step-up bonds (1) Bonds in which the coupon rate is low at first (and may even be zero) and later steps up to a higher level. Such bonds are usually callable just prior to the time when the coupon steps up. This creates an incentive for the issuer to call them. (2) Floating rate notes that pay a spread over the reference rate. The spread increases in a prespecified fashion. For example, the floating coupon might pay LIBOR + 50 bps for the first two years and then step up to LIBOR + 75 bps. In such structures, there can be a number of such steps up.

step-up swap Two distinct meanings: (1) An interest rate swap in which the swap coupon (fixed rate) periodically steps up to a new higher level. The other leg is usually LIBOR. (2) A swap in which the notional principal gets larger at preset points in time or in response to the occurrence of specified events.

sticky floater See *ratchet floater.*

stochastic models Models that place a value on future cash flows in which the size, the timing, or both the size and the timing of said cash flows are uncertain. This is in contrast to deterministic models in which future cash flows are certain with respect to both size and timing.

stochastic process An equation that describes or captures the behavior of a stochastic variable and conveys information about its probable future value.

stochastic variables Variables whose future value is uncertain.

stock Equity interests in a corporation. See *common stock* and *preferred stock* for further discussion.

stock basket An index of stocks usually including a relatively small number of constituents (e.g., 5–50 stocks) and representing an industry sector or some narrow market niche.

stock dividend The issuance of additional shares of stock in lieu of a cash dividend. For example, a corporation desiring to pay a $2 dividend on stock trading at $50 (i.e., a 4% dividend yield) could instead issue an investor 4 new shares of stock for every 100 shares the investor holds.

stock index An index formed from a number of stocks and intended to indicate the overall level or performance of the broad stock market or some subset of it. Stock indexes are often used as benchmarks for assessing the performance of portfolio managers. There are two main methods of construction: *price weighting* and *value weighting.* See these terms for further discussion of their methods of computation.

stock option (1) A standardized option written on a specific underlying stock. Such options are listed on option exchanges and trade with standardized terms. They normally cover one round lot of stock (i.e., 100 shares). In the United States, such options are almost always of the American type. There are five exchanges trading stock options within the United States: The Chicago Board Options Exchange, the American Stock Exchange, the Pacific Stock Exchange, the Philadelphia Stock Exchange, and the International Securities Exchange. All such options clear through the Option Clearing Corporation. (2) OTC options written on common stock.

stock split The issuance of additional shares of stock to an individual shareholder and a corresponding reduction in the price of each share so that the value of the position is preserved. A two-for-one stock split would involve the issuance of one new share for each old share that an individual possesses with the reduction in the share price by one half. For example, if an individual held 100 shares of a stock worth $50 a share and the stock split two-for-one, the individual would have 200 shares worth $25 a share. Stock splits often occur after a stock has risen substantially in value. Empirical evidence suggests that abnormal positive returns are associated with stock split announcements.

stock-index futures Futures contracts written on stock indexes. All such contracts are cash settled based on the value of the underlying index at the time of the final settlement. Such futures were first introduced in 1982. Today, such futures exist on the S&P 500 index, the Dow Jones Industrials, the NASDAQ composite, and various other U.S. and non–U.S. stock indexes.

stock-index option Any option written on a stock index. The most heavily traded of such options are calls and puts on the S&P 100, known widely as the OEX.

stop loss order See *stop order*.

stop order Originally called *stop loss orders*. These are orders usually intended to get an investor out of a position when the price of the asset held is moving in a direction contrary to the investor's interests. For example, an investor holding a long position will suffer a loss if the price of the asset declines. In this case, the investor could place a sell stop below the current market price of the asset. If the asset trades at or below the *stop price*, the stop order converts to a market order to liquidate the position before the loss gets any greater. Stop orders can also be used to get an investor into a new position.

stop out bid The highest accepted competitive bid in terms of yield on a competitive auction of debt securities. The term is most often used in connection with the Treasury's periodic auction of bills, notes, and bonds.

stop out price The lowest accepted price on a competitive auction of securities. This is obtained from the stop out bid. See *stop out bid*.

stop price The price that triggers a stop order.

stopping time The expected length of time until the first breaching of a barrier on a barrier option. Stopping time is inversely related to volatility. That is, the greater the volatility of the underlying asset the shorter the stopping time.

storage cost One component of carrying cost. The cost of keeping a commodity in storage stated either on a per unit basis or as a percentage of the commodity's market value.

straddle The most common combination option strategy. A straddle consists of both a call option and a put option written on the same underlying, having the same expiry and the same strike price. Both the call and the put are either held long (called a long straddle) or held short (called a short straddle). Long straddle positions are often used to speculate that volatility will increase (as manifested by a large change in the price of the underlying) relative to the implied volatility embedded in the prices of the straddle's components. Short straddle positions are often used to speculate that the underlying's price will not change much from its current level (i.e., volatility will be lower than that implied by the current prices of the straddle's components).

straight bond A plain vanilla coupon-bearing bond. Straight bonds pay a fixed coupon rate, are non-amortizing, and do not have any embedded optionality (i.e., there are no call or put options embedded within the bond).

straight-line method of depreciation A method of depreciating a capital asset that assigns the same dollar amount of depreciation to the asset each year. There is often an adjustment for the first and last year to account for the fact that the asset may not have been in service for the full year. This is in contrast to accelerated methods of depreciation that take more depreciation expense in the early years and less in the later years. See *modified accelerated cost recovery system* for comparison.

strangle A combination option strategy that involves buying both a call and a put (long strangle) or selling both a call and a put (short strangle). Both options are written on the same underlying and both have the same expiration date. Similar to a straddle, but the call strike is higher than the put strike.

strap A combination option strategy involving two calls and one put on the same underlying with the same expiry and the same strike price. All options are held long (called a long strap) or all options are held short (called a short strap).

strategic asset allocation Generally used to mean a long-term asset allocation strategy to be employed by an investment advisor in the management of a client's assets. It usually specifies some percentage or range of percentages for each asset class in which the investment advisor may invest. For example, the strategic asset allocation might be 55–60% stock and 40–45% bonds. The strategic asset allocation will generally not focus on the mix of industry groups within the stock component or the types or durations of the bonds within the bond component. These latter issues are the realm of *tactical asset allocation*. See *asset allocation* and *tactical asset allocation*.

Street, The The term "the Street" originally referred to all of the member firms of the New York Stock Exchange. Today the term is interpreted to include any firm involved in the securities industry.

Street name Securities that are registered in the name of a brokerage firm rather than in the name of the actual owner of the securities (i.e., the customer of the brokerage firm). Registering securities in Street name makes it much easier to sell the securities because obtaining the beneficial owner's signature is not necessary to transfer ownership. Most securities are held in Street name with a central depository used as custodian of the securities.

stress testing The testing of risk measurement and/or risk management models under extreme market conditions including such things as a sharp increase in the correlations among different variables. The purpose of stress testing is to better understand how risk measures and risk management models might perform during volatile markets in which historic relationships might breakdown.

strike See *strike price*.

strike price Also known as the *exercise price*, the *striking price*, and simply the *strike*. In the case of a call option, the amount that the option holder must pay the option writer for each unit of the underlying asset covered by the option in the event that the option holder (i.e., the party long the option) chooses to exercise the option. In the case of a put option, the amount that the option writer must pay the option holder for each unit of the underlying covered by the option in the event that the option holder (i.e., the party long the option) chooses to exercise the option. The strike price is written into the option contract and is fixed on standardized options. Some non-standard options, however, employ floating strikes.

striking price See *strike price*.

strip (futures) A series of successive contracts of a particular type and their accompanying price structure. The most important is the IMM strip. This is the set of Eurodollar futures traded on the IMM and often used to price swaps and forward rate agreements.

strip (options) A combination option strategy involving two puts and one call on the same underlying with the same expiry and strike. Both are held long (called a long strip) or both are held short (called a short strip).

strip and stack hedging A combination of strip hedging and stack hedging that is used when a strip hedge is desired but cannot be fully implemented because the futures contract series do not go far enough out or there is insufficient liquidity in the back months. For example, a multi-period exposure to jet fuel prices going out say 18 months might be hedgeable in a strip hedge out to 12 months but not beyond. The residual portion of the hedge (i.e., for months 13 through18) could be stack hedged in the futures contract that is 12 months out. See also *strip hedge* and *stack hedge*.

strip hedge A hedge structured to offset a multi-period risk exposure by simultaneously holding hedge positions in a series of successively maturing futures contracts or options contracts. For example, the payments on a floating rate note that pays three-month LIBOR quarterly for three years (a total of 12 payments) could be hedged by the issuer by shorting an appropriate number of Eurodollar futures contracts in each of the 12 successive Eurodollar futures series. Each position hedges one and only one of the payments. This structure is in contrast to a stack and roll hedge. See *stack and roll hedging*. A strip hedge involves less basis risk than a stack and roll hedge but has the disadvantage of requiring portions of the hedge to be in back months (i.e., more forward futures) where there is less liquidity.

stripping Deconstructing a security. That is, breaking the cash flow components associated with a security into their component parts. The best example is removing the coupons from a conventional fixed rate bond to create a collection of zero coupon bonds. See *STRIPS*.

STRIPS An acronym for *Separate Trading of Registered Interest and Principal Securities*. These are generic zero coupon Treasury bonds created by stripping off the coupons from conventional Treasury bonds.

structured finance Financial products and lending facilities that are highly structured. The term is often used to refer to asset-backed securities. Indeed, the term is sometimes used synonymously with asset-backed securities.

structured notes Structured debt securities. See *structured products*.

structured products Financial instruments that are designed or engineered to meet specific financial or investment objectives. Thus, they are engineered to meet the needs of both the issuers and the investors. Such instruments combine traditional securities with various types of derivative instruments including forwards, swaps, and options.

structured shelf and equity distribution program Allows issuers and shareholders to continuously sell large amounts of common stock into the market, at such times and prices as desired, off a shelf registration filed under the SEC's Rule 415. Issuers can raise funds through common stock sales by registering new shares on either an equity shelf registration statement filed with the SEC or the common stock portion of a universal shelf. Control persons and holders of restricted stock or stock received in an acquisition can also sell their holdings using the off-the-shelf transactions.

structuring A nontraditional process of creating and fabricating a wide variety of financial products whose values are linked to or derived from one or more underlying assets, such as equities, bonds, commodities, currencies, or other economic interests.

structuring fees A commission-like fee assessed to a client for structuring a transaction. See also *arrangement fee*.

sub-LIBOR financing The ability of some parties to borrow money on a floating-rate basis at rates below LIBOR. Sub-LIBOR financing is often achieved by synthesizing the floating rate by issuing fixed rate and then using an interest rate swap to swap into floating rate. In some cases, this process can exploit inefficiencies in the market and/or comparative borrowing advantages.

submajors The smallest of the investment banks make up what is called the submajor bracket. While small, they are many. They are also known as *regionals*. In order of size, the largest firms make up the special bracket, the next largest make up the major bracket, and the smallest firms make up the submajor bracket.

subordinated Ranking below another in a hierarchy of claims. See *senior* for contrast.

subordinated debentures A security in which the holder's claims on the assets

of the issuer rank behind the claims of other debt holders for purposes of repayment in the event of liquidation. Debentures are bonds that lack any specific collateral.

subordinated debt Any debt instrument that is subordinated to another debt instrument with respect to the hierarchy of claims on the issuer.

subscription price The strike price contained within a subscription right. See *subscription rights*.

subscription rights Most often called *rights*. A corporation that plans to issue additional shares of stock to raise additional equity capital might first offer the shares to existing shareholders in proportion to their current percentage interest in the corporation's equity. For example, if a corporation has 100 million shares of stock outstanding and decides to issue 10 million new shares, the corporation may offer each existing shareholder the right, but not the obligation, to buy 1 new share for each 10 old shares the investor owns. The offer to buy the stock is made at a fixed price (called the *subscription price*) and is good for a limited time. Subscription rights are similar to call options.

substitution option See *quality option*.

substitution swap A type of bond swap (not a derivative transaction) in which a portfolio manager removes one bond from his portfolio and replaces it with another bond having nearly identical terms and ratings but which is more attractively priced. The substitution of one bond for another has no net effect on the overall characteristics of the bond portfolio but results in some yield pick up.

suitability A determination of the appropriateness of a particular investment for a specific investor. Factors considered include net worth, investment experience, and income. When used with respect to restricted stock transactions, factors considered include an investor's relationship with the company who issued the stock, the number of shares proposed for a transaction, the daily trading volume of the stock, the length of time the stock has been held, the stock's price volatility, and other legal and regulatory constraints.

suitor A corporation that seeks to acquire another corporation (the target) on friendly terms (i.e., a friendly takeover). The term "suitor" is intended to convey the friendly nature of the effort. This is in contrast to a hostile takeover effort in which the acquirer is often referred to as a *raider.*

supervening illegality A change in applicable law, the imposition of foreign exchange controls by a government, or any similar condition such that a counterparty to a financial transaction is prohibited from performing under the terms of the contract.

support bonds See *companion bonds.*

swap (1) In the context of derivatives, a contractual agreement providing for a series of exchanges of cash flows over time in the same or different currencies. At a more general level, the term includes the exchange of fixed-for-floating payments on a given quantity of notionals. See also *interest rate swap, currency swap, commodity swap,* and *equity swap.* (2) In the context of bonds, the sale of one bond having real principal and the purchase of another bond having real principal. This swap is often called a *bond swap* to distinguish it from a derivative swap.

swap assignment The transfer of a counterparty's rights and obligations under a swap agreement to another party. Generally speaking, swaps are not freely assignable. However, language can be included in a swap agreement to allow for assignment under specified circumstances.

swap book A swap dealer's portfolio of swaps. At the beginning of the swap market, swap banks acted in the capacity of swap brokers. That is, they would arrange a swap between two end-user counterparties in exchange for a commission from both counterparties. In the early 1980s, swap banks began to insert themselves between the counterparties, doing a deal with each counterparty independently of the other. In this way, they transformed themselves from swap brokers to swap dealers. The process required dealers to take and hold positions in swaps, called *warehousing* the swaps. The portfolio of swaps that are warehoused constitutes the swap book.

swap broker An agent acting on behalf of one or more end users that finds parties with matching swap needs in exchange for a commission. The swap is then written between the two end users. The swap broker does not become a counterparty to the swap.

swap coupon The fixed rate of interest on the fixed-rate side of an interest rate or currency swap. Determining the fair swap coupon is one of the most important components of running a swap dealing operation. Swap dealers typically quote two swap coupons for each tenor swap. The lower is the dealer's pay rate (sometimes called a bid rate) and the higher is the dealer's receive rate (sometimes called an offer rate). In the case of USD interest rate swaps, the swap coupon is usually quoted as a spread over Treasuries of the same average life.

swap curve A curve depicting the fixed swap coupons that can be swapped for six-month LIBOR for a range of maturities from six months out to many years. The curve is usually drawn with respect to the mid-rate, which is the midpoint between the pay-rate swap coupon and the receive-rate swap coupon. For the market, the swap curve is an average of the mid-rates obtained from many dealers plotted against the maturities of the swaps.

swap dealer Also known as a *market maker*. A financial intermediary that makes a market in swaps and profits from its bid-offer spread. The bid-offer spread is often called a pay-receive spread. Unlike a swap broker, the swap dealer becomes a counterparty to each swap.

swap driven A term loosely used to describe pricing behaviors in non-swap instruments that are influenced through a linkage to the swap market. Examples include price movements in the Eurobond markets.

swap intermediary The broker-dealer or other dealer who structures the transaction, values and prices the cash flows, documents the transaction, and collects fees from one or more counterparties involved in a swap transaction.

swap rate See *swap coupon.*

swap yield curve See *par swap curve and swap curve.*

swaption An option on a swap. The swaption purchaser has the right to enter a specific swap (with all terms prespecified) for a defined period of time. If not exercised by the expiry date, the option expires. Swaptions are most often written on interest rate swaps, but can be written on any type of swap. Swaptions can also be structured to cancel existing swaps. There are two basic types: *payer swaptions* and *receiver swaptions.* See these terms for details.

switch A term used in the United Kingdom to mean a bond swap. See *bond swap.*

switching option A special case of a quality option that allows the substitution of one delivery instrument on a futures contract for another after the close of the market on the last day of trading. See also *quality option.*

syndicate A group of investment banks that buys a new security issue (called underwriting) and then resells the issue to investors. The syndicate is led by a manager, often called the lead underwriter. The syndicate shares the risk that the offering will not be well received. For its services, the syndicate keeps a portion of the proceeds of the sale.

syndicate invitations An offer from the lead manager of a securities offering to join the underwriting or selling group as a comanager or regular member.

synthetic equity A reference to the conversion of the cash flows on a single bond or a debt portfolio into equity-like cash flows by way of an equity swap. For example, an entity holding a specific Treasury bond can enter into a swap in which the entity pays the total return on the Treasury bond and receives the total return on either a specific equity security or an equity index. The total return received by the entity is offset by the total return paid on the swap, leaving only the total return on the equity leg of the swap. As such, the portfolio consisting of the position in the Treasury bond and the position in the swap are mathematically equivalent to having a long position in equity.

The portfolio then constitutes synthetic equity.

synthetic instruments Also known as synthetic securities. Cash flow streams structured to mimic the cash flow stream of some target security. Such streams can be engineered by an appropriate combination or decomposition of other instruments.

synthetic options The replication of option-like payoffs by taking positions in the cash market or the futures market together with positions in the risk-free asset (i.e., Treasury bills) and periodically changing the size of the positions in order to replicate the behavior of the option. Because the strategy requires continuous adjustments to the size of the cash market positions and the risk-free position, the strategy is often called *dynamic asset replication* and sometimes called *dynamic hedging*. The term *dynamic asset allocation* is also used to describe dynamic option replication.

systematic risk The degree to which the fluctuations in value of a financial instrument are associated with fluctuations in the value of the market more generally for instruments of that particular type. This is in contrast to unsystematic risk, which is risk that is specific to a specific instrument and not associated with the market more generally. In the stock market, systematic risk is measured with the aid of *beta coefficients*. In the bond markets, systematic risk is measured with the aid of *durations*.

systemic risk The idea that a complex intertwining of financial positions across thousands of individuals, banks, and corporations could give rise to the possibility that a shock to the financial markets originating with any one of the individuals, banks, or corporations could spill over from one to another until the damage spreads uncontrollably throughout the financial system. Some believe that derivative instruments lay a foundation for future systemic crises in the financial system. Others believe that derivatives have precisely the opposite effect because they are principally used to hedge risk exposures and thus mitigate the impact of shocks to the system.

tack The time remaining on restricted stock before the party granted the stock can sell it. Restricted stock may not be sold for two years after being granted. Another investor taking the stock must hold the stock or *tack* the remainder of the two-year holding period onto any time left before open market sale is permitted. See *restricted stock*.

tactical asset allocation An asset allocation strategy having a shorter focus than strategic asset allocation. For example, the strategic asset allocation strategy may specify that the investment advisor maintain from 55% to 60% of the portfolio in stocks and from 40% to 45% of the portfolio in bonds at all times. Within the stock component, however, the investment advisor would be free to move about within different industry groups (e.g., sell technology stocks and purchase consumer product stocks) and to move among different groups of bonds or bonds with different durations (e.g., sell long duration

Treasury bonds and purchase short du-ration corporate bonds). Tactical asset allocation views opportunities within asset classes over a shorter term than is employed in strategic asset allocation. See also *asset allocation* and *strategic asset allocation*.

tail The difference between the average price and the stop-out price in a competitive auction of securities.

tailing a hedge The term is most often used in conjunction with strip hedging using Eurodollar futures. It refers to the determination of the correct size of the futures hedge in order to properly offset the risk associated with a cash market position. For example, suppose that a corporation has issued a $100 million floating rate note (FRN) paying three-month LIBOR quarterly. The corporation would like to hedge the exposure associated with the payment to be made two years from today by taking a position in Eurodollar futures. To hedge the exposure, the corporation would sell futures. Each futures contract covers $1 million of Eurodollar deposits. At first glance, it would appear that it would take 100 contracts to hedge the exposure associated with the payment to be made two years out, but it actually takes fewer. The reason for this is that changes in a forward LIBOR on a floating rate note have to be discounted to their present value. However, changes in the LIBORs implied by Eurodollar futures do not get discounted. The result is that the dollar value of a single basis point change in a futures contract is larger than the dollar value of a single basis point change in an FRN for the same amount of principal. Thus it takes fewer than 100 futures to hedge the exposure.

take down Also called the take-down concession. The amount of discount that a member of an underwriting syn-dicate is allowed to take in exchange for selling the securities. Also known as a *selling concession*.

takedown See *shelf registration*.

takeover The acquisition of one company by another. If the takeover is part of a negotiated deal between the boards of the two companies, the takeover is said to be friendly. If the takeover involves a tender offer made directly to the target firm's shareholders with the implication that the target firm's senior management will likely lose their jobs, the takeover is generally described as hostile.

target A company that another company seeks to acquire through a takeover effort. The purchasing company is the acquirer (called a *raider* if the effort is hostile and a *suitor* if the effort is friendly) and the company that is to be purchased is called the target.

targeted amortization class bonds Known by the acronym *TACs*. A class of CMO tranches that has a relatively high degree of certainty with respect to the rate of principal amortization. This is possible only because some other class of CMO tranches takes on greater uncertainty with respect to principal amortization. These latter bonds are called *companion bonds*.

targeted block repurchase A decision by a corporation's board of directors to buy back the stock of the corporation held by a specific shareholder, usually at above market price and for the purpose of obtaining a specific agreement from that shareholder. Often associated with greenmail. See *greenmail*.

tax anticipation notes Also known by the acronym *TAN*. Notes issued in anticipation of tax revenues to be collected. These notes are usually retired from the taxes collected.

tax exempt bonds Bonds on which the coupon interest is exempt from federal, state, and local income taxes. The tax exemption does not extend to any capital gain or loss on the sale of the bond. The term "tax exempt" is often confused with "tax-free." In fact, tax exempt instruments afford a lower yield than taxable instruments and this difference represents implicit taxation. Thus, tax exempt bonds are free of explicit, but not implicit, taxation. The term "tax-exempt bond" is sometimes used synonymously with "municipal bond," but this is not wise. Some municipal bonds, especially private purpose issues may, be subject to taxation.

tax exempt swap A swap in which the cash flows have been structured to mimic the cash flows on a tax exempt instrument, such as a municipal bond.

tax-driven swaps Asset-based swaps that are used to alter the tax character of a cash flow stream or to shelter a position from taxation.

Taylor series A process for determining the change in the value of a function resulting from a change in the independent variable by exploiting each of the function's derivatives with respect to that variable (i.e., first derivative, second derivative, third derivatives, etc.). Often called a Taylor series expansion. Frequently, less than all of the derivatives are employed resulting in an approximation of the change in the function's value. This is called a Taylor series approximation.

teaser rate An artificially low (and temporary) initial interest rate on an adjustable-rate mortgage or other adjustable-rate loan. Used to induce borrowers to opt for an adjustable-rate mortgage as opposed to a conventional fixed-rate mortgage.

technical analysis A method of forecasting the future direction of an asset's price based on historical transactions data including, but not limited to, past price data and past volume data. Technical analysis relies on the belief that asset prices trend or form patterns that predict future direction. This is in contrast to fundamental analysis. Technical analysis makes use of charts, moving averages, and various "character of the market" indicators.

TED spread The difference between the interest rate on Treasury bills and the interest rate on Eurodollar deposits of similar maturities. The definition applies to both cash instruments and futures contracts.

temporal arbitrage An arbitrage across time, as opposed to space. For example, one could buy the underlying asset on a futures contract in the cash market and simultaneously sell the futures contract for later delivery. This will lock in a profit if the difference between the futures price and the spot price of the cash commodity exceeds the cost of carrying the asset forward through time.

tender offer An offer made to the holders of a specific security to buy those securities. The tender offer will state the price the offerer is willing to pay, the length of time before the tender offer expires, and any conditions attached to the tender offer. Tender offers are often used as a way to gain control of a public corporation.

tenor The length of the life of a multiperiod derivative instrument such as a cap, a floor, or a swap. Often called the *maturity*.

term Definition depends on context. (1) For bonds, refers to the term to maturity. (2) For options and warrants, refers to the specific period of time that an option or warrant is in effect.

term repo A repurchase agreement having a maturity of 30 days or more.

term structure of default probabilities The probability of default for each year from the present to the end of the life of a bond (or other debt instrument). For example, a B-rated bond might have a 4.5% probability of default in the first year, a 5.2% probability of default in the second year, and so forth. Default probabilities can be stated as marginal, conditional, or cumulative probabilities.

term structure of interest rates The relationship between the maturities of debt instruments and the yields on those debt instruments. The phrase "term structure of interest rates" encompasses all information embedded within the yield/maturity relationship including spot (i.e., zero coupon) interest rates and forward interest rates.

term structure of volatility See *volatility term structure.*

terminal value The value of a financial instrument at its maturity.

termination The cancellation of a swap agreement. Usually involves one party paying the other party a termination fee equal to the mark-to-market value (also known as replacement cost) of the swap. Termination might result from a negotiation leading to mutual consent to terminate, or from the occurrence of a terminating event or an event of default, as defined within the swap contract.

termination clauses Provisions in a swap agreement that provide for the assessment of damages in the event of early termination due to the occurrence of an event of default or a terminating event.

termination date Also known as *maturity date.* The date on which a swap terminates.

termination event Any event other than those indicative of credit problems that results in automatic termination of a swap contract. Unlike an event of default, a termination event terminates only the affected swaps.

terms currency The currency in which an exchange rate is stated. For example, if the price of a euro was stated at $1.0200, then the dollar is the terms currency. The euro would be called the *commodity currency.*

term-to-maturity Also referred to as *term.* The length of time from the present until an instrument matures.

theta (option time decay) The dollar amount by which an option's price changes due to the passage of time. That is, as time passes and the option's time to expiry grows shorter, the option loses value. This loss of value is measured as the option's theta. Theta is one of the risk measures associated with options. Collectively, these risk measures make up the option Greeks.

third generation options See *exotic options.*

third market A reference to over-the-counter trading in securities that are listed on an exchange.

third-party guarantee A situation in which a debt obligation has been guaranteed by a party other than the primary obligor. The obligation of the third party is in addition, and second, to the obligation of the main obligor. Third-party guarantees are a form of credit enhancement.

30/360 A day-count convention for purposes of accruing interest that treats each month as having 30 days and a year as having 360 days. The 31st day of a month does not accrue any interest and the 28th day of February in a non-leap year accrues 3 days' interest. This is the day-count convention employed on corporate bonds, municipal bonds, and agency bonds in the United States. Treasury bonds, however, use an *actual/actual* day count convention.

thrifts Depository institutions other than commercial banks. In the United States, the thrifts consist of savings and loan associations, mutual savings banks, and credit unions. The term derives from the savings function of these institutions.

tick The smallest allowable price change for a traded asset. The term derives from the sound made by a stock ticker-tape machine.

TIGRs See *Treasury Investment Growth Receipts.*

time basis The portion of the difference between the spot price of a cash commodity and a futures price on that same commodity that is attributable to the cost of carry. See also *basis*. The shorter the time to the delivery of the futures, the smaller the time basis.

time decay See *theta.*

time diversification The idea that risky portfolios (i.e., portfolios on which the return is highly volatile from year to year) are less risky if held for long periods because the unusually good years and the unusually bad years tend to cancel each other out over time. Investment advisors generally consider time diversification to be an important factor in investment planning. Some leading academics have argued that time diversification is a fallacy, but others endorse the concept.

time spread See *horizontal spread.*

time to expiration Also called *time to expiry.* The period of time from the present until an option contract expires. Usually stated in terms of years. For example, an option with six months remaining would have a time to expiry of 0.5 years.

time to expiry See *time to expiration.*

time value Two distinct meanings: (1) That portion of an option's premium in excess of the option's intrinsic value. Time value is a function of time to expiration, price volatility of the underlying asset, the amount by which the option is in-the-money, and the level of interest rates. (2) The difference between the present value and the future value of future cash flow.

time value decay The gradual loss of the time value component of an option's premium as time passes and the option grows ever nearer to expiry. At expiry, the time value is zero. Time value decay, also known as *time value erosion,* is decidedly nonlinear with respect to the passage of time. The rate of decay accelerates as the option gets closer to expiry.

time value erosion See *time value decay.*

timing and exercise risk Option contracts should expire on days and at times of day that allow traders to set or unwind hedges. The possibility that foreign holidays and time zone differences may make that impossible represents timing and exercise risk.

timing option The right of the short in some futures contract to choose the point in time when he/she will make delivery of the underlying within some allowable delivery period.

tombstone A published announcement that an offering of securities is being made. The name derives from the announcement's similarity in appearance to a gravestone. The tombstone provides a summary description of the securities, identifies the lead underwriters, and lists the members of the underwriting syndicate who can be contacted to obtain a prospectus.

total return The percentage return on an investment over a given period of time (not necessarily one year) that takes into consideration the current income generated by the instrument (i.e., coupons and/or dividends) and the price appreciation (i.e., gain or loss) where the return is stated as a percentage of the starting value of the investment. For example, if a bond paying a coupon of 8% sa, is purchased for 90 and if at the end of six months the bond is priced at 93, then the total return is 7.78% for the six-month period [(4 + 3) ÷ 90]. Total return can be stated for a multi-year period, in which case it is often called *cumulative total return*. Cumulative total returns usually take into consideration the effect of compounding.

total return swaps Swaps in which the floating leg pays the total return on some specific asset or index. Equity swaps were the earliest type of total return swap. On these swaps, the equity leg paid the total return on an equity index. Later forms of total return swaps included total returns on bonds and bond indexes. A total return swap can pay a total return on both swap legs. For example, one leg might pay the total return on an equity index and the other leg might pay the total return on a bond index. Credit swaps were a 1990s evolutionary product growing out of total return swaps.

tracking error A measure of the deviations of the returns earned by an actual portfolio relative to the returns on some benchmark index portfolio. Tracking error is particularly important when measuring the performance of passively managed portfolios (e.g., index funds).

trademarks In a securities industry context, the name given to the proprietary products of investment banks and commercial banks. The term refers to the fact that these names have been registered with the U.S. Patent & Trademark Office.

trading ahead of a client See *front running*.

trailing floors Put options that protect the value of a cash position should the market price of the cash position decline. The floor is a trailing floor if the put's strike price is adjusted upward when the spot price of the cash position rises. Trailing floors are sometimes built into floating rate notes.

tranche From the French word for "slice." One of two or more instruments governed by the same documentation even though they may have different terms. The term is most often associated with collateralized mortgage obligations (CMO). For example, in the CMO structure, the issuer issues a bond, collateralized by a pool of mortgages. The bond is divided into several distinct tranches. Each tranche receives periodic interest but only one tranche receives principal. When the principal on the first tranche is fully amortized, the tranche terminates and the principal begins to pass to the second tranche, and so forth.

transaction costs The costs associated with engaging in a financial transaction. These include explicit costs (such as commissions and front-end fees) and indirect costs (such as a bid-ask spread and market impact costs). Market impact costs, sometimes called *slippage,* are incurred when large transactions move the price unfavorably for the party trying to buy or sell.

transfer pricing rate Often abbreviated *TRP*. The cost to a department within a bank for intrabank borrowing of funds or securities. Also sometimes called the *cost of carry* although the latter term has other uses as well.

translation exposure The potential to suffer a loss when balance sheet positions are translated from one currency to another. For example, a parent corporation having a foreign subsidiary will ordinarily employ the currency of the subsidiary's country as the subsidiary's functional currency. However, at year-end, the subsidiary's balance sheet must be consolidated into the parent's balance sheet. This requires that the subsidiary's balance sheet positions be translated from the subsidiary's functional currency to the parent's functional currency. This translation can give rise to a gain/loss that is recorded on the parent's balance sheet as an "adjustment arising from the translation of foreign currency."

Treasury bills Also known as *T-bills.* Short-term securities sold at a discount from face value by the U.S. Treasury as part of its ongoing funding operations. Offered in maturities of 13 weeks, 26 weeks, and 52 weeks. Yields on these instruments are quoted on a bank discount basis.

Treasury bond futures Futures contracts on Treasury bonds traded on the Chicago Board of Trade. These contracts are unusual because they allow for the delivery of more than one underlying bond. The exchange publishes a set of numbers called *conversion factors* intended to equalize the values of the different delivery instruments. However, market conditions generally result in one Treasury bond being cheaper for the short to deliver than any other Treasury bond. This bond is called the *cheapest-to-deliver.*

Treasury bonds Also known as *T-bonds.* Long-term coupon-bearing securities sold at periodic auctions by the U.S. Treasury to fund its ongoing operations. Offered in 30-year maturities, although other maturities have been issued from time to time. The yield on these instruments is quoted on a semiannual bond basis.

Treasury coupons A reference to coupon-bearing Treasury securities, which include both Treasury notes and Treasury bonds, to distinguish them from the discounted Treasury products, like Treasury bills.

Treasury Investment Growth Receipts Known by the acronym *TIGRs*. An early Treasury-based zero coupon bond created by Merrill Lynch by stripping the coupons off coupon Treasury bonds, placing them in a trust, and then issuing units in the trust as pro rata claims on the coupons. These units were the TIGRs.

Treasury note futures Similar to Treasury bond futures but written on Treasury notes. See *Treasury bond futures.*

Treasury notes Also known as *T-notes*. Intermediate-term coupon-bearing securities sold at periodic auctions by the U.S. Treasury to fund its ongoing operations. Offered in 2-year, 5-year, and 10-year maturities. Like Treasury bonds, the yield on these instruments is quoted on a semiannual bond basis. Treasury notes and bonds together are sometimes called *Treasury coupons* to distinguish them from discounted instruments like Treasury bills.

Treasury receipts A Treasury-based, generic zero coupon product which has been superseded by the STRIPS program.

treasury stock Shares of stock that a corporation has issued and then repurchased. Such shares remain issued but are not outstanding.

tree A method of depicting the evolution of a price by assuming that the initial value can change to only one of a small number of new values with the passage of each time period. Binomial models employ binomial trees (one value becomes two values) and trinomial models employ trinomial trees (one value becomes three values) Such models are widely used to describe the price evolution of the underlying asset in an attempt to price options.

trigger option See *barrier options*.

triple witching hour A name give to the final hour of trading on days when stock index futures, stock options, and stock index options expire simultaneously. Unusual price behavior has often characterized these time periods, hence the name.

true variance See *variance*.

trust A legal "container" often used to transform the cash flows associated with securities. Essentially, the trust's sponsor deposits securities to the trust or the trust simply purchases securities. These become assets of the trust. The trust then finances the purchased securities by issuing its own debt or equity. Equity interests in a trust are called units. Such a trust structure was used by Merrill Lynch to create the first Treasury-based zero coupon bonds called TIGRs. It was also used by Salomon Brothers to create the first CMOs. Trusts can engage in derivatives transactions to further alter the nature of the cash flows.

trust deed See *indenture*.

trust structures (for restricted stock) Legal "container" into which restricted stock can be deposited or pledged and resold as units to other investors. The original investor retains voting rights, partially monetizes a concentrated equity position, hedges price risk, and defers potential tax payments during the life of the trust.

trust units The securities that represent ownership interests in a trust.

trustee An institution or individual appointed to look after the interests of another institution or individual. Trustees are appointed to look after the interests of the unit holders of trusts, to oversee endowment funds, and to protect the interests of bondholders.

tunnel options A combination of a long (short) cap option and a short (long) floor option to produce a multi-period collar. Tunnel options are usually structured to be zero cost. They are used to place a lower limit on a rate received on a floating rate instrument at the cost of placing an upper limit on the same rate. See also *collar*.

turnover In the context of the mortgage markets, prepayments on mortgages that occur for reasons other than refinancings. This would include prepayments because the home is sold and the mortgage is paid off out of the sale proceeds.

twist risk The potential to suffer financial loss as a consequence of a change in the shape of the yield curve, such as a steepening or a flattening. A specific type of yield curve risk.

two-dollar brokers Persons who own or lease seats on an exchange in order to earn commissions from transacting on behalf of others. Unlike floor brokers, however, two-dollar brokers are independents (i.e., not affiliated with a brokerage house). Instead, they handle overflow volume that regular floor brokers cannot handle in a timely fashion. The term "two dollar broker" stems from the fact that for many years the standard fee paid to these persons was two dollars per trade handled. This is no longer the case, but the name persists.

U.S. Treasury securities Also called Treasurys, sometimes called *governments* and, in market slang, *govies*. The latter two terms are often used to include federal agency securities in addition to those issued by the Treasury. Debt issues of the U.S. Treasury consist primarily of Treasury bills (T-bills), Treasury notes (T-notes), and Treasury bonds (T-bonds).

unbiased expectations theory See *expectations theory*.

underlyer See *underlying asset*.

underlying See *underlying asset*.

underlying asset The asset on which an option, futures, swap, or other derivative is written. The underlying is the source from which the value of the derivative is derived. The underlying asset might be an asset in the usual sense, or it might be a rate (such as an interest or exchange rate), an index value (such as a stock or bond index), or a reference credit (in the case of credit derivatives).

The underlying asset is often simply referred to as the *underlying* or the *underlyer*.

underwriter One who commits to purchase securities from an issuer for a guaranteed price for the purpose of distributing the securities in resale. Generally, an investment banking activity but also practiced, on a limited scale, by commercial banks. More generally, one who assumes another's risk.

underwriter's discount Also called the *gross spread*. The difference between the offering price for securities and the sum promised to the issuer by the underwriter. This sum does not necessarily accrue to the underwriter, who may find it necessary to sell the securities below the offering price.

underwriter's liability The obligations incumbent upon comanagers to share in the pro rata costs of an offering and, more important, in any potential damages claimed by and awarded (through arbitration or legal action) to investors, resulting from material omissions from or misrepresentations in the offering document (i.e., the red herring or the prospectus supplement, if a shelf take-down).

underwriting The process of organizing, registering, marketing, and selling securities by investment banks that oversee the offering process.

underwriting discount See *gross spread.*

underwriting fee Part of the gross spread. The underwriting fee is allocated to cover the lead manager's costs in bringing the deal (i.e., legal, printing, and other offering costs). Any amount over such costs is usually split among the comanagers, along with the management fee, on a negotiated basis.

underwriting spread See *gross spread.*

undivided interest A property in which multiple parties share an ownership interest and, on a pro rata basis, revenues and expenses. Each party may transfer his interest to another party, but the property itself is not physically divisible.

unregistered stock Stock that may not be sold to the public until it is registered with the SEC or otherwise meets an exemption from registration.

unsystematic risk The extent to which the fluctuations in an instrument's value are not associated with fluctuations in the value of the market more generally for instruments of that particular type. As a result, this risk grows progressively smaller as a portfolio becomes more diversified. It is also known as *diversifiable risk, nonsystematic risk,* and *company-specific risk.*

unwind The cancellation of a swap or other over-the-counter derivative prior to its maturity date by the payment of a lump sum by one party to the other. Also known as a *close-out sale.* See also *termination.*

up tick A price change to the upside.

up-and-away options See *up-and-out options.*

up-and-in options A type of barrier option in which the option is activated (i.e., comes into existence) if the underlying's price crosses a prespecified barrier level. The barrier is set above the spot price of the underlying at the time the option is written. Note: If the barrier were set below the spot price, then the option would be called a *down-and-in option.* See also *knock-in options.*

up-and-out options A type of barrier option in which the option extinguishes (i.e., ceases to exist) if the underlying's price crosses a prespecified barrier level. The barrier is set above the spot price of the underlying at the time the option is written. Note: If the barrier were set below the spot price, then the option would be called a *down-and-out.* Up-and-out options are sometimes called *up-and-away options.* See also *knock-out options.*

upstairs market making The securities buying and selling activities engaged in by the trading desks of broker-dealers. This is in contrast to the market-making activities of an exchange floor specialist.

upward sloping yield curve Also called an *ascending yield curve.* The shape of the yield curve when short-maturity instruments have lower yields than long-maturity instruments. Upward sloping yield curves are considered normal in the sense that that shape has prevailed more often than any other.

value date The date a swap or other instrument commences in the sense that it begins to accrue interest. It is also known as the *effective date*.

value diagram A graphic device used to depict the value of a derivative instrument as of some specific date over a range of values for the underlying asset. In the case of options, the profit diagram will differ from the value diagram by the amount of premium paid or received for the option.

value weighting Any weighting scheme that employs value-based weights to determine an index value. For example, some stock indexes are computed using the capitalizations of the various stocks in the index. Larger cap stocks are given more weight in the index than are small cap stocks. Value weighting is also known as *capitalization weighting*.

value-at-risk Also known by the acronym VaR or VAR. Value-at-risk is a measure of risk that boils risk down to a single easy-to-understand number. Simply put, a firm's VaR is the maximum number of dollars that the firm might lose over a specified period of time (called the risk horizon) at a specified level of confidence. A firm's VaR can be measured for different risk horizons and different levels of confidence. It can be measured for a single trader, a single group of traders (a desk), a single division (group of desks), or for the firm as a whole. VaR is used as a risk-monitoring tool but can also be used as a risk management tool. It can be measured in three basic ways: parametric VaR (often called variance-covariance VaR), historic VaR, and simulation VaR (often called Monte Carlo

VaR). Parametric VaR takes a Markowitz-type portfolio approach to measuring VaR. Its major weakness is that it is best suited for linear positions. Options are decidedly nonlinear, so parametric VAR is generally inappropriate for a portfolio having options or embedded options. Historic VaR takes the approach that the future will be similar to the past and is therefore inappropriate if the firm's positions in the future will be different from those in the past and/or the correlations and volatilities are different from what they were in the past. Simulated VaR is based on Monte Carlo–types of simulations in which the value drivers are identified and various paths are simulated. From the results, the change in the value of the firm can be computed. By repeating this process numerous times, one gets a distribution of value changes for the firm, from which the VaR can be estimated.

variable interest rate An interest rate payable on an instrument where said interest rate periodically changes to reflect current market conditions. Such interest rates are pegged to some reference rate. Instruments paying variable rates are also referred to as floating rate and adjustable rate.

variable rate debt See *floating-rate debt*.

variable write See *ratio write*.

variance A widely used statistic that measures deviations from a central or mean value. Often converted to a standard deviation by taking the square root of the variance. Assuming one knows all possible values a random variable might take and the probability associated with each possible value, the variance can be computed by taking each value, subtracting the mean from the value, and then squaring the difference. Each squared difference is then multiplied by the associated probability and the products are summed. The sum is the true variance, also known as the population variance. When all the possible values and/or their associated probabilities are not known, a sample variance can be computed from repeated trials. The sample variance serves as an estimate of the true variance.

variance rate The square of a volatility when the volatility is measured as the annualized standard deviation of the percentage change continuously compounded. See *volatility*.

variance-covariance matrix An array depicting the covariances between different pairs of random variables. Along the columns, the array would contain the names of the variables in sequential order (e.g., X_1, X_2, X_3, etc.). Along the rows, the array would contain the same variable names in the same sequential order (e.g., X_1, X_2, X_3, etc.). At each intersection of a row and a column would be a covariance. For example, where the variables X_1 and X_2 intersect, the number that appears is the covariance between variable X_1 and variable X_2. Along the principal diagonal of the matrix are matched pairs of variables (e.g., X_1 and X_1; X_2 and X_2). The numbers associated with these matched pairs are variances. Variance-covariance matrices are symmetrical. That is, the upper right triangle is the mirror image of the lower left triangle.

variation margin Two meanings: (1) Money added to or subtracted from a futures account to reflect daily changes in the value of the position as a consequence of daily marking-to-market. (2) The amount of margin necessary to bring a futures margin account back to its initial level.

vega One of the option Greeks. Vega is defined as the dollar amount of change in an option's price that would result from a change in the implied volatility of the underlying asset's price. Volatility is measured as the standard deviation of the annual percentage price change continuously compounded. An option's vega gets smaller as the option gets closer to expiry. Vega is also known as *kappa* and is sometimes called *lambda* and *sigma*.

vega neutral A reference to an option portfolio that has been hedged against vega risk so that a change in the implied volatility of the underlying asset does not cause a change in the value of the option portfolio.

venture capitalists Investors or investment firms that provide capital to start-up businesses and/or to businesses early in their developmental or growth stage. Because start ups are usually considered high risk, they generally cannot borrow from banks. Because of their small size and insufficient profitability, they cannot tap the capital markets (i.e., stock and bond markets). Venture capitalists generally demand a substantial equity stake for the financing they provide and look to earn a very high rate of return. The high rate of return is, in part, necessary because many start-up businesses result in a total loss of the investment capital.

vertical bear spread A vertical spread in options in which the spreader is long the higher strike option and short the lower strike option. See *vertical spread* for more general discussion.

vertical bull spread A vertical spread in options in which the spreader is long the lower strike option and short the higher strike option. See *vertical spread* for more detail.

vertical merger A merger of two firms that are in the same industry but which occupy different stages of the production process. For example, if an oil producer merged with an oil refiner, the merger would be described as a vertical merger.

vertical spread Also called a price spread and a money spread. An option position involving simultaneous long and short positions in options of the same class. Both options have the same expiration date but different strike prices.

view Market jargon for a forecast. For example, if a speculator believed that interest rates were likely to fall, he would be inclined to buy bonds. We would say that he is exploiting the view that rates will rise. Views can be far more complex than a forecast of the direction of a price. For example, a bond trader might have a view on the future shape of the yield curve, or on the size of the credit spread between risky corporate bonds and risk-free Treasury bonds. An option trader might have a view on future volatility of the underlying asset.

VIX Abbreviation for CBOE volatility index. A volatility index that provides a value for the market's perceived volatility for a stock index where the value of the volatility index represents the implied volatility of a synthetic at-the-money option with a constant maturity (i.e., a constant time to expiry). This is accomplished using a matrix approach that weights the implied volatilities of out-of-the-money and in-the-money options and the implied volatilites of far and near options. From these values, the desired volatility is synthesized.

vol As used in option pricing, a vol is the standard deviation of the annual percentage change continuously compounded. Because vol is a percentage, it would be correct to say, for example, the vol is 13%. However, market convention is to drop the % symbol and just say, for example, the "vol is 13," in which case the percent symbol is understood. Note: vol is derived from the term volatility unit.

volatility A measure of the frequency and intensity of changes in an asset price or a rate. Volatility can be measured in a number of ways but, for purposes of valuing an option or an instrument containing an embedded option, volatility is usually measured as the standard deviation of the annual percentage change when that percentage is continuously compounded. Volatility can be measured from historic data to get an *historic volatility* or it can be extracted from the price of an option with the use of an appropriate option pricing model to get an *implied volatility*.

volatility matrix A table depicting the implied volatilities for a particular class of options written on a particular underlying where both the strike prices and the time to expiry are allowed to vary. This same information can be presented in graphical form, in which case it is called a *volatility surface*. See also *volatility surface*.

volatility skew A volatility smile in which the plot is not symmetrical. That is, the implied volatilities are extracted from a number of options on the same underlying with the same expiration date but with different strike prices. If a plot of the implied volatilities (vertical axis) against the strike prices (horizontal axis) is asymmetric, the volatility smile is referred to as a volatility skew. See also *volatility smile*.

volatility smile When implied volatilities are extracted from a number of options written on the same underlying and having the same expiration but different strike prices, the implied volatilities are often different. It is common for the at-the-money option to have a lower implied volatility than both the in-the-money options and the out-of-the-money options. When graphed, this gives rise to a curve that is lower in the center and higher at the ends, hence the reference to a smile. The plot is not always symmetric. When it is asymmetric, the volatility smile is often called a volatility skew. See also *volatility skew*.

volatility spreads The difference between the price an option can be sold for and the price at which a hedge can be purchased to partially or fully offset the risk of the option.

volatility surface A visual depiction of the implied volatilities associated with all the options of a single class written on the same underlying asset but with different strike prices and different expiration dates. In essence, it combines a volatility smile with volatility term structure to produce a three-dimensional depiction. This same information can be depicted in a matrix form, in which case it is called a *volatility matrix*. See also *volatility smile* and *volatility term structure*.

volatility swaps A type of derivative contract in which one party pays a sum based on the realized volatility in the market price of some asset and the other party pays a fixed sum. The realized volatility is based on historic performance over the life of the swap.

volatility term structure Also known as the *term structure of volatility*. A visual depiction of the implied volatilities associated with a given class of options written on the same underlying and having the same strike price (usually at-the-money) but different times to expiry.

volatility unit See *vol*.

vulture capitalists Individuals who invest in the securities of troubled companies or other securities whose values are significantly depressed. Closely related are the terms *bottom fisher* and *grave dancer*.

warehouse receipts Documentation representing ownership of goods (including commodities) held in a public warehouse. Often used as the mechanism for transferring ownership of stored commodities. The transfer of warehouse receipts is the customary manner in which commodities are delivered on commodity futures contracts.

warehousing Also called *running a book*. Refers to the act of managing a portfolio of some specific type of instrument. Warehousing swaps, for example, means holding a portfolio of swaps without making an attempt to offset each swap with an identical swap having mirror image terms.

warrant valuation The value of a warrant can be analyzed using standard option pricing parameters (strike, interest rate, dividend/coupon rate, term, volatility, and underlying security price).

However, since the credit backing a warrant obligation is of a specific issuer and not an exchange or clearinghouse (which is usually considered to be a risk-free rate), the borrowing rate of the issuing or guaranteeing corporation must be reflected in the valuation.

warrants The economic equivalent of owning the underlying asset in the form of long-term options that can be privately issued or listed on worldwide stock exchanges. Unlike standard listed options, which are guaranteed by an exchange or clearinghouse, warrants are backed by the credit of the issuer. Warrants are often sold as part of a package that might contain common stock and warrants, preferred stock and warrants, or a bond and warrants. When sold as a package, the warrants are often detachable (i.e., they can be separated from the other components of the package and traded separately).

watch list A list of corporations that an investment bank is negotiating deals with or engaged in business on behalf of. Employees of these investment banks are not allowed to trade securities on the watch list if they are privy to information concerning the relationship. A more restrictive form is called a *restricted list*. This is a list of companies that the investment bank is acting on behalf of and none of the investment bank's employees may trade the securities of these companies.

WEBS An acronym for *world equity benchmark shares*. They are similar in design to SPDRs but are based on the Morgan Stanley world equity index and allow an investor to trade a world benchmark as a single unit.

weighted-average coupon The weighted average of the coupon rates on a bond portfolio where the weights on each bond are the percentage of the par value of the overall portfolio represented by each bond. The term is also used in the context of a pool of mortgages in which case the weighted average coupon is the average coupon of the different mortgages included in the pool where the weight on each mortgage is obtained from that mortgage's outstanding balance relative to the outstanding balance of the entire mortgage pool.

weighted-average maturity Can be used for either a portfolio of bonds or a pool of mortgages. It is the average maturity of the portfolio or pool formed by taking the remaining maturity of each of the components of the portfolio or pool and weighting by the par value or principal outstanding as a percentage of the total portfolio par value or total mortgage principal outstanding.

when issued market Also known as the *wi market*. The term is often used with respect to Treasury securities that begin trading before they are actually issued. The Treasury announces the size and date of the issuance prior to the issuance and then accepts competitive bids. The issue, however, begins trading in the secondary market before the primary market transaction has taken place. Treasury securities trading in the secondary market prior to issuance are called *when issued securities*. The term can also be applied to other securities that are trading subsequent to announcement of a forthcoming issuance but prior to actual issuance.

when issued securities See *when issued market*.

white knight A corporation that agrees to a friendly takeover of another corporation (i.e., the target) in order to prevent the target corporation from being taken over by a different would-be acquirer via a hostile takeover.

wholesale market Any financial market specifically geared to handling large transactions in order to service the institutional investor. This is in contrast to a retail market that is intended for small transactions usually involving individuals.

wi market See *when issued market*.

Wiener process A type of stochastic process in which each successive change in the random variable is normally distributed with a mean of zero and a variance equal to the length of time over which the change takes place.

wild card option Certain futures contracts involve a gap between the time the market closes for the day and the time at which the short must notify the clearinghouse of the short's intention to deliver (should the short choose to do so). The short can deliver at the day's settlement price even if the decision to exercise is made later in the day. Because it is possible for new information to develop, the short has, essentially, a fixed price at which it can exercise its decision to deliver. This opportunity to benefit from this fixed price is called the *wild card option*. It is sometimes called a *wild card play*.

wild card play See *wild card option*.

workout The process of resolving the debts and other issues associated with a financially troubled firm. Often involves creditors accepting a settlement that represents less than the full amount that is owed them. See *recovery rate*.

worse-of options Also known as *alternative options*, but this latter term also includes better-of options. Options that pay off based on the worst performing of several assets or indexes. The payoff would be given by $min[S_1, S_2, S_3,...,S_n]$. Where $min[\ ]$ denotes the min function and S_i denotes the ith underlying at the time of option expiration. This is in contrast to a better-of option. For contrast, see *better-of option*.

writer The person who sells an option, provided that he did not already own the option. That is, the person who, by selling the option, participates in its creation. A writer is said to be short the option. Writers of options are also known as *grantors*, but the latter term is more common in Europe than the United States.

Yankee bonds Bonds issued by non-U.S. corporations but denominated in dollars and sold to American investors in the United States. Counterparts exist in other countries. See, for example, *samurai bonds* and *bulldogs*.

yield (1) Used in a general sense to refer to the annual rate of return (expressed as a percentage) on a financial instrument. In this usage, the rate can refer to any yield measure that is customary for quoting the instrument in question. (2) More narrowly, used to mean the *yield-to-maturity* when a bond is a straight bond and the *yield-to-worst* when the bond has embedded options.

yield beta The historic change in the yield of one instrument (subject instrument) divided by the historic change in the yield of another instrument (usually a benchmark instrument). Obtained by a regression of the former on the latter. For example, a yield beta of 0.8 implies that when there is a 1 basis point change in the yield on the benchmark instrument, there is only a 0.8 basis point change in the yield on the subject instrument.

yield curve A graphic portrayal of the relationship between the yields-to-maturity on conventional bonds of a given risk class and the terms-to-maturity of those same bonds. The benchmark yield curve is usually drawn with respect to bond issues of the sovereign government. In the United States the benchmark yield curve is drawn with respect to Treasury bonds. See also *term structure of interest rates*.

yield curve options Options that allow an investor to exploit a view that the shape of the yield curve will change. They are most often structured to pay off the difference between the yields for two different bonds on the benchmark yield curve. For example, a yield curve option might be structured to pay off as follows:

$$max[1/2 \times \{(y_{10} - y_2) - 50 \text{ bps}\}, 0] \times NP$$

where y_{10} denotes the yield on the 10-year Treasury and y_2 denotes the yield on the 2-year Treasury, both observed as of some specific future date (e.g., the option's expiration date). This equation says that if the yield on the 10-year bond exceeds the yield on the 2-year bond by at least 50 basis points, the bond will have a positive pay off. If not, the bond pays nothing. Note that the payoff is based on half the yield differential because the yields are quoted on the assumption of a semiannual payment frequency. Also note that the size of the payoff is a function of the notional principal (NP) on which the option is written. Yield curve options can

be structured to be of the average price variety so that the payoff is based on the difference between the average yield on the 10-year bond and the average yield on the 2-year bond as observed over some period of time.

yield curve risk The risk that there will be a shift in the yield curve or a change in the slope of the yield curve. The latter is sometimes called *twist risk*.

yield curve swaps An interest rate swap in which both legs are floating. One leg is periodically reset to the yield on a constant maturity Treasury bond having a relatively short maturity (say 2 years) and the other leg is periodically reset to the yield on a constant maturity Treasury bond having a relatively long maturity (say 10 years). These types of swaps can be used to exploit a view on the future shape of the yield curve. For example, if a party believes that the yield curve is going to flatten, he would want to pay the yield on the 10-year bond and receive the yield on the 2-year bond. Yield curve swaps can be constructed from two constant maturity Treasury swaps (i.e., CMT swaps).

yield enhancement The term is most often used to mean the creation of a synthetic security that has the same investment characteristics as the real security but provides a yield in excess of that provided by the real security. It is sometimes possible, for example, to synthesize a Treasury bill by selling a futures contract short and simultaneously buying the underlying asset. Together these positions replicate a T-bill. This would only make sense if the yield on the synthetic instrument exceeds the yield on the real instrument—which implies the existence of an arbitrage opportunity.

yield spread The difference between the yields on two instruments. The two instruments could be of the same asset class but have different maturities (a *maturity spread*) or have the same maturity but belong to different asset classes (a *credit spread*). See *maturity spread* and *credit spread* for more detail.

yield-to-call The discount rate that equates the present value of the cash flow stream associated with an instrument (usually a bond) through one of the instrument's call dates. The calculation must use the call price as the redemption amount in lieu of the instrument's par value. An instrument will have as many yields-to-call as it has call dates.

yield-to-maturity Also called *yield*. The discount rate that equates the present value of the cash flow stream associated with an instrument (usually a bond) through its maturity date to the bond's current market price. This calculation assumes that cash flows can be reinvested to earn the same rate.

yield-to-workout A collective term that incorporates all of a bond's yields-to-call and its yield-to-maturity.

yield-to-worst The lowest of all of a bond's yields-to-workout. Also known as the *promised yield*.

"you choose" options and warrants See *chooser option*.

Z bond A tranche of a CMO that behaves, at least for a time, like a zero coupon bond. Also known as an *accrual bond* and as an *accretion bond*. See *accretion bond*.

zebra basis risk swap See *actual rate swap*.

zebra swap See *actual rate swap*.

zero See *zero coupon bond*.

zero coupon bond Also called a *zero*. A bond that does not pay periodic coupons. In lieu of periodic coupons, such bonds are sold at a steep discount from par and redeemed at par. Zero coupon bonds were first synthesized by Merrill Lynch in 1977 by stripping coupons from conventional coupon bonds and placing them in trusts. Units in these trusts, called Treasury Investment Growth Receipts (TIGRs), were

then sold to investors. This structure was copied by other banks. In 1982, the U.S. Treasury launched the STRIPS programs to allow banks to streamline the stripping of coupons from bonds for purposes of creating zero coupon bonds.

zero coupon curve See *spot curve*.

zero coupon yield curve A graphic portrayal of the relationship between zero coupon rates (also called spot rates) and maturity when the instruments involved are zero coupon bonds. Usually drawn for Treasury-based zeros. Also known as a spot curve. This curve can be derived from conventional coupon-bearing bonds via an iterative procedure called *bootstrapping*. See *spot curve*.

zero coupon-for-fixed swap A variant of the fixed-for-floating interest rate swap in which the floating rate paying party does not pay the periodically observed reference rate but continues to receive the fixed rate. Instead of the normal floating payment, the floating rate of interest accumulates with compounding and is paid in a lump sum at the maturity of the swap.

zero coupon-for-floating swap A variant of the fixed-for-floating interest-rate swap in which the fixed-rate paying party does not pay a periodic coupon but instead pays all coupon interest, after compounding, upon the maturity of the swap. Such swaps can be used to create synthetic zero coupon bonds by coupling them to a rollover strategy employing short-term money market instruments.

zero tick A transaction made at the same price as the previous transaction in the same asset. If a zero tick follows an up tick, the tick is often referred to as a zero up tick. Similarly, if the tick follows a down tick, the tick is often referred to as a zero down tick.

zero-cost collar A combination of a short call (or cap) and a long put (or floor), such that the premium collected from the sale of the call exactly equals the premium paid for the put. These positions together make up the zero-cost collar. However, the presumption is usually that the purchaser of the collar also holds a long position in the underlying. The structure has a variety of other names including *forward band* and *min-max structure*. See also specific types of zero-cost collars such as for floating rate instruments and for equity.

zero-cost collar (equity) Frequently, investors holding large positions in a specific corporation's stock may wish to reduce their exposure to the unsystematic risk associated with the security. The most direct way to do this is simply to sell a portion of the position and invest the proceeds elsewhere. However, there may be good reasons why this is not a desirable solution (a sale might result in a large capital gains tax, or in the loss of voting rights necessary to retain control, or in a negative signaling effect). Alternatively, the investor might be prohibited from selling the stock because the stock is restricted or controlled. In order to avoid "constructive sales" rules that might apply if the investor did a short against the box or employed an equity swap to convert the character of the return to some other form, the investor can simply wrap a collar around the position. This collar would involve purchasing a put option with a strike below the current price of the stock and writing a call option with a strike above the current price of the stock. The strikes would be set so that the premium received from the sale of the call would equal the premium paid for the put.

zero-cost collar (floating rate instrument) A combination of a call option and a put option (if multi-period, may be a cap and a floor instead of a call and a put) such that protection on the downside is purchased at the expense of surrendering upside beyond a certain level. The put/floor strike and the call/cap strike are set so that the premium paid for the put/floor is exactly equal to the premium received from the sale of the call/cap. This is what makes the structure "zero cost." See also *collars*.

zero-premium option A general term referring to any option in which there is no premium, either because the option provides for some form of profit sharing with the writer of the option or because another option is sold and the premium of the option purchased is fully offset by the premium of the option sold.

zero-sum game An economic term used to describe any type of financial transaction in which the profits to the winners exactly equal the losses of the losers. Futures and options trading are examples of zero-sum games if one ignores transaction costs. So are most forms of gambling.

Appendices

ABBREVIATIONS/ACRONYMS

for Security and Futures Exchanges

Agrarische Termijnmarkt Amsterdam (ATA)
American Stock Exchange (AMEX)
Australian Financial Futures Market (AFFM)
Australian Options Market (AOM)
Australian Stock Exchange (ASX)
Beijing Commodity Exchange (BCE)
Belgian Futures & Options Exchange (BELFOX)
Bolsa de Mercadorias y Futuros, Brazil (BM&F)
Bolsa de Valores do Rio de Janeiro (BVRJ)
Chicago Board of Trade (CBOT)
Chicago Board Options Exchange (CBOE)
Chicago Mercantile Exchange (CME)
Coffee, Sugar & Cocoa Exchange, New York (CSCE)
Commodity Exchange, New York (COMEX)
Copenhagen Stock Exchange (FUTOP)
Deutsche Termin Borse (DTB)
European Options Exchange (EOE)
Financial Instrument Exchange (FINEX)
Financiele Termijnmarkt Amsterdam (FTA)
Finnish Options Market (FOM)
Garantifonden for Danske Optioner og Futures (FUTOP)
Hong Kong Futures Exchange (HKFE)
International Markets Index (IMI)
International Petroleum Exchange, London (IPE)
International Securities Exchange (ISE)
International Stock Exchange of London (ISE)
Irish Futures & Options Exchange (IFOX)
Kansas City Board of Trade (KCBT)
Kobe Rubber Exchange (KRE)
Kuala Lumpur Commodity Exchange (KLCE)
London Commodity Exchange (LCE)
London International Financial Futures and Options Exchange (LIFFE)
London Metal Exchange (LME)

London Securities and Derivatives Exchange (OMLX)
Major Market Index (MMI)
Manila International Futures Exchange (MIFE)
Marche a Terme International de France (MATIF)
Marche des Options Negociables de Paris (MONEP)
MEFF Renta Fija and Variable, Spain (MEFF)
Mercado de Futuros y Opciones S.A., Argentina (MERFOX)
Mercato Italiano Futures (MIF)
MidAmerica Commodity Exchange (MidAm)
Minneapolis Grain Exchange (MGE)
Montreal Exchange (ME)
Nagoya Stock Exchange (NSE)
New York Cotton Exchange (NYCE)
New York Futures Exchange (NYFE)
New York Mercantile Exchange (NYMEX)
New York Stock Exchange (NYSE)
New Zealand Futures & Options Exchange (NZFOE)
OM Stockholm Fond AB (OM)
Osaka Grain Exchange (OGE)
Osaka Securities Exchange (OSA)
Oslo Stock Exchange (OSLO)
Osterreichische Terminund Optionborse (OTOB)
OTOB Aktiengesellschaft Austria (OTOB)
Pacific Stock Exchange (PSE)
Philadelphia Stock Exchange (PHLX)
Singapore International Monetary Exchange (SIMEX)
South Africa Futures Exchange (SAFEX)
Stockholm Options Market (OM)
Swiss Options & Financial Futures Exchange (SOFFEX)
Sydney Futures Exchange (SFE)
Tel Aviv Stock Exchange (TASE)
Tokyo Commodity Exchange (TOCOM)
Tokyo Grain Exchange (TGE)
Tokyo International Financial Futures Exchange (TIFFE)
Toronto Futures Exchange (TFE)
Toronto Stock Exchange (TSE)
Vancouver Stock Exchange (VSE)
Winnipeg Commodity Exchange (WCE)

 **PPENDIX A**

Fixed Income Analytics:
Forward Rates, Spot Rates, and
Option Adjusted Spreads

 INTRODUCTION

Fixed income analytics has advanced considerably over the past two decades and today represents a significant part of the toolkit of the modern financial engineer. At the heart of much of the new analytics are better ways to value bonds using spot rates and forward rates. These new bond valuation methodologies have been combined with option analytics to address the complexities introduced when fixed income securities contain embedded options.

One of the most important of these new tools is option adjusted spread, or OAS, analysis. It is very useful for assessing the incremental return on a bond or other fixed income security for the purpose of ascertaining whether said incremental return is sufficient compensation for the credit risk associated with the bond. Earlier measures, such as yield-to-worst, have been difficult to interpret and often produced inconsistent and unstable results.

Examples of instruments that contain embedded options include callable bonds, puttable bonds, convertible bonds, most structured securities, mortgages, and mortgage-backed securities such as collateralized-mortgage obligations (CMOs) and passthrough certificates. Indeed, the prepayment options embedded in traditional fixed-rate mortgages are one of the most difficult types of options to understand, making the valuation of mortgage-backed securities problematic at best. This is one of the reasons that mortgage-backed securities (MBS) have been at the center of many large losses reported by financial institutions and fixed income portfolio managers over the last decade. It is also the reason that OAS analysis initially became popular among buyers and sellers of MBS.

In order to appreciate the benefits of OAS analysis as a way to measure incremental return, one should first understand the difficulties associated with the traditional approach to analyzing fixed income securities having embedded options (called embedded optionality). For this reason we begin our tutorial by reviewing basic concepts associated with measuring incremental return and interest rate risk. These concepts are initially applied to straight bonds, i.e., bonds having no embedded optionality, and then reapplied to bonds having embedded optionality. This exercise will reveal the inherent shortcomings of applying traditional approaches to valuing fixed income securities with embedded optionality. We then introduce the necessary concepts for understanding OAS analysis including spot zero rates, forward rates, and short rates. Finally, we combine these concepts with techniques developed to value options. What emerges is OAS analysis.

OAS analysis can be used to measure the incremental return and to assess the interest rate risk associated with a bond that does not contain embedded options. In this case, however, the results are not meaningfully different from more traditional measures. Nevertheless, the fact that OAS is always applicable—while more traditional methodologies are only truly applicable in the absence of embedded options—suggests that OAS is destined to become the standard method for assessing incremental return and interest rate risk.

All terms used in this paper will be defined as simply and clearly as possible. The authors apologize for the somewhat pedantic result. Throughout this article we will refer to the fixed income security as a "bond" and we will use a callable bond to illustrate the OAS analysis. One of the most widely employed analytic resources for calculating OAS for bonds is Bloomberg. For this reason the terminology employed in this paper and the analytical process described are drawn largely from Bloomberg publications. We will illustrate the process making use of rather simple assumptions. The reader is forewarned that actual OAS models often invoke considerably more complex assumptions than are employed in this paper.

ADVANTAGES OF OAS ANALYSIS

There are at least three advantages of OAS analysis:

- Relative to other approaches, OAS provides a more comprehensive and more reliable measure of the risk premium associated with risky non-bullet bonds—bonds that are not scheduled to return all of their principal in a single lump sum at maturity but instead return principal periodically throughout the bond's life, e.g., a bond with amortizing principal;
- OAS provides a rational basis for valuing the options embedded in many bonds;
- OAS leads to more stable and more reliable measures of interest rate risk associated with bonds having embedded options, relative to traditional methods. At the same time, these measures are analogous to and consistent with more traditional measures of interest rate risk applicable to bullet bonds—bonds that pay their full principal at maturity.

THE EVOLUTION OF BOND VALUATION METHODOLOGIES

To fully appreciate the OAS approach we first need to review the evolution of bond valuation. The evolution of bond valuation has had three major stages:

yield-to-workout methodology, spot rate methodology, and option adjusted spread methodology. The first two stages are reviewed here in section 3, while OAS analysis is tackled in section 4. Initially, however, an understanding of the different types of bonds is required.

TYPES OF BONDS

Bullet bond: A conventional bond paying a fixed periodic coupon and having no embedded optionality. Such bonds are nonamortizing, i.e., the principal remains the same throughout the life of the bond and is repaid in its entirety at maturity. Bullet bonds are also called straight bonds. In the United States such bonds usually pay a semiannual coupon. The coupon rate (CR) is stated as an annual rate (usually with semiannual compounding) and paid on the bond's par value (Par). Thus, a single coupon payment is equal to $1/2 \times CR \times Par$.

Benchmark bullet bond: A bullet bond issued by the sovereign government and assumed to have no credit risk (e.g., Treasury bond).

Non-benchmark bullet bond: A bullet bond issued by an entity other than the sovereign and which, therefore, has some credit risk.

Callable bond: A bond where the issuer has the right, but not the obligation, to call back/repurchase the bond at one or more specified points over the bond's life. If called, the issuer pays the investor the pre-specified call price. The call price is usually higher than the bond's par value. The difference between the call price and par value is called the call premium.

Zero coupon bonds: Zero coupon bonds do not pay periodic coupons. These bonds generate one and only one cash flow at some point in the future. This sum is received when the bond is redeemed at maturity. For example, a six-month zero produces one cash flow when the bond matures six months from today. Because they do not pay periodic coupons, zero coupon bonds always trade at a discount from their par value. The discount rate that equates the redemption value of the zero coupon bond to its current market price is called the bond's spot zero rate. This rate is often called the zero rate or spot rate. Spot zero rates must be distinguished from forward zero rates, which are rates expected to prevail on zero coupon bonds at various points in the future.

Pure discount bonds: These are zero coupon bonds that are free of credit risk. They are zeros that are issued by the sovereign (e.g., zero coupon Treasury bonds).

YIELD-TO-WORKOUT METHODOLOGY

This is the traditional methodology for valuing bonds. Essentially, all cash flows are discounted at the same rate. This rate is called the yield-to-workout (or simply the yield). In the case of a bond paying a semiannual coupon, and assuming that today is a coupon payment date, the present value of the bond is given by:

$$PV_{bond} = \frac{\frac{1}{2} \times CR \times Par}{\left(1 + \frac{y}{2}\right)^1} + \frac{\frac{1}{2} \times CR \times Par}{\left(1 + \frac{y}{2}\right)^2} + \ldots + \frac{\frac{1}{2} \times CR \times Par}{\left(1 + \frac{y}{2}\right)^{2T}} + \frac{Redemption}{\left(1 + \frac{y}{2}\right)^{2T}}$$

(Eq. A.1)

Where y denotes the bond's yield-to-workout

CR denotes the coupon rate (annual rate)

Par denotes the par value of the bond (we will assume throughout that this is $100)

Redemption is the bond's par amount if the bond is held to maturity, or it is the relevant call price if the bond is called

T denotes the number of years to the bond's workout date.

This valuation equation is applicable if today is one of the bond's coupon payment dates. This is an assumption we will make throughout because it simplifies the illustrations. Note that if we know the bond's yield we can calculate the bond's present value. The price of the bond should be equal to its present value. Equivalently, if we know the bond's price we can work backwards (in an iterative fashion) to obtain the bond's yield. Thus price and yield are interchangeable concepts.

The yield-to-workout method for valuing a bond clearly assumes that each cash flow (i.e., the coupon payments and the redemption amount) should be discounted at the same rate. This rate, called the bond's yield-to-workout, is stated as an annual rate but with semiannual compounding (s.a.). If we assume that the bond will not be called, then T will be the years to maturity and the redemption amount is par. Here the yield-to-workout is called a yield-to-maturity.

If we assume that the bond will be called on a particular call date, then T is the number of years to the call date and the redemption amount represents the call price associated with that call date. In this case the yield-to-workout is known as a yield-to-call.

It cannot be known in advance whether a callable bond will be called and, if so, on which of its call dates it will be called. The traditional practice therefore, is to use the bond's current market price to calculate all of its yields-to-workout and then to make the conservative assumption that the return on the bond is the lowest of all the yields-to-workout. The lowest of all the yields-to-workout is called the bond's yield-to-worst or its promised yield. For example, suppose that a callable corporate bond matures at par in 20 years and pays a 9.00% s.a. coupon. The bond is currently priced at $108.25. It has three call dates. One is 5 years from today, the second is 10 years from today, and the last is 15 years from today. If not called on one of its three call dates, the bond would be redeemed for par at maturity. We have the following information:

When redeemable	Redemption amount	Implied yield-to-workout
5 years	$107.50 (call price)	yield to first call
10 years	103.50 (call price)	yield to second call
15 years	100.50 (call price)	yield to third call
20 years	100.00 (par)	yield to maturity

To calculate the yield-to-worst, we use equation 1 and enter the current price of the bond, $108.25, for its present value (PV_{bond}). We then input the coupon rate of 9.00%, the relevant number of years to call or redemption T (e.g., 5 for the first call date), and the relevant redemption amount corresponding to that call or redemption date (e.g., $107.50 for the first call date). We then iterate to solve for y, which we interpret as the yield to the first call. We then repeat this process while using the information for the second call date and so forth. This produces the information below:

When redeemable	Redemption amount	Implied yield-to-workout at a price of $108.25	
5 years	$107.50	yield to first call	= 8.1992%
10 years	103.50	yield to second call	= 8.0197% = yield to worst
15 years	100.50	yield to third call	= 8.0601%
20 years	100.00	yield to maturity	= 8.1566%

It may be prudent to employ the yield-to-workout methodology in order to measure the incremental return associated with bonds having credit risk, *but not embedded options*. Anything other than a benchmark bond, such as a corporate bond, will have at least some credit risk.

Essentially, when an investor purchases a corporate bond the investor is assuming some credit risk relative to the credit risk-free benchmark bond. Because such bonds expose the investor to additional credit risk, they should provide additional return. This additional return is usually called the credit spread.[1] Credit spreads represent a type of risk premium.

Credit spreads are measured as the difference between the yield on a risky bond and the yield on a comparable-maturity benchmark bond. These credit spreads are measured in basis points. For example, suppose that the yield on

---

[1] The credit spread is not necessarily entirely explained by additional credit risk. There are other factors as well. These include the liquidity of the bond issue, any unusual covenants the bond indenture might contain, and tax factors. The latter are particularly important. The interest on risk-free Treasury bonds is exempt from state and local income taxes but the interest on corporate bonds is generally not exempt from these taxes. Also, the coupon interest on municipal securities can be exempt from federal, state, and local income taxes and this will significantly affect their yields.

a 10-year A-rated corporate bullet bond is 8.23%, while the yield on a 10-year Treasury bullet bond is 7.50%. The difference between these two yields is 73 basis points (bps). Thus the credit spread on the corporate is 73 bps and may be interpreted (albeit cautiously) as the risk premium earned for bearing the bond's incremental credit risk.

While this is a reasonable way to measure the risk premium for a non-callable corporate bullet bond (i.e., direct comparison to a non-callable bullet benchmark bond), it is not judicious to apply this method to a callable corporate bond. The problem of course is that there can be many yields-to-workout associated with a callable bond (or other security with embedded optionality). Which of the yields-to-workout is the "right" yield to use to determine the credit spread? There is no good answer to this question in the yield-to-workout methodology. The standard approach is to take the yield-to-workout that represents the bond's yield-to-worst and to treat the bond as though it has a maturity corresponding to the call date associated with the yield-to-worst. Then the yield on a benchmark bullet bond having a comparable maturity is deducted from the yield-to-worst on the callable bond. The difference between these two yields is the credit spread. While this approach seems reasonable at first blush, it is not. The yield-to-workout representing the yield-to-worst can suddenly change as a result of even a small change in the bond's price. For example, in the corporate bond discussed above the yield-to-second-call represents the yield-to-worst and we would treat the bond as though it had a maturity of 10 years. The credit spread would be found by taking the difference between the corporate bond yield-to-worst and the yield on the comparable-maturity 10-year benchmark bond. But if the price of the corporate bond were to fall to $106, then the yield-to-worst would shift to the yield-to-third-call and the credit spread would be found by taking the difference between the bond's yield-to-worst and the yield on the 15-year benchmark bond:

When redeemable	Redemption amount	Implied yield-to-workout		
5 years	$107.50	yield to first call	= 8.7230%	
10 years	103.50	yield to second call	= 8.3350%	
15 years	100.50	yield to third call	= 8.3100%	yield-to-worst
20 years	100.00	yield to maturity	= 8.3760%	

The yield-to-workout methodology has a number of other weaknesses and inconsistencies. First, the method assumes that all cash flows should be discounted at the same rate. This is inconsistent with anything other than a completely flat spot rate curve. That is, an upward sloping spot rate curve implies that cash flows to be received later should be discounted at a higher rate than cash flows to be received sooner. The interpretation we give this is that a yield-to-workout is not really the right rate at which to discount any of the cash flows that the bond will generate. Rather it is a weighted-average of the rates at which the individual cash flows should be discounted. In other words, we accept the idea that we are discounting all the individual cash flows at the wrong rate, because it is "right on average." For some purposes this is an acceptable treatment. For other purposes it can be critically flawed.

Second, the yield-to-workout methodology implicitly assumes that cash flows generated by the instrument can be reinvested to return the same yield-to-workout. Again, this is not likely to be a reasonable assumption unless the spot rate curve is flat.

Third, as we have already demonstrated the yield-to-workout can be unstable when bonds are callable with the result that if the bond price changes, sometimes by only a little, the call date corresponding to the yield-to-worst can change abruptly. This has at least two serious implications: It can cause an abrupt and misleading change in the credit spread, and it causes the bond's duration—a traditional measure of interest rate risk—to be quite unreliable.

Fourth and finally, it can be demonstrated that the yield-to-workout methodology is incapable of addressing, in a precise manner, the volatility of interest rates.

THE SPOT RATE METHODOLOGY

An important insight of Caks[2] is that conventional bonds are simply portfolios of zero coupon bonds. That is, each coupon payment and the final redemption payment may be viewed as separate instruments. Each of these separate instruments may be viewed as a zero coupon bond.

While this argument seems obvious today, it was a revolutionary idea at the time. It was this realization that led Merrill Lynch to begin breaking up bullet Treasury bonds into zero coupon bonds. Merrill discovered that investors were willing to pay more for the zeros than it cost Merrill to create them from bullet Treasury bonds, giving rise, at least for a time, to an arbitrage opportunity.

When viewed as a portfolio of zeros, it becomes obvious that the proper way to value a bullet bond is to value each component zero separately by discounting it at the appropriate spot zero rate. The value of the bond is then the sum of these individual present values. Assuming semiannual coupon payments and that today is a coupon payment date, the valuation equation would look as follows:

$$PV_{bond} = \frac{\frac{1}{2} \times CR \times Par}{\left(1 + \frac{_0z_1}{2}\right)^1} + \frac{\frac{1}{2} \times CR \times Par}{\left(1 + \frac{_0z_2}{2}\right)^2} + \ldots + \frac{\frac{1}{2} \times CR \times Par}{\left(1 + \frac{_0z_{2T}}{2}\right)^{2T}} + \frac{Redemption}{\left(1 + \frac{_0z_{2T}}{2}\right)^{2T}}$$

(Eq. A.2)

Where $_0z_t$ denote the spot zero rates that are applicable for discounting zero coupon bonds at time 0 (now) that will mature t periods from now. Here we assume that a period is six months in length and that the spot rate is stated as an annual rate with semiannual compounding.

---

[2] John Caks. "The Coupon Effect on Yield to Maturity," *Journal of Finance*, v32(1), 103-115.

The spot rate methodology is theoretically superior to the yield-to-workout methodology because it uses a correct, though different, discount rate for each cash flow. Thus if each cash flow is discounted at the correct rate, the sum of the present values is the correct value of the bond.

The spot rate methodology corrects for the first and second weaknesses of the yield-to-workout methodology, but it does not, by itself, address the third and fourth weaknesses. This is where OAS analysis picks up. First, however, we need to briefly introduce the concept of short rates.

SHORT RATES

Short rates are zero coupon rates that are limited to zero coupon bonds having a maturity of just one period. A "period" is defined by the context. For our purposes a period is six months. As each new period begins, a short rate for that period is realized. For example, suppose that we are measuring time in six-month intervals starting from today. Suppose that today is January 1, 1999. Then the current short rate is the six-month zero coupon rate applicable to a zero coupon bond maturing on July 1, 1999. The next short rate, i.e., the one associated with the six-month zero coupon bond that will exist on July 1 and mature on January 1, 2000, is not yet realized but will be realized on July 1, 1999.

 ## OPTION ADJUSTED SPREADS ANALYSIS

OAS analysis makes use of forward rates of interest. This requires some explanation and some notation. Before beginning, keep in mind that time is divided into six-month intervals throughout this discussion. Thus a "period" is six months in length.

FORWARD RATES

The term forward rate is used by different people to mean different things, so great care should be taken when using it. In general, a forward rate refers to an expectation of a rate of interest that will prevail at some point in the future.

One type of forward rate is the forward yield-to-maturity on a coupon-bearing bond. These types of forward rates are often called coupon forwards. For example, we might be interested in the yield-to-maturity on a five-year coupon-bearing bond two years from today. This could be described as a two-year forward five-year coupon yield.

Most frequently, however, the term forward rate is used to refer to a forward zero rate. This rate could be any number of periods forward and applicable to any maturity zero coupon bond. Here a forward zero rate will be denoted $_jz_t$. This is interpreted as the t-period zero rate expected to prevail j periods from today (i.e., t periods from period j). For instance, the notation $_3z_4$ would imply the zero rate expected to prevail on four-period zero coupon bonds three periods from today.

Recall that $_0z_t$ denotes the rate of discount applicable now (time 0) to a zero coupon bond that matures t periods later. We earlier called this a spot zero rate. It should be clear that a spot zero rate is just a special case of a forward zero rate where j = 0.

FORWARD SHORT RATES

There is one special set of forward zero rates that is critical to OAS analysis, namely, forward short rates. Forward short rates, most often just called forward rates, are forward rates on zero coupon bonds where each zero coupon bond has a maturity of just one period. Forward short rates may be viewed as forecasts of the future short rates. It is important to appreciate that a forecast is just that, a forecast. The actual short rate that is realized for a particular period will almost certainly differ from the forward short rate. Indeed, the forward short rate is continuously changing to reflect new information until such time as the future becomes the present—at which time the forward short rate becomes the realized short rate.

The full set of forward short rates is given by $_0z_1, _1z_1, _2z_1, _3z_1, _4z_1, \cdots$ Notice that the first forward short rate is simply the one-period spot zero rate, otherwise known as the current short rate.

Using a time line, these forward rates can be visualized in Exhibit A.1.

OBTAINING SPOT RATES AND FORWARD SHORT RATES

Under a widely employed theory of term structure, called the expectations theory, forward short rates can be derived from a series of spot zero rates. Essentially, the expectations theory holds that spot zero rates are the geometric average of successive forward short rates. That is:

$$\left(1+\frac{_0z_t}{2}\right)^t =\left(1+\frac{_0z_1}{2}\right)\times\left(1+\frac{_1z_1}{2}\right)\times\left(1+\frac{_2z_1}{2}\right)\times...\times\left(1+\frac{_{t-1}z_1}{2}\right)$$

Thus, if one knows the spot zero rates, one can sequentially derive the forward short rates. The spot zero rates can either be observed from Treasury zero coupon bonds (called STRIPS) or derived from the current term structure (yield curve) through a process commonly known as bootstrapping.[3]

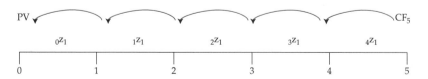

EXHIBIT A.1 Sequential discounting at forward short rates

---

[3] For a discussion of bootstrapping see John F. Marshall and Vipul K. Bansal, *Financial Engineering: A Complete Guide to Financial Innovation*, New York Institute of Finance, 1992, pp 430–433.

If we accept the expectations theory of term structure, the following will be true:

$$PV_{bond} = \frac{\frac{1}{2} \times CR \times Par}{\left(1 + \frac{_0z_1}{2}\right)^1} + \frac{\frac{1}{2} \times CR \times Par}{\left(1 + \frac{_0z_2}{2}\right)^2} + \ldots + \frac{\frac{1}{2} \times CR \times Par}{\left(1 + \frac{_0z_{2T}}{2}\right)^{2T}} + \frac{Redemption}{\left(1 + \frac{_0z_{2T}}{2}\right)^{2T}}$$

$$\left[\left(1 + \frac{_0z_1}{2}\right) \times \left(1 + \frac{_1z_1}{2}\right)\right]$$

$$\left[\left(1 + \frac{_0z_1}{2}\right) \times \left(1 + \frac{_1z_1}{2}\right) \times \ldots \times \left(1 + \frac{_{2T-1}z_1}{2}\right)\right]$$

This allows us to express the value of a bond in terms of forward short rates rather than in terms of spot zero rates.

Notice that this formulation implies that the discounting of cash flows is a process by which each future cash flow is sequentially discounted period-by-period at each single period's applicable short rate until we obtain its present value.

Now notice that the first short rate (i.e., the one-period spot zero rate $_0z_1$) is known with certainty. However, the next period short rate is uncertain and will remain uncertain until one period has elapsed. Thus the short rate that will be realized one period from today is likely to be different from the current one-period forward short rate ($_1z_1$). Similarly, the short rate that will be realized two periods from today is likely to be different from the current two-period forward short rate ($_2z_1$). Notice also that the short rate to be realized two periods from now is more uncertain than the short rate to be realized one period from now, and so on. Indeed, the further out we project the short rates, the greater the likelihood that the realized rate will deviate from the current estimate (i.e., the forward short rate). This is where OAS analysis becomes important. OAS analysis provides a systematic framework for factoring in the uncertainty (i.e., volatility) of the forward short rates.

THE EIGHT STEPS OF OAS ANALYSIS

There are eight steps associated with OAS analysis. We assume that we are applying the method to a callable bond:

1. Derive the set of risk-free spot zero rates (via bootstrapping) from the benchmark yield curve. (We will assume that this has already been done.)
2. Derive the risk-free forward short rates from the benchmark spot zero rates by exploiting the expectations theory of term structure. (We will assume that this too has already been done.)

3. Build a binomial tree depicting the possible future values of the short rates and also determine their probabilities.[4]
4. Apply the binomial tree to value the cash flows on a benchmark bullet bond.
5. Calibrate the model by adjusting the binomial tree values until the model's predicted price matches the actual market price of the bond.
6. Apply the same set of calibrated rates to value a callable bond by adding the same number of basis points (the spread factor) to all short rates in the tree. Adjust this spread factor until the model's predicted price equals the actual market price. The result is the bond's OAS.
7. Apply the same OAS to value a bullet bond with terms identical to the callable bond (except that the bullet bond is not callable).
8. Take the difference between the value obtained for the callable bond and the value obtained for the non-callable bullet bond. This difference is the value of the embedded call option.

BUILDING A BINOMIAL TREE OF SHORT RATES

We begin at step 3, building a binomial tree of forward short rates. We make a number of simplifying assumptions to illustrate the process. The more important of these assumptions are that the annual volatility of forward short rates is the same for all forward short rates and that this annual volatility is constant. We also assume that forward rates evolve via a random walk process.

In order to have a set of rates with which to illustrate the process, assume that we have the following four forward short rates, all expressed with semiannual compounding:

$$_0z_1 = 6.000\%$$
$$_1z_1 = 7.200\%$$
$$_2z_1 = 8.150\%$$
$$_3z_1 = 8.836\%$$

Assume that annual volatility of the forward short rates is 15%.[5] We need to describe how, over time, the estimates of future short rates might evolve from the current estimates of those future short rates (the current estimates of the future short rates are the forward rates). Under a standard binomial approach, we assume that with each passing time period, the estimate of a future short rate can go either up to one and only one higher level or down to one and only one lower level (see Exhibit A.2).

---

[4] It is at this stage that the option analytics approach enters the methodology. Binomial models to value options are widely used. They constitute one of the numeric approaches to option valuation. Other numeric approaches could be used in lieu of a binomial approach and sometimes are used. Examples of other numeric approaches are simulation and finite difference methods.

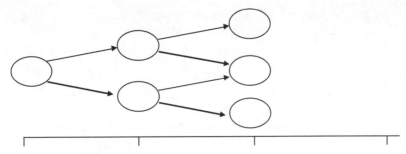

EXHIBIT A.2   Evolution of forward short rates

As noted earlier, we are denoting the t-period forward short rate by $_tz_1$. Suppose we are interested in where this forward rate will be j periods from now. Denote this by $_t^jz_1$. Thus one period from now the estimate of the t-period short rate (currently $_tz_1$) will be $_t^1z_1$. There would be two such values (one higher than $_tz_1$ and one lower than $_tz_1$). Similarly, two periods from now the estimate of the t-period short rate (currently $_tz_1$) will be $_t^2z_1$. There will be three such values. Note that when j = t the forward short rate has become the realized short rate. We need to know all possible short rates that might be realized for each period.

For example, suppose that time is divided into six-month intervals, today is January 1, 1999, and I ask "what is the current estimate of the short rate that will prevail on July 1, 2000?" What I am asking for is $_3z_1$.

And now suppose that I ask "what will be the estimate of the July 1, 2000 short rate on July 1, 1999?" The answer would be $_3^1z_1$. Similarly, if I ask "what will be the estimate of the July 1, 2000 short rate on January 1, 2000?" then I am asking for $_3^2z_1$.

We will assume that the probability of the forward short rate rising each period and the probability of the forward short rate declining each period are the same.

Denote the higher possible value of the future t-period short rate one period from now by $_t^1z_1^H$ and the lower possible value of the future t-period short rate one period from now by $_t^1z_1^L$.

The following relationship between the higher and lower rates will hold:

$$_t^1z_1^H = \exp(2 \times \sigma \times \sqrt{\tau}) \times _t^1z_1^L \qquad \text{(Eq. A.3)}$$

Where exp($\bullet$) is the exponential function, and τ denotes the fraction of a year covered by each single period (this is 0.5 in this case as we have assumed six-month intervals).

---

[5] Annual volatility is defined as the standard deviation of the annual percentage change in the forward rate, when that percentage change is continuously compounded. This is the usual way to measure volatility in applications involving option valuation.

Substituting the given values for σ (.15) and τ (.5), Equation A.3 becomes:

$$\frac{1}{t} z_1^H = \exp(2 \times .15 \times \sqrt{.5}) \times \frac{1}{t} z_1^L$$

$$= 1.23631 \times \frac{1}{t} z_1^L \qquad \text{(Result 1)}$$

Intuitively, it would be expected that the statistical expectation of the next period value of the forward short rate should be equal to the current forward rate. This relationship is given by Equation A.4:

$$(.5 \times \frac{1}{t} z_1^H) + (.5 \times \frac{1}{t} z_1^L) = {}_t z_1 \qquad \text{(Eq. A.4)}$$

Substituting Result 1 into Equation 4 allows us to solve for $\frac{1}{t} z_1^H$ and $\frac{1}{t} z_1^L$ in terms of $_t z_1$:

$$\frac{1}{t} z_1^H = 1.10567 \times {}_t z_1$$

and

$$\frac{1}{t} z_1^L = 0.89433 \times {}_t z_1$$

These results allow us to express each subsequent evolution of a forward rate in terms of its value in the prior period.

Consider the value $_1 z_1$ (7.200%). What might its realized values be one period from now ($\frac{1}{1} z_1$) (see Exhibit A.3)?

$$\frac{1}{t} z_1^H = 1.10567 \times 7.200\% = 7.961\%$$

and

$$\frac{1}{t} z_1^L = 0.89433 \times 7.200\% = 6.439\%$$

Now consider what the realized values of the short rate two periods from now (i.e., $\frac{2}{2} z_1$) might be (see Exhibit A.4).

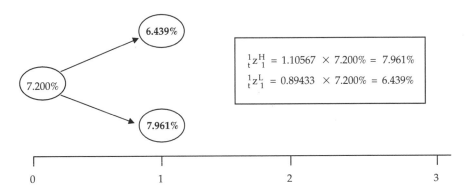

$$\frac{1}{t} z_1^H = 1.10567 \times 7.200\% = 7.961\%$$

$$\frac{1}{t} z_1^L = 0.89433 \times 7.200\% = 6.439\%$$

EXHIBIT A.3 Evolution of a one-period forward short rate to the realizable short rates

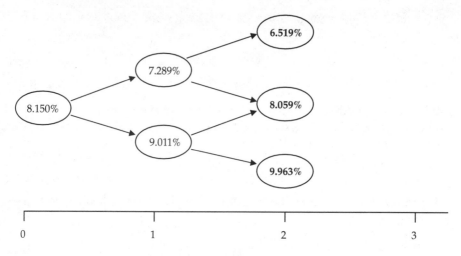

EXHIBIT A.4 Evolution of a two-period forward short rate to the realizable short rates

Finally, consider what the realized value of the short rate three periods from now (i.e., $_3^3z_1$) might be (see Exhibit A.5).

We are not interested in the intermediate values associated with arriving at the set of possible realizable values of each short rate, but rather just the realizable values per se. We now gather all of the realizable values and place them on the appropriate nodes of a binomial tree. This is called the binomial tree of risk-free short rates. It is depicted in Exhibit A.6.

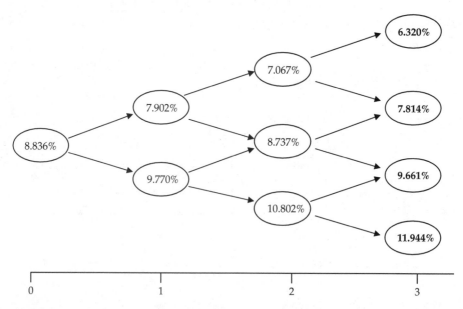

EXHIBIT A.5 Evolution of a three-period forward short rate to the realizable short rates

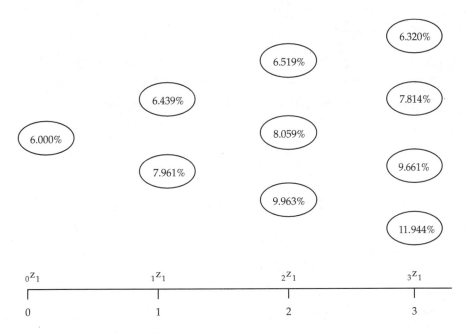

EXHIBIT A.6 Binomial tree of risk-free short rates

We are now ready to employ the range of possible values the various short rates might take on to value a bond. We begin with a benchmark bullet bond (recall that it is credit risk free and non-callable). Suppose that the bond pays a 7.50% annual coupon in two semiannual installments of $3.75 (per $100 of par) and that the bond currently has 24 months (four periods) to maturity. Given the forward short rates we have assumed, this bond should be priced exactly at par (100.0000), which we will assume it is.

The first coupon of $3.75 will be received in exactly one period, i.e., six months. What is the value now (present value) of this future payment? We obtain this by building a "price tree" for this payment. Because this payment is only one period away and the short rate associated with this one period is known with certainty, this is a trivial matter (see Exhibit A.7).

Next, we use the short rates to determine the value of the $3.75 coupon payment that will be received two periods (12 months) from now by building a price tree for the second cash flow. This requires that we discount sequentially backward through every possible path of potentially realizable short rates (see Exhibit A.8).

Next, we use the short rates to determine the value of the $3.75 coupon payment that will be received three periods from now by building a price tree for the third cash flow. Again, this requires that we discount sequentially backward through every possible path of potentially realizable short rates (see Exhibit A.9).

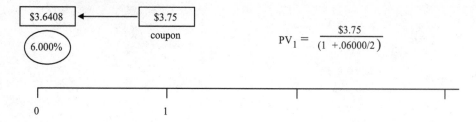

$$PV_1 = \frac{\$3.75}{(1 + .06000/2)}$$

EXHIBIT A.7 Price tree for first cash flow

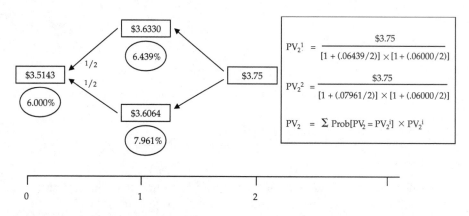

$$PV_2^1 = \frac{\$3.75}{[1 + (.06439/2)] \times [1 + (.06000/2)]}$$

$$PV_2^2 = \frac{\$3.75}{[1 + (.07961/2)] \times [1 + (.06000/2)]}$$

$$PV_2 = \Sigma \, Prob[PV_2 = PV_2^i] \times PV_2^i$$

EXHIBIT A.8 Price tree for second cash flow

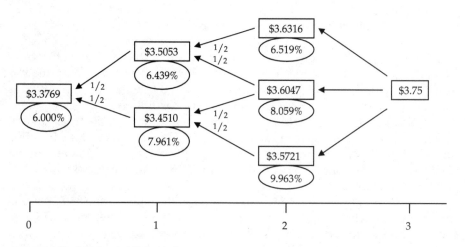

EXHIBIT A.9 Price tree for third cash flow

Finally, we use the binomial tree of short rates in the same manner to calculate the expected present value of the final cash flow. This final cash flow, which occurs two years from today, includes the final coupon payment of $3.75 and the bond's par value of $100. Thus, the final cash flow is $103.75 (see Exhibit A.10).

VALUING THE BOND FROM ITS CASH FLOWS

We have calculated the present values of the individual cash flows by way of the price trees. We now sum these present values to obtain the value of the bond (representing step 4 in the eight-step OAS process):

Period	Cash flow	Present value
1	$3.75	$3.6408
2	$3.75	$3.5143
3	$3.75	$3.3769
4	$103.75	$89.4842
		$100.0162

Notice that the actual market price of the bond is par ($100.0000). The value we obtained above for the bond is greater than par. Thus our model contains an error. What is the source of this error and how can we correct it?

The error is caused by a combination of two factors. The first is the convexity of present value functions and the second is the volatility of the forward rates that leads to multiple realizable values for the short rates. To understand the convexity problem we need to illustrate the relationship between the present value of a cash flow and the rate at which that cash flow is discounted. This is illustrated in Exhibit A.11.

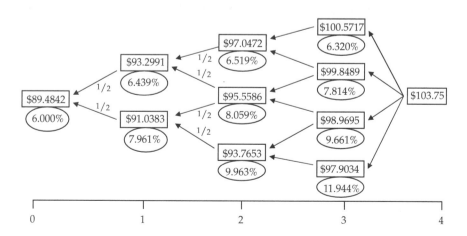

EXHIBIT A.10 Price tree for final cash flow

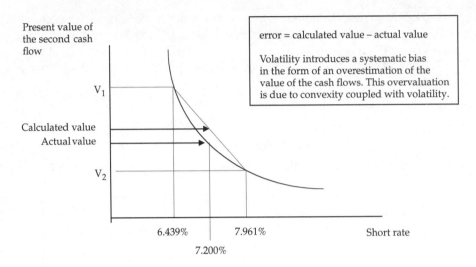

EXHIBIT A.11 Convexity and volatility induced error

Notice that the present value curve depicted in Exhibit A.11 is not linear. That is, it has some curvature to it. This curvature is called convexity and it, together with the volatility of interest rates, is the source of the error. To see this, consider the second cash flow on the bond above. This cash flow is a coupon payment of $3.75. If this cash flow is discounted for one period at the one-period forward short rate, $_1z_1$, which is 7.200%, and then again at the spot short rate $(_0z_1)$ of 6.000%, we get the actual value depicted in Exhibit A.11. (Note that the exhibit illustrates only the first discounting but both sequential discountings are implied.) Instead, if the cash flow is discounted at the two different short rates that might be realized in one period (6.439% and 7.961%), and then the resulting values are discounted again at the spot short rate of 6.000%, we obtain the two values labeled V_1 and V_2 in Exhibit A.11. The value of the cash flow, labeled the "calculated value" in the exhibit, is an average of these two values. Note that this average is higher than the actual value.

CALIBRATING THE BINOMIAL TREE OF SHORT RATES

Correcting the error in the valuation of cash flows requires a sequential process called calibrating the binomial tree of short rates (step 5). The calibration process involves raising the estimates of the future short rates by an amount just sufficient so that the average of the calculated present value for the cash flow exactly equals the actual value of the cash flow. As this is done, we must simultaneously preserve the relationship between the different values that the short rates might take on, as given by Equation A.3.

This calibration process is an iterative sequential process. First we calibrate the values at the first node in the binomial tree of short rates. Once this

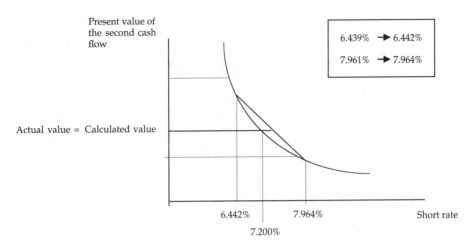

EXHIBIT A.12 Calibrating the binomial tree of short rates

is finished, we calibrate the second set of nodes in the binomial tree of short rates, and so forth.

The solution to the first set of nodes is illustrated in Exhibit A.12.

The fully calibrated binomial tree of risk-free short rates that correspond to our data is illustrated in Exhibit A.13. Here the calibrated rates appear in the ellipses while the non-calibrated rates appear in brackets below the ellipses for comparison.

When the cash flows associated with the benchmark bond are obtained by discounting through this calibrated tree of risk-free short rates, the sum of present values is precisely the value of the bond. This is depicted below:

Period	Cash flow	Present value
1	$3.75	$3.6408
2	$3.75	$3.5143
3	$3.75	$3.3766
4	$103.75	$89.4683
		$100.0000

CALCULATING A BOND'S OPTION ADJUSTED SPREAD

The calibrated binomial tree of short rates we have just derived is applicable to valuing a benchmark bullet bond. Now we consider how this same calibrated binomial tree could be adapted to value a non-benchmark callable bond (step 6). A callable corporate bond is an example of such a bond. To simplify the analysis, we assume that a corporation incurs no transactions costs either when it calls a bond or when it issues a new bond and that it will always call a bond if it is rational to do so.

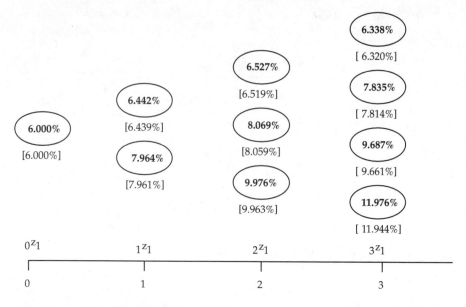

EXHIBIT A.13 Fully calibrated binomial tree of risk-free short rates

Suppose that we have a 24-month corporate bond paying an annual coupon of 10.50% in two semiannual installments. Thus each coupon is $5.25. The bond is callable in 18 months (three periods) at $101.00. Suppose that the bond's offer price is $103.75. This is the price at which you could buy this bond. Our goal is to come up with this same value by way of our model. We begin by developing the price tree for each of this bond's cash flows using the previously derived calibrated binomial tree of short rates.

The price trees for the first, second, and third cash flows are illustrated in Exhibits A.14, A.15, and A.16, respectively. Now consider the price tree for the final cash flow on this bond. This is depicted in Exhibit A.17.

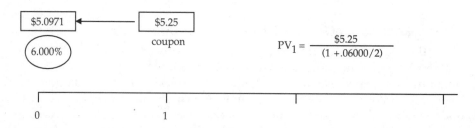

EXHIBIT A.14 Price tree for the first cash flow of callable bond

Now notice that the value of the fourth cash flow on the bond's call date may be any one of four different values: $102.0173, $101.2822, $100.3878, or $99.3038. As the bond is callable on this date at $101 and we have assumed that the issuer incurs no transaction costs when calling or issuing a bond, the rational thing for this issuer to do is to call the bond if the value on the call date is above $101. This condition is satisfied if the value on the call date is either $102.0173 or $101.2822, but not satisfied if the value is either $100.3878 or $99.3038. To see why this is so, consider the issuer's behavior if the bond's value is $102.0173: Because the bond is a liability to the issuer, the issuer is able to eliminate a liability worth $102.0173 at a cost of $101.

At all short rates that give rise to values that would cause the issuer to call the bond, the investor must assume that the bond would be called and the value would then be only the call price, in this case $101.

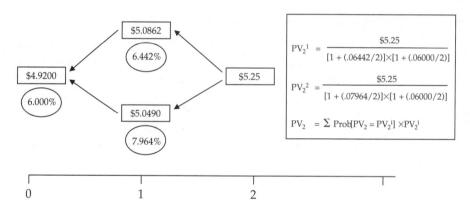

EXHIBIT A.15 Price tree for the second cash flow of callable bond

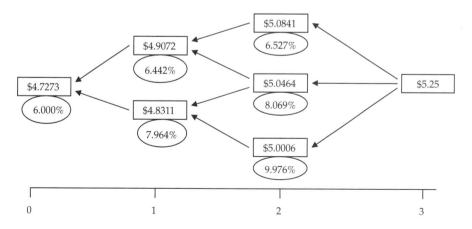

EXHIBIT A.16 Price tree for the third cash flow of callable bond

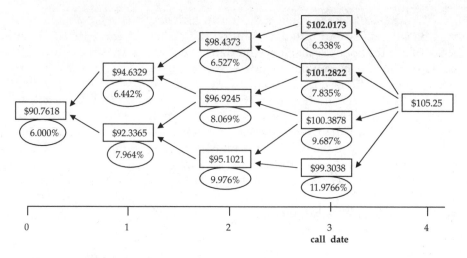

EXHIBIT A.17 Price tree for the final cash flow of callable bond

Thus, we must substitute the call price for the value of the cash flow on the call date in any case in which the value of the cash flow exceeds the call price. This is depicted in Exhibit A.18.

We can now sum the present values obtained from the price trees for the four individual cash flows, using the call-adjusted replacement tree for the fourth cash flow, to obtain the model's predicted price (MPP). This value is $105.2948.

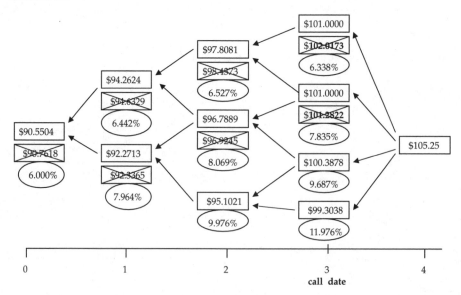

EXHIBIT A.18 Adjusted price tree for final cash flow of callable bond

Period	Cash flow	Present value
1	$5.25	$5.0971
2	$5.25	$4.9200
3	$5.25	$4.7273
3	$105.25	$90.5504
		$105.2948

Notice that the MPP of $105.2948 is higher than the actual market price of $103.75. Our model has clearly overestimated the value of the bond. The explanation for this is simple. The calibrated binomial tree of short rates that was used to value the bond was for risk-free bonds (e.g., recall that it was derived for valuing credit risk-free Treasury bonds). The rates at which bonds with credit risk should be discounted must clearly be higher than these risk-free rates. To deal with this, we go back to the calibrated binomial tree of risk-free short rates and add the same number of basis points to each short rate in the tree.

The number of basis points we add is called a spread factor. Spread factors are measured in basis points. This number is obtained in an iterative fashion. Suppose, for example, we add 50 basis points to each short rate in the calibrated tree and re-value the cash flows. We have:

Period	Cash flow	Present value
1	$5.25	$5.0874
2	$5.25	$4.8962
3	$5.25	$4.6933
4	$105.25	$89.7921
		$104.4690

Because the MPP is still higher than the observed market price of $103.75, the spread factor we used is too low. So we try a higher spread factor. Suppose that we try 100 basis points. In this case, the MPP is $103.5791. This, of course, is lower than the observed market price of $103.7500. Thus the 100 basis points is too high a spread factor. This process is repeated until the MPP matches (to a nearly exact amount) the observed market price. In our case this occurs with a spread factor of 90.465 basis points:

Period	Cash flow	Present value
1	$5.25	$5.0748
2	$5.25	$4.8772
3	$5.25	$4.6659
4	$105.25	$89.1321
		$103.7500

The solution of 90.465 basis points is called the bond's option adjusted spread. Essentially, we interpret the OAS as the number of basis points that must be added to each and every rate in the calibrated binomial tree of risk-free short rates to obtain a MPP that precisely equals the observed market value of the bond. These basis points represent the risk premium for bearing the credit risk associated with the bond. The same sort of analysis could have been performed if the bond had contained an embedded put option.

USING OAS ANALYSIS TO VALUE THE EMBEDDED OPTION

We can use the OAS to determine the value of the option that is embedded in a callable bond (steps 7 and 8). To accomplish this task we ask "what would the value of the bond be *at the same OAS* if the bond had *not* been callable.[6] In this case, the answer is $103.8143.

A callable bond may be viewed as a portfolio consisting of a long position in a bullet bond and a short position in a call option on a bullet bond that begins on the option's call date. Therefore,

$$B_{callable} = B_{bullet} - C_{bullet}$$
$$103.7500 = 103.8143 - C_{bullet}$$
$$\text{implying that } C_{bullet} = 0.0643$$

Thus the option is worth $0.0643 for every $100 of par.

EFFECTIVE DURATION

As mentioned earlier in this paper, when a bond contains embedded options modified duration is a poor indicator of the interest rate risk associated with holding the bond. The OAS approach, by specifically taking the optionality of the bond into consideration as well as taking the sources of an option's value into consideration (i.e., volatility), makes it possible to derive a better measure of interest rate risk. This measure is called the bond's effective duration or option adjusted duration.

The most intuitive way to calculate an effective duration is to first calculate the callable bond's fair value using the OAS approach, as we did above. Next, we assume that the benchmark yield curve shifts upward by exactly one basis point. We then re-derive the benchmark spot rates, re-derive the forward rates, and re-derive the calibrated binomial tree of risk-free short rates.

Next, using the *same* OAS previously derived we calculate what the value of the callable bond would be. The new value is deducted from the original value of the bond to obtain the bond's option-adjusted dollar value of a basis point or DV01.[7]

---

[6] For this particular bond, this is simply a matter of not substituting the call price of $101 for the value of the fourth period cash flow at the third node when that value exceeds $101.

[7] The dollar value of a basis point is also called the price value of a basis point or the present value of a basis point. It is defined as the dollar amount by which the price of a $100 par value bond will decline if the yield curve shifts up by one basis point.

For a non-callable bond, the following relationship holds between a bond's modified duration (D_M) and its DV01:

$$DV01 = D_M \times Price_{\$100\ par} \times 0.0001$$

implying that

$$D_M = \frac{DV\,01}{Price_{\$100\ par} \times 0.0001}$$

A similar relationship will hold for effective duration (D_E), whether the bond is callable or not, provided that the DV01 is derived via OAS analysis in the manner described above:

$$D_E = \frac{DV\,01_{option\ adjusted}}{Price_{\$100\ par} \times 0.0001} \tag{Eq. A.5}$$

It should be clear that for a non-callable bond, the bond's modified duration and the bond's effective duration are identical. But they are not identical for a callable bond (or any bond with embedded optionality for that matter).

In the case of the corporate bond for which we calculated an OAS of 90.465 basis points, we add one basis point to all maturities on the benchmark yield curve. We then re-derive the spot rates, re-derive the forward rates, and then re-derive the calibrated binomial tree of risk-free short rates. Finally, using the same OAS previously derived (90.465 basis points), we calculate the value of the bond and find it to be 103.73190. Thus, the option-adjusted DV01 is found to be:

$$DV01_{option\ adjusted} = 103.7500 - 103.7319$$

$$= \$0.0181.$$

That is, a one basis point parallel upward shift in the benchmark yield curve will cause this corporate bond to decline in value by $0.0181 for every $100 of par value.[8]

We can now obtain this bond's effective duration from Equation A.5. The effective duration is found to be 1.745.

For comparison to the traditional yield-to-workout methodology described earlier in this article, this bond's yield-to-maturity is 8.4235% and its yield-to-call is 8.4258%. Clearly, the yield-to-maturity is this bond's yield-to-worst. Based on this yield-to-worst and the fact that it corresponds to a redemption date 24 months out, this bond would have a modified duration of 1.7829. Notice the difference between this bond's unreliable modified duration and its far-more reliable effective duration. While this difference may not seem

---

[8] This assumes that corporate bond yields shift in the same direction and by the same number of basis points as the bonds that make up the benchmark yield curve.

significant, it has to be remembered that this bond has a very short maturity. For bonds with longer maturities, the difference can be very significant.

PORTFOLIO PROPERTIES OF EFFECTIVE DURATION

Effective duration has the same basic portfolio properties as does modified duration. Specifically, the effective duration of a bond portfolio is a weighted-average of the effective durations of the individual components of the portfolio, where the weights are the ratios of the present values of the individual components to the total present value of the portfolio.

 SUMMARY

This paper has presented the basics of OAS analysis. It has described the necessary steps to compute the credit spread, adjusted for embedded optionality, of a risky debt instrument such as a callable corporate bond. Still, OAS analysis can be significantly more complicated in practice than was illustrated here.

OAS analysis is an important valuation tool that can be used to determine if option-embedded securities are transacted at arms-length prices. For instance, in *ACM v. Commissioner* (commonly known as the "Colgate case"), the government argued that certain transactions undertaken by the partnership were sham transactions conducted at off-market prices as part of a complicated scheme to shield former capital gain income. Some of the securities transacted contained embedded options. In order to determine, therefore, whether or not said securities were traded at-market, OAS analysis was used to transform the securities to straight debt. The option adjusted yields on these securities were then compared to the yields of straight-debt instruments of a similar risk class and maturity that were trading in the market at the time. If the option adjusted yields and the yields of comparable straight-debt instruments were not substantially different, then one could conclude that the transactions in question were at-market. Otherwise, the conclusion would be that the transactions were not arms-length. In its ruling the Court found that certain transactions undertaken by ACM were not at-market. The ultimate effect of this finding was to preclude the taxpayer from shielding past gains.

APPENDIX B

From Portfolio Theory to Complex Constructs: Financial Engineering Comes of Age

Financial engineering is the development and creative application of financial technology to solve financial problems and exploit financial opportunities.

Any true science goes through three stages in its development. The first is description, the second is analysis, and the final—the mature stage—is engineering. Most would agree that the transformation of finance from a descriptive discipline to an analytical science began with the seminal work of Harry Markowitz[1] who, in 1952, provided the theoretical foundations of modern portfolio theory.[2] In the 1960s, the seeds planted by Markowitz began to take root as academics nurtured the theory—developing the capital asset pricing model and the rudiments of hedging theory. Practitioners began to employ the new theory and the tools that grew from it in portfolio selection and hedging strategies.

As the 1960s progressed, analytical thinking and methodology slowly but surely replaced the more descriptive approach of earlier scholars and practitioners. The new approach is probably most clearly seen in the work of Fischer Black and Myron Scholes who, in 1973, published the first complete option pricing model.[3] In that same year, the Chicago Board Options Exchange introduced listed stock options.

The pace of analytical development in finance accelerated considerably following publication of the Black/Scholes option pricing model and theoretical breakthroughs came ever more rapidly. At the same time, innovation in the

---

[1] Markowitz, "Portfolio Selection," 7 J. Finance 77 (1952).

[2] This is not to overlook the earlier development of present-value arithmetic and the important interest rate risk measure called duration, both of which precede Markowitz's work by many years.

[3] Black and Scholes, "The Pricing of Options and Corporate Liabilities," 31 J. Political Economy 637 (May/June 1973).

market-place, inspired in part by opportunity and in part by necessity, took on a new urgency. The opportunity was brought about by the rapid advances in financial theory, the development of computer science and telecommunications, a more highly educated and analytical work force, and changes in the regulatory environment that were more conducive to innovation. The necessity included a more volatile exchange rate and interest rate environment, and a globalization of the marketplace. Among the market innovations were the rise of the Eurobond market, the development of the repurchase agreement market, the explosive growth of new types of financial instruments, and the emergence of new types of investment vehicles—e.g., money market mutual funds.

Of the new financial instruments to make their appearance, perhaps the most important were derivatives. Derivatives can be divided into two subgroups: elemental derivatives and derivative securities. Elemental derivatives include forward-like instruments (forwards, futures, and swaps) and option-like instruments (puts and calls, caps and floors, warrants, and exotic options). Derivative securities are similar to more traditional instruments, like stocks and bonds, but contain a derivative component—often called an embedded derivative. Examples of this type include convertible bonds, mortgage-backed securities, and structured notes.

Forward contracts are the oldest form of derivative, but futures contracts were, until recently, the best known. Forwards and futures are similar instruments but forwards are customized contracts that trade in a largely unregulated OTC environment while futures are highly standardized and regulated contracts that trade exclusively on organized exchanges. Futures trading was introduced in the U.S. by the Chicago Board of Trade in the 1860s. Until the 1970s, however, futures trading was limited to the trading of contracts on commodities, particularly agricultural commodities. During the 1970s, the nature of the derivatives markets began to change. Listed stock options were introduced in 1973. Futures contracts on currencies were introduced around the same time. In 1975, the CBOT introduced the first interest rate futures contract. But the most important market innovations were still a few years away.

In 1979, the first currency swap was done. This was followed, in 1981, by the first interest rate swap. These two products marked the birth of the modern OTC derivatives market.[4] In 1982, stock index futures made their debut and options on futures followed shortly. In 1986, commodity swaps were introduced and multi-period OTC options began to appear. In 1989, equity swaps came on the scene. The first of a long line of "exotic" options were introduced about the same time.

---

[4] Because forward contracts are also OTC derivatives, and because forwards predate swaps by several centuries, it is not literally true that currency swaps mark the beginning of the OTC derivatives market. But they certainly do mark the beginning of the modern era.

Within a few years of the introduction of swaps, industrious financial engineers began to create variants. The early variants were rather simple modifications of the original plain vanilla structures, but more novel forms were gradually introduced to better serve end-users' needs. The number of variants of interest rate and currency swaps may now number more than a thousand. This gave rise to a complex and colorful lexicon which was further embellished by the introduction of commodity and equity swaps, exotic options, and structured securities.

By the late 1980s, financial scholars realized that finance, as a science, was undergoing a second fundamental transformation. This time, it was transforming from an analytical science to an engineering science. In the late 1980s, for example, Hayne Leland and Mark Rubinstein, the originators of portfolio insurance—a dynamic hedging strategy—began talking about the "new science of financial engineering."[5] In 1988, John Finnerty formally defined financial engineering in the context of corporate finance.[6] Leland, Rubinstein, and Finnerty were among the first, but were not the only, scholars to recognize the engineering orientation of the new finance.[7] By the early 1990s, many finance practitioners had adopted "financial engineer" as a job title, and a handful of financial institutions, including Chemical Securities and Bank of America, created financial engineering departments.

The growing realization that finance was becoming ever-more an engineering science eventually led academics and practitioners to collaborate in founding the first professional society for financial engineers: the International Association of Financial Engineers (IAFE). This organization, founded in 1991, grew rapidly and now it has nearly 2,000 members. The IAFE defines "financial engineering" as the "development and creative application of financial technology to solve financial problems and exploit financial opportunities." This definition makes no explicit mention of derivatives though, clearly, derivatives are an important component of the technology.

Others have defined "financial engineering" much more narrowly. Some, for example, equate financial engineering exclusively with financial risk management. This would fall within the broader definition used by the IAFE, but it would not be exclusive. An interesting definition that is also a bit narrow but is nevertheless consistent with the IAFE's definition can be found in Gary Gas-

---

[5] Leland and Rubinstein, "The Evolution of Portfolio Insurance," *Portfolio Insurance: A Guide to Dynamic Hedging* (Luskin, ed., John Wiley & Sons, 1988), at 3.

[6] Finnerty, "Financial Engineering in Corporate Finance: An Overview," Financial Management (Winter 1988), at 14.

[7] Other early references to "financial engineering" can be found in Smith and Smithson, *The Handbook of Financial Engineering* (Harper Business, 1990) and Marshall and Bansal, *Financial Engineering* (Allyn & Bacon, 1991).

tineau's 1992 dictionary of financial risk management.[8] Gastineau defines "financial engineering" as "the art (with contributions from science) of creating desirable cash flow and/or market value patterns from existing instruments or new instruments to meet an investment or risk management need. The creations of financial engineers are typically based on traditional instruments such as bonds and notes with forward and futures contracts, options, and swap components added."

The products, structures, and strategies developed by financial engineers often look formidable, but the most complex structures are usually nothing more than combinations (portfolios) of simpler instruments. The easiest way to understand these complex structures is to decompose them into their building blocks. This is not a simple endeavor and can, depending on the nature of the undertaking, require extensive knowledge of mathematics, management science, statistics, accounting and tax rules, securities law, financial theory, institutional practice, market microstructure, a host of financial products, data processing, telecommunications, economics, and a variety of other disciplines.

Derivatives are one of the tools of choice for financial engineers because they can make all assets fungible: Dollars become Euros, floating rates become fixed, equity becomes debt, short-term debt becomes long-term debt, etc. In this column, which will appear in each issue of *Derivatives*, David Bizer and I, together with various authors, will explain, in as non-quantitative a way as possible, the constructs of today's financial engineers by analyzing the markets, products, strategies, and structures developed by financial engineers. In this manner, we hope to demystify financial engineering, particularly as it pertains to derivatives.

---

[8] Gastineau, *Dictionary of Financial Risk Management* (Probus Publishing, Swiss Bank Corporation, 1992), at 108.

APPENDIX C

What Are Swaps?
A Look at Plain Vanilla Varieties

Swap markets are now measured in trillions of dollars yet the uses to which swaps can be put are only now beginning to be understood.

In the 14 years since they were first introduced, swaps and related OTC derivative instruments have become one of the most important components of the technology used by modern financial engineers. Swaps can be used to reduce finance costs, hedge price risks, synthesize any type of security, arbitrage market imperfections and asymmetries, better manage seasonal cash flows, reduce or defer taxes, reduce transaction costs, create synthetic barter, manage business cycle risks, and much more. The plain vanilla swaps described here are typically the earliest forms of the several major swap classes, but hundreds of special-purpose variants of each class have evolved.

 BASIC TERMINOLOGY

A swap is a general term for a legally binding contract between two parties, called counterparties, in which the two parties agree to exchange cash flows (i.e., payments) at designated intervals for some period of time. The life of the instrument is called the "tenor" (or maturity) of the swap. The cash flows may be fixed in size or varying in size. If varying, the payments are said to be floating and are pegged to a "benchmark" interest rate, commodity price, or index of some sort. The benchmark is also called the reference rate or reference price. In the plain vanilla form, one counterparty typically pays a fixed rate (or price) and the other party pays a floating rate (or price) on some quantity of underlying assets, called "notionals." The two payment sides of the swap are called the "fixed leg" and the "floating leg," respectively.

Most often, at least one of the counterparties to the swap is a swap dealer. A swap dealer is a financial institution that is prepared to enter into a swap as either fixed-rate-payor/floating-rate-receiver, or as floating-rate-payor/fixed-rate-receiver. The swap dealer profits from a very small difference between the fixed rate it receives on those swaps in which it is the fixed-rate receiver, and the fixed rate it pays on those swaps in which it is the fixed-rate payor. The difference is called the "pay-receive spread" and generally ranges from 3 to 5 basis points on the more liquid swaps. In theory, swap dealers would like to match precisely each swap to which they are a counterparty with another swap having identical, but opposite, terms. In practice, however, it is much more efficient for swap dealers to warehouse swaps and hedge residual risks associated with the swap portfolio (which, in market parlance, is a "swap book").

The major classes of swaps are (1) currency swaps, (2) interest rate swaps, (3) equity swaps, (4) commodity swaps, (5) macroeconomic swaps, and (6) what may loosely be called "other" swaps. The largest class is that of the interest rate swap.

INTEREST RATE SWAPS

In interest rate swaps the underlying asset is a quantity of money called "notional principal." The term "notional" is intended to convey the fact that the underlying asset is purely hypothetical and only exists for purposes of calculating the size of the interest payments.

In a plain vanilla interest rate swap, one party pays a fixed rate of interest on the notional principal while the other party pays a floating rate of interest on the same amount of notional principal. This floating rate is pegged to some standard reference rate, usually the London Interbank Offered Rate, or LIBOR. Payments might be made annually, semiannually, quarterly, or monthly. For purposes of illustration, assume (1) payments are made semiannually, (2) the reference rate of interest for the floating leg of the swap is six-month (6-M) LIBOR, (3) the tenor of the swap is four years, (4) the fixed rate is 4.88%, and (5) the notional principal on the swap is $32 million. The swap commences on December 15, 1995, and terminates on December 15, 1999. The cash flows on this swap are depicted in Exhibit C.1.

Interest is usually understood to represent a payment for the use of someone else's money. The cash flow diagram in Exhibit C.1 does not depict any transfers of principal between counterparties. The reason for this is that each

EXHIBIT C.1 Cash flows under a typical plain vanilla interest rate swap

counterparty may be viewed as having made a loan of $32 million to the other counterparty. While they could each give the other $32 million at the commencement of the swap and then repay these "loans" of principals on the termination of the swap, the exchanges would actually be pointless since they are the same sum in the same currency. It is for this reason that the exchanges of principals are usually dispensed with and the principals are called "notional." (The only exception to this full offset of principal flows involves currency swaps, because the notional principals in such swaps are in different currencies.)

To see who pays whom what, let's examine what happens to the reference rate as the years pass. The reference rate is observed, for purposes of setting the floating rate, at the start of each payment period on what are called the "reset dates." In this swap, the first observation of the reference rate (6-M LIBOR) is made on December 15, 1995. Suppose that 6-M LIBOR is 3.625% on this first reset date. Six months later, on June 15, 1996, the floating-rate payor will make a payment of $589,667 to the floating-rate receiver and the fixed-rate payor will make a payment of $780,800 to the fixed-rate receiver. Because each party is making a payment to the other in the same currency, only the difference need be paid by the higher-paying counterparty to the lower-paying counterparty. This practice of transferring only the difference between the two payments is called "netting."

To complete the example, suppose that over the course of the four-year tenor of the swap eight payments are made. The net is represented in Exhibit C.2 as the sum the fixed-rate payor pays (if positive) or receives (if negative). The calculation of the fixed-rate payment is made by the formula:

$$\text{rate} \times \text{notional principal} \times \text{1/2 year} =$$
$$4.88\% \times \$32 \text{ million} \times 0.5 = \$780,800$$

EXHIBIT C.2   Payments under a $32 million interest rate swap

Reset date	6-M LIBOR	Payment date	Fixed pay	Floating pay	Net
12/15/95	3.625%	6/15/96	$788,000	$589,667	$191,133
6/15/96	3.750	12/15/96	780,800	610,000	170,800
12/15/96	4.125	6/15/97	780,800	667,333	113,467
6/15/97	5.375	12/15/97	780,800	874,333	(93,533)
12/15/97	5.125	6/15/98	780,800	829,111	(48,311)
6/15/98	5.500	12/15/98	780,800	894,667	(113,867)
12/15/98	6.250	6/15/99	780,800	1,011,111	(230,311)
6/15/99	6.125	12/15/99	780,800	996,333	(215,533)

The calculation of the first floating rate payment (in the first payment period) is:

$$\text{rate} \times \text{notional principal} \times \text{number of days} \div 360 =$$
$$3.625\% \times \$32 \text{ million} \times 183 \div 360 = \$589{,}667.$$

The fixed-rate side pays a half year's interest while the floating-rate side pays slightly more than a half year's interest (183/360). This is because the fixed-rate side is usually quoted on a "bond basis" while LIBOR is quoted on a "money market basis." Money market basis pays interest each day but calculates the daily rate as though a year has only 360 days. (This particular period would ordinarily have only 182 days in it, but 1996 happens to be a leap year.) During the next six-month interval, the floating-rate side would pay interest based on 183 days (i.e., 183/360). Subsequent periods would alternate between 182 days and 183 days.

The interest rate swap described above implicitly assumed that the notional principal which underlies the swap remains unchanged over the swap's tenor. That is, it is "non-amortizing." Nonamortizing notionals is a standard assumption in plain vanilla swap structures. Variants of the plain vanilla swap can be formed by making the notionals amortizing (getting smaller over time) or accreting (getting larger over time, sometimes called negative amortization), varying the reference rate (using the T-bill rate instead of LIBOR, for example), varying the payment frequency (quarterly or monthly, for example), and in dozens of other ways.

● OTHER PLAIN VANILLA CATEGORIES

Interest rate swaps are the dominant swap form in that the total of notional principals outstanding on these types of swaps dwarf those on all other swap classes, but other swap classes are also very important. Currency swaps are similar to interest rate swaps except that the notional principals on which the interest payments are calculated are in two different currencies. One counterparty, for example, might pay a fixed rate of interest on D-Mark principal while the other counterparty pays a floating rate of interest on yen principal. An equity swap would typically pay the "total return" on an equity index, such as the S&P 500, on one leg of the swap and a floating rate of interest, such as LIBOR, on the other leg of the swap. (Total return is defined as the percentage change in the value of the index plus dividend yield.) A commodity swap would pay a floating rate (i.e., the spot price of the commodity) on one leg and a fixed price on the other. A macroeconomic swap would pay a fixed sum on the fixed leg and would pay a sum determined by the performance of a macroeconomic index, such as gross domestic product (GDP), on the other leg. Such swaps could be used by cyclically sensitive industries, such as the automotive industry, to hedge exposures to variations in the business cycle.

The class which we loosely categorized as "other" would include all other types of swaps, such as swaps in which one leg is pegged to insurance casualty losses, or to a real estate index, or to the market value of pollution rights, or some other exotic index.

 ## CONCLUSION

The uses to which swaps can be put are really only now beginning to be understood. At the same time, swap markets are exploding and are now measured, globally, in the trillions of dollars of notionals. The shear size of the market, its apparent complexity, and a seemingly intractable web of interrelationships among market participants have raised concerns about the potential for the market to engender systemic risks. The authors believe that these concerns are misplaced and that derivatives, when properly used, insulate end users and financial institutions alike from the vagaries of the markets. Thus, they serve to ameliorate systemic risk, not to exacerbate it.

 PPENDIX D

Creative Engineering with Interest Rate Swaps

Interest rate swaps can be used to lower finance costs, hedge interest rate risks, manage the seasonality of cash flows, take speculative positions on the future shape of the yield curve, alter the investment characteristics of a portfolio, and synthesize other types of securities.

Two issues back, this column looked at the structure and terminology of plain vanilla interest rate swaps, along with some discussion of currency, commodity, equity, and macroeconomic swaps.[1] Here, a few of the more common, slightly exotic, variants of the interest rate swaps will be examined, along with a sampling of the applications for these instruments.

 ## COMMON VARIANTS OF THE INTEREST RATE SWAP

In the plain vanilla interest rate swap, the notional principal is nonamortizing, the payments are made semiannually, the reference rate for determining the floating leg payments is six-month LIBOR, and the swap is not callable or puttable. Innumerable variants can be created, some by simply changing the reference rate. This could be any standard short-term rate, such as the T-bill rate, the CD rate, a commercial paper rate, COFI, and so on. Alternatively, the reference rate can be pegged to a long-term rate, such as a five-year T-note rate or a two-year T-note rate. That is to say, a swap can be constructed so that on each reset date, the floating leg is reset to pay the yield on the par five-year T-note or the yield on the par two-year T-note. Because these swaps employ a reference rate tied to a specific maturity on the Treasury yield curve, they are called "constant maturity Treasury swaps" or, more simply, CMT swaps. Of course, it may be that, on a given reset date, there is no appropriate par Treasury of the correct maturity. To deal with this, the required yield is interpolated from existing instruments.

Another way to create a swap variant is to make both legs floating. For example, both legs can be tied to a short-term rate. This is called a basis swap.

---

[1] Marshall and Wynne, "What Are Swaps? A Look at Plain Vanilla Varieties," 1 DERIVATIVES 128 (January/February 1996).

Or, both rates can be pegged to long-term rates. This is called a yield curve swap. Basis swaps can be synthesized from two fixed-for-floating swaps:

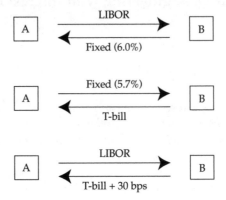

Yield curve swaps can be synthesized from two CMT swaps:

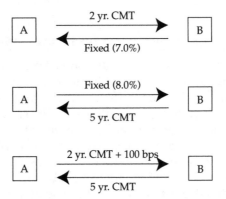

Another way to create a variant is to alter the payment frequency. Thus, instead of making the payments semiannually, the payments could be made annually, quarterly, or monthly. The swaps can also be structured so that one party pays on one payment frequency (say monthly) while the other party pays on a different payment frequency (say semiannually). This structure, of course, limits the ability to net payments and exposes at least one of the counterparties to additional credit risk.

Still another way to create a variant is to make the notional principal amortizing (getting smaller over time) or to make it accreting (getting larger over time). The former is common when the purpose of the swap is to hedge a mortgage portfolio. The latter is common when the purpose of the swap is to hedge a construction loan.

A particularly interesting variant of the basis swap is to tie the two legs to short-term rates in *different* currencies. This is not to be confused with a currency swap. In this type of interest rate swap, called a "rate differential swap," or "diff swap," the notional principals are in the *same* currency (e.g., dollars) but the floating rates of interest are drawn from two different currency markets, such as 6-M USD LIBOR (six-month LIBOR on Eurodollars) and 6-M DEM LIBOR (six-month LIBOR on Euro-deutschemarks). Of course, 6-M USD LIBOR and 6-M DEM LIBOR are unlikely to be the same. If, on average, DEM LIBOR is less than USD LIBOR, then a rate differential will have to be added to DEM LIBOR or deducted from USD LIBOR to make the present values of the two legs the same. (Hence the name of this swap.) The rate differential is depicted thus:

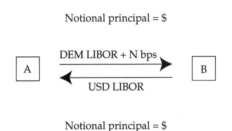

Another common swap variant is to make the swap callable or puttable. A callable swap is a swap in which the fixed-rate payor has the right to terminate the swap prior to its maturity. A puttable swap (also sometimes "putable") is a swap in which the floating-rate payor has the right to terminate the swap early. In both of the structures one of the parties has the *right but not the obligation* to terminate the swap early. This is the essence of an option. Thus, callable and puttable swaps are in fact portfolios consisting of a plain vanilla swap and an option on a plain vanilla swap. To make this a bit more concrete, consider a five-year fixed-for-floating interest rate swap that is callable after three years. This is really no different from a five-year plain vanilla swap and a three-year call option on a two-year plain vanilla swap (an option on a swap is called a "swaption"). That is to say, the fixed-rate paying counterparty has a five-year swap on which he is a fixed-rate payor. The option gives him the right, exercisable in three years, to enter into a two-year swap having identical, but opposite, terms. If, after three years, he exercises his option, the two-year swap he acquires offsets the remainder of the existing five-year swap.

One of the key themes that has been running through this discussion of swap variants is the idea that exotic swaps can be replicated by combining a number of simpler structures. Indeed, some would say that this is the essence of financial engineering—building complex special purpose structures from relatively simple components. Of special interest is the well-known fact that, while many different portfolios can replicate the same set of cash flows, and therefore be deemed economically equivalent, they do not necessarily have the same tax and accounting consequences.

 COMMON APPLICATIONS OF INTEREST RATE SWAPS

The two most common applications of interest rate swaps are to reduce financing costs and to hedge interest rate risks. Other applications include managing the seasonality of cash flows, taking speculative positions on the future shape of the yield curve, altering the investment characteristics of a portfolio, and synthesizing other types of securities. We will consider a simple example of each of the first four of these uses.

LOWERING FINANCING COSTS

Consider a firm that needs to finance a new production facility that will cost $50 million to construct. The firm would like to lock in its financing costs by issuing seven-year fixed-rate debt. This would likely take the form of seven-year notes paying a semiannual coupon. The firm, which has a single A rating, determines that it could sell $50 million of new notes at par if it pays a coupon of 8.5%.

As an alternative, the firm could issue $50 million of six-month commercial paper, paying the investment-grade commercial paper rate (CP), and roll this paper over 13 times to achieve a seven-year financing. This, of course, has the effect of creating a floating-rate liability rather than the desired fixed-rate liability. Suppose, instead, that a swap dealer is currently prepared to write a plain vanilla interest rate swap (six-month LIBOR against fixed) with the dealer as fixed-rate receiver at a swap coupon rate of 7.85%, and that the same (or another) dealer is prepared to enter into a LIBOR/CP basis swap with the dealer as CP payor/LIBOR receiver with the LIBOR leg set at LIBOR + 18 basis points. The firm could then achieve a financing that is economically equivalent to seven-year fixed rate by issuing six-month commercial paper, using a basis swap to swap into LIBOR, and using a fixed-for-floating interest rate swap to lock into fixed:

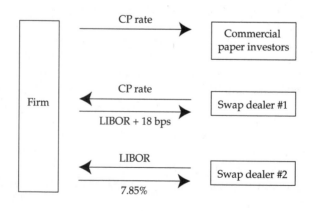

After all the legs have cancelled, the final cost to the firm is approximately 8.03%. This final cost compares quite favorably to issuing fixed-rate directly. Indeed, this synthetic fixed rate saves the firm approximately 47 basis points a year. (Approximate because LIBOR, CP, and the swap coupon are all stated using different yield conventions and some adjustments are necessary to get the true funding costs.) The two swaps employed in this structure would most likely be collapsed into a single swap of CP against fixed.

There are a number of ancillary considerations. The synthetic fixed-rate financing described above is economically equivalent to the direct fixed rate only if it is assumed that all other things are equal, or, as economists like to say, *ceteris paribus*. Unfortunately, this will generally not be the case. These other factors, often described as "qualitative factors," may work in favor of the synthetic financing or against it. Examples include the risk that the synthetic fixed rate will be affected by a downgrading (or upgrading) of the firm's credit, the length of time it takes to get the synthetic financing into place versus the time it takes to get the direct financing into place, the number of counterparties one has to deal with, how the two financings are recorded on the firm's balance sheet, and so forth.

Consider the impact of a down-grading. The CP-based swap will be tied to a particular quality of commercial paper (investment grade). Suppose that the firm, which is currently investment grade, is down-graded at one or more points over the seven-year period of the synthetic financing. The firm's CP rate would then go up on subsequent rollovers relative to the investment-grade CP rate to which the swap is tied. The possibility of changes in the firm's credit quality introduces some residual uncertainty into the firm's cost of funds. The firm does not have this residual uncertainty with a direct fixed-rate financing. This residual risk works in favor of the direct financing.

Next, consider the length of time it will take to get the financing in place. If a public offering is involved, direct fixed-rate financing will generally take from several weeks to several months to effect (assuming the firm does not have a shelf registration already in place and that the securities will be sold in the U.S. to U.S. investors). A commercial paper issuance, coupled with swaps, can generally be effected in a few days. This favors synthetic financing.

Next, consider the number of counterparties involved. In the case of the direct financing, the relationship is simply between the firm, as issuer, and the investors. In the synthetic financing, the multiple components result in multiple relationships that must be serviced. If the number of counterparties involved in a financial structure is a concern, the direct financing has an advantage.

Last, consider how these two forms of debt might be interpreted for balance sheet purposes. The direct fixed rate debt is clearly long-term debt of the issuer and might, therefore, be treated as debt capital of the firm. The CP issuance, if not viewed in conjunction with the swap (which is off balance sheet), is short-term debt and would not, therefore, generally be included in capital unless specific attention is drawn to the linkage between the commercial paper and the swaps.

Thus, the size and timing of the cash flows, both of which are quantitative factors, are not, in and of themselves, sufficient to judge the merits of synthetic financing relative to a direct financing. The qualitative, or ancillary, factors should also be considered.

HEDGING RISK

As a second application of interest rate swaps, consider a firm that enters into a swap to hedge a particular risk. For example, consider an automobile finance company that makes relatively long-term (four-year) fixed-rate loans to car buyers and which funds these loans in the commercial paper market using three-month commercial paper. The finance company has considerable risk exposure. It is lending at a fixed rate and borrowing at a floating rate—a recipe for disaster. By entering into a CP-linked interest rate swap, it can dramatically reduce its risks. This is a classic case of using swaps to hedge. The structure is depicted as in Exhibit D.1.

MANAGING SEASONAL CASH FLOWS

Many businesses have heavy seasonality to their cash flow streams. Examples would include the toy industry, the snow removal equipment industry, the garment industry, the credit card franchising industry, and the travel industry. Firms in such industries experience regular surges in cash flow followed by plunges in cash flow. To deal with this, classic corporate finance teaches to prepare cash budgets in order to predict the surpluses of cash that can be *lent* or the deficien-

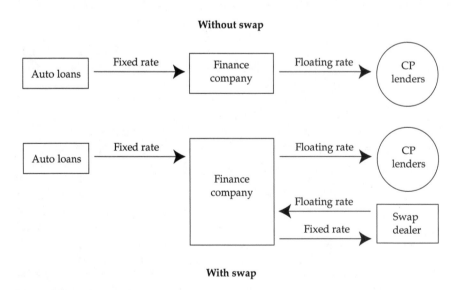

Without swap

With swap

EXHIBIT D.1 CP-linked interest rate swap

cies of cash that must be *financed*. This leads to alternating periods of lending and borrowing. The cost of this strategy may be defined as the difference between the borrowing rates and the lending rates. Swaps can be used to reduce these costs by eliminating much of the seasonality of cash flows. This could be done, for example, by entering into a specially structured interest rate swap designed to remove seasonality. Such swaps are sometimes called "seasonal swaps."

EXAMPLE.

A firm has two cash flow peaks and two cash flow troughs each year. The firm enters into a *fixed-for-fixed* interest rate swap having mismatched payment dates. That is, each counterparty to the swap pays a semiannual fixed rate but the payment dates are intentionally mismatched so that the firm is a net receiver on the swap during its cash cycle troughs and a net payor on the swap during its cash cycle peaks, as indicated in Exhibit D.2.

SPECULATING ON YIELD CURVES

For yet another application, suppose that the Treasury yield curve is such that the two-year Treasury note is yielding 6% and the five-year Treasury note is yielding 6.40%. An investor believes that the yield curve will steepen considerably over the next few years (i.e., the difference between the five-year rate and the two-year rate will widen) and would like to structure an investment that would pay off in accordance with this view. The investor determines that a swap dealer is prepared to enter a three-year swap tied to two-year CMT as fixed-rate payor at a swap coupon of 6.38% and that the same (or another) swap dealer is prepared to enter into a three-year swap tied to five-year CMT as fixed-rate receiver at a swap coupon of 6.90%. (These rates reflect the forward values of two-year CMT and five-year CMT respectively, not the current rates.) These two swaps are depicted in Exhibit D.3.

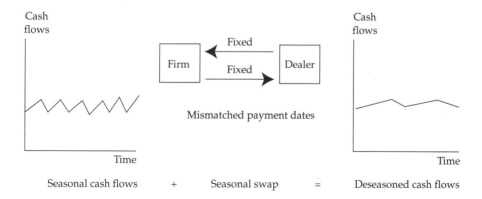

EXHIBIT D.2 Seasonal swap

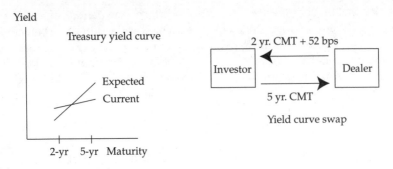

EXHIBIT D.3 Yield curve swap

These two swaps can be collapsed into a single swap with the two-year CMT on one leg and the five-year CMT on the other leg. This can be done simply by adding an appropriate number of basis points to the two-year CMT leg. This swap will now generate a profit if the five-year Treasury note rate rises relative to the two-year Treasury note rate. Thus, the swap allows the investor to structure an investment strategy around an anticipated change in the shape of the yield curve.

 ## CONCLUSION

All the strategies and structures described above can be achieved without resort to swaps (or any other derivative for that matter). Swaps, however, often allow us to structure (or engineer) a desired outcome with less cost. The simplicity and cost-effectiveness of achieving required or desired outcomes using derivatives is undoubtedly a principal explanation for the rapid growth of these markets.

Nevertheless, users need to be aware that solutions that are economically equivalent in a quantitative sense are not necessarily equivalent in a qualitative sense. The ancillary considerations, a few of which have been enumerated here, can be just as important—sometimes even more important—than any savings or efficiencies that can be achieved with the use of derivatives. These should, therefore, not be ignored.

Currency Swaps, Commodity Swaps, and Equity Swaps

Macroeconomic swaps can reduce a cyclically-sensitive firm's cash flow volatility due to variations in the general level of economic activity.

In an earlier column, we examined the basic interest rate swap and considered some of its applications.[1] Next we considered some variant forms of the interest rate swap, we explored some of the slightly more exotic structures, and we considered a number of now common applications of these structures.[2] Here, we turn our attention to other types of swaps including currency swaps, commodity swaps, and equity swaps. We also briefly describe a new class of swaps called macroeconomic swaps. As before, we consider applications as we introduce the products.

The principal use for swaps is to hedge price risks. For example, in our earlier look at plain vanilla swaps, we saw that an end user could employ an interest rate swap to convert a floating rate obligation to a fixed rate obligation by entering into a swap with itself as floating-rate receiver/fixed-rate payor. The floating rate would be pegged to six-month LIBOR and the swap would have semiannual payments. If the original obligation to be converted had a five-year maturity and principal of $80 million, then the swap would have a five-year tenor and notional principal of $80 million.

The end-user would most likely effect the swap with a swap dealer. The dealer, in turn, would either fold the swap into its portfolio as part of its overall effort at running a matched book, or, alternatively, it would hedge any residual risks in the futures markets. The motivation for the swap dealer is to capture a few basis points on the notional amount of the swap from the difference between its pay/receive rates on swaps of each tenor.

While still privately negotiated contracts, swaps are typically documented using industry-developed master agreements. The International Swaps and De-

---

[1] Marshall and Wynne, "What Are Swaps? A Look at Plain Vanilla Varieties," 1 DERIVATIVES 128 (January/February 1996).

[2] Marshall and Wynne, "Creative Engineering With Interest Rate Swaps," 1 DERIVATIVES 233 (May/June 1996).

rivatives Association (ISDA) is the principal author of these documents but it is not without competitors. The majority of swap dealers in the U.S. are either investment banks or money center commercial banks, but a few insurance companies have become major players. Because market regulation in the U.S. is based on industry, rather than function, regulation is often not consistent across participants—a sore point with many in the industry.

CURRENCY SWAPS

Currency swaps, also called cross-currency swaps, were introduced in 1979. Interest rate swaps were introduced two years later. The early currency swaps were called "exchanges of borrowings" and only later came to be called swaps. Like interest rate swaps, currency swaps typically have one floating leg and one fixed leg. The fixed leg pays a fixed rate of interest on notional principal in *one* currency while the floating leg pays a floating rate of interest on notional principal in a *different* currency. It is the different currency denominations of the notional principals that distinguish a currency swap from an interest rate swap. The relationship between the notionals is determined by the exchange rate prevailing at the time the swap is initiated. For example, one leg might pay six-month USD LIBOR on $50 million of notional principal while the other leg might pay a fixed rate of 7.42% on £76.75 million. Currency swaps can also be structured so that both legs have a fixed rate. In the latter case, the fixed rates reflect the current market conditions in the two countries whose currencies are involved in the swap.

Currency swaps are an effective tool for hedging foreign exchange risk when the exposure is recurring (also called multi-period). This is in contrast to the use of futures or forwards, which are more appropriate when the exposure is not recurring (single period). Of course, a series of futures or forwards could be strung together to achieve multi-period exchange rate risk management and, therefore, swaps must compete for market share with these other instruments.

EXAMPLE

A U.S. multinational (MNC) needs floating-rate dollar financing. The MNC considers all of the ways it might achieve this financing and concludes that, under current market conditions, the most cost effective is to issue fixed-rate samurai bonds in the Japanese markets. The principal received from the offering and the interest rate obligation created are both in yen. To hedge the resultant exchange rate risk associated with the bond offering, the MNC enters into a yen/dollar fixed-for-floating currency swap. The transactions are illustrated in the diagram in Exhibit E.1. This swap will likely involve an initial exchange of notional principals and a terminal re-exchange of notional principals (only the interest payments are shown). In this sense, it must be differentiated from an interest rate swap, where the notionals are never exchanged.

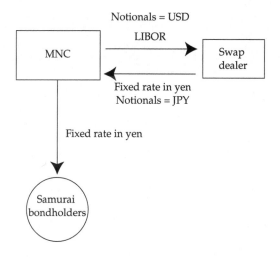

EXHIBIT E.1 Currency swap

Alternatively, the MNC could use foreign exchange forward contracts or currency futures to hedge its exposure, but the multi-period nature of the exposure and the relatively long maturity of the obligation make the swap solution more attractive. Nevertheless, the MNC should consider these alternative vehicles for hedging its exchange rate risk.[3] As an aside, it is likely that the swap dealer will use the futures market to hedge its positions in the swap until such time as it can offset the risks in other swaps.

Consider a second case. Exhibit E.2 illustrates a U.S. multinational that wanted to hedge its currency exposure on a financing subsidy it had received as an inducement by the French government to contract with a French firm to build an oil refinery. The U.S. firm, which is an oil producer, had agreed to make semiannual payments at a fixed rate of 3.58% in French francs. But, the firm would prefer that its obligations be in the form of fixed rate dollars. To meet its franc interest and principal obligations, the firm had been exchanging dollars for francs in the spot foreign exchange market. This exposed the firm to considerable currency risk.

To better manage this risk, the firm entered a currency swap. It agreed to pay dollar LIBOR in exchange for receiving a fixed rate in French francs. While this swap converted the financing from a franc obligation to a dollar obligation, thereby removing the currency risk, it did not provide the U.S. firm with

---

[3] Ira Kawaller recently contrasted forward and futures solutions to exchange rate risk hedging, "Combining Futures and Forwards for Managing Currency," 1 DERIVATIVES 196 (May/June 1996).

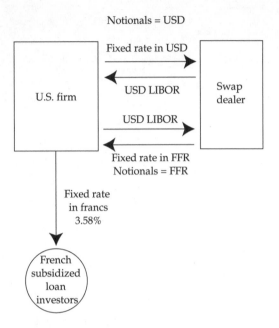

EXHIBIT E.2   Fixed-for-fixed currency swap

the type of interest obligation it desired, i.e., fixed rate. To achieve the latter, the firm entered an interest rate swap separately from the currency swap. This is depicted in Exhibit E.2.

The combination of the fixed-for-floating currency swap coupled with a fixed-for floating interest rate swap produces a fixed-for-fixed currency swap. A dealer writing such swaps would typically fold the two swaps into a single swap having two fixed legs.

COMMODITY SWAPS

Commodity swaps were first introduced in 1986 by the Chase Manhattan Bank. Shortly thereafter, the CFTC questioned their legality. The resultant uncertainty cast a pall over the market with the result that the business was moved overseas. In 1989, the CFTC granted commodity swaps, indeed all swaps, an exemption from the laws governing futures trading and commodity swaps were reborn.

EXAMPLE

In the first half of 1996, the price of copper rose dramatically and the futures market became seriously inverted (front months were trading at a significant premium to back months), which is typical of a market squeeze. A copper producer comes to believe that the current level of copper prices is unusually at-

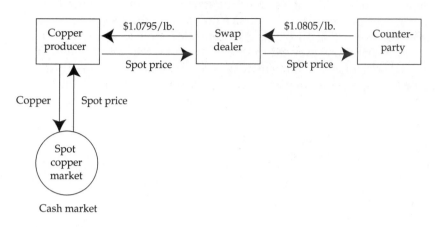

Notionals = 2 million pounds of copper

Cash market

EXHIBIT E.3 A copper swap

tractive and decides that it can assure itself of long-term profitability by locking in the high prices now. A commodity swap dealer offers a five-year commodity swap under which it will pay the producer a fixed price of $1.0795 per pound in exchange for the spot price of copper. (At the time, this rate is lower than the price on near-month futures but higher than the price on back-month futures.) The copper swap requires quarterly payments on 2 million notional pounds of copper. With the swap in place the producer is insulated from further volatility in the price of copper, at least for the tenor of the swap.

As it happens the price of copper rises further and the producer seems, for a time, to have locked in to a fixed price a bit prematurely, but on June 11, the price of copper plunges by 6% on fears that Sumitomo Corporation, a large Japanese metals trading firm, would unload sizable positions. It falls further in the days that follow and the producer's hedge proves quite fortuitous. The hedge is illustrated in Exhibit E.3.

The commodity swap dealer, like the interest rate swap dealer, looks to profit from the difference between its pay rate and its receive rate. Both rates are quoted against the spot copper price. This too is illustrated in Exhibit E.3. As with interest rate swaps, the key to pricing and hedging the dealer's positions is the futures markets.

Commodity swaps can be combined with other swaps to achieve unique outcomes. For example, with two plain vanilla commodity swaps, a plain vanilla currency swap, and a plain vanilla interest rate swap, one could create *synthetic barter*.[4]

---

[4] For more detail on this structure and the background for its application, see Marshall and Wynne, "Synthesizing Countertrade Solutions with Swaps," Global Finance Journal 1996, forthcoming.

EXAMPLE

A country produces oil that it sells on the spot oil market for dollars. It uses the proceeds from oil sales to purchase rice in Japan for the spot rice price in yen. Neither the dollar nor the yen is the domestic currency of this country. The country ("Nation"), is exposed to three price risks: the price of oil in dollars, the price of rice in yen, and the price of yen in dollars. All of these risks can be removed by a properly engineered structure, as indicated in Exhibit E.4.

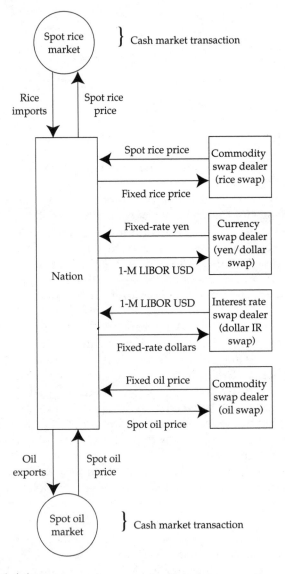

EXHIBIT E.4 Synthetic barter

EQUITY SWAPS

Equity swaps are swaps in which at least one leg of the swap pays a floating rate that is linked to the return on an equity or equity index. The other leg could be fixed rate, also linked to an equity or equity index, or linked to a floating rate of interest such as LIBOR. Equity swaps typically reset quarterly.

Most equity swaps are linked to the *total return* on the equity or equity index. (Total return includes both dividend return and capital appreciation.) But, an equity swap can be structured to pay only the dividend yield or only the capital appreciation on the equity or equity index. The notional principals of the two legs of an equity swap are routinely in the same currency, but equity swaps can be structured so that the two legs are in different currencies by combining equity swaps with currency swaps.

Equity swaps have a great many uses. Perhaps the most obvious is to convert an equity portfolio into a fixed income portfolio or into a money market portfolio. For example, an equity for-LIBOR swap could be used by a portfolio manager to convert an equity portfolio to a money market portfolio without the necessity of selling the stocks. By avoiding the sale of the stocks, the portfolio manager also avoids the transactions costs. This is depicted in Exhibit E.5.

Equity swaps can also be used to effect all variety of asset allocation strategies. For example, a portfolio manager holding a U.S. equities portfolio providing an S&P-like return could convert his portfolio into a synthetic Japanese stock portfolio by paying the total return on the S&P 500 and receiving the total return on the Nikkei 225. Returns on the Nikkei would need to be measured

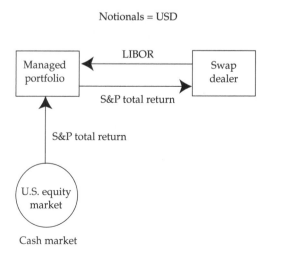

EXHIBIT E.5 An equity-for-floating equity swap

on a dollar basis, rather than a yen basis, to replicate the actual holding of a Japanese stock portfolio. That is, the recipient should receive the total return on the Nikkei *after* the conversion to dollars. This exposes the portfolio's owners to exchange rate risk in the same way that holding an actual Japanese stock portfolio would expose them to exchange rate risk. Importantly, derivatives dealers will write swaps with the Japanese stock return on a yen basis, instead of a dollar basis. This removes the exchange rate risk, and is called a *quantoed* structure.

To see the difference between an equity swap that is quantoed and one that is not quantoed, consider two swaps of the type just described. Suppose that, for a given quarter, the S&P 500 provides a total return of 4% (in dollars) and the Nikkei provides a total return of 6% (in yen). For the same period, however, the yen loses 5% against the dollar.

If the swap was not quantoed, the U.S. portfolio manager would pay out 4% on the S&P leg and receive about 0.7% on the Nikkei leg [(1 + .06)(1 − .05) − 1]. Thus, he is a net payer of 3.3%. If the swap was quantoed, however, he would pay 4% on the S&P leg but receive 6% on the Nikkei. Thus he would be a net receiver of 2%. This is depicted in Exhibit E.6.

Using equity swaps to synthesize foreign equity returns has become a common financial engineering activity. The advantages of this approach may include maturity matching, tax avoidance, arbitrage, and regulatory circumvention. Nevertheless, before employing a swap solution, the investor would be wise to contrast the strategy with more traditional methods of achieving international diversification. Traditional methods include purchasing foreign securities directly, holding American Depository Receipts (ADRs), and holding futures contracts on foreign stock indexes.

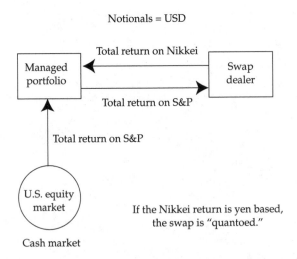

EXHIBIT E.6 Using an equity swap to synthesize foreign equity from domestic equity

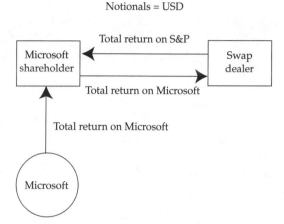

Notionals = USD

EXHIBIT E.7 Using an equity swap to diversify a risk

Equity swaps can also be used by corporate insiders to diversify away the unsystematic risk associated with holding a large equity position in a firm without actually having to sell the stake in the firm. This kind of structure is very useful for founders of successful high technology firms. For example, an owner of Microsoft stock might swap the total return on Microsoft for the total return on the S&P 500, as diagrammed in Exhibit E.7.

 MACROECONOMIC SWAPS

The development of the swap contracts led, in 1991, to the idea that business cycle risk might also be hedged with swaps. Swaps designed for this purpose are linked to macroeconomic indices and are called, not surprisingly, macroeconomic swaps. If properly structured, macroeconomic swaps can be used to reduce a cyclically sensitive firm's cash flow volatility attributable to variations in the general level of economic activity. A typical macroeconomic swap, using an automobile manufacturer as the end-user is depicted in Exhibit E.8. The manufacturer is paying the swap dealer a rate that is indexed to gross domestic product (GDP). At high GDP growth rates the manufacturer is a net payer on the swap. With low or negative GDP growth rates, the manufacturer is a net receiver on the swap. This allows the automobile manufacturer to manage the impact of recessions on the profitability of the firm. Of course, the presence of the swap dampens the firm's profitability during expansionary periods.

A major problem with macroeconomic swaps is the difficulty that the swap dealer has in hedging the risk. Since most businesses are procyclical, it is virtually impossible for a dealer to run a matched book. This is a problem because there are presently no GDP futures contracts in which to hedge the dealer's risks. One possible solution is to hold a proxy portfolio of futures or

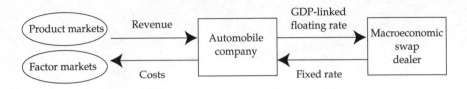

EXHIBIT E.8 Macroeconomic derivatives

stocks such that the portfolio mimics the GDP index. To date, it has not been possible to create proxy portfolios having a high enough degree of correlation with GDP to make this solution viable.

 ## CONCLUSION

Currency, commodity, and equity swaps can be used to engineer solutions, some of which have been discussed here, to an assortment of financial problems. Macroeconomic swaps can also hedge business cycle risk. In a future column, we will examine a few of the more common types of exotic options and consider how swaps and options can be embedded in structured notes to simultaneously satisfy the financing needs of issuers and the investment needs of investors when the needs of the two parties are different.

Options 101: The Basics

Financial engineers go to great lengths to develop valuation models. The first analytical solution developed was the Black/Scholes model, while the first lattice model was the binomial option pricing model.

This column continues our series of tutorials on derivatives and their applications. Previously we have provided tutorials that have examined the evolution of financial engineering (Sep/Oct 1995), basic swap structures (Jan/Feb 1996), interest rate swap variants (May/Jun 1996), and other types of swaps including currency, commodity, equity, and macroeconomic swaps (Sep/Oct 1996). This column now focuses on options. Options are, at one and the same time, a very simple and a very complex subject—simple if one concentrates on the basic structures and the basic uses, but complex if one concentrates on their valuation and risk characteristics.

Our purpose in this first column on options is simply to describe their basic types, the terminology that surrounds them, and the payoffs from holding them. We limit ourselves to the simplest types of options known as calls and puts. In a future issue of DERIVATIVES, we will examine how the simple options described here can be used for risk management purposes. In later articles we will examine some of the more complex types of options and some of the more sophisticated applications of options.

 A BRIEF HISTORY

Most people believe that options trading in the U.S. began in 1973. In fact, options have a much longer history. The confusion stems from the fact that the options of old were not called options, but rather were called "privileges." Additionally, a type of call option called a warrant has also been around for a much longer time.

Nevertheless, the options markets were not of any significant note until the birth of the first modern options exchange. This was the Chicago Board Options Exchange (CBOE), which introduced listed call options on common stocks using a standardized format in 1973. Put options on common stocks were introduced shortly thereafter. Subsequently, other exchanges, including a number of stock exchanges, also introduced listed options on common stocks.

The listed stock options markets grew steadily with more contracts on stocks added each year. Trading volume grew as well. In the 1980s, listed options on futures contracts and on stock indexes were introduced. Also in the 1980s, OTC options made their debut. The market for the latter has grown explosively over the last ten years, largely because the OTC market provides flexibility in contract design (at the expense of liquidity and counterparty risk).

 ## THE MOST BASIC TYPES OF OPTIONS

A financial option is most often described very generally as the "right but not the obligation to buy or sell something at a pre-determined price." The key words are the "right but not the obligation." This is what differentiates an option from other types of derivatives. Technically, this definition is a little too general. The holder (i.e., the purchaser) of the option has a right *but not* an obligation. The writer (i.e., the seller) of the option has an absolute obligation. The two most basic types of options are calls and puts. We will describe these options in their original form—i.e., deliverable options on common stock. But the descriptions would be very similar for calls and puts written on any underlying asset.[1]

A call option grants its holder the right, but not the obligation, to buy a specified number of units of some asset from the option writer for a defined period of time for a specified price. The asset on which the option is written is called the "underlying asset" or simply the "underlying." The period of time that the option right is valid is called "the time to expiry" or the "time to expiration." The actual day of expiration is called the "expiration date" or "expiry." In this article, we will use the phrase "at the end of the option's life" to mean the last possible moment that the option can be exercised before it expires. The price at which the option can be exercised is called the "strike price." Most people just say "strike." The strike price is also known as the "exercise price" and sometimes is called the "striking price."

Most exchange-traded stock options in the U.S. cover 100 shares of the underlying stock. Even though the option covers many shares, we always speak of it as though it covers only one. Most stock options expire on the Saturday following the third Friday of the expiration month. The third Friday itself is the last trading day. For example, a *June 95 call on IBM* would describe a call option on 100 shares of IBM common stock that expires on the Saturday following the third Friday of June. If the option holder chooses to exercise the option,

---

[1] For example, an option could be written on a bond, or on a commodity, or on a stock index. Some options are cash settled instead of deliverable. This means that these options settle up for a sum of money equal to the value that would be captured if the option had been deliverable.

he would have to give the option writer $95 for each share of IBM stock (for a total of $9,500) and the option writer would be obligated to deliver 100 shares of IBM. Clearly, if the market price of IBM is greater than $95 at the end of the option's life, the holder is better off if exercising the option. Even if he does not really want IBM stock, he is better off if he exercises the option because he can always sell the stock for more than $95. For example, if the price of IBM is $98, the option holder would buy the stock for $95 and then sell it again in the market for $98, thereby capturing $3 (for each share). On the other hand, if the market price of IBM is below $95 at the end of the option's life, the option holder should not exercise the option—even if he does want IBM stock because he could buy the stock more cheaply in the market.

Put options grant their holders the right but not the obligation to *sell* the underlying asset to the option writer. The terminology for puts is the same as the terminology for calls. For example, a *June 95 put on IBM* would give the option holder the right to sell to the option writer 100 shares of IBM stock for $95 a share even if the price of IBM stock is less than $95 in the market at that time. Suppose, for example, that the price of IBM is $92 a share. The option holder will exercise the option and sell the stock for $95 a share. He will do this even if he does not have the stock. He would purchase the stock in the market for $92 and then exercise the option and deliver the stock for $95. The option writer has no choice but to take the stock at that price.

Clearly, the holder of a call benefits if the market price of the underlying asset goes up and the holder of a put benefits if the market price of the underlying asset goes down.

AMERICAN-TYPE VERSUS EUROPEAN-TYPE OPTIONS

Options are usually classified as either American-type or European-type. The terminology has nothing to do with the trading location, but it does explain the geographic origins of the different types. The difference between these types of options has to do with when they can be exercised. American-type calls and puts can be exercised by their holder anytime the holder wants—literally from the moment he buys the option until the moment the option expires. Of course, once the option has expired, it is no longer exercisable. A European-type option, on the other hand, can only be exercised during a short period of time that occurs just before the end of the option's life.

For options written on some underlying assets, the difference between American-type and European-type options is not very important. But for options written on other underlying assets the difference can be very important. For example, consider the case of a call option written on common stock that is scheduled to go ex-dividend a few weeks prior to the option's expiration date. On the ex-dividend date, the underlying stock's market price will drop by the amount of the declared dividend. In such a situation, it might be advantageous to exercise the call prior to the drop in the market price of the underlying stock. With an American-type option you can exercise the option early, but with a European-type option you cannot. Thus, the two options will have different values.

MONEYNESS

Options are often described as "in-the-money," "at-the-money," or "out-of-the-money." These terms refer to the current relationship between the option's strike price and the price of the underlying asset. In the case of a call option, if the underlying asset's market price exceeds the strike price of the option, the option is said to be "in-the-money." If they are the same, it is "at-the-money." If the underlying asset's price is below the strike, it is "out-of-the-money." The descriptions are reversed for put options.

NO FREE LUNCH: THE OPTION PREMIUM

The beauty of an option is in the asymmetry of the payoff. For example, if you hold a June 95 call on IBM until the end of its life, it will pay off a sum equal to the difference between the market price of IBM stock and the strike price of the option—but only if that difference is positive. If the difference is negative, the option holder would simply allow the option to expire. Thus, in a sense, you can win, but you can't lose. This payoff is most often represented by a *max* function. For example, if the underlying asset's market price is denoted by A, and the strike price of the option is denoted by S, then the payoff to the holder of a call option at the end of the option's life is given by: Payoff = $max[A-S, 0]$. The *max* function means we take the larger of the two numbers in brackets. Notice that the payoff cannot be negative (you simply let the option expire if exercising it would result in a loss of value). Thus, if A is greater than S, the payoff is positive. If A is less than or equal to S, the payoff is zero.

A similar relationship would hold for a put option, except the option holder profits if the underlying asset's price declines. The payoff is given by: Payoff = $max[S-A, 0]$.

All of this can lead one to conclude that options are a "no lose situation," at least for the option holder. But, if this were the case, why would anyone write one? After all, for the holder to win, the writer has to lose. The answer is simple: *options are not free*. To get the option, the option purchaser has to pay a market-determined sum to the option writer. This sum is called the "option premium." The option premium is paid up front and it is separate from the option's strike price. The term "premium" stems from the fact that options are often likened to insurance policies, particularly when options are used as risk management tools.

It does not matter if one is buying a call option or a put option, a premium must still be paid to the option writer to acquire the option. Determining what is a fair premium for an option is probably the most mathematically complex subject in all of finance. Unfortunately, there is no single formula that works for all options.

Financial engineers go to great lengths to develop valuation models that accurately reflect the fair values of options. There are a number of ways to go about this. One way is to derive what financial engineers call an "analytical," also known as a "closed form," solution. This is an equation that specifies the precise relationship between the value of the option and the various factors that determine its value. Such equations are rigorously derived and are based upon a set of carefully defined and rigid assumptions about the behavior of the underlying asset's price and the behaviors of the other variables that influence the option's value. The first such analytical solution to be developed was the Black/Scholes model. This was published by Fischer Black and Myron Scholes in 1973 and has long been the workhorse of option traders.[2]

A very different approach to valuing options uses numeric methods rather than rigorous derivations. The most widely used of these approaches are lattice models, the first of which was the binomial option pricing model. This approach is not as elegant mathematically, but if used properly, it will produce the same result as an analytical model. It has the advantages of being intuitively simple and extremely flexible because it allows for alternative assumptions. As a result, it can be applied easily to value many different types of options. The binomial approach was popularized by John Cox, Stephen Ross, and Mark Rubinstein in 1979, but others contributed as well.[3] The method has the disadvantages of being computationally intensive, often requiring many millions of calculations to achieve a solution. As a result, the widespread application of this methodology had to wait for the advent of high-speed microprocessors.

VALUING OPTIONS

Regardless of the approach taken, option valuation must capture the various factors that influence an option's value. In the case of simple options on common stock, the value of the options will be determined by six factors. These are the current market price of the underlying asset, the strike price of the option, the time to expiry (as a fraction of a year), the interest rate, the future volatility of the price of the underlying asset (measured on an annual basis in percentage form), and the expected dividends. Assuming for simplicity that the stock on which the option is written will not pay any dividends before the expiration date of the option, the value of the option can be expressed as a function of the remaining five variables as follows: $C = f(A, S, T, R, V)$, where C is the premium on a call option, A is the current price of the underlying asset, S is the strike price of the option, T is the time to expiry, R is the rate of interest, and V is the volatility of the underlying.

---

[2] Black and Scholes, "The Pricing of Options and Corporate Liabilities," 81 Journal of Political Economy May/June 1973, pp. 637–659.

[3] Cox, Ross, and Rubinstein, "Options Pricing: A Simplified Approach," 7(3) Journal of Financial Economics 229–264

Four of the five variables, *A*, *S*, *T*, and *R*, are directly observable. Only *V*, the future volatility of the underlying, is not directly observable. Thus, when one is pricing an option, what one is really pricing is the volatility. That is, a volatility estimate implies a specific premium and, similarly, a market-observed premium implies a specific volatility. This is why options traders often describe themselves as "trading volatility" or "volatility traders."

THE GREEKS

Probably the scariest aspect for novices in any discussion of options are references to the option's Greeks. This is not so formidable as it first appears. Since the option premium is a function of five input variables, we can ask the following question: "what will happen to the premium on the option if *one* of the input variables changes by a small amount?" Let's illustrate this in the context of call options on IBM.

We ask "what will happen to the fair value of the call option if the price of IBM stock rises by $1?" Let's suppose that the option valuation model tells us the answer is that the option premium will go up by $0.45. That is, a $1 change in the price of the underlying causes a $0.45 change in the option premium. This change is called the option's "delta." That is, an option's delta is defined as the dollar amount the option premium would change if the underlying's price changes by $1. In this case, the delta is $0.45. Similarly, we can ask how the option's premium would change if time to expiry changed (called the option's "theta"), or how the option's premium would change if the interest rate changed (called the option's "rho"), or how the option premium would change if volatility changed (called the option's "vega"). Delta, theta, rho, and vega are, collectively, the option's Greeks.[4]

PAYOFF PROFILES

An option's value is often divided into two fundamental components. The first is called its "intrinsic value." An option's intrinsic value is nothing more than the larger of the amount by which it is in-the-money or zero. Thus, it is given by the *max* function we examined earlier. This intrinsic value is the value that would be captured if the option were exercised immediately.

The second value component is called the option's "time value." Time value is value in excess of the intrinsic value and it reflects the potential for the price of the underlying asset to move favorably (meaning the intrinsic value goes up) prior to the option's expiration. For example, consider again the June 95 call on IBM. Suppose that this option has one month before it expires and

---

[4] Some of the Greeks have more than one name. And, there are other, less often discussed, Greeks as well. One of these is an option's gamma. Gamma is a measure of how an option's delta changes.

suppose that the current price of IBM is $96. The intrinsic value of the option is, of course, $1 (i.e., *max*[96-95,0]). But is that all you would be willing to pay for it? The answer is no. With a full month before expiration, there is considerable opportunity for the price of IBM to rise and for the option to become more deeply in the money—that is, acquire more intrinsic value. The time value of the option captures this potential. The term "time value" is used because, all other things being equal, this extra value declines as the option approaches expiration. Thus, it is a function of time.

The premium of a call option can then be defined as the sum of the two components as follows:

$$C = \text{intrinsic value} + \text{time value}$$
$$C = max[A\text{-}S,0] + \text{time value}$$

The time value of an option gets smaller as the option get more deeply in-the-money but it also gets smaller as the option gets more deeply out-of-the-money. Thus, time value is at a maximum when the option is at-the-money.[5]

We often have a reason to want to visually examine the payoffs from holding options. That is, we want to look at what is called the payoff profile or the value diagram. This is a visual depiction of the value of the option as a function of the price of the underlying asset—holding both the annual volatility and the interest rate constant. The trouble is that there are actually an infinite number of such diagrams, each corresponding to a different amount of time until expiration.

The most common way around this problem is to draw the payoff profile as of the very end of the option's life. At this point in time, the option has lost all of its time value and only intrinsic value remains. This is depicted for the holder of a call and for the holder of a put in Exhibits F.1 and F.2.

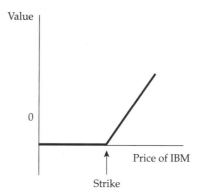

EXHIBIT F.1 Payoff to the holder of a call (at expiration)

---

[5] The reasons for these behaviors can be found in any good book on the subject.

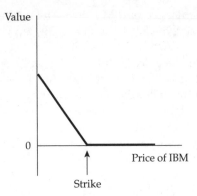

EXHIBIT F.2 Payoff to the holder of a put (at expiration)

Prior to the end of the option's life, the payoffs would look like those in Exhibits F.3 and F.4. These reflect the presence of positive time value. Notice that the curves are not linear. This is why options are often called "nonlinear contracts."

It is important to appreciate that these payoff profiles do not depict profit. To obtain profit, we would have to deduct the premium that was paid for the option. When we deduct the option premium, these diagrams are called profit diagrams.[6] Typical profit diagrams, drawn as of the end of the option's life, are depicted in Exhibits F.5 and F.6.

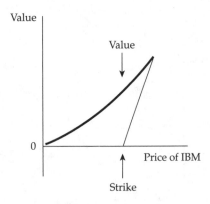

EXHIBIT F.3 Value for the holder of a call (prior to expiration)

---

[6] Sometimes payoff profiles are drawn to reflect the cost of the option. In these cases, profit diagrams and payoff profiles are the same, but differ from value diagrams which never reflect the cost of the option.

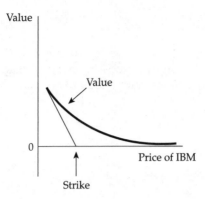

EXHIBIT F.4 Value for the holder of a put (prior to expiration)

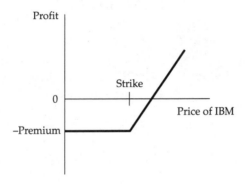

EXHIBIT F.5 Profit diagram for the holder of a call (at expiration)

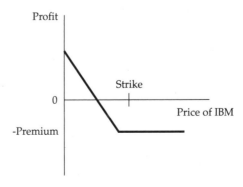

EXHIBIT F.6 Profit diagram for the holder of a put (at expiration)

CONCLUSION

With this introduction to basic option terminology and concepts complete, we are now ready to look at applications. In our next column, we will examine some of the ways that options can be used to hedge.

APPENDIX G

Options Can Be Tailored to Hedge Single and Multiple Exposure Periods

If the firm has a strong view on the direction of interest rates, options may be the best hedge.

This column continues our series of tutorials on derivative instruments and their applications. In our previous column (January/February 1997), we examined the basics of options. Most of our discussion in that column involved two types of single-period options called *calls* and *puts*. While that discussion was cast in terms of options on common stock, the principles are equally applicable to options on other underlying assets. Here, we will expand the discussion to include:

- Simple multi-period options.
- Several types of interest rate options.
- Some common hedging applications.

All of the options that we discuss and employ in this column are considered "plain vanilla." We will also highlight the difference between hedging with futures and hedging with options.

 ### A BRIEF REVIEW

An option is a contract in which one party, called the *writer,* sells to another party, called the *holder,* the right, but not the obligation, to buy or sell the *underlying asset* for a limited period of time at a preset price, called the option's *strike price.* If the contract grants the holder the right to *buy* the underlying asset, the option is called a *call.* If the option grants the holder the right to *sell* the underlying asset, the option is called a *put.* The remaining life of the option is called its *time to expiration.* For the right that the option conveys, the holder pays the option writer a nonrefundable fee called a *premium.* This fee is paid at the time the option is purchased. In the case of a call, if the option holder chooses to exercise the option, the holder will pay the writer the option's strike price and receive from the writer the underlying asset. In the case of a put, if the option holder chooses to exercise the option, the holder will receive from the writer the option's strike price and deliver to the writer the underlying asset.

An option's value is the sum of its *intrinsic value* and its *time value*. Time value represents the potential for the option to acquire more intrinsic value before it expires. At the very end of an option's life, there is no more potential to acquire additional intrinsic value and, hence, the time value at the end of an option's life is zero. At this point, only the intrinsic value remains. In the case of a deliverable option, such as an option written on common stock, the intrinsic value is captured by exercising the option and simultaneously acquiring or disposing of the underlying asset in the underlying asset's cash market.[1] For example, with a call option on stock, the option holder would exercise the option—thereby buying the stock for the option's strike price—and then sell the stock in the market. Similarly, for a put, the option holder would buy the stock in the market and then exercise the option to force the writer to take the stock for the option's strike price. Since the option holder would never voluntarily exercise an option that is out-of-the-money, the option can never have negative value.[2]

The payoff to the option holder can be calculated at the end of the option's life, when only the option's intrinsic value remains. The payoff formulas are given below. Here, A denotes the market price of the underlying and S denotes the strike price of the option.

$$\text{Payoff on a call:} \quad \text{payoff} = max[A-S, 0]$$
$$\text{Payoff on a put:} \quad \text{payoff} = max[S-A, 0]$$

The underlying assets on which options can be written are not limited to common stocks. They can be bonds (such as Treasury bonds), commodities, futures contracts, etc. In all of these cases, however, the underlying is deliverable if the option is exercised.

 ## CASH SETTLED OPTIONS

Options do not have to be deliverable. That is, we could write an option on some underlying asset but specify that, in lieu of delivery, the option will settle for a cash payment equal to the intrinsic value of the option at the very end

---

[1] The term "cash market" refers to the market in which the underlying asset trades for immediate delivery. Immediate delivery means whatever length of time is the usual and customary settlement period on a transaction. For example, the New York Stock Exchange would be a cash market for stocks. Immediate delivery means three business days.

[2] Exercising an out-of-the-money option would result in a loss beyond the option premium already paid. This loss need not be sustained because the option holder can simply allow the option to expire.

of the option's life. The payoff would be the same as if the option was deliverable, but the cash market transactions in the underlying are dispensed with.

Examples of cash-settled options include options written on stock indexes and options on interest rates. Consider briefly one example of each. Suppose that you wanted to place a bet on the entire stock market, as represented by an index. To accomplish this, you buy a call option on the S&P 500. At the end of the option's life, the writer of the option will simply pay you a sum of money equal to the amount by which the S&P 500 index exceeds the strike specified in the option contract. Of course, the actual payoff is based on "some number of units" of the underlying asset, so the contract must also specify the number of units. This might, for example, be 100. Thus, the actual payoff would be 100 times the $max[A-S, 0]$, where A is the value of the S&P 500 index at the very end of the option's life, and S is the strike price of the option. The key to making cash-settled options work is having some objective reference index. This reference index could be a price, an interest rate, a stock index and so forth. The reference index is sometimes called the benchmark. In this case, the reference index is the value of the S&P 500 index.

A second example of cash-settled options is options written on interest rates. For example, we could write an option on LIBOR, on the prime rate of interest, on the Treasury-bill rate, etc. Options written on LIBOR are widely used. LIBOR is an acronym for the London Interbank Offered Rate. It is, essentially, the rate of interest on Eurocurrency deposits. If we do not specify otherwise, it is understood to be dollar (USD) LIBOR. That is, it is the interest rate on Eurodollar deposits. There are also deutschemark LIBOR, yen LIBOR, and so on. When quoting LIBOR, we have to specify the deposit period as well as the currency. For example, LIBOR is quoted for one-month deposits, three-month deposits, six-month deposits, and one-year deposits, among others. Thus, we need to identify the specific deposit term we are interested in. This might be, for example, 6-mo LIBOR, which means the interest rate on a six-month Eurodollar deposit. On these options, the strike takes the form of a "strike rate" rather than a strike price.

Consider a June call on 6-mo LIBOR with a strike of 7% and notional principal of $100 million. This says that on a certain day in June, we will observe the value of 6-mo LIBOR as quoted in London at 11 A.M. London time. The number of days covered by that quote would typically be 182 or 183. Suppose that it is 182. For this option, the purchaser pays the writer a premium—usually expressed as a percentage of the notional principal. This might be 0.40%. Thus, the premium paid upfront to acquire the option would be $400,000, found by multiplying the premium by the notional principal (0.4% × $100 million).

At the end of this option's life, i.e., on the expiration date, the option would cash settle for a sum given by:

$$\text{Payoff} = max[\text{6-mo LIBOR} - 7.00\%, 0] \times 182/360 \times \$100 \text{ million}$$

and

$$\text{Profit = payoff} - \text{premium paid =}$$
$$\{max[\text{6-mo LIBOR} - 7.00\%, 0] \times 182/360 \times \$100 \text{ million}\} - \$400,000$$

If 6-mo LIBOR is greater than 7.00%, the payoff is positive; otherwise it is zero. The payoff requires multiplication by 182/360 because LIBOR is quoted "actual/360," which means the year is assumed to have 360 days but the interest is paid each and every day. Since the underlying Eurodollar deposit is for six months but interest rates are quoted on an annual basis, this adjustment is necessary.[3]

 ## MULTI-PERIOD OPTIONS

Whether deliverable or cash settled, call options and put options are, essentially, single-period options in the sense that they are structured to have a single payoff or settlement, after which they cease to exist. There is no reason, however, that we cannot write an option that settles up repeatedly using the standard option payoff formula. That is to say, the option can have a long life, called its *tenor*. During this life, it settles up and pays off, using the standard call or the standard put payoff formula, at regular intervals, perhaps once every six months. For example, we could have an option that pays off every six months for four years. Only after the eighth payoff does the option cease to exist. These sorts of options are, collectively, called multi-period options.

The two simplest types of multiperiod options are caps and floors. Caps are often described as multiperiod call options while floors are often described as multi-period put options. Caps and floors, like all options, are named after the underlying on which they are written. Thus, we have S&P caps, LIBOR caps, prime caps, and so forth. A LIBOR cap would have a payoff exactly like that of the LIBOR call discussed in the preceding section, except the payoff would be repeated on a series of designated settlement dates. The premium on the cap is paid in a lump sum up front, but only a portion of the premium is applicable to each payoff sequence. Thus, the premium can be viewed as amortizing over the life of the option with a portion of the premium attributable to each settlement.

 ## YIELDS AND PRICES

Interest rate options include both options written directly on an interest rate (such as a LIBOR call or a LIBOR cap) and options written on bond (or note)

---

[3] There are some minor subtleties that we are glossing over. For example, LIBOR on real Eurodollar deposits is paid in arrears. That is, the interest is paid at the end of the deposit period, but the options described here settle up at the same time LIBOR is observed. Thus, they settle up at the beginning of the hypothetical Eurodollar deposit period. To keep things fair, we have to discount the actual payoff to reflect the present value of the future payoff. These subtleties are not critical to understanding the basics of these markets, so we will ignore them.

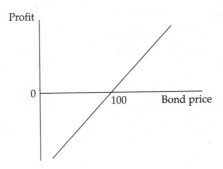

EXHIBIT G.1 Payoff profile for a bond position (long)

prices. Bond prices are determined by bond yields. If we know a bond's price, we know its yield. If we know the change in its yield, we know the change in its price. Thus, an option that is written on a bond (meaning on a bond's price) could just as easily be restated as an option written on the bond's yield. There are occasionally reasons that we might want to do this.

Futures that are written on bonds can also be restated as futures written on bond yields. That is, we could illustrate the profit/loss with respect to the bond's price (the usual way) or we could re-express the profit/loss with respect to the bond's yield.

Whether talking about cash bonds, futures on bonds, or options on bonds, when we re-express the payoff profile in terms of the bond's yield, it causes the payoff to take on a different appearance. Consider the following figures illustrating the payoff from holding a long position in T-bonds (or T-bond futures). Both figures indicate the profit per $100 of par value for a bond having a 20-year maturity, an 8.00% coupon, and purchased at par.

Exhibit G.1 has the upward slope that we usually associate with a long position. Exhibit G.2 has the downward slope that we usually associate with a short position. Both figures actually illustrate the payoffs for a *long* position in

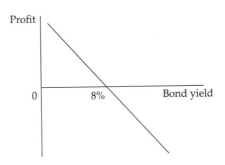

EXHIBIT G.2 Payoff profile for a bond position (long)

bonds. What has happened in Exhibit G.2 is that we have re-expressed the horizontal axis in terms of yield, rather than price. Since a bond's yield and a bond's price are inversely related, the curve is flipped over, but it still conveys the same information.[4]

 ## USE OF OPTIONS IN HEDGING

There are a number of ways that options can be used by risk managers to hedge market exposures. Some situations call for the use of single-period options while others require the use of multi-period options. We will consider two cases of the former and one of the latter. All of the cases involve hedging interest rate exposures.

CASE 1: HEDGING WITH PUT OPTIONS ON T-BONDS

A corporation's Board has been asked to approve the issuance of $100 million of fixed rate debt in the form of 20-year mortgage bonds. The proceeds from the bond offering would be used to finance the construction of a new production facility. Suppose that at the time the request is put to the Board, the firm's CFO informs the Board that, if issued today, the bonds can be sold at par if the firm attaches a coupon of 9.00%. The bonds would be distributed through a public offering which requires registration with the SEC. The registration process will take 12 weeks to complete. The Board approves the bond offering conditional on the issuance not requiring a coupon greater than 9.25% to sell at par.

The problem for the CFO, of course, is that interest rates might rise significantly between now and the final approval of the offering by the SEC. If rates rise, the CFO might not be able to issue the bonds with a coupon not exceeding 9.25% and still sell the bonds at par. The risk is depicted in Exhibit G.3. Such graphic depictions of risk exposures are often called *risk profiles*. If interest rates rise, the firm loses. If interest rates fall, the firm wins.

The CFO could hedge away all of the firm's interest rate risk in interest-rate futures contracts—in which case the firm locks in a rate of approximately 9.00%. He would do this by going short an appropriate number of T-bond futures.[5] Let's suppose that the appropriate number of T-bond futures is 850. A *short* position in T-bond futures would have the payoff depicted in Exhibit G.4.

---

[4] When profit is illustrated as a function of yield, the payoff is no longer linear. Instead, the payoff is convex. We can create the illusion of linearity by spacing the yields unevenly along the horizontal axis. This has been done in these figures to avoid addressing the complex issue of convexity and the problems it introduces.

[5] Determining the quantity of T-bond futures to go short to properly hedge a specific offering is not a simple task. It requires the careful calculation of a hedge ratio, which, in this case, is based on durations.

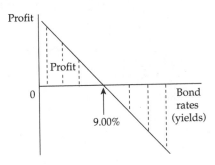

EXHIBIT G.3   Risk profile

The curve is upward sloping moving left to right. This is the shape that we usually associate with a long position. This is only a visual trick. The horizontal axis is drawn in terms of *yield*, rather than in terms of bond prices, causing a reversal of the way the profile would normally look. Now, if we combine the firm's risk profile with the payoff from the futures we get Exhibit G.5.[6] The futures hedge locks in a cost of 9.00%, which is represented by the flat profile depicted in Exhibit G.5.

Suppose, however, that the CFO decides that rates are more likely to decline significantly than to rise significantly over the next 12 weeks. That is, he has a strong view on interest rates. Clearly, if his view proves correct, the firm would be best off if the CFO does not hedge. Unfortunately, the CFO cannot take the chance that his view on rates is wrong.

This is an ideal situation for an option hedge. Suppose that 12-week put options on T-bonds having a strike price that implies a strike rate of 9.00% can be purchased for a premium that equates to 20 basis points (20 bps = 0.20%) a year over the life of the bond that is to be issued.[7] Assume that it will take 850 put options on T-bonds to fully hedge the exposure.

With this option hedge in place, the worst case scenario for the firm is a financing cost of 9.20%. This is the sum of the implied option strike rate and the cost of the option, and it is less than the 9.25% limit imposed by the Board. On the other hand, if interest rates drop over the next 12 weeks as the CFO ex-

---

[6] To be precise, since we are hedging a corporate bond issuance in Treasury bonds, (or Treasury bond futures) we would need to restate the payoff on the Treasury bond in terms of the corporate bond's yield, not the Treasury bond's yield. There are standard tools to make such a conversion, but we ignore this complicating factor here. The same would be true for an option's hedge.

[7] Options can be purchased on T-bonds directly or on T-bond futures. In either case, the underlying T-bonds trade in terms of price, not yield. But each yield implies a unique price and each price implies a unique yield. Thus, a given strike price implies a specific strike yield.

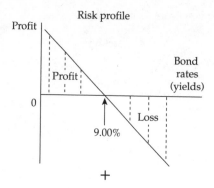

EXHIBIT G.3   Repeated

+

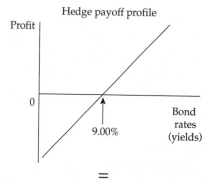

EXHIBIT G.4   Hedge payoff profile

=

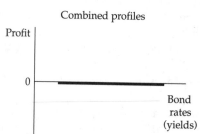

EXHIBIT G.5   Combined profiles

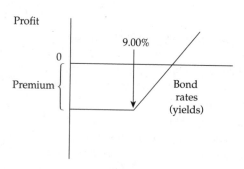

EXHIBIT G.6   Payoff profile on put option on T-bonds

pects, the firm can still enjoy the lower financing costs by simply allowing the options to expire. The profit diagram for the options is in Exhibit G.6. Again, we have drawn the profile for the options with yields on the horizontal axis rather than the underlying bond's price. This has the effect of making the profit diagram for these put options look like the profit diagram for call options. By combining the risk profile of the firm with the profit diagram on the put option hedge, the firm is able to achieve the new profile given by Exhibit G.7.

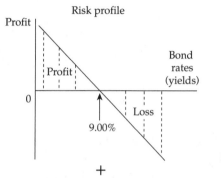

Risk profile

EXHIBIT G.3 Repeated

+

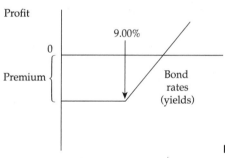

Payoff profile on put option on T-bonds

EXHIBIT G.6 Repeated

=

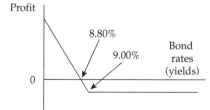

Combined profiles

EXHIBIT G.7 Combined profiles

Exhibit G.7 resembles the payoff profile for a call option on T-bonds (after we recognize that the horizontal axis is expressed in terms of yield rather than in terms of prices). Essentially, by combining an exposure to corporate bond interest rates (or yields) with long positions in put options on T-bonds, we have replicated a call option. Thus, the firm's exposure is now equivalent to holding call options on bonds. This is a manifestation of a well-known relationship in finance called put/call parity.

Before proceeding to our second example, we should reflect for a moment on the nature of risk. In finance, the term "risk" is most often understood to mean *any* deviation from an expected outcome. In the context of the example above, this definition would treat favorable deviations from the expected interest rate level as equivalent to unfavorable deviations from the expected interest rate level. Futures hedges, if properly structured, will remove the potential for both types of deviation. The reality, however, is that favorable deviations from expected interest rate levels are actually desirable. It is only the unfavorable deviations that we would like to protect against. The trade-off in futures hedging is that we surrender the potential to benefit from favorable deviations to obtain protection against unfavorable deviations.

This is where the option hedge comes in. The option hedge allows a risk manager to remove the potential for unfavorable deviations while preserving the opportunity to enjoy some of the benefits from a favorable deviation. Of course, there are no free lunches and the benefits associated with option hedging come at the price of the option premium.

CASE 2: HEDGING WITH PUT OPTIONS ON EURODOLLAR FUTURES

A bank funds its short-term dollar loans in the Eurodollar markets at LIBOR. Today is January 15, and the bank has a customer in need of a $10 million three-month loan commencing on the third Wednesday of March. The bank would ordinarily charge this customer 125 basis points above its own funding costs. That is, it would charge LIBOR + 1.25%.

The customer wants the bank to make a rate commitment today for a loan that would commence in March. (Why the customer needs the rate commitment from the bank is irrelevant to the problem.) The loan commitment would be binding on both the bank and the customer.

The bank could lock in its cost of funds by buying March Eurodollar futures on the IMM.[8] These futures are priced by taking 100 and subtracting the market's expectation of the future 3-mo LIBOR rate. That is, $F_{ED} = 100 -$ LIBOR, where F_{ED} denotes the futures price and LIBOR is the 3-mo LIBOR rate

---

[8] The IMM is the International Monetary Market, a division of the Chicago Mercantile Exchange. These futures are sometimes referred to as IMM Eurodollar futures and sometimes referred to as CME Eurodollar futures.

stated as a percentage. The futures price then implies a forward LIBOR rate.[9] That is, LIBOR = $100 - F_{ED}$.

Suppose that the March Eurodollar futures are currently trading at 94.75. This implies that the bank can lock in LIBOR financing at 5.25% (i.e., 100 − 94.75). Since the bank adds a spread of 125 basis points, it would be willing to commit to a rate of 6.50% on the loan to its customer. As it happens, the bank's funding unit strongly believes that interest rates are far more likely to fall over the next few months than they are to rise. The funding unit would like to take advantage of its interest rate forecast, but still protect the bank from downside risk (defined in this case as a rise in funding costs). So, they buy ten March puts on Eurodollar futures, each covering $1 million, having a strike price of 94.75. These options are at-the-money. Let's suppose that they currently command a premium that is equivalent to 25 basis points per year.

Consider two possible outcomes. First, suppose that the funding unit's forecast turns out to be wrong and March 3-mo LIBOR rises by 100 basis points so that the March futures are priced, at the terminal point in the option's life, at 93.75. In this case, the options have a terminal value of 100 basis points and the payoff is, therefore, 75 bps (after deducting the 25 bps premium paid for the options). The bank's final cost of funds is 5.50%. This is the cost of funding the loan in the Eurodollar markets (6.25%) less the 75 bps (0.75%) profit on its option hedge. The bank's spread on its committed lending is 100 basis points (i.e., 6.50% − 5.50%). This same outcome would have resulted from any final LIBOR rate above 5.25% (equivalent to any final futures price below 94.75).

Now, consider the outcome for the bank if March LIBOR declines, as the funding unit expects. Suppose, for example, that March LIBOR falls to 4.20% so that the March Eurodollars are priced at 95.80. In this case, the options expire out-of-the-money and are worthless; but, the bank obtains its funding at a cost of 4.20%. The bank's spread is then 2.05%.

$$\text{Spread} = \text{lending rate} - \text{cost of funds in Eurodollar market} - \text{cost of option} = 6.50\% - 4.20\% - 0.25\%.$$

At any March Eurodollar futures price above 95.00, the bank will come out better with the option hedge than with the futures hedge. This value reflects the initial Eurodollar futures price (94.75) plus the cost of the option (0.25). The bank's potential profit on this lending, after reflecting the hedge outcomes and cost, is depicted in Exhibit G.8.

There is another good reason why an option hedge is sometimes superior to a futures hedge when managing interest rate risk. To see this, consider again the bank in the preceding example. We had explicitly assumed that both the bank's and the customer's commitments to the loan were binding so that

---

[9] A forward LIBOR is the rate that the market, in its collective wisdom, expects to prevail at a certain point in the future (in this case March) for a particular deposit period (in this case three months).

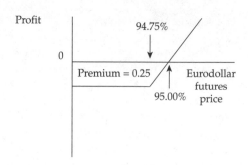

EXHIBIT G.8 Profile after option hedge has been placed

neither could back out. Suppose, instead, that the customer needs the bank's loan rate commitment to formulate a bid for some business on which it is competing. The firm does not know if its bid will be successful and therefore requires a firm commitment from the bank (should the bid be successful), but it does not itself want to make a firm commitment to the bank to take the loan, in case it is not the successful bidder. Additionally, it might simply want to preserve the opportunity to benefit from cheaper financing should rates fall before March.

In this latter case, the customer is looking to obtain a *guarantee* from the bank that is not binding on the firm. If the firm's bid is successful *and* rates rise, it will exercise its loan-rate guarantee. If, on the other hand, the firm's bid is unsuccessful *or* rates fall, it will allow its guarantee to expire. Clearly, the guarantee that the bank is providing to its customer is really an interest rate option. This option is equivalent to a put option on Eurodollars futures. Here, a futures hedge would be inappropriate for the bank, but a hedge consisting of a long put on March Eurodollar futures would also be appropriate. Since the bank must pay for its option hedge, it will charge the customer for the option that the bank is writing. The bank might, for example, charge the customer 30 bps for the option and then cover itself at a cost of 25 bps.

CASE 3: USING A CAP TO ACHIEVE A MULTI-PERIOD HEDGE

Consider now a firm that has entered into a five-year floating-rate financing by selling a floating rate note. The note pays 6-mo LIBOR + 40 bps. The firm is comfortable with this arrangement provided that its payout does not rise above 8.00%. To eliminate the risk, the firm prices several five-year caps on 6-mo LIBOR with semiannual settlements. The firm finds that it can purchase a 7.20% LIBOR cap for a premium that amortizes to 35 bps per year. If it buys this cap, its cost for any period cannot exceed 7.95%. On the other hand, when LIBOR is below 7.20%, the cost to the firm is now LIBOR + 75 bps, rather than LIBOR + 40 bps, reflecting the per-annum cost of the cap. These periodic payouts are summarized by the equation below.

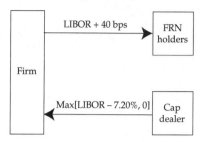

Result: capped floating rate

Cost of cap = 35 bps per annum

EXHIBIT G.9   Result: capped floating rate debt

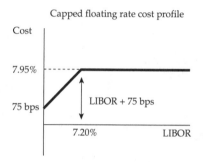

Capped floating rate cost profile

EXHIBIT G.10   Capped floating rate cost profile

$$\text{Cost} = \text{payout on the FRN} - \text{payoff on the cap} + \text{per annum cost of the cap} =$$
$$\text{LIBOR} + 40 \text{ bps} - max[\text{LIBOR} - 7.20\%, 0] + 35 \text{ bps}$$

The cash flows on this structure are depicted in Exhibit G.9 and the cost is graphically depicted, in the form of a combined cost profile, in Exhibit G.10. The cap is appropriate in this case because the risk exposure is recurring. That is, it arises every six months and is therefore multi-period. This contrasts with our first two examples, which were both single-period exposures.

 CONCLUSION

All three of these examples illustrate how options can hedge interest rate risk. Some of these options are exchange traded, such as the puts on T-bonds and the puts on Eurodollar futures. Others, such as the cap, are privately negotiated as over the counter transactions with derivatives dealers. Similar structures to the ones presented here can be used to hedge commodity price risk, foreign exchange risk, and equity risk. In our next column, we will examine more exotic types of options.

# APPENDIX H

Exotic Options Are Not as Exotic as They Once Were

Exotic or non-standard options are unusual for their underlying assets, strike price calculations, payoff mechanisms, or expiration conditions.

In our last two articles in this column, we provided tutorials on the most basic types of single-period options, i.e., calls and puts,[1] and on the multi-period analogs of calls and puts called caps and floors.[2] We also provided illustrations of how these relatively simple single-period and multi-period instruments could be used for risk management purposes. Now, we will look at an assortment of options that are considerably more varied and complex, exotic options, though our examination will be largely non-quantitative. Our intent is to explain the structure, logic, and uses of the products. We do not address the valuation arithmetic (which is complex) or the trading and dealer-hedging issues (which are also complex).

 ### EXOTIC OPTIONS

Exotic options are any of a wide variety of options with unusual underlying assets, strike price calculations, payoff mechanisms, or expiration conditions. They are also known as non-standard options. Essentially, exotic options include all options that do not fit neatly into our traditional call/put or cap/floor models. They share certain fundamental characteristics with more traditional options and are, therefore, still options.

Exotic options first appeared in the late 1980s. The number of types and variants have since exploded. We will limit our discussion in this article to some of the more easy-to-understand types. Exotic options can be single-period in nature (like traditional calls and puts) or multi-period in nature (like caps and

---

[1] Marshall and Wynne, "Options 101: The Basics," 2 DERIVATIVES 147 (January/February 1997).

[2] Marshall and Wynne, "Options Can Be Tailored to Hedge Single And Multiple Exposure Periods," 2 DERIVATIVES 260 (May/June 1997).

floors).[3] They can also be path dependent or non-path dependent. This distinction has not been made in our prior columns and needs some additional explanation.

PATH DEPENDENT VS. NON-PATH DEPENDENT EXOTIC OPTIONS

Consider the payoff associated with a single period plain vanilla option to buy an underlying asset. For example, let's make it a cash settled call option on the raw S&P 500 index. Suppose that today is September 15 and we buy a three-month call option (expiration date December 15) on the S&P having a strike price of 900. The option covers 500 units of the S&P. The final payoff on this option would reflect the value of the S&P 500 index on December 15:

$$\text{Payoff} = max[\text{S\&P} - 900, 0] \times \$500$$

For example, if, at the close of business on December 15, the S&P stands at 920, the option holder would receive from the option writer $10,000 (i.e., $max[920 - 900, 0] \times \$500$). If the S&P stood at 940, the holder would receive $20,000, and so forth. At any S&P value equal to or less than 900 on December 15, the holder receives nothing and the option expires worthless.

Consider again the first outcome. That is, the S&P stands at 920 on December 15 and the option holder gets $10,000. For purposes of the final payoff, it did not matter whether the S&P rose between September 15 and December 15 or if it fell between September 15 and December 15. All that matters is that the S&P is 920 on December 15. That is, the terminal value of the option is not dependent on the path that the underlying asset's price took in arriving at its final (settlement day) value. Thus, we say it is path independent or non-path dependent. This is illustrated in Exhibit H.1.

Now consider a very different type of option. Suppose that the option's payoff is determined by the average value of the asset as observed on October 15, November 15, and December 15. Denote this average by $\overline{\text{S\&P}}$. The payoff is structured as follows:

$$\text{Payoff} = max[\overline{\text{S\&P}} - 900, 0] \times \$500$$

For example, suppose that the S&P is 900 on October 15, 910 on November 15, and 920 on December 15. The "average" value of the underlying is then 910 and the option pays $5,000. Now suppose instead of the values 900, 910, and 920 on October 15, November 15, and December 15, respectively, the values are 940, 930, and 920. Then the average value of the S&P is 930 and the option pays $15,000. In both cases, the terminal value of the underlying was 920 (i.e., the value on December 15) but the payoffs on the option are nevertheless different. The payoffs are clearly dependent upon the path the underlying asset's price took in arriving at its terminal value. Thus, these options, a type of exotic op-

---

[3]Ibid.

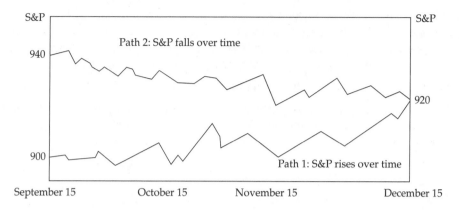

EXHIBIT H.1 Path independent or non-path dependent S&P option

tion falling into a group called "average-rate" options, are path dependent. These are not the only type of average-rate options, but they illustrate the basic distinction between options that are path dependent and those that are non-path dependent.

There are many types of exotic options that are path dependent and there are many types that are not path dependent. The difference has considerable implications for the value of the options. For example, one would generally expect an average rate option to be cheaper (smaller premium to purchase it) than an otherwise equivalent option that is not an average rate because the averaging process tends to dampen the extreme outcomes. Extreme outcomes mean extreme payoffs.

DIGITAL OPTIONS

Another commonly used group of exotic options are the digital options. These are also known as "binary options." The names come from the fact that these options can take on only one of two possible outcomes on their settlement date. These outcomes are 1 and 0. Digital options can be single-period (calls and puts) or multi-period (caps and floors). For example, we could have a digital call, a digital cap, a digital put, or a digital floor. The payoff to the holder of a digital call or cap on the S&P having a strike of 900, would look as follows:

$$\text{Payoff} = max[\text{S\&P} - 900, 0]/(\text{S\&P} - 900) = [0, 1]$$

It is easy to see that if the S&P is greater than 900 on the contract's settlement date, the contract will pay off 1 because the numerator and denominator are identical. On the other hand, if the S&P is less than or equal to 900, then the numerator is zero and the option payoff is zero.

A digital put or floor would be analogous:

$$\text{Payoff} = max[900 - \text{S\&P}, 0]/(900 - \text{S\&P}) = [0, 1]$$

Now, one might wonder why an option would be written to pay off 1 or 0. Suppose that the payoff on an option was written as the terminal value of a digital option (i.e., 1 or 0) times either a fixed dollar amount or the market value of some specific asset. In the first case, the payoff might look like this:

$$\text{Payoff} = (\text{value of digital option}) \times \$200{,}000$$

This says that if the option is in-the-money at expiration, the payoff is $200,000. If it is out-of-the-money, the payoff is zero. That is, you either get all of the $200,000 or you get none of it. In the second case, the payoff might look like this:

$$\text{Payoff} = (\text{value of digital option}) \times \text{S\&P}$$

This says that the option will pay off the entire value of the S&P, whatever that happens to be, or none of it. Consider one more application. Suppose that we write a digital option on one asset with the payoff taking the form of the "all or nothing" value of some other asset. For example, suppose that someone bought an option having the following payoff:

$$\text{Payoff} = max[\text{S\&P} - 900{,}0]/(\text{S\&P} - 900) \times \text{price of a barrel of oil} \times 100{,}000$$

This payoff function says that the option will pay off the market value of 100,000 barrels of oil, or nothing, on the option's settlement date depending on whether the S&P is above or below 900 on that date.

Notice that all of the last several variations of digital option applications have had the characteristic of paying "all or nothing." For this reason, these options are grouped together and described as "all or nothing options." Such options are very useful for building certain types of structured securities and for hedging certain types of balance sheet exposures.

BARRIER OPTIONS

Another widely used group of exotic options are called barrier options.[4] These are options in which something dramatic happens if the underlying asset's price crosses a prespecified threshold. Common types of barrier options include up-and-in, up-and-out, down-and-in, and down-and-out. All of these have other names as well.

To see how such an option might work, consider an "up-and-out-call" option on IBM. This option might be written on September 15 with an expiration date of December 15. Suppose that it has a strike price of $180, but it "goes out of existence" if IBM trades above $200 a share prior to October 15. If IBM trades above $200 (crosses the barrier) before October 15, the option ceases to exist.

---

[4] Kat, "Barrier Options Can Reduce Cost Of Effective Risk Management," 2 DERIVATIVE 210 (March/April 1997).

Thus, the price went up and the option went out of existence (up and out). No matter what the value of IBM on the option's December 15 settlement date, the option has no payoff. On the other hand, if the price of IBM does not exceed $200 on or before October 15, the option behaves as a normal call would behave after October 15.

Just as an option can be written to go out of existence if the prespecified barrier is crossed, we can also write one to come into existence if a barrier gets crossed. For example, the option could be written to come into existence if IBM trades above $200 any time before October 15. If it does, the option behaves like a normal call would behave after October 15. If IBM does not trade above $200 prior to October 15, the option never comes into existence, and, therefore, has no value on December 15, irrespective of IBM's price on December 15.

Down-and-in and down-and-out options are analogous to up-and-in and up-and-out options, respectively, except that the barrier is set below rather than above, the current price. Clearly, barrier options are path dependent.

OUTPERFORMANCE OPTIONS

Outperformance options are options that pay off based on more than one underlying asset. For example, suppose that an international equities portfolio manager is torn between investing $5 mm in the U.S. markets or the Japanese markets, both of which he thinks will do well over the next six months. He could, of course, divide the funds between the two markets. Instead, however, suppose that he invests the proceeds in T-bills and then purchases a six-month option with the following payoff:

$$\text{Payoff} = max[\text{TR}_{S\&P}, \text{TR}_{NIK}, 0] \times \$5 \text{ mm}$$

where TR denotes the percentage total return earned by the index over the six-month period, S&P denotes the S&P 500 (a U.S. index), and NIK denotes the Nikkei 225 (a Japanese stock index).

This option has two underlying assets: the total return on the S&P and the total return on the Nikkei. It also has two strike prices, but they both happen to be zero in this case. Clearly, this option will pay off the better of the returns on the two stock indices, so that the portfolio manager will turn out to be in the better of the two markets, irrespective of which market performs better. If both markets perform badly, the portfolio manager does not lose because zero is the worst-case outcome. Of course, this notion of "not losing" overlooks the fact that the portfolio manager had to pay an up-front premium to acquire the option and that this premium will likely be substantial.

Options of this type are referred to loosely as outperformance options because they pay off based on which of the underlyings performed the best. There is no reason why such options need be limited to two underlyings. We could, for example, have included a German stock index, a Hong Kong index, and as many more as we like.

CONCLUSION

There are many other types of exotic options and new ones seem to be introduced almost daily. Accounting and legal practitioners should become familiar with what is meant by an exotic option, the difference between path and non-path dependent options, a few of the specific types of exotic options, and at least a smattering of the uses to which these options might be put. We will look more closely at those uses in a future tutorial in this space.

APPENDIX I

How Financial Engineers Create Structured Notes to Satisfy Cash Flow Needs of Issuers and Investors

Since the issuer can broadly tap the investor community by tailoring pay-offs for each segment of that community, it can reduce the cost of financing while still having the type of liability it desires.

Previously in this journal, the authors have discussed plain vanilla swaps, plain vanilla options, several variants of the plain vanilla swap, and exotic options. Our discussion of each of these groups of instruments was necessarily limited to a sampling of a few of the many types. Here, we see how these derivative instruments can be combined with traditional securities to custom design a structured security in such a way as to simultaneously satisfy an issuer and an investor when the needs of the issuer (in the sense of the cash flows it wants to pay) are very different from the needs of the investor (in the sense of the cash flows it wants to receive).

These securities are often, but not always, sold through a private placement. In the U.S., the securities are structured or engineered by the structured products group of an investment bank or the securities subsidiary of a commercial bank. The bank's structured products group works closely with the bank's corporate finance desk, which speaks with corporate issuers, and with the sales and trading desk, which speaks most directly with institutional and retail investors.

The job of the structured products group is to combine various instruments, including derivatives, so that the final product meets both the issuers' and the investors' needs. Because the resultant securities are constructed, in part, from derivatives, they are often called *derivative securities*, but that term is a little too general. It includes structured notes, but also mortgage-backed securities, asset-backed securities, and various forms of more traditional debt like convertible bonds and callable bonds. We will limit ourselves to structured notes.

 TRUST STRUCTURES: THE PRECURSOR TO STRUCTURED NOTES

Structured notes evolved from trust structures. The latter involve the use of trusts to alter the character of the cash flows. These structures are cumbersome and costly, but they did work and they are still used. Structured notes are a more streamlined and cost effect vehicle to accomplish the same basic objective. Nevertheless, it is useful to look at trust structures first in order to give structured notes an historical perspective.

A financially engineered product generally begins with an investment bank or commercial bank sponsoring the creation of a trust. A trust is an entity set up for a special investment purpose. Its trustees protect the interests of the parties with a beneficial interest in the trust. The trust can issue debt, in the form of bonds or notes, or it can issue ownership interests, called units. Units are similar in nature to common stock. After creating the trust, the sponsor arranges for the trust to acquire (purchase) securities having some type of cash flow. The trust then issues its own securities, either equity or debt. These securities are sold to investors. The trust-issued securities held by the investors provide cash flows to them that are different than the cash flows that the trust is receiving on the securities it holds as assets. The cash flows are altered either by the way in which the trust's own debt and equity are structured, or by derivative transactions entered into by the trust. The securities issued by the trust are, generally, marketed by the financial institution that sponsored the trust, acting in the capacity of underwriter. The financial institution, of course, receives underwriting fees. It also, generally, makes a secondary market in the securities issued by the trust. The structure is depicted in Exhibit I.1.

To make this a little more concrete, suppose that an issuer of securities would like to fund itself by issuing a traditional fixed rate bond, paying a semiannual coupon. There are investors for these bonds. But, there are also investors who do not want traditional bonds that pay periodic coupons because these

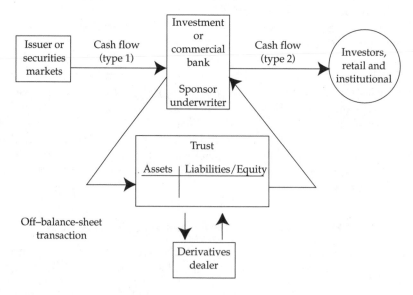

EXHIBIT I.1 Structured products using trusts

investors have no immediate need for the coupon payments they would receive and they do not want to bear the reinvestment risk. Reinvestment risk is the risk that the coupon will have to be reinvested when received and the reinvestment rates are not known at the time the initial bond is purchased. Thus, the investor's wealth at the time the bond matures has an element of uncertainty. For these investors, the ideal investment instrument is a zero coupon bond.

Until 1977, zero coupon bonds did not exist in the U.S. to any meaningful degree. Thus, investors had no choice but to hold a fixed-coupon bond which, for some, was a less than optimal instrument. Then, in 1977 Merrill Lynch used a trust structure to alter the character of a conventional coupon-bearing U.S. Treasury bond in such a way as to generate zero coupon bonds with different maturity dates. In essence, it set up a trust and deposited coupon-bearing bonds as assets. These bonds would pay the trust known fixed coupons at specific later dates. The trust then issued *units* to investors. These units were such that a specific unit had a specific maturity date. The maturity dates of the various series of units were matched to the coupon payment dates of the bond held by the trust. For example, suppose that the bond will pay the trust a coupon six months from today. When received by the trust, these coupons are paid out to the holders of one unit series on a pro rata basis. Once these unit holders have received their payment, that series of units terminates. The next series of units gets the second coupon, and so on. Thus, each series of units constitutes a synthetic zero coupon bond. This structure made it possible to synthesize zero coupon bonds backed by U.S. Treasury securities in denominations suitable for retail investors.

Merrill Lynch called these securities Treasury Investment Growth Receipts (or TIGRs). They proved very popular and were soon copied by other securities firms. While trusts predate Merrill Lynch's TIGRs, it was this structure that led early financial engineers to realize that trusts made it possible to structure cash flows.

The creation of synthetic zeros proved very profitable to the firms that created them. The reason was simple. Investors were now able to get an instrument that better matched their needs (i.e., reinvestment risk removed). They were willing to pay for this risk reduction in the form of accepting a lower yield. The difference between the cost of the raw Treasury bond used as input, and what the investors were willing to pay for the products that could be carved out of it, was a source of profit to the firm that sponsored the trust.

The trust structure, as an engineering tool to alter the characteristics of cash flows, got another big boost in 1982 when a Salomon Brothers bond trader—Lewis Ranieri—used the same vehicle to create the first collateralized mortgage obligations, or CMOs. In this case, the trust purchased whole mortgages. It held these mortgages as assets. The trust then issued its own debt to fund the purchase of the mortgages. The bonds that the trust issued, which it sold to investors, were divided into a series of different bonds. In a sense, they were sliced up and the French word for slice, *tranche*, was used to describe them.

The principal problems with mortgage investing is that (1) mortgages have very long lives, generally 30 years, and (2) the mortgagors have the right to prepay the mortgage principal in whole or in part, without penalty, whenever they wish. If mortgagors behave rationally, they can be expected to prepay their mortgages when interest rates decline (i.e., they refinance at lower rates). The mortgage investor then suddenly receives his money back sooner than he wants it. To make matters worse, he will get his money back and have to reinvest it precisely at the worst time, i.e., when interest rates are low.

Under the CMO trust structure, the trust receives regular principal and interest payments from the banks and/or savings and loans that are servicing the mortgages held by the trust. The trust then pays interest to each tranche but only pays principal to the first tranche. This tranche is called the *fastest-pay tranche*. Because the fastest-pay tranche is getting all of the principal, the holders of that tranche will be fully repaid within a very short period of time, perhaps two to three years. Once they are fully repaid, the tranche terminates, and the principal payments begin flowing to the second tranche, which becomes the fastest-pay tranche. When the second tranche is fully repaid, the principal shifts to the third tranche, and so on. Through this structure, the trust is able to take a single-class input instrument (whole mortgages) and create multi-class output instruments (i.e., CMO tranches with different average lives).

STRUCTURED NOTES: A MORE STREAMLINED APPROACH

Trust structures proved very versatile. Over time, more complex structures emerged to achieve an ever more varied universe of investment alternatives. But the structures were costly to construct and cumbersome to administer. This led to a more streamlined and efficient vehicle—structured notes.

In a structured note, the issuer works with the corporate finance desk of a financial institution (either an investment bank or a commercial bank), which in turns works with the structured products group and the sales and trading desk, to (1) identify what investors really want to own, and then (2) structure a security that gives the investors precisely the kind of cash flows they want, while also allowing the issuer to pay the type of cash flow it wants to pay. This is accomplished, most often, with derivatives (i.e., OTC options and swaps).

Consider the following scenario. A corporate issuer wants to pay a fixed rate (semiannual coupon) on a two-year financing. The investor, on the other hand, wants to receive a floating rate tied to LIBOR. The issuer agrees to issue a *floating rate note* tied to LIBOR, but swaps this LIBOR payment for a fixed payment. The end result: the issuer pays fixed but the investor receives floating. This is depicted in Exhibit I.2.

Consider another scenario. An investor wants to receive a floating rate tied to LIBOR. But, the investor does not believe that LIBOR will go above 7% over the two-year period. He is willing to bet that it won't go over 7% by accepting a cap on LIBOR at 7%. In exchange, he gets a premium over LIBOR when LIBOR is below 7%. This is called a *capped floating rate note*, or *capped floater*

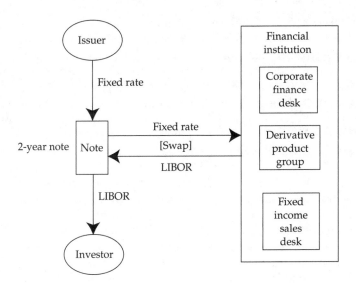

EXHIBIT I.2 Structured securities (floating rate note)

and is created with a plain vanilla interest rate swap and an interest rate cap. In essence, the investor has sold an option. His extra yield comes from the premium associated with the option he sold. This is depicted in Exhibit I.3.

Consider now an investor that would like his interest to take the form of the total return on the S&P 500 stock index. That is, instead of getting a float-

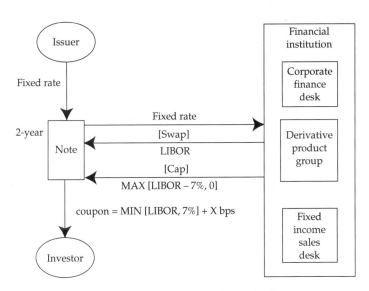

X bps = amortized premium from sale of cap

EXHIBIT I.3 Structured securities (capped floating rate note)

ing rate of interest tied to LIBOR, the investor wants his interest to be a function of the S&P total return. Total return is the sum of the dividend and capital appreciation, stated as a percentage. Of course, it is possible for the total return on the S&P to be negative for a given six-month period. This would require the investor to pay the issuer the negative return on the S&P or to reduce the principal by the amount of the negative S&P return. Neither is acceptable. So, the note is structured so that the note pays a percentage of the total return on the S&P to the investor but only when the total return on the S&P is positive. When it is negative, the investor is not affected. This is referred to as a *principal-protected equity-linked note*. It is created, essentially, by having the investor, indirectly, buy an S&P floor (a type of multi-period put). The long floor is, in essence, structured into the note. Because this option has to be paid for, the investor does not get all of the S&P total return when the S&P total return is positive. He gets something less, say 60%. The difference may be viewed as the cost of the option. This is depicted in Exhibit I.4.

Consider now a structure in which an investor wants a floating rate note but he does not want to take the risk that LIBOR goes below 4%. To get downside protection, he buys an interest rate floor (analogous to the S&P floor in the preceding example). He has to pay for this floor in the form of a lower interest rate on his note (say LIBOR – 25 basis points). While he likes the downside protection, he doesn't like giving up the 25 basis points. So, he agrees to accept a cap on LIBOR at 7%, like the capped floating rate note in the earlier example. He now has both a cap and a floor. (He is short the cap and long the floor.) He

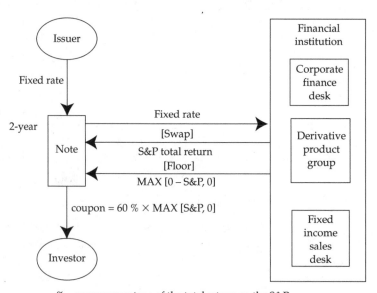

% = some percentage of the total return on the S&P

EXHIBIT I.4 Structured securities (principal protected equity-linked note)

will get LIBOR when LIBOR is between 4% and 7%. If LIBOR goes below 4%, he will continue to get 4%. If LIBOR goes above 7%, he will only get 7%. This structure is depicted in Exhibit I.5. Notice that this structure involves three different derivatives: a plain vanilla swap, a plain vanilla interest rate cap (sold), and a plain vanilla interest rate floor (purchased). This structure is called a *collared floating rate note* or a *collared floater*.

As a final example, consider a structure that is often confused with a collared floating rate note, but is, in actuality, quite different. It is called a *range floater*. There are many variations of the range floater. We will only consider the simplest form. Imagine that an investor has a view that the floating rate of interest, which we will again suppose is LIBOR, will stay within a specific range. Let's suppose that this range is 4.00% to 7.00%. That is, the investor does not believe that LIBOR will go below 4.00% or above 7.00% over the two-year life of the note. Assume that he feels very confident in this view. He, therefore, agrees to give up all of LIBOR when LIBOR is above 7.00% and also to give up all of LIBOR when LIBOR is below 4.00%. That is, he receives *nothing* when LIBOR is above 7.00% and he also receives *nothing* when LIBOR is below 4.00%.

In this case, the investor has, in effect, sold two options. One of these is an *all-or-nothing cap* and the other is an *all-or-nothing floor*. It will be recalled from the description provided in this journal in the September/October 1997

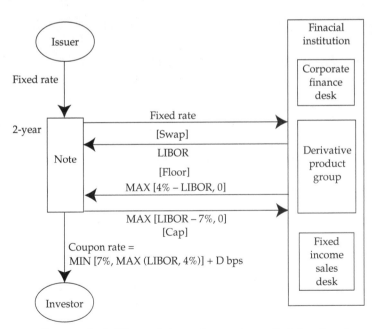

D = amortized difference between the premium collected on the sale of the cap and the premium paid on purchase of the floor

EXHIBIT I.5 Structured securities (collared floating rate note)

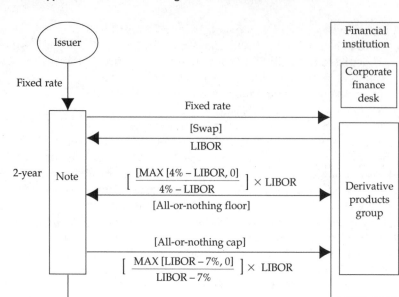

X bps = the amortized value of the sum of the premiums collected on the sale
of the all-or-nothing floor and the sale of the all-or-nothing cap

EXHIBIT I.6 Structured securities (range floater)

issue[1] that all-or-nothing caps and floors are a type of *digital option*. Because the
investor has, in effect, sold both options, he is entitled to collect premiums from
both. These two premiums are then amortized over the life of the two-year note
and expressed as a percentage. Thus, while investors in floating rate notes are
getting LIBOR, this investor is getting LIBOR plus some number of basis points,
provided that LIBOR stays within the forecasted range. The premium might
easily amount to 50 basis points or more per year. This structure is depicted in
Exhibit I.6. The collared floater and the range floater are compared in terms of
their payoff profiles in Exhibit I.7.

A few years ago, a money market mutual fund manager, in an effort to
augment the fund's return, purchased a range floater. The reference rate moved
out of the designated range and, suddenly, the fund went from earning the ref-

---

[1] Marshall and Wynne, "Exotic Options Are Not as Exotic as They Once Were," at
p. 38.

Return on structured note

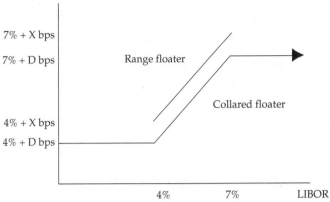

EXHIBIT I.7 Payoff profiles (range floater vs. collared floater)

erence rate plus a premium on the range floater to earning virtually nothing. To make matters worse, once the reference rate moved significantly out of the designated range, the instrument behaved like a zero coupon bond. That is, no further payments were expected until redemption at maturity. Zero coupon bonds trade at discounts to par. As a consequence, the value of the range floater in the portfolio dropped sharply, and the share price of the fund fell below the benchmark price of $1.00 a share. In the jargon of investing, the fund "broke the buck," probably the worst sin a money fund can commit.

 CONCLUSION

This completes our look at structured notes. Of course, we have only presented a smattering of the many forms of structured notes that have been created. The key point to realize is that by tailoring the payoff to fit the desires of the investor, the issuer is able to reduce the cost of financing while still having the type of liability it desires. This is so because the issuer is able to tap each segment of the investor community. There is no reason, for example, why the issuer in need of $5 billion of fixed rate financing cannot tap the fixed rate note market for part of it, the floating rate note market for part of it, the principal-protected equity-linked note market for part of it, the capped floater market for part of it, the collared floater market for part of it, and the range floater market for part of it, in all cases swapping back into fixed rate. There are issuers, most notably the Federal Home Loan Bank, that have issued over a hundred different debt variants, all engineered from the component parts described in this article and in earlier articles in this series.